The
Design and Evolution
of
C++

Bjarne Stroustrup

AT&T Bell Laboratories
Murray Hill, New Jersey

ADDISON-WESLEY PUBLISHING COMPANY

Reading, Massachusetts · Menlo Park, California · New York
Don Mills, Ontario · Wokingham, England · Amsterdam · Bonn · Sydney
Singapore · Tokyo · Madrid · San Juan · Milan · Paris

Library of Congress Cataloging-in-Publication Data

Stroustrup, Bjarne.
  The Design and Evolution of C++ / Bjarne Stroustrup.
     p.   cm.
  Includes bibliographical references and index.
  ISBN 0-201-54330-3
  1. C++ (Computer program language) I. Title.
II. Title: Design and Evolution of C plus plus.
QA76.73.C153S79 1994
005.13'3—dc20   93-50758
                                                CIP

 AT&T

This book was typeset in Times Roman and Courier by the author.

Reprinted with corrections April, 1995

3 4 5 6 7 8 9 10-MA-9695

Preface

He who does not plow,
must write.
– Martin A. Hansen

The ACM HOPL-2 conference on the History of Programming Languages asked me to write a paper on the history of C++. This seemed a reasonable idea and a bit of an honor, so I started writing. To get a more comprehensive and balanced view of C++'s growth, I asked a few friends from the early days of C++ for their recollections. That caused news of this project to travel through the grapevine. There, the story mutated, and one day I received a message from a friend asking where he could buy my new book on the design of C++. That email message is the real origin of this book.

Traditional books about programming and programming languages explain *what* a language is and how to use it. However, many people are also curious about *why* a language is the way it is and how it came to be that way. This book answers these last two questions for C++. It explains how C++ evolved from its first design to the language in use today. It describes the key problems, design aims, language ideas, and constraints that shaped C++, and how they changed over time.

Naturally, C++ and the ideas about design and programming that shaped it didn't just mutate by themselves. What really evolved was the C++ users' understanding of their practical problems and of the tools needed to help solve them. Consequently, this book also traces the key problems tackled using C++ and the views of the people who tackled them in ways that influenced C++.

C++ is still a young language. Some of the issues discussed here are yet unknown to many users. Many implications of decisions described here will not become obvious for years to come. This book presents my view of how C++ came about, what it is, and what it ought to be. I hope this will be of help to people trying to understand how best to use C++ and in the continuing evolution of C++.

The emphasis is on the overall design goals, practical constraints, and people that shaped C++. The key design decisions relating to language features are discussed and put into their historical context. The evolution of C++ is traced from C with Classes through Release 1.0 and 2.0 to the current ANSI/ISO standards work and the explosion of use, interest, commercial activity, compilers, tools, environments, and libraries. C++'s relationship to C and Simula is discussed in detail. C++'s relationship to other languages is discussed briefly. The design of major language facilities such as classes, inheritance, abstract classes, overloading, memory management, templates, exception handling, run-time type information, and namespaces are discussed in some detail.

The primary aim of this book is to give C++ programmers a better idea of the background and fundamental concepts of their language and hopefully to inspire them to experiment with ways of using C++ that are new to them. This book can also be read by experienced programmers and students of programming languages and might help them decide whether using C++ might be worth their while.

Acknowledgments

I am very grateful to Steve Clamage, Tony Hansen, Lorraine Juhl, Peter Juhl, Brian Kernighan, Lee Knight, Doug Lea, Doug McIlroy, Barbara Moo, Jens Palsberg, Steve Rumsby, and Christopher Skelly for reading complete drafts of this book. Their constructive comments caused major changes to the contents and organization of this book. Steve Buroff, Martin Carroll, Sean Corfield, Tom Hagelskjær, Rick Hollinbeck, Dennis Mancl, and Stan Lippman helped by commenting on selected chapters. Also, thanks to Archie Lachner for asking for this book before I had thought of writing it.

Naturally, I owe thanks to the many people who helped make C++. In a sense, this book is a tribute to them and some of their names can be found throughout the chapters and in the index. Should I single out individuals, it must be Brian Kernighan, Andrew Koenig, Doug McIlroy, and Jonathan Shopiro, each of whom has been a steady source of help, encouragement, and ideas for more than a decade. Also, thanks to Kristen Nygaard and Dennis Ritchie as the designers of Simula and C from which the key ingredients of C++ were borrowed. Over the years, I have come to appreciate them not only as brilliant and practical language designers, but also as gentlemen and thoroughly likable individuals.

Murray Hill, New Jersey   *Bjarne Stroustrup*

Contents

0

Notes to the Reader

*Writing is the only art
that must be learned by wrote.*
– anon

Main themes of this book — how to read this book — a timeline for C++
— C++ and other programming languages — references.

Introduction

C++ was designed to provide Simula's facilities for program organization together
with C's efficiency and flexibility for systems programming. It was intended to
deliver that to real projects within half a year of the idea. It succeeded.

At the time, mid-1979, neither the modesty nor the preposterousness of that goal
was realized. The goal was modest in that it did not involve innovation, and prepos-
terous in both its time scale and its Draconian demands on efficiency and flexibility.
While a modest amount of innovation did emerge over the years, efficiency and flexibility have been maintained without compromise. While the goals for C++ have been
refined, elaborated, and made more explicit over the years, C++ as used today directly
reflects its original aims.

The purpose of this book is to document those aims, track their evolution, and present C++ as it emerged from the efforts of many people to create a language that
served its users according to those aims. In doing so, I try to balance historical facts
(such as names, places, and events) against technical issues of language design,
implementation, and use. It is not my aim to document every little event, but to focus
on the key events, ideas, and trends that actually influenced the definition of C++ or
might influence its further evolution and use.

Wherever events are presented, I try to describe them as they happened rather than
how I or others might have liked them to have happened. Where reasonable, I use

quotes from papers to illustrate the aims, principles, and features as they appeared at the time. I try not to project hindsight into events; rather, retrospective comments and comments about the implications of a decision are presented separately and are explicitly marked as retrospective. Basically, I abhor revisionist history and try to avoid it. For example, I mention that ''I had found Pascal's type system worse than useless – a straitjacket that caused more problems than it solved by forcing me to warp my designs to suit an implementation-oriented artifact.'' That I thought that at the time is a fact, and it is a fact that had important implications for the evolution of C++. Whether that harsh judgement on Pascal was fair and whether I would make the same judgement today (more than a decade later) is irrelevant. I could not delete the fact (say, to spare the feelings of Pascal fans or to spare myself embarrassment or controversy) or modify it (by providing a more complete and balanced view) without warping the history of C++.

I try to mention people who contributed to the design and evolution of C++, and I try to be specific about their contribution and about when it occurred. This is somewhat hazardous. Since I don't have a perfect memory, I will overlook some contributions. I offer my apologies. I name the people who caused a decision to be made for C++. Inevitably, these will not always be the people who first encountered a particular problem or who first thought of a solution. This can be unfortunate, but to be vague or to refrain from mentioning names would be worse. Feel free to send me information that might help clarify such points.

Where I describe historical events, there is a question of how objective my descriptions are. I have tried to compensate for unavoidable bias by obtaining information about events I wasn't part of, by talking to other people involved in events, and by having several of the people involved in the evolution of C++ read this book. Their names can be found at the end of the preface. In addition, the History of Programming Languages (HOPL-2) paper [Stroustrup,1993] that contains the central historical facts from this book was extensively reviewed and deemed free of unsuitable bias.

How to Read this Book

Part I goes through the design, evolution, use, and standardization of C++ in roughly chronological order. I chose this organization because during the early years, major design decisions map onto the timeline as a neat, logical sequence. Chapters 1, 2, and 3 describe the origins of C++ and its evolution through C with Classes to Release 1.0. Chapter 4 describes the rules that guided C++'s growth during that period and beyond. Chapter 5 provides a chronology of post-1.0 developments, and Chapter 6 describes the ANSI/ISO C++ standards effort. To provide perspective, Chapters 7 and 8 discuss applications, tools, and libraries. Finally, Chapter 9 presents a retrospective and some thoughts on the future.

Part II presents the post-Release-1.0 development of C++. The language grew within a framework laid down around the time of Release 1.0. This framework included a set of desired features, such as templates and exception handling, and rules guiding their design. After Release 1.0, chronology didn't matter much to the development of C++. The current definition of C++ would have been substantially the same had the chronological sequence of post-1.0 extensions been different. The actual sequence in which the problems were solved and features provided is therefore of historical interest only. A strictly chronological presentation would interfere with the logical flow of ideas, so Part II is organized around major language features instead. Part II chapters are independent, so they can be read in any order: Chapter 10, memory management; Chapter 11, overloading; Chapter 12, multiple inheritance; Chapter 13, class concept refinements; Chapter 14, casting; Chapter 15, templates; Chapter 16, exception handling; Chapter 17, namespaces; Chapter 18, the C preprocessor.

Different people expect radically different things from a book on the design and evolution of a programming language. In particular, no two people seem to agree on what level of detail is appropriate for a discussion of this topic. *Every* review I received on the various versions of the HOPL-2 paper (well over a dozen reviews) was of the form, "This paper is too long ... please add information on topics X, Y, and Z." Worse, about a third of the reviews had comments of the form, "Cut the philosophical/religious nonsense and give us proper technical details instead." Another third commented, "Spare me the boring details and add information on your design philosophy."

To wiggle out of this dilemma, I have written a book within a book. If you are not interested in details, then at first skip all subsections (numbered §$x.y.z$, where x is the chapter number and y is the section number). Later, read whatever else looks interesting. You can also read this book sequentially starting at page one and carry on until the end. Doing that, you might get bogged down in details. This is not meant to imply that details are unimportant. On the contrary, no programming language can be understood by considering principles and generalizations only; concrete examples are essential. However, looking at the details without an overall picture to fit them into is a way of getting seriously lost.

As an additional help, I have concentrated most of the discussion of new features and features generally considered advanced in Part II. This allows Part I to concentrate on basics. Almost all of the information on nontechnical aspects of C++'s evolution is found in Part I. People with little patience for "philosophy" can break up the discussion in Chapters 4 through 9 by looking ahead to the technical details of language features in Part II.

I assume that some will use this book as a reference and that many will read individual chapters without bothering with all preceding chapters. To make such use feasible, I have made the individual chapters relatively self-contained for the experienced C++ programmer and been liberal with cross references and index terms.

Please note that I don't try to define the features of C++ here, I present only as much detail as is necessary to provide a self-contained description of how the features came about. I don't try to teach C++ programming or design either; for a tutorial, see [2nd].

C++ Timeline

This C++ timeline might help you keep track of where the story is taking you:

1979	May	Work on C with Classes starts
	Oct	1st C with Classes implementation in use
1980	Apr	1st internal Bell Labs paper on C with Classes [Stroustrup,1980]
1982	Jan	1st external paper on C with Classes [Stroustrup,1982]
1983	Aug	1st C++ implementation in use
	Dec	C++ named
1984	Jan	1st C++ manual
1985	Feb	1st external C++ release (Release E)
	Oct	Cfront Release 1.0 (first commercial release)
	Oct	*The C++ Programming Language* [Stroustrup,1986]
1986	Aug	The "whatis paper" [Stroustrup,1986b]
	Sep	1st OOPSLA conference (start of OO hype centered on Smalltalk)
	Nov	1st commercial Cfront PC port (Cfront 1.1, Glockenspiel)
1987	Feb	Cfront Release 1.2
	Nov	1st USENIX C++ conference (Santa Fe, NM)
	Dec	1st GNU C++ release (1.13)
1988	Jan	1st Oregon Software C++ release
	June	1st Zortech C++ release
	Oct	1st USENIX C++ implementers workshop (Estes Park, CO)
1989	June	Cfront Release 2.0
	Dec	ANSI X3J16 organizational meeting (Washington, DC)
1990	May	1st Borland C++ release
	Mar	1st ANSI X3J16 technical meeting (Somerset, NJ)
	May	*The Annotated C++ Reference Manual* [ARM]
	July	Templates accepted (Seattle, WA)
	Nov	Exceptions accepted (Palo Alto, CA)
1991	June	*The C++ Programming Language (second edition)* [2nd]
	June	1st ISO WG21 meeting (Lund, Sweden)
	Oct	Cfront Release 3.0 (including templates)
1992	Feb	1st DEC C++ release (including templates and exceptions)
	Mar	1st Microsoft C++ release
	May	1st IBM C++ release (including templates and exceptions)
1993	Mar	Run-time type identification accepted (Portland, OR)
	July	Namespaces accepted (Munich, Germany)
1994	Aug	ANSI/ISO Committee Draft registered

Focus on Use and Users

This book is written for C++ users, that is, for programmers and designers. I have tried (believe it or not) to avoid truly obscure and esoteric topics to give a user's view of the C++ language, its facilities, and its evolution. Purely language-technical discussions are presented only if they shed light on issues that directly impact users. The discussions of name lookup in templates (§15.10) and of lifetime of temporaries (§6.3.2) are examples.

Programming language specialists, language lawyers, and implementers will find many tidbits in this book, but the aim is to present the large picture rather than to be precise and comprehensive about every little detail. If precise language-technical details is what you want the definition of C++ can be found in *The Annotated C++ Reference Manual* (the ARM) [ARM], in *The C++ Programming Language (second edition)* [2nd], and in the ANSI/ISO standards committee's working paper. However, the details of a language definition are incomprehensible without an understanding of the purpose of the language. The language, details and all, exists to help build programs. My intent with this book is to provide insights that can help in this endeavor.

Programming Languages

Several reviewers asked me to compare C++ to other languages. This I have decided against doing. Thereby, I have reaffirmed a long-standing and strongly held view: Language comparisons are rarely meaningful and even less often fair. A good comparison of major programming languages requires more effort than most people are willing to spend, experience in a wide range of application areas, a rigid maintenance of a detached and impartial point of view, and a sense of fairness. I do not have the time, and as the designer of C++, my impartiality would never be fully credible.

I also worry about a phenomenon I have repeatedly observed in honest attempts at language comparisons. The authors try hard to be impartial, but are hopelessly biased by focusing on a single application, a single style of programming, or a single culture among programmers. Worse, when one language is significantly better known than others, a subtle shift in perspective occurs: Flaws in the well-known language are deemed minor and simple workarounds are presented, whereas similar flaws in other languages are deemed fundamental. Often, the workarounds commonly used in the less-well-known languages are simply unknown to the people doing the comparison or deemed unsatisfactory because they would be unworkable in the more familiar language.

Similarly, information about the well-known language tends to be completely up-to-date, whereas for the less-known language, the authors rely on several-year-old information. For languages that are worth comparing, a comparison of language X as defined three years ago vs. language Y as it appears in the latest experimental implementation is neither fair nor informative. Thus, I restrict my comments about languages other than C++ to generalities and to very specific comments. This is a book about C++, its design, and the factors that shaped its evolution. It is not an attempt to contrast C++ language features with those found in other languages.

To fit C++ into a historical context, here is a chart of the first appearances of languages that often crop up in discussions about C++:

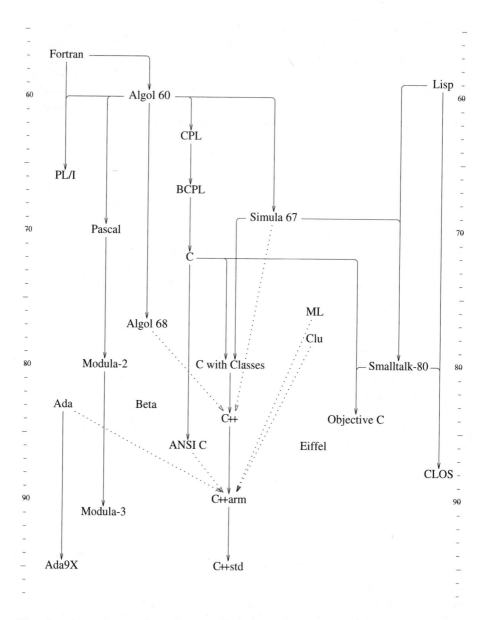

The chart is not intended to be anywhere near complete except for significant influences on C++. In particular, the chart understates the influence of the Simula class concept; Ada [Ichbiah,1979] and Clu [Liskov,1979] are weakly influenced by Simula [Birtwistle,1979]; Ada9X [Taft,1992], Beta [Madsen,1993], Eiffel [Meyer,1988], and Modula-3 [Nelson,1991] are strongly influenced. C++'s influence on other languages is left unrepresented. Solid lines indicate an influence on the structure of the language; dotted lines indicate an influence on specific features. Adding lines to show this for every language would make the diagram too messy to be useful. The dates for the languages are generally those of the first usable implementation. For example, Algol68 [Woodward,1974] can be found by the year 1977 rather than 1968.

One conclusion I drew from the wildly divergent comments on the HOPL-2 paper – and from many other sources – is that there is no agreement on what a programming language really is and what its main purpose is supposed to be. Is a programming language a tool for instructing machines? A means of communicating between programmers? A vehicle for expressing high-level designs? A notation for algorithms? A way of expressing relationships between concepts? A tool for experimentation? A means of controlling computerized devices? My view is that a general-purpose programming language must be all of those to serve its diverse set of users. The only thing a language cannot be – and survive – is a mere collection of "neat" features.

The difference in opinions reflects differing views of what computer science is and how languages ought to be designed. Ought computer science be a branch of mathematics? Of engineering? Of architecture? Of art? Of biology? Of sociology? Of philosophy? Alternatively, does it borrow techniques and approaches from all of these disciplines? I think so.

This implies that language design parts ways from the "purer" and more abstract disciplines such as mathematics and philosophy. To serve its users, a general-purpose programming language must be eclectic and take many practical and sociological factors into account. In particular, every language is designed to solve a particular set of problems at a particular time according to the understanding of a particular group of people. From this initial design, it grows to meet new demands and reflects new understandings of problems and of tools and techniques for solving them. This view is pragmatic, yet not unprincipled. It is my firm belief that *all* successful languages are grown and not merely designed from first principles. Principles underlie the first design and guide the further evolution of the language. However, even principles evolve.

References
This section contains the references from every chapter of this book.

[2nd]   see [Stroustrup,1991].

[Agha,1986]   Gul Agha: *An Overview of Actor languages*. ACM SIGPLAN Notices. October 1986.

[Aho,1986]   Alfred Aho, Ravi Sethi, and Jeffrey D. Ullman: *Compilers: Principles, Techniques, and Tools*. Addison-Wesley, Reading, MA. 1986. ISBN 0-201-10088-6.

[ARM]   see [Ellis,1990].

[Babcisky,1984] Karel Babcisky: *Simula Performance Assessment*. Proc. IFIP WG2.4 Conference on System Implementation Languages: Experience and Assessment. Canterbury, Kent, UK. September 1984.

[Barton,1994]   John J. Barton and Lee R. Nackman: *Scientific and*

                    *Engineering C++: An Introduction with Advanced Techniques
                    and Examples.* Addison-Wesley, Reading, MA. 1994. ISBN
                    0-201-53393-6.

[Birtwistle,1979]   Graham Birtwistle, Ole-Johan Dahl, Björn Myrhaug, and Kris-
                    ten Nygaard: *SIMULA BEGIN.* Studentlitteratur, Lund, Swe-
                    den. 1979. ISBN 91-44-06212-5.

[Boehm,1993]   Hans-J. Boehm: *Space Efficient Conservative Garbage Collec-
                    tion.* Proc. ACM SIGPLAN '93 Conference on Programming
                    Language Design and Implementation. ACM SIGPLAN
                    Notices. June 1993.

[Booch,1990]   Grady Booch and Michael M. Vilot: *The Design of the C++
                    Booch Components.* Proc. OOPSLA'90. October 1990.

[Booch,1991]   Grady Booch: *Object-Oriented Design.* Benjamin Cummings,
                    Redwood City, CA. 1991. ISBN 0-8053-0091-0.

[Booch,1993]   Grady Booch: *Object-oriented Analysis and Design with Appli-
                    cations, 2nd edition.* Benjamin Cummings, Redwood City,
                    CA. 1993. ISBN 0-8053-5340-2.

[Booch,1993b]   Grady Booch and Michael M. Vilot: *Simplifying the C++
                    Booch Components.* The C++ Report. June 1993.

[Budge,1992]   Ken Budge, J.S. Perry, and A.C. Robinson: *High-Performance
                    Scientific Computation using C++.* Proc. USENIX C++ Con-
                    ference. Portland, OR. August 1992.

[Buhr,1992]   Peter A. Buhr and Glen Ditchfield: *Adding Concurrency to a
                    Programming Language.* Proc. USENIX C++ Conference.
                    Portland, OR. August 1992.

[Call,1987]   Lisa A. Call, et al.: *CLAM – An Open System for Graphical
                    User Interfaces.* Proc. USENIX C++ Conference. Santa Fe,
                    NM. November 1987.

[Cameron,1992]   Don Cameron, et al.: *A Portable Implementation of C++
                    Exception Handling.* Proc. USENIX C++ Conference. Port-
                    land, OR. August 1992.

[Campbell,1987]   Roy Campbell, et al.: *The Design of a Multiprocessor Operat-
                    ing System.* Proc. USENIX C++ Conference. Santa Fe, NM.
                    November 1987.

[Cattell,1991]   Rich G.G. Cattell: *Object Data Management: Object-Oriented
                    and Extended Relational Database Systems.* Addison-Wesley,
                    Reading, MA. 1991. ISBN 0-201-53092-9.

[Cargill,1991]   Tom A. Cargill: *The Case Against Multiple Inheritance in
                    C++.* USENIX Computer Systems. Vol 4, no 1, 1991.

[Carroll,1991]   Martin Carroll: *Using Multiple Inheritance to Implement
                    Abstract Data Types.* The C++ Report. April 1991.

[Carroll,1993]   Martin Carroll: *Design of the USL Standard Components.* The
                    C++ Report. June 1993.

[Chandy,1993]   K. Mani Chandy and Carl Kesselman: *Compositional C++:*

Compositional Parallel Programming. Proc. Fourth Workshop on Parallel Computing and Compilers. Springer-Verlag. 1993.

[Cristian,1989]   Flaviu Cristian: *Exception Handling.* Dependability of Resilient Computers, T. Andersen, editor. BSP Professional Books, Blackwell Scientific Publications, 1989.

[Cox,1986]   Brad Cox: *Object-Oriented Programming: An Evolutionary Approach.* Addison-Wesley, Reading, MA. 1986.

[Dahl,1988]   Ole-Johan Dahl: Personal communication.

[Dearle,1990]   Fergal Dearle: *Designing Portable Applications Frameworks for C++.* Proc. USENIX C++ Conference. San Francisco, CA. April 1990.

[Dorward,1990]   Sean M. Dorward, et al.: *Adding New Code to a Running Program.* Proc. USENIX C++ Conference. San Francisco, CA. April 1990.

[Eick,1991]   Stephen G. Eick: *SIMLIB - An Object-Oriented C++ Library for Interactive Simulation of Circuit-Switched Networks.* Proc. Simulation Technology Conference. Orlando, FL. October 1991.

[Ellis,1990]   Margaret A. Ellis and Bjarne Stroustrup: *The Annotated C++ Reference Manual.* Addison-Wesley, Reading, MA. 1990. ISBN 0-201-51459-1.

[Faust,1990]   John E. Faust and Henry M. Levy: *The Performance of an Object-Oriented Threads Package.* Proc. ACM joint ECOOP and OOPSLA Conference. Ottawa, Canada. October 1990.

[Fontana,1991]   Mary Fontana and Martin Neath: *Checked Out and Long Overdue: Experiences in the Design of a C++ Class Library.* Proc. USENIX C++ Conference. Washington, DC. April 1991.

[Forslund,1990]   David W. Forslund, et al.: *Experiences in Writing Distributed Particle Simulation Code in C++.* Proc. USENIX C++ Conference. San Francisco, CA. April 1990.

[Gautron,1992]   Philippe Gautron: *An Assertion Mechanism based on Exceptions.* Proc. USENIX C++ Conference. Portland, OR. August 1992.

[Gehani,1988]   Narain H. Gehani and William D. Roome: *Concurrent C++: Concurrent Programming With Class(es).* Software—Practice & Experience. Vol 18, no 12, 1988.

[Goldberg,1983]   Adele Goldberg and David Robson: *Smalltalk-80, The Language and its Implementation.* Addison-Wesley, Reading, MA. 1983. ISBN 0-201-11371-6.

[Goodenough,1975]   John Goodenough: *Exception Handling: Issues and a Proposed Notation.* Communications of the ACM. December 1975.

[Gorlen,1987]   Keith E. Gorlen: *An Object-Oriented Class Library for C++ Programs.* Proc. USENIX C++ Conference. Santa Fe, NM. November 1987.

[Gorlen,1990]   Keith E. Gorlen, Sanford M. Orlow, and Perry S. Plexico: *Data Abstraction and Object-Oriented Programming in C++*. Wiley. West Sussex. England. 1990. ISBN 0-471-92346-X.

[Hübel,1992]   Peter Hübel and J.T. Thorsen: *An Implementation of a Persistent Store for C++*. Computer Science Department. Aarhus University, Denmark. December 1992.

[Ichbiah,1979]   Jean D. Ichbiah, et al.: *Rationale for the Design of the ADA Programming Language*. SIGPLAN Notices Vol 14, no 6, June 1979 Part B.

[Ingalls,1986]   Daniel H.H. Ingalls: *A Simple Technique for Handling Multiple Polymorphism*. Proc. ACM OOPSLA Conference. Portland, OR. November 1986.

[Interrante,1990] John A. Interrante and Mark A. Linton: *Runtime Access to Type Information*. Proc. USENIX C++ Conference. San Francisco 1990.

[Johnson,1992]   Steve C. Johnson: Personal communication.

[Johnson,1989]   Ralph E. Johnson: *The Importance of Being Abstract*. The C++ Report. March 1989.

[Keffer,1992]   Thomas Keffer: *Why C++ Will Replace Fortran*. C++ Supplement to Dr. Dobbs Journal. December 1992.

[Keffer,1993]   Thomas Keffer: *The Design and Architecture of Tools.h++*. The C++ Report. June 1993.

[Kernighan,1976]   Brian Kernighan and P.J. Plauger: *Software Tools*. Addison-Wesley, Reading, MA. 1976. ISBN 0-201-03669.

[Kernighan,1978]   Brian Kernighan and Dennis Ritchie: *The C Programming Language*. Prentice-Hall, Englewood Cliffs, NJ. 1978. ISBN 0-13-110163-3.

[Kernighan,1981]   Brian Kernighan: *Why Pascal is not my Favorite Programming Language*. AT&T Bell Labs Computer Science Technical Report No 100. July 1981.

[Kernighan,1984]   Brian Kernighan and Rob Pike: *The UNIX Programming Environment*. Prentice-Hall, Englewood Cliffs, NJ. 1984. ISBN 0-13-937699-2.

[Kernighan,1988]   Brian Kernighan and Dennis Ritchie: *The C Programming Language (second edition)*. Prentice-Hall, Englewood Cliffs, NJ. 1988. ISBN 0-13-110362-8.

[Kiczales,1992]   Gregor Kiczales, Jim des Rivieres, and Daniel G. Bobrow: *The Art of the Metaobject Protocol*. The MIT Press. Cambridge, Massachusetts. 1991. ISBN 0-262-11158-6.

[Koenig,1988]   Andrew Koenig: *Associative arrays in C++*. Proc. USENIX Conference. San Francisco, CA. June 1988.

[Koenig,1989]   Andrew Koenig and Bjarne Stroustrup: *C++: As close to C as possible – but no closer*. The C++ Report. July 1989.

[Koenig,1989b]   Andrew Koenig and Bjarne Stroustrup: *Exception Handling for*

C++. Proc. "C++ at Work" Conference. November 1989.

[Koenig,1990]   Andrew Koenig and Bjarne Stroustrup: *Exception Handling for C++ (revised)*. Proc. USENIX C++ Conference. San Francisco, CA. April 1990. Also, Journal of Object-Oriented Programming. July 1990.

[Koenig,1991]   Andrew Koenig: *Applicators, Manipulators, and Function Objects*. C++ Journal, vol. 1, #1. Summer 1990.

[Koenig,1992]   Andrew Koenig: *Space Efficient Trees in C++*. Proc. USENIX C++ Conference. Portland, OR. August 1992.

[Krogdahl,1984]   Stein Krogdahl: *An Efficient Implementation of Simula Classes with Multiple Prefixing*. Research Report No 83. June 1984. University of Oslo, Institute of Informatics.

[Lea,1990]   Doug Lea and Marshall P. Cline: *The Behavior of C++ Classes*. Proc. ACM SOOPPA Conference. September 1990.

[Lea,1991]   Doug Lea: Personal Communication.

[Lea,1993]   Doug Lea: *The GNU C++ Library*. The C++ Report. June 1993.

[Lenkov,1989]   Dmitry Lenkov: *C++ Standardization Proposal*. #X3J11/89-016.

[Lenkov,1991]   Dmitry Lenkov, Michey Mehta, and Shankar Unni: *Type Identification in C++*. Proc. USENIX C++ Conference. Washington, DC. April 1991.

[Linton,1987]   Mark A. Linton and Paul R. Calder: *The Design and Implementation of InterViews*. Proc. USENIX C++ Conference. Santa Fe, NM. November 1987.

[Lippman,1988]   Stan Lippman and Bjarne Stroustrup: *Pointers to Class Members in C++*. Proc. USENIX C++ Conference. Denver, CO. October 1988.

[Liskov,1979]   Barbara Liskov, et al.: *CLU Reference manual*. MIT/LCS/TR-225. October 1979.

[Liskov,1987]   Barbara Liskov: *Data Abstraction and Hierarchy*. Addendum to Proceedings of OOPSLA'87. October 1987.

[Madsen,1993]   Ole Lehrmann Madsen, et al.: *Object-Oriented Programming in the Beta Programming Language*. Addison-Wesley, Reading, MA. 1993. ISBN 0-201-62430.

[McCluskey,1992]   Glen McCluskey: *An Environment for Template Instantiation*. The C++ Report. February 1992.

[Meyer,1988]   Bertrand Meyer: *Object-Oriented Software Construction*. Prentice-Hall, Englewood Cliffs, NJ. 1988. ISBN 0-13-629049.

[Miller,1988]   William M. Miller: *Exception Handling without Language Extensions*. Proc. USENIX C++ Conference. Denver CO. October 1988.

[Mitchell,1979]   James G. Mitchell, et.al.: *Mesa Language Manual*. XEROX

PARC, Palo Alto, CA. CSL-79-3. April 1979.

[Murray,1992]   Rob Murray: *A Statically Typed Abstract Representation for C++ Programs.* Proc. USENIX C++ Conference. Portland, OR. August 1992.

[Nelson,1991]   Nelson, G. (editor): *Systems Programming with Modula-3.* Prentice-Hall, Englewood Cliffs, NJ. 1991. ISBN 0-13-590464-1.

[Rose,1984]   Leonie V. Rose and Bjarne Stroustrup: *Complex Arithmetic in C++.* Internal AT&T Bell Labs Technical Memorandum. January 1984. Reprinted in AT&T C++ Translator Release Notes. November 1985.

[Parrington,1990]   Graham D. Parrington: *Reliable Distributed Programming in C++.* Proc. USENIX C++ Conference. San Francisco, CA. April 1990.

[Reiser,1992]   John F. Reiser: *Static Initializers: Reducing the Value-Added Tax on Programs.* Proc. USENIX C++ Conference. Portland, OR. August 1992.

[Richards,1980]   Martin Richards and Colin Whitby-Strevens: *BCPL – the language and its compiler.* Cambridge University Press, Cambridge, England. 1980. ISBN 0-521-21965-5.

[Rovner,1986]   Paul Rovner: *Extending Modula-2 to Build Large, Integrated Systems.* IEEE Software Vol 3, No 6, November 1986.

[Russo,1988]   Vincent F. Russo and Simon M. Kaplan: *A C++ Interpreter for Scheme.* Proc. USENIX C++ Conference. Denver, CO. October 1988.

[Russo,1990]   Vincent F. Russo, Peter W. Madany, and Roy H. Campbell: *C++ and Operating Systems Performance: A Case Study.* Proc. USENIX C++ Conference. San Francisco, CA. April 1990.

[Sakkinen,1992]   Markku Sakkinen: *A Critique of the Inheritance Principles of C++.* USENIX Computer Systems, vol 5, no 1, Winter 1992.

[Sethi,1980]   Ravi Sethi: *A case study in specifying the semantics of a programming language.* Seventh Annual ACM Symposium on Principles of Programming Languages. January 1980.

[Sethi,1981]   Ravi Sethi: *Uniform Syntax for Type Expressions and Declarators.* Software – Practice and Experience, Vol 11. 1981.

[Sethi,1989]   Ravi Sethi: *Programming Languages – Concepts and Constructs.* Addison-Wesley, Reading, MA. 1989. ISBN 0-201-10365-6.

[Shopiro,1985]   Jonathan E. Shopiro: *Strings and Lists for C++.* AT&T Bell Labs Internal Technical Memorandum. July 1985.

[Shopiro,1987]   Jonathan E. Shopiro: *Extending the C++ Task System for Real-Time Control.* Proc. USENIX C++ Conference. Santa Fe, NM. November 1987.

[Shopiro,1989]   Jonathan E. Shopiro: *An Example of Multiple Inheritance in C++: A Model of the Iostream Library*. ACM SIGPLAN Notices. December 1989.

[Schwarz,1989]   Jerry Schwarz: *Iostreams Examples*. AT&T C++ Translator Release Notes. June 1989.

[Snyder,1986]   Alan Snyder: *Encapsulation and Inheritance in Object-Oriented Programming Languages*. Proc. OOPSLA'86. September 1986.

[Stal,1993]   Michael Stal and Uwe Steinmüller: *Generic Dynamic Arrays*. The C++ Report. October 1993.

[Stepanov,1993]   Alexander Stepanov and David R. Musser: *Algorithm-Oriented Generic Software Library Development*. HP Laboratories Technical Report HPL-92-65. November 1993.

[Stroustrup,1978]   Bjarne Stroustrup: *On Unifying Module Interfaces*. ACM Operating Systems Review Vol 12 No 1. January 1978.

[Stroustrup,1979]   Bjarne Stroustrup: *Communication and Control in Distributed Computer Systems*. Ph.D. thesis, Cambridge University, 1979.

[Stroustrup,1979b]   Bjarne Stroustrup: *An Inter-Module Communication System for a Distributed Computer System*. Proc. 1st International Conf. on Distributed Computing Systems. October 1979.

[Stroustrup,1980]   Bjarne Stroustrup: *Classes: An Abstract Data Type Facility for the C Language*. Bell Laboratories Computer Science Technical Report CSTR-84. April 1980. Revised, August 1981. Revised yet again and published as [Stroustrup,1982].

[Stroustrup,1980b]   Bjarne Stroustrup: *A Set of C Classes for Co-routine Style Programming*. Bell Laboratories Computer Science Technical Report CSTR-90. November 1980.

[Stroustrup,1981]   Bjarne Stroustrup: *Long Return: A Technique for Improving The Efficiency of Inter-Module Communication*. Software Practice and Experience. January 1981.

[Stroustrup,1981b]   Bjarne Stroustrup: *Extensions of the C Language Type Concept*. Bell Labs Internal Memorandum. January 1981.

[Stroustrup,1982]   Bjarne Stroustrup: *Classes: An Abstract Data Type Facility for the C Language*. ACM SIGPLAN Notices. January 1982. Revised version of [Stroustrup,1980].

[Stroustrup,1982b]   Bjarne Stroustrup: *Adding Classes to C: An Exercise in Language Evolution*. Bell Laboratories Computer Science internal document. April 1982. Software: Practice & Experience, Vol 13. 1983.

[Stroustrup,1984]   Bjarne Stroustrup: *The C++ Reference Manual*. AT&T Bell Labs Computer Science Technical Report No 108. January 1984. Revised, November 1984.

[Stroustrup,1984b]   Bjarne Stroustrup: *Operator Overloading in C++*. Proc. IFIP WG2.4 Conference on System Implementation Languages:

	Experience & Assessment. September 1984.
[Stroustrup,1984c]	Bjarne Stroustrup: *Data Abstraction in C.* Bell Labs Technical Journal. Vol 63, No 8. October 1984.
[Stroustrup,1985]	Bjarne Stroustrup: *An Extensible I/O Facility for C++.* Proc. Summer 1985 USENIX Conference. June 1985.
[Stroustrup,1986]	Bjarne Stroustrup: *The C++ Programming Language.* Addison-Wesley, Reading, MA. 1986. ISBN 0-201-12078-X.
[Stroustrup,1986b]	Bjarne Stroustrup: *What is Object-Oriented Programming?* Proc. 14th ASU Conference. August 1986. Revised version in Proc. ECOOP'87, May 1987, Springer Verlag Lecture Notes in Computer Science Vol 276. Revised version in *IEEE Software Magazine.* May 1988.
[Stroustrup,1986c]	Bjarne Stroustrup: *An Overview of C++.* ACM SIGPLAN Notices. October 1986.
[Stroustrup,1987]	Bjarne Stroustrup: *Multiple Inheritance for C++.* Proc. EUUG Spring Conference, May 1987. Also, USENIX Computer Systems, Vol 2 No 4. Fall 1989.
[Stroustrup,1987b]	Bjarne Stroustrup and Jonathan Shopiro: *A Set of C classes for Co-Routine Style Programming.* Proc. USENIX C++ Conference. Santa Fe, NM. November 1987.
[Stroustrup,1987c]	Bjarne Stroustrup: *The Evolution of C++: 1985-1987.* Proc. USENIX C++ Conference. Santa Fe, NM. November 1987.
[Stroustrup,1987d]	Bjarne Stroustrup: *Possible Directions for C++.* Proc. USENIX C++ Conference. Santa Fe, NM. November 1987.
[Stroustrup,1988]	Bjarne Stroustrup: *Type-safe Linkage for C++.* USENIX Computer Systems, Vol 1 No 4. Fall 1988.
[Stroustrup,1988b]	Bjarne Stroustrup: *Parameterized Types for C++.* Proc. USENIX C++ Conference, Denver, CO. October 1988. Also, USENIX Computer Systems, Vol 2 No 1. Winter 1989.
[Stroustrup,1989]	Bjarne Stroustrup: *Standardizing C++.* The C++ Report. Vol 1 No 1. January 1989.
[Stroustrup,1989b]	Bjarne Stroustrup: *The Evolution of C++: 1985-1989.* USENIX Computer Systems, Vol 2 No 3. Summer 1989. Revised version of [Stroustrup,1987c].
[Stroustrup,1990]	Bjarne Stroustrup: *On Language Wars.* Hotline on Object-Oriented Technology. Vol 1, No 3. January 1990.
[Stroustrup,1990b]	Bjarne Stroustrup: *Sixteen Ways to Stack a Cat.* The C++ Report. October 1990.
[Stroustrup,1991]	Bjarne Stroustrup: *The C++ Programming Language (2nd edition).* Addison-Wesley, Reading, MA. 1991. ISBN 0-201-53992-6.
[Stroustrup,1992]	Bjarne Stroustrup and Dmitri Lenkov: *Run-Time Type Identification for C++.* The C++ Report. March 1992. Revised version: Proc. USENIX C++ Conference. Portland, OR. August

1992.

[Stroustrup,1992b]   Bjarne Stroustrup: *How to Write a C++ Language Extension Proposal*. The C++ Report. May 1992.

[Stroustrup,1993]   Bjarne Stroustrup: *The History of C++: 1979-1991*. Proc. ACM History of Programming Languages Conference (HOPL-2). April 1993. ACM SIGPLAN Notices. March 1993.

[Taft,1992]   S. Tucker Taft: *Ada 9X: A Technical Summary*. CACM. November 1992.

[Tiemann,1987]   Michael Tiemann: *"Wrappers:" Solving the RPC problem in GNU C++*. Proc. USENIX C++ Conference. Denver, CO. October 1988.

[Tiemann,1990]   Michael Tiemann: *An Exception Handling Implementation for C++*. Proc. USENIX C++ Conference. San Francisco, CA. April 1990.

[Weinand,1988]   Andre Weinand, et al.: *ET++ – An Object-Oriented Application Framework in C++*. Proc. OOPSLA'88. September 1988.

[Wikström,1987]   Åke Wikström: *Functional Programming in Standard ML*. Prentice-Hall, Englewood Cliffs, NJ. 1987. ISBN 0-13-331968-7.

[Waldo,1991]   Jim Waldo: *Controversy: The Case for Multiple Inheritance in C++*. USENIX Computer Systems, vol 4, no 2, Spring 1991.

[Waldo,1993]   Jim Waldo (editor): *The Evolution of C++*. A USENIX Association book. The MIT Press, Cambridge, MA. 1993. ISBN 0-262-73107-X.

[Wilkes,1979]   M.V. Wilkes and R.M. Needham: *The Cambridge CAP Computer and its Operating System*. North-Holland, New York. 1979. ISBN 0-444-00357-6.

[Woodward,1974]   P.M. Woodward and S.G. Bond: *Algol 68-R Users Guide*. Her Majesty's Stationery Office, London. 1974. ISBN 0-11-771600-6.

Part I

Part I describes the origins of C++ and its evolution through C with Classes to Release 1.0. It also describes the rules that guided C++'s growth during that period and beyond. A chronology of post-1.0 developments is provided, and the C++ standardization effort is described. To provide perspective, the use of C++ is discussed. Finally, a retrospective and some thoughts on the future is presented.

Chapters

1

The Prehistory of C++

In olden days,
when EVIL ruled!
– Kristen Nygaard

Simula and distributed systems — C and systems programming — the influence of mathematics, history, philosophy, and literature.

1.1 Simula and Distributed Systems

The prehistory of C++ – the couple of years before the idea of adding Simula-like features to C occurred to me – is important because during this time, the criteria and ideals that later shaped C++ emerged. I was working on my Ph.D. Thesis in the Computing Laboratory of Cambridge University in England. My aim was to study alternatives for the organization of system software for distributed systems. The conceptual framework was provided by the capability-based Cambridge CAP computer and its experimental and continuously evolving operating system [Wilkes,1979]. The details of this work and its outcome [Stroustrup,1979] are of little relevance to C++. What is relevant, though, was the focus on composing software out of well-delimited modules and that the main experimental tool was a relatively large and detailed simulator I wrote for simulating software running on a distributed system.

The initial version of this simulator was written in Simula [Birtwistle,1979] and ran on the Cambridge University computer center's IBM 360/165 mainframe. It was a pleasure to write that simulator. The features of Simula were almost ideal for the purpose, and I was particularly impressed by the way the concepts of the language helped me think about the problems in my application. The class concept allowed me to map my application concepts into the language constructs in a direct way that made my code more readable than I had seen in any other language. The way Simula classes can act as co-routines made the inherent concurrency of my application easy to express. For example, an object of class `computer` could trivially be made to work in pseudo-parallel with other objects of class `computer`. Class hierarchies were used to express variants of application-level concepts. For example, different types of computers could be expressed as classes derived from class `computer` and different types of inter-module communication mechanisms could be expressed as classes derived from class `IPC`. The use of class hierarchies was not heavy, though; the use of classes to express concurrency was much more important in the organization of my simulator.

During writing and initial debugging, I acquired a great respect for the expressiveness of Simula's type system and its compiler's ability to catch type errors. I observed that type errors almost invariably reflected either a silly programming error or a conceptual flaw in the design. The latter was by far the most significant and a help that I had not experienced in the use of more primitive ''strong'' type systems. In contrast, I had found Pascal's type system to be worse than useless – a straitjacket that caused more problems than it solved by forcing me to warp my designs to suit an implementation-oriented artifact. The contrast I perceived between the rigidity of Pascal and the flexibility of Simula was essential for the development of C++. Simula's class concept was seen as the key difference, and ever since I have seen classes as the proper primary focus of program design.

I had used Simula before (during my studies at the University of Aarhus, Denmark), but was very pleasantly surprised by the way the mechanisms of the Simula language became increasingly helpful as the size of the program increased. The class and co-routine mechanisms and the comprehensive type checking ensured that problems and errors did not (as I – and I guess most people – would have expected) grow more than linearly with the size of the program. Instead, the total program acted more like a collection of very small programs than a single large program and was therefore easier to write, comprehend, and debug.

The implementation of Simula, however, did not scale in the same way. As a result, the whole project came close to disaster. My conclusion at the time was that the Simula implementation (as opposed to the Simula language) was geared to small programs and was inherently unsuitable for larger programs [Stroustrup,1979]. Link times for separately compiled classes were abysmal: It took longer to compile 1/30th of the program and link it to a precompiled version of the rest than it took to compile and link the program as a monolith. This I believe, was more a problem with the mainframe linker than with Simula, but it was still a burden. On top of that, the run-time performance was such that there was no hope of obtaining useful data from the simulator. The poor run-time characteristics were a function of the language and its implementation rather than a function of the application. The overhead problems were fundamental to Simula and could not be remedied. The cost arose from several language features and their interactions: run-time type checking, guaranteed initialization of variables, concurrency support, and garbage collection of both user-allocated objects and procedure activation records. For example, measurements showed that more than 80% of the time was spent in the garbage collector despite the fact that resource management was part of the simulated system so that no garbage was ever produced. Simula implementations are better these days (15 years later), but the order-of-magnitude improvement in run-time performance still has not (to the best of my knowledge) materialized.

To avoid terminating the project – and thus having to leave Cambridge without a Ph.D. – I rewrote the simulator in BCPL and ran it on the experimental CAP computer. The experience of coding and debugging the simulator in BCPL [Richards,1980] was horrible. BCPL makes C look like a very high-level language and provides absolutely no type checking or run-time support. The resulting simulator did, however, run suitably fast and gave a whole range of useful results that clarified many issues for me and provided the basis for several papers on operating system issues [Stroustrup,1978,1979b,1981].

Upon leaving Cambridge, I swore never again to attack a problem with tools as unsuitable as those I had suffered while designing and implementing the simulator. The significance of this to C++ was the notion I had evolved of what constituted a ''suitable tool'' for projects such as writing a significant simulator, an operating system, and similar systems programming tasks:

[1] A good tool would have Simula's support for program organization – that is, classes, some form of class hierarchies, some form of support for concurrency, and strong (that is, static) checking of a type system based on classes. This I saw (as I still see it today) as support for the process of inventing programs, as support for design rather than just for implementation.

[2] A good tool would produce programs that run as fast as BCPL programs and share BCPL's ability to easily combine separately compiled units into a program. A simple linkage convention is essential for combining units written in languages such as C, Algol68, Fortran, BCPL, assembler, etc., into a single program so that programmers can avoid getting caught by inherent limitations in a single language.

[3] A good tool should also allow for highly portable implementations. My experience was that the ''good'' implementation I needed would typically not be available until ''next year'' and then only on a machine I couldn't afford. This implied that a tool must have multiple sources of implementations (no monopoly would be sufficiently responsive to users of ''unusual'' machines or to poor graduate students), that there should be no complicated run-time support system to port, and that there should be only very limited integration between the tool and its host operating system.

These criteria were not fully formed when I left Cambridge. Some matured only on further reflection on my experience with the simulator, on programs written over the next couple of years, and on the experiences of others that I learned of through discussions and reading of code. C++ as defined at the time of Release 2.0 strictly fulfills these criteria; the fundamental tensions in the effort to design templates and exception handling mechanisms for C++ arise from the need to depart from some aspects of these criteria. I think the most important aspect of these criteria is that they are only loosely connected with specific programming language features. Instead, they specify constraints on a solution.

At the time I was there, the Cambridge Computing Laboratory was headed by Maurice Wilkes. I received my main technical guidance from my supervisor, David Wheeler, and from Roger Needham. My background in operating systems and my interest in modularization and communication had permanent effects on C++. The C++ model of protection, for example, is based on the notion of granting and transferring access rights; the distinction between initialization and assignment has its root in thoughts about transferring capabilities; C++'s notion of `const` is derived from hardware read/write access protection mechanisms; and the design of C++'s exception handling mechanism was influenced by work on fault-tolerant systems done by Brian Randell's group in Newcastle during the seventies.

1.2   C and Systems Programming

I had briefly encountered C in London in 1975 and acquired some respect for it compared to other languages of the kind referred to as systems programming languages, machine-oriented languages, or low-level languages. Of those, I knew PL360, Coral, Mary, and others, but my main experience with languages of this class was BCPL. In addition to being a BCPL user, I had once implemented BCPL by microcoding its intermediate form, O-code, so I had a detailed understanding of the low-level efficiency implications of this class of languages.

After finishing my Ph.D. Thesis in Cambridge and getting a job at Bell Labs, I (re)learned C from [Kernighan,1978]. Thus, at the time, I was not a C expert and saw C primarily as the most modern and prominent example of the systems programming languages. Only later did I achieve a fuller understanding of C based on personal experience and discussion with people such as Stu Feldman, Steve Johnson, Brian Kernighan, and Dennis Ritchie. The general idea of a systems programming language thus determined the growth of C++ to at least the same extent as did the specific language-technical details of C.

I knew Algol68 [Woodward,1974] pretty well from using it for minor projects in Cambridge. I appreciated the relationship between its constructs and those of C, and sometimes find it useful to consider C constructs as specialized versions of Algol68's more general concepts. Curiously enough, I did not see Algol68 as a systems programming language (despite having used an operating system written in Algol68). I suspect the reason was the emphasis I placed on portability, ease of linkage to code written in other languages, and run-time efficiency. I have on occasion described my dream language as Algol68 with Simula-like classes. However, for building a practical tool, C seemed a much better choice than Algol68.

1.3 General Background

It is often claimed that the structure of a system reflects the structure of the organization that created it. Within reason, I subscribe to that idea. It follows that when a system is primarily the work of an individual, the system reflects the fundamental outlook of that individual. In retrospect, I think the overall structure of C++ was shaped as much by my general "world view" as it was shaped by the detailed computer science concepts used to form its individual parts.

I studied pure and applied mathematics so that my Danish "masters degree" (a Cand.Scient. degree) is in mathematics and computer science. This left me with an appreciation of the beauty of mathematics, but also with a bias towards mathematics as a practical tool for problem solving as opposed to an apparently purposeless monument to abstract truth and beauty. I have a lot of sympathy for the student Euclid reputedly had evicted for asking, "But what is mathematics for?" Similarly, my interest in computers and programming languages is fundamentally pragmatic. Computers and programming languages can be appreciated as works of art, but aesthetic factors should complement and enhance utility, not substitute for or compromise utility.

My long-term (continuous for at least 25 years) hobby is history, and I spent significant time in university and later studying philosophy. This has given me a rather conscious view of where my intellectual sympathies lie and why. Among the long-standing schools of thought, I feel most at home with the empiricists rather than with the idealists – the mysticists I just can't appreciate. That is, I tend to prefer Aristotle to Plato, Hume to Descartes, and shake my head sadly over Pascal. I find comprehensive "systems" like those of Plato and Kant fascinating, yet fundamentally unsatisfying in that they appear to me dangerously remote from everyday experiences and the essential peculiarities of individuals.

I find Kierkegaard's almost fanatical concern for the individual and keen psychological insights much more appealing than the grandiose schemes and concern for humanity in the abstract of Hegel or Marx. Respect for groups that doesn't include respect for individuals of those groups isn't respect at all. Many C++ design decisions have their roots in my dislike for forcing people to do things in some particular way. In history, some of the worst disasters have been caused by idealists trying to force people into "doing what is good for them." Such idealism not only leads to suffering among its innocent victims, but also to delusion and corruption of the idealists applying the force. I also find idealists prone to ignore experience and experiment that inconveniently clashes with dogma or theory. Where ideals clash and sometimes even when pundits seem to agree, I prefer to provide support that gives the programmer a choice.

My preferences in literature have reinforced this unwillingness to make a decision based on theory and logic alone. In this sense, C++ owes as much to novelists and essayists such as Martin A. Hansen, Albert Camus, and George Orwell, who never saw a computer, as it does to computer scientists such as David Gries, Don Knuth, and Roger Needham. Often, when I was tempted to outlaw a feature I personally disliked, I refrained from doing so because I did not think I had the right to force my views on others. I know that much can be achieved in a relatively short time by the energetic pursuit of logic and by ruthless condemnation of "bad, outdated, and confused habits of thought." However, the human cost is often high. A high degree of tolerance and acceptance that different people do think in different ways and strongly prefer to do things differently is to me far preferable.

My preference is to slowly – often painfully slowly – persuade people to try new techniques and adapt the ones that suit their needs and tastes. There are effective techniques for achieving "religious conversions" and "revolutions," but I have fundamental qualms about those techniques and grave doubts about their effects in the long term and on a large scale. Often, if someone can be easily converted to "religion" X, a further conversion to "religion" Y is likely, and the gain ephemeral. I prefer skeptics to "true believers." I value a small piece of solid evidence over most theories, and a solid experimental result over most logical arguments.

These views could easily lead to fatalistic acceptance of status quo. After all, one cannot make an omelet without cracking a few eggs and most people do not actually want to change – at least "not just now" or in ways that will disrupt their everyday lives. This is where respect for facts comes in – and a modicum of idealism. Things in programming and in the world in general really aren't in a very good state, and much can be done to improve them. I designed C++ to solve a problem, not to prove a point, and it grew to serve its users. The underlying view is that it is possible to achieve improvements through gradual change. The ideal situation is to maintain the greatest rate of change that improves the welfare of the individuals involved. The main difficulties are to determine what constitutes progress, to develop techniques to smooth transitions, and to avoid excesses caused by over-enthusiasm.

I'm willing to work hard for the adoption of ideas that I have become convinced will be of help to people. In fact, I consider it the obligation of scientists and intellectuals to ensure that their ideas are made accessible and thus useful to society instead of being mere playthings for specialists. However, I'm not willing to sacrifice people to ideas. In particular, I do not try to enforce a single style of design through a narrowly defined programming language. People's ways of thinking and working are so diverse that an attempt to force a single style would do more harm than good. Thus, C++ is deliberately designed to support a variety of styles rather than a would-be "one true way."

Chapter 4 presents the more detailed and practical rules that guided the design of C++. In those rules, you can find the echoes of the general ideas and ideals mentioned here.

A programming language can be the most important factor in a programmer's day. However, a programming language is really a very tiny part of the world, and as such, it ought not be taken too seriously. Keep a sense of proportion and – most importantly – keep a sense of humor. Among major programming languages, C++ is the richest source of puns and jokes. That is no accident.

Philosophy, like discussion of language features, does tend to get overly serious and preachy. For this, I apologize, but I felt like acknowledging my intellectual roots and I guess this is harmless – well, mostly harmless. And no, my preferences in literature are not limited to writers emphasizing philosophical and political themes; those are just the ones who left the most obvious traces in the fabric of C++.

2

C with Classes

Specialization is for insects.
– R.A.Heinlein

C++'s immediate predecessor, C with Classes — key design principles — classes — run-time and space efficiency — the linkage model — static (strong) type checking — why C? — syntax problems — derived classes — living without virtual functions and templates — access-control mechanisms — constructors and destructors — my work environment.

2.1 The Birth of C with Classes

The work on what eventually became C++ started with an attempt to analyze the UNIX kernel to determine how it could be distributed over a network of computers connected by a local area network. This work started in April 1979 in the Computing Science Research Center of Bell Laboratories in Murray Hill, New Jersey. Two subproblems soon emerged: how to analyze the network traffic that would result from the kernel distribution and how to modularize the kernel. Both required a way to express the module structure of a complex system and the communication pattern of the modules. This was exactly the kind of problem that I had become determined never again to attack without proper tools. Consequently, I set about developing a proper tool according to the criteria I had formed in Cambridge.

In October 1979 I had a running preprocessor, called Cpre, which added Simula-like classes to C, and by March 1980 this preprocessor had been refined to the point where it supported one real project and several experiments. My records show the preprocessor was in use on 16 systems by then. The first key C++ library, the task system supporting a co-routine style of programming [Stroustrup,1980b] [Stroustrup,1987b] [Shopiro,1987], was crucial to these projects. The language accepted by the preprocessor was called ''C with Classes.''

During the April to October period the transition from thinking about a *tool* to thinking about a *language* had occurred, but C with Classes was still thought of primarily as an extension to C for expressing modularity and concurrency. A crucial decision had been made, though. Even though support of concurrency and Simula-style simulations was a primary aim of C with Classes, the language contained no primitives for expressing concurrency; rather, a combination of inheritance (class hierarchies) and the ability to define class member functions with special meanings recognized by the preprocessor was used to write the library that supported the desired styles of concurrency. Please note that ''styles'' is plural. I considered it crucial – as I still do – that more than one notion of concurrency should be expressible in the language. There are many applications for which support for concurrency is essential, but there is no one dominant model for concurrency support; thus, when support is needed, it should be provided through a library or a special-purpose extension so that a particular form of concurrency support does not preclude other forms.

The language thus provided general mechanisms for organizing programs, rather than support for specific application areas. This was what made C with Classes – and later, C++ – a general-purpose language rather than a C variant with extensions to support specialized applications. Later, the choice between providing support for specialized applications or general abstraction mechanisms has come up repeatedly. Each time the decision has been to improve the abstraction mechanisms. Thus, C++ does not have built-in complex number, string, or matrix types, or direct support for concurrency, persistence, distributed computing, pattern matching, or file system manipulation, to mention a few of the most frequently suggested extensions. Instead, libraries supporting those needs exist.

An early description of C with Classes was published as a Bell Labs technical report in April 1980 [Stroustrup,1980] and in SIGPLAN Notices [Stroustrup,1982]. A more detailed Bell Labs technical report, *Adding Classes to the C Language: An Exercise in Language Evolution* [Stroustrup,1982b] was published in *Software: Practice and Experience*. These papers set a good example by describing only features that were fully implemented and had been used. This was in accordance with Bell Labs Computing Science Research Center tradition. That policy was modified only when more openness about the future of C++ became needed to ensure a free and open debate over the evolution of C++ among its many non-AT&T users.

C with Classes was explicitly designed to allow better organization of programs; ''computation'' was considered a problem solved by C. I was very concerned that improved program structure was not achieved at the expense of run-time overhead compared to C. The explicit aim was to match C in terms of run-time, code compactness, and data compactness. To wit: Someone once demonstrated a 3% systematic decrease in overall run-time efficiency compared with C caused by the use of a spurious temporary introduced into the function return mechanism by the C with Classes preprocessor. This was deemed unacceptable and the overhead promptly removed. Similarly, to ensure layout compatibility with C and thereby avoid space overhead, no ''housekeeping data'' was placed in class objects.

Another major concern was to avoid restrictions on the domain where C with Classes could be used. The ideal – which was achieved – was that C with Classes could be used for whatever C could be used for. This implied that in addition to matching C in efficiency, C with Classes could not provide benefits at the expense of removing "dangerous" or "ugly" features of C. This observation/principle had to be repeated often to people (rarely C with Classes users) who wanted C with Classes made safer by increasing static type checking along the lines of early Pascal. The alternative way of providing "safety," inserting run-time checks for all unsafe operations, was (and is) considered reasonable for debugging environments, but the language could not guarantee such checks without leaving C with a large advantage in run-time and space efficiency. Consequently, such checks were not provided for C with Classes, although some C++ environments do provide such checks for debugging. In addition, users can and do insert run-time checks (see §16.10 and [2nd]) where needed and affordable.

C allows low-level operations, such as bit manipulation and choosing between different sizes of integers. There are also facilities, such as explicit unchecked type conversions, for deliberately breaking the type system. C with Classes and later C++ follow this path by retaining the low-level and unsafe features of C. In contrast to C, C++ systematically eliminates the need to use such features except where they are essential and performs unsafe operations only at the explicit request of the programmer. I strongly felt then, as I still do, that there is no one right way of writing every program, and a language designer has no business trying to *force* programmers to use a particular style. The language designer does, on the other hand, have an obligation to encourage and support a variety of styles and practices that have proven effective and to provide language features and tools to help programmers avoid the well-known traps and pitfalls.

2.2 Feature overview

The features provided in the initial 1980 implementation can be summarized:
- [1] Classes (§2.3)
- [2] Derived classes (but no virtual functions yet, §2.9)
- [3] Public/private access control (§2.10)
- [4] Constructors and destructors (§2.11.1)
- [5] Call and return functions (later removed, §2.11.3)
- [6] `friend` classes (§2.10)
- [7] Type checking and conversion of function arguments (§2.6)

During 1981, three more features were added:
- [8] Inline functions (§2.4.1)
- [9] Default arguments (§2.12.2)
- [10] Overloading of the assignment operator (§2.12.1)

Since a preprocessor was used for the implementation of C with Classes, only new features (that is, features not present in C) had to be described and the full power of C

was available to users. Both aspects were appreciated at the time. Having C as a subset dramatically reduced the support and documentation work needed. This was most
important because for several years I did all of the C with Classes and C++ documentation and support in addition to doing the experimentation, design, and implementation. Having all C features available further ensured that no limitations introduced
through prejudice or lack of foresight on my part would deprive a user of features
already available in C. Naturally, portability to machines supporting C was ensured.
Initially, C with Classes was implemented and used on a DEC PDP/11, but soon it
was ported to machines such as the DEC VAX and Motorola 68000 based machines.

    C with Classes was still seen as a dialect of C rather than as a separate language.
Furthermore, classes were referred to as ''an abstract data type facility'' [Strous-
trup,1980]. Support for object-oriented programming was not claimed until the provision of virtual functions in C++ in 1983 [Stroustrup,1984].

2.3 Classes

Clearly, the most important aspect of C with Classes – and later of C++ – was the
class concept. Many aspects of the C with Classes class concept can be observed by
examining a simple example from [Stroustrup,1980]†:

```
class stack {
    char    s[SIZE];  /* array of characters */
    char*   min;      /* pointer to bottom of stack */
    char*   top;      /* pointer to top of stack */
    char*   max;      /* pointer to top of allocated space */
    void    new();    /* initialize function (constructor) */
public:
    void    push(char);
    char    pop();
};
```

A class is a user-defined data type. A class specifies the type of class members that
define the representation of a variable of the type (an object of the class), the set of
operations (functions) that manipulate such objects, and the access users have to these
members. Member functions are typically defined ''elsewhere:''

```
char stack.pop()
{
    if (top <= min) error("stack underflow");
    return *(--top);
}
```

Objects of class `stack` can now be defined and used:

---

† I have retained the original C with Classes syntax and style in the examples. The differences from C++
and modern style should not cause problems with comprehension and may be of interest to some readers. I
have, however, fixed obvious bugs and added comments to compensate for the lack of the original context.

```
class stack s1, s2;          /* two stack variables */
class stack * p1 = &s2;      /* p1 points to s2 */
class stack * p2 = new stack; /* p2 points to stack object
                                 allocated on free store */


s1.push('h');    /* use object directly */
p1->push('s');   /* use object through pointer */
```

Several key design decisions are reflected here:

[1] C with Classes follows Simula in letting the programmer specify types from which variables (objects) can be created, rather than, say, the Modula approach of specifying a module as a collection of objects and functions. In C with Classes (as in C++), a class is a type (§2.9). This is a key notion in C++. When class means user-defined type in C++, why didn't I call it type? I chose class primarily because I dislike inventing new terminology and found Simula's quite adequate in most cases.

[2] The representation of objects of the user-defined type is part of the class declaration. This has far-reaching implications (§2.4, §2.5). For example, it means that true local variables of a user-defined type can be implemented without the use of free store (also called heap store and dynamic store) or garbage collection. It also means that a function must be recompiled if the representation of an object it uses directly is changed. See §13.2 for C++ facilities for expressing interfaces that avoid such recompilation.

[3] Compile-time access control is used to restrict access to the representation. By default, only the functions mentioned in the class declaration can use names of class members (§2.10). Members (usually function members) specified in the public interface – the declarations after the public: label – can be used by other code.

[4] The full type (including both the return type and the argument types) of a function is specified for function members. Static (compile-time) type checking is based on this type specification (§2.6). This differed from C at the time, where function argument types were neither specified in interfaces nor checked in calls.

[5] Function definitions are typically specified ''elsewhere'' to make a class more like an interface specification than a lexical mechanism for organizing source code. This implies that separate compilation for class member functions and their users is easy and the linker technology traditionally used for C is sufficient to support C++ (§2.5).

[6] The function new() is a constructor, a function with a special meaning to the compiler. Such functions provided guarantees about classes (§2.11). In this case, the guarantee is that the constructor – known somewhat confusingly as a new-function at the time – is guaranteed to be called to initialize every object of its class before the first use of the object.

[7] Both pointers and non-pointer types are provided (as in both C and Simula).

Like C and unlike Simula, pointers can point to objects of both user-defined and built-in types (§2.4).

[8] Like C, objects can be allocated in three ways: on the stack (automatic storage), at a fixed address (static storage), and on the free store (on the heap, dynamic storage). Unlike C, C with Classes provides specific operators `new` and `delete` for free store allocation and deallocation (§2.11.2).

Much of the further development of C with Classes and C++ can be seen as exploring the consequences of these design choices, exploiting their good sides, and compensating for the problems caused by their bad sides. Many, but by no means all, of the implications of these design choices were understood at the time; [Stroustrup,1980] is dated April 3, 1980. This section tries to explain what was understood at the time and gives pointers to sections that explain consequences and later realizations.

2.4 Run-Time Efficiency

In Simula, it is not possible to have local or global variables of class types; that is, every object of a class must be allocated on the free store using the `new` operator. Measurements of my Cambridge simulator had convinced me this was a major source of inefficiency. Later, Karel Babcisky from the Norwegian Computer Centre presented data on Simula run-time performance that confirmed my conjecture [Babcisky,1984]. For that reason alone, I wanted global and local variables of class types.

In addition, having different rules for the creation and scope of built-in and user-defined types is inelegant, and I felt that on occasion my programming style had been cramped by the absence of local and global class variables from Simula. Similarly, I had missed the ability to have pointers to built-in types in Simula, so I wanted the C notion of pointers to apply uniformly over user-defined and built-in types. This is the origin of the notion that over the years grew into a rule of thumb for the design of C++: User-defined and built-in types should behave the same relative to the language rules and receive the same degree of support from the language and its associated tools. When the ideal was formulated built-in types received by far the best support, but C++ has overshot that target so that built-in types now receive slightly inferior support compared to user-defined types (§15.11.3).

The initial version of C with Classes did not provide inline functions to take further advantage of the availability of the representation. Inline functions were soon provided, though. The general reason for the introduction of inline functions was concern that the cost of crossing a protection barrier would cause people to refrain from using classes to hide representation. In particular, [Stroustrup,1982b] observes that people had made data members public to avoid the function call overhead incurred by a constructor for simple classes where only one or two assignments are needed for initialization. The immediate cause for the inclusion of inline functions into C with Classes was a project that couldn't afford function call overhead for some classes involved in real-time processing. For classes to be useful in that application, crossing the protection barrier had to be free. Only the combination of having the representation available in the class declaration and having the calls of the public (interface) functions inlined could deliver that.

Over the years, considerations along these lines grew into the C++ rule that it was not sufficient to provide a feature, it had to be provided in an affordable form. Most definitely, *affordable* was seen as meaning "affordable on hardware common among developers" as opposed to "affordable to researchers with high-end equipment" or "affordable in a couple of years when hardware will be cheaper." C with Classes was always considered as something to be used *now* or *next month* rather than simply a research project to deliver something in a couple of years hence.

2.4.1 Inlining

Inlining was considered important for the utility of classes. Therefore, the issue was more *how* to provide it than *whether* to provide it. Two arguments won the day for the notion of having the programmer select which functions the compiler should try to inline. First, I had had poor experiences with languages that left the job of inlining to compilers "because clearly the compiler knows best." The compiler only knows best if it has been programmed to inline and it has a notion of time/space optimization that agrees with mine. My experience with other languages was that only "the next release" would actually inline, and it would do so according to an internal logic that a programmer couldn't effectively control. To make matters worse, C (and therefore C with Classes and later C++) has genuine separate compilation so that a compiler never has access to more than a small part of the program (§2.5). Inlining a function for which you don't know the source appears feasible given advanced linker and optimizer technology, but such technology wasn't available at the time (and still isn't in most environments). Furthermore, techniques that require global analysis, such as automatic inlining without user support, tend not to scale well to very large programs. C with Classes was designed to deliver efficient code given a simple, portable implementation on traditional systems. Given that, the programmer had to help. Even today, the choice seems right.

In C with Classes, only member functions could be inlined and the only way to request a function to be inlined was to place its body within the class declaration. For example:

```
class stack {
    /* ... */
    char pop()
    {   if (top <= min) error("stack underflow");
        return *--top;
    }
};
```

The fact that this made class declarations messier was observed at the time and seen as a good thing in that it discourages overuse of inline functions. The `inline` keyword and the ability to inline nonmember functions came with C++. For example, in C++ one can write the example like this:

```
class stack {  // C++
    // ...
    char pop();
};

inline char stack::pop()  // C++
{
    if (top <= min) error("stack underflow");
    return *--top;
}
```

An `inline` directive is only a hint that the compiler can and often does ignore. This is a logical necessity because one can write recursive inline functions that cannot at compile time be proven not to cause infinite recursions; trying to inline one of those would lead to infinite compilations. Leaving `inline` a hint is also a practical advantage because it allows the compiler writer to handle ''pathological'' cases by simply not inlining.

C with Classes required – as its successor still requires – that an inline function must have a unique definition in a program. Defining a function like `pop()` above differently in different compilation units would lead to chaos by subverting the type system. Given separate compilation, it is extremely hard to guarantee that such subversion hasn't taken place in a large system. C with Classes didn't check, and most C++ implementations still don't try to guarantee that an inline function hasn't been defined differently in separate compilation units. However, this theoretical problem has not surfaced as a real problem largely because inline functions tend to be defined in header files together with classes – and class declarations also need to be unique in a program.

2.5 The Linkage Model

The issue of how separately compiled program fragments are linked together is critical for any programming language and to some extent determines the features the language can provide. One of the critical influences on the development of C with Classes and C++ was the decision that

[1] Separate compilation should be possible with traditional C/Fortran UNIX/DOS style linkers.

[2] Linkage should be type safe.

[3] Linkage should not require any form of database (although one could be used to improve a given implementation).

[4] Linkage to program fragments written in other languages such as C, assembler, and Fortran should be easy and efficient.

C uses header files to ensure consistent separate compilation. Declarations of data structure layouts, functions, variables, and constants are placed in header files that are typically textually included into every source file that needs the declarations.

Consistency is ensured by placing adequate information in the header files and ensuring that the header files are consistently included. C++ follows this model up to a point.

The reason that layout information can be present in a C++ class declaration (though it doesn't *have* to be; see §13.2) is to ensure that the declaration and use of true local variables is easy and efficient. For example:

```
void f()
{
    class stack s;
    int c;
    s.push('h');
    c = s.pop();
}
```

Using the `stack` declaration from §2.3 and §2.4.1, even a simple-minded C with Classes implementation can ensure that no use is made of free store for this example, that the call of `pop()` is inlined so that no function call overhead is incurred and that the non-inlined call of `push()` can invoke a separately compiled function. In this, C++ resembles Ada.

At the time, I felt there was a trade-off between having separate interface and implementation declarations (as in Modula-2) plus a tool (linker) to match them up, and having a single class declaration plus a tool (a dependency analyzer) that considered the interface part separately from the implementation details for the purposes of recompilation. It appears I underestimated the complexity of the latter and that the proponents of the former approach underestimate the cost (in terms of porting problems and run-time overhead) of the former.

I also made matters worse for the C++ community by not properly explaining the use of derived classes to achieve the separation of interface and implementation. I tried (see for example [Stroustrup,1986,§7.6.2]), but somehow I never got the message across. I think the reason for this failure was primarily that it never occurred to me that many (most?) C++ programmers and non-C++ programmers looking at C++ thought that because you *could* put the representation right in the class declaration that specified the interface, you *had* to.

I made no attempt to provide tools to enforce type-safe linkage for C with Classes; that had to wait for Release 2.0 of C++. However, I remember talking to Dennis Ritchie and Steve Johnson to establish that type safety across compilation boundaries was considered a part of C. We just lacked the means of enforcement for real programs and had to rely on tools such as Lint [Kernighan,1984].

In particular, Steve Johnson and Dennis Ritchie affirmed that C was intended to have name equivalence rather than structural equivalence. For example:

```
struct A { int x, y; };
struct B { int x, y; };
```

defines two incompatible types A and B. Further:

```
struct C { int x, y; }; // in file 1
struct C { int x, y; }; // in file 2
```

defines two different types, both called C, and a compiler that can do checking across compilation unit boundaries should give a ''double definition'' error. The reason for this rule is to minimize maintenance problems. Such identical declarations are unlikely to occur except through copying. Once copied into different source files, however, the declarations are unlikely to stay identical forever. The moment one declaration – and not the other – is changed, the program will mysteriously fail to work correctly.

As a practical matter, C and therefore C++ guarantees that similar structures such as A and B have similar layout so that it is possible to convert between them and use them in the obvious manner:

```
extern f(struct A*);

void g(struct A* pa, struct B* pb)
{

    f(pa);   /* fine */
    f(pb);   /* error: A* expected */

    pa = pb;                /* error:  A* expected */
    pa = (struct A*)pb;   /* ok: explicit conversion */

    pb->x = 1;
    if (pa->x != pb->x) error("bad implementation");
}
```

Name equivalence is the bedrock of the C++ type system and the layout compatibility rules ensure that explicit conversions can be used to provide low-level services that in other languages have been supplied through structural equivalence. I prefer name equivalence over structural equivalence because I consider it the safest and cleanest model. I was therefore pleased to find that this decision didn't get me into compatibility problems with C and didn't complicate the provision of low-level services.

This later grew into the ''one-definition rule:'' every function, variable, type, constant, etc., in C++ has exactly one definition.

2.5.1 Simple-Minded Implementations

The concern for simple-minded implementations was partly a necessity caused by the lack of resources for developing C with Classes and partly a distrust of languages and mechanisms that required clever techniques. An early formulation of a design goal was that C with Classes ''should be implementable without using an algorithm more complicated than a linear search.'' Wherever that rule of thumb was violated – as in the case of function overloading (§11.2) – it led to semantics that were more complicated than I felt comfortable with. Frequently, it also led to implementation complications.

The aim – based on my Simula experience – was to design a language that would be easy enough to understand to attract users and easy enough to implement to attract implementers. A relatively simple implementation had to be able to deliver code that compared favorably with C code in correctness, run-time speed, and code size. A relatively novice user in a relatively unsupportive programming environment had to be able to use this implementation for real projects. Only when both of these criteria were met could C with Classes and later C++ expect to survive in competition with C. An early formulation of that principle was that "C with Classes has to be a weed like C or Fortran because we cannot afford to take care of a rose like Algol68 or Simula. If we deliver an implementation and go away for a year, we want to find several systems running when we come back. That will not happen if complicated maintenance is needed or if a simple port to a new machine takes more than a week."

This was part of a philosophy of fostering self-sufficiency among users. The aim was always – and explicitly – to develop local expertise in all aspects of using C++. Most organizations must follow the opposite strategy. They keep users dependent on services that generate revenues for a central support organization, consultants, or both. In my opinion, this contrast is a fundamental difference between C++ and many other languages.

The decision to work in the relatively primitive – and almost universally available – framework of the C linking facilities caused the fundamental problem that a C++ compiler must always work with only partial information about a program. An assumption made about a program could possibly be violated by a program written tomorrow in some other language (such as C, Fortran, or assembler) and linked in – possibly after the program has started executing. This problem surfaces in many contexts. It is hard for an implementation to guarantee that

[1] Something is unique.

[2] Information is consistent (in particular, that type information is consistent).

[3] Something is initialized.

In addition, C provides only the feeblest support for the notion of separate namespaces so that avoiding namespace pollution by separately written program segments becomes a problem. Over the years, C++ has tried to face all of these challenges without departing from the fundamental model and technology that gives portability and efficiency, but in the C with Classes days we simply relied on the C technique of header files.

Through the acceptance of the C linker came another rule of thumb for the development of C++: C++ is just one language in a system and not a complete system. In other words, C++ accepts the role of a traditional programming language with a fundamental distinction between the language, the operating system, and other important parts of the programmer's world. This delimits the role of the language in a way that is hard to do for a language, such as Smalltalk or Lisp, that is conceived as a complete system or environment. It makes it essential that a C++ program fragment can call program fragments written in other languages and that a C++ program fragment can itself be called by program fragments written in other languages. Being "just a language'' also allows C++ implementations to benefit directly from tools written for other languages.

The need for a programming language and the code written in it to be just a cog in a much larger machine is of utmost importance to most industrial users. Yet such coexistence with other languages and systems was apparently not a major concern to most theoreticians, would-be perfectionists, and academic users. I believe this to be one of the main reasons for C++'s success.

C with Classes was almost source-compatible with C. However, it was never 100% C compatible; for example, words such as class and new are perfectly good identifier names in C, but they are keywords in C with Classes and its successors. It was, however, link compatible. C functions could be called from C with Classes, C with Classes functions could be called from C, a struct had the same layout in both languages so that passing both simple and composite objects between the languages was simple and efficient. This link compatibility has been maintained for C++ (with a few simple and explicit exceptions that can be avoided by programmers when necessary (§3.5.1). Over the years, my experience and that of my colleagues has been that link compatibility is much more important than source compatibility. This, at least, is the case when identical source code gives the same results on both C and C++ or alternatively fails to compile or link in one of the languages.

2.5.2 The Object Layout Model

The basic model of an object was fundamental to the design of C with Classes in the sense that I always maintained a clear view of what an object looked like in memory and considered how language features affected operations on such objects. The evolution of the object model is fundamental to the evolution of C++.

A C with Classes object was simply a C structure. Thus, the layout of

```
class stack {
    char s[10];
    char* min;
    char* top;
    char* max;
    void new();
public:
    void push();
    char pop();
};
```

is the same as for

```
struct stack { /* generated C code */
    char s[10];
    char* min;
    char* top;
    char* max;
};
```

that is

```
char s[10]
char* min
char* top
char* max
```

A compiler may add some "padding" between and after the members for alignment, but otherwise the size of the object is the sum of the sizes of the members. Thus, memory usage is minimized.

Run-time overhead is similarly minimized by a direct mapping from a call of a member function

```
void stack.push(char c)
{
    if (top>max) error("stack overflow");
    *top++ = c;
}

void g(class stack* p)
{
    p->push('c');
}
```

to the call of an equivalent C function in the generated code:

```
void stack__push(this,c) /* generated C code */
struct stack* this;
char c;
{
    if ((this->top)>(this->max)) error("stack overflow");
    *(this->top)++ = c;

}

void g(p) struct stack* p; /* generated C code */
{
    stack__push(p,'c');
}
```

In every member function, a pointer called this refers to the object for which the member function was called. Stu Feldman remembers that in the very first C with Classes implementation, the programmer couldn't refer directly to this. After he pointed that out to me, I promptly remedied the problem. Without this or some equivalent mechanism, member functions cannot be used for linked list manipulation.

The this pointer is C++'s version of the Simula THIS reference. Sometimes, people ask why this is a pointer rather than a reference and why it is called this rather than self. When this was introduced into C with Classes, the language didn't have references, and C++ borrows its terminology from Simula rather than from Smalltalk.

Had `stack.push()` been declared `inline`, the generated code would have looked like this:

```
void g(p) /* generated C code */
struct stack* p;
{
    if ((p->top)>(p->max)) error("stack overflow");
    *(p->top)++ = 'c';
}
```

This is of course exactly the code a programmer would have written in C.

2.6 Static Type Checking

I have no recollection of discussions, no design notes, and no recollection of any implementation problems concerning the introduction of static (''strong'') type checking into C with Classes. The C with Classes syntax and rules, the ones subsequently adopted for the ANSI C standard, simply appeared fully formed in the first C with Classes implementation. After that, a minor series of experiments led to the current (stricter) C++ rules. Static type checking was to me, after my experience with Simula and Algol68, a simple *must* and the only question was exactly how it was to be added.

To avoid breaking C code, I decided to allow the call of an undeclared function and not perform type checking on such undeclared functions. This was of course a major hole in the type system, and several attempts were made to decrease its importance as the major source of programming errors before finally – in C++ – the hole was closed by making a call of an undeclared function illegal. One simple observation defeated all attempts to compromise, and thus maintain a greater degree of C compatibility: As programmers learned C with Classes, they lost the ability to find run-time errors caused by simple type errors. Having come to rely on the type checking and type conversion provided by C with Classes, they lost the ability to quickly find the silly errors that creep into C programs through the lack of checking. Further, they failed to take the precautions against such silly errors that good C programmers take as a matter of course. After all, ''such errors don't happen in C with Classes.'' Thus, as the frequency of run-time errors caused by uncaught argument type errors decreases, their seriousness and the time spent finding them increases. The result was seriously annoyed programmers demanding further tightening of the type system.

The most interesting experiment with ''incomplete static checking'' was the technique of allowing calls of undeclared functions, but noting the type of the arguments used so that a consistency check could be done when further calls were seen. When Walter Bright many years later independently discovered this trick he named it *autoprototyping*, using the ANSI C term *prototype* for a function declaration. The experience was that autoprototyping caught many errors and initially increased a programmer's confidence in the type system. However, since consistent errors and errors in a function called only once in a compilation were not caught, autoprototyping ultimately destroyed programmer confidence in the type checker and induced a sense of paranoia even worse than I have seen in C or BCPL programmers.

C with Classes introduced the notation f(void) for a function f that takes no arguments as a contrast to f() that in C declares a function that can take any number of arguments of any type without any type check. My users soon convinced me, however, that the f(void) notation wasn't elegant, and that having functions declared f() accept arguments wasn't intuitive. Consequently, the result of the experiment was to have f() mean a function f that takes no arguments, as any novice would expect. It took support from both Doug McIlroy and Dennis Ritchie for me to build up the courage to make this break from C. Only after they used the word *abomination* about f(void) did I dare give f() the obvious meaning. However, to this day, C's type rules are much more lax than C++'s, and ANSI C adopted "the abominable f(void)" from C with Classes.

2.6.1 Narrowing Conversions

Another early attempt to tighten C with Classes' type rules was to disallow "information destroying" implicit conversions. Like others, I had been badly bitten by examples equivalent to (but naturally not as easy to spot in a real program) as these:

```
void f()
{
    long int lng = 65000;
    int i1 = lng;    /* i1 becomes negative (-536)   */
                     /* on machines with 16 bit ints */

    int i2 = 257;
    char c = i2;     /* truncates: c becomes 1       */
                     /* on machines with 8 bit chars */
}
```

I decided to try to ban all conversions that were not value preserving, that is, to require an explicit conversion operator wherever a larger object was stored into a smaller:

```
void g(long lng, int i) /* experiment */
{
    int i1 = lng;      /* error: narrowing conversion */
    i1 = (int)lng;     /* truncates for 16 bit ints   */

    char c = i;        /* error: narrowing conversion */
    c = (char)i;       /* truncates                   */
}
```

The experiment failed miserably. Every C program I looked at contained large numbers of assignments of ints to char variables. Naturally, since these were working programs, most of these assignments were perfectly safe. That is, either the value was small enough not to become truncated, or the truncation was expected or at least harmless in that particular context. There was no willingness in the C with Classes community to make such a break from C. I'm still looking for ways to compensate for these problems (§14.3.5.2).

2.6.2 Use of Warnings

I considered introducing run-time checks for the values assigned, but that would imply a high cost in time and code size, and also detect the problems far too late for my taste. Therefore, run-time checks for conversions – and more importantly, in general – were relegated to the category of "ideas for future debugging support." Instead, I used a technique that was to become standard for dealing with what I considered deficiencies in the C language that were too serious to ignore, but too ingrained in the structure of C to remove. I made the C with Classes preprocessor (and later my C++ compiler) issue warnings:

```
void f(long lng, int i)
{
    int i1 = lng;     // implicit conversion: warning
    i1 = (int)lng;    // explicit conversion: no warning

    char c = i;       // too common to repair: no warning
}
```

Unconditional warnings were (and still are) issued for *long–>int* and *double–>int* conversions, because I really don't see any excuse for having such conversions legal. They are simply a result of the historical accident that floating point arithmetic was introduced into C before explicit conversions were. I have had no complaints about these warnings, and I and others have been saved by them many times. The *int–>char* conversion, however, I didn't feel able to do anything about. To this day, such conversions pass the AT&T C++ compiler without even a warning.

The reason for this is that I decided to use unconditional warnings exclusively for things that "had a higher than 90% chance of actually catching an error." This reflected the experience that C-compiler and Lint warnings more often than not are "wrong" in the sense that they warn against something that doesn't in fact cause the program to misbehave. This leads programmers to ignore warnings from C compilers or to heed them only under protest. My intent was to ensure that ignoring a C++ warning would be seen as a dangerous folly; I feel I succeeded. Thus, warnings are used to compensate for problems that cannot be fixed through language changes because of C compatibility requirements and also as a way of easing the transition from C to C++. For example:

```
class X {
    // ...
}
```

```
g(int i, int x, int j)
        // warning:  class X defined as return type for g()
        // (did you forget a ';' after '}' ?)
        // warning:  j not used
{
  if (i = 7) {  // warning: constant assignment
                // in condition
    // ...
  }
    // ...
  if (x&077 == 0) {  // warning:  == expression
                     // as operand for &
    // ...
  }
}
```

Even the first Cfront release (§3.3) produced these warnings. They were the result of a design decision and not an afterthought.

Much later, the first of these warnings was made into an error by banning the definition of new types in return types and argument types.

2.7 Why C?

A common question at C with Classes presentations was ''Why use C? Why didn't you build on, say, Pascal?'' One version of my answer can be found in [Stroustrup,1986c]:

''C is clearly not the cleanest language ever designed nor the easiest to use so why do so many people use it?

[1] C is *flexible*: It is possible to apply C to most every application area and to use most every programming technique with C. The language has no inherent limitations that preclude particular kinds of programs from being written.

[2] C is *efficient*: The semantics of C are ''low level''; that is, the fundamental concepts of C mirror the fundamental concepts of a traditional computer. Consequently, it is relatively easy for a compiler and/or a programmer to efficiently utilize hardware resources for C programs.

[3] C is *available*: Given a computer, whether the tiniest micro or the largest super-computer, chances are that there is an acceptable quality C compiler available and that that C compiler supports an acceptably complete and standard C language and library. Libraries and support tools are also available, so that a programmer rarely needs to design a new system from scratch.

[4] C is *portable*: A C program is not automatically portable from one machine (and operating system) to another, nor is such a port necessarily easy to do. It is, however, usually possible and the level of difficulty is such that

porting even major pieces of software with inherent machine dependencies is typically technically and economically feasible.

Compared with these first-order advantages, the second-order drawbacks like the curious C declarator syntax and the lack of safety of some language constructs become less important. Designing "a better C" implies compensating for the major problems involved in writing, debugging, and maintaining C programs *without compromising the advantages of C*. C++ preserves all these advantages and compatibility with C at the cost of abandoning claims to perfection and of some compiler and language complexity. However, designing a language from scratch does not ensure perfection and the C++ compilers compare favorably in run-time, have better error detection and reporting, and equal the C compilers in code quality."

This formulation is more polished than I could have managed in the early C with Classes days, but it does capture the essence of what I considered important about C and that I did not want to lose in C with Classes. Pascal was considered a toy language [Kernighan,1981], so it seemed easier and safer to add type checking to C than to add the features considered necessary for systems programming to Pascal. At the time, I had a positive dread of making mistakes of the sort where the designer, out of misguided paternalism or plain ignorance, makes the language unusable for real work in important areas. The ten years that followed clearly showed that choosing C as a base left me in the mainstream of systems programming where I intended to be. The cost in language complexity has been considerable, but manageable.

At the time, I considered Modula-2, Ada, Smalltalk, Mesa [Mitchell,1979], and Clu as alternatives to C and as sources for ideas for C++ [Stroustrup,1984c] so there was no shortage of inspiration. However, only C, Simula, Algol68, and in one case BCPL left noticeable traces in C++ as released in 1985. Simula gave classes, Algol68 operator overloading (§3.6), references (§3.7), and the ability to declare variables anywhere in a block (§3.11.5), and BCPL gave / / comments (§3.11.1).

There were several reasons for avoiding major departures from C style. I saw the merging of C's strengths as a systems programming language with Simula's strengths for organizing programs as a significant challenge in itself. Adding significant features from other sources could easily lead to a "shopping list" language and destroy the integrity of the resulting language. To quote from [Stroustrup,1986]:

"A programming language serves two related purposes: it provides a vehicle for the programmer to specify actions to be executed and a set of concepts for the programmer to use when thinking about what can be done. The first aspect ideally requires a language that is "close to the machine," so that all important aspects of a machine are handled simply and efficiently in a way that is reasonably obvious to the programmer. The C language was primarily designed with this in mind. The second aspect ideally requires a language that is "close to the problem to be solved" so that the concepts of a solution can be expressed directly and concisely. The facilities added to C to create C++ were primarily designed with this in mind."

Again, this formulation is more polished than I could have managed during the early

stages of the design of C with Classes, but the general idea was clear. Departures
from the known and proven techniques of C and Simula would have to wait for further experience with C with Classes and C++ and for further experiments. I firmly
believe – and believed then – that language design is not just design from first principles, but an art that requires experience, experiments, and sound engineering tradeoffs. Adding a major feature or concept to a language should not be a leap of faith,
but a deliberate action based on experience and fitting into a framework of other features and ideas of how the resulting language can be used. The post-1985 evolution
of C++ shows the influence of ideas from Ada (templates, §15; exceptions, §16;
namespaces, §17), Clu (exceptions, §16), and ML (exceptions, §16).

2.8 Syntax Problems

Could I have ''fixed'' the most annoying deficiencies of the C syntax and semantics
at some point before C++ was made generally available? Could I have done so without removing useful features (to C with Classes' users in their environments – as
opposed to an ideal world) or introducing incompatibilities that were unacceptable to
C programmers wanting to migrate to C with Classes? I think not. In some cases, I
tried, but I backed out my changes after receiving complaints from outraged users.

2.8.1 The C Declaration Syntax

The part of the C syntax I disliked most was the declaration syntax. Having both prefix and postfix declarator operators is the source of a fair amount of confusion. For
example:

```
int *p[10]; /* array of 10 pointers to int, or */
            /* pointer to array of 10 ints?    */
```

Allowing the type specifier to be omitted (meaning int by default) also led to complications. For example:

```
            /* C style (proposed banned):    */

static a;   /* implicit: type of 'a' is int */
f();        /* implicit: returns int          */

            // proposed C with Classes style:
static int a;
int f();
```

The negative reaction to changes in this area from users was very strong. They considered the ''terseness'' allowed by C essential to the point of refusing to use a ''fas-
cist'' language that required them to write redundant type specifiers. I backed out the
change. I don't think I had a choice. Allowing that implicit int is the source of
many of the annoying problems with the C++ grammar today. Note that the pressure
came from users, not management or arm-chair language experts. Finally, ten years

later, the C++ ANSI/ISO standard committee (§6) has decided to deprecate implicit `int`. That means that we may get rid of it in another decade or so. With the help of tools and compiler warnings, individual users can now start protecting themselves from confusions caused by implicit `int`, such as

```
void f(const T);   // const argument of type T, or
                   // const int argument named T?
                   // (it's a const argument of type T)
```

The function definition syntax with the argument types within the function parentheses was, however, used for C with Classes and C++, and later adopted for ANSI C:

```
f(a,b) char b;   /* K&R C style function definition */
{
    /* ... */
}

int f(int a, char b)   // C++ style function definition
{
    // ...
}
```

Similarly, I considered the possibility of introducing a linear notation for declarators. The C trick of having the declaration of a name mimic its use leads to declarations that are hard to read and write, and maximizes the opportunity for humans and programs to confuse declarations and expressions. Many people had observed that the problem with C's declarator syntax was that the declarator operator `*` (''pointer to'') is prefix, whereas the declarator operators `[]` (''array of'') and `()` (''function returning'') are postfix. This forces people to use parentheses to disambiguate cases such as:

```
              /* C style:                  */
int* v[10];   /* array of pointers to ints */
int (*p)[10]; /* pointer to array of ints  */
```

Together with Doug McIlroy, Andrew Koenig, Jonathan Shopiro, and others I considered introducing postfix ''pointer to'' operator `->` as an alternative to the prefix `*`:

```
               // radical alternative:
v: [10]->int ; // array of pointers to ints
p: ->[10]int;  // pointer to array of ints

               // less radical alternative:
int v[10]->;   // array of pointers to ints
int p->[10];   // pointer to array of ints
```

The less radical alternative has the advantage of allowing the postfix `->` declarator to coexist with the prefix `*` declarator during a transition period. After a transition period the `*` declarator and the redundant parentheses could have been removed from the language. A noticeable benefit of this scheme is that parentheses are only needed to express "function" so that an opportunity for confusion and grammar subtleties could be removed (see also [Sethi,1981]). Having all declarator operators postfix would ensure that declarations can be read from left to right. For example:

```
int f(char)->[10]->(double)->;
```

meaning a function f returning a pointer to an array of pointers to functions returning a pointer to int. Try to write that in straight C/C++! Unfortunately, I fumbled the idea and didn't ever deliver a complete implementation. Instead, people build up complicated types incrementally using typedef:

```
typedef int* DtoI(double);   // function taking a double and
                             // returning a pointer to int
typedef DtoI* V10[10];       // array of 10 pointers to DtoI
V10* f(char);                // f takes a char and returns
                             // a pointer to V10
```

My eventual rationale for leaving things as they were was that any new syntax would (temporarily at least) add complexity to a known mess. Also, even though the old style is a boon to teachers of trivia and to people who want to ridicule C, it is not a significant problem for C programmers. In this case, I'm not sure if I did the right thing, though. The agony to me and other C++ implementers, documenters, and tool builders caused by the perversities of syntax has been significant. Users can – and do – of course insulate themselves from such problems by writing in a small and easily understood subset of the C/C++ declaration syntax (§7.2).

2.8.2 Structure Tags vs. Type Names

A significant syntactic simplification for the benefit of users was introduced into C++ at the cost of some extra work to implementers and some C compatibility problems. In C, the name of a structure, a "structure tag," must always be preceded by the keyword struct. For example

```
struct buffer a;   /* 'struct' is necessary in C */
```

In the context of C with Classes, this had annoyed me for some time because it made user-defined types second-class citizens syntactically. Given my lack of success with other attempts to clean up the syntax, I was reluctant and only made the change – at the time C with Classes evolved into C++ – at the urging of Tom Cargill. The name of a struct, union, or class is a type name in C++ and requires no special syntactic identification:

```
buffer a;   // C++
```

The resulting fights over C compatibility lasted for years (see also §3.12). For example, the following is legal C:

```
struct S { int a; };
int S;
```

```
void f(struct S x)
{
    x.a = S;   // S is an int variable
}
```

It is also legal C with Classes and legal C++, yet for years we struggled to find a formulation that would allow such (marginally crazy, but harmless) examples in C++ for
compatibility. Allowing such examples implies that we must reject

```
void g(S x)   // error: S is an int variable
{
    x.a = S;   // S is an int variable
}
```

The real need to address this particular issue came from the fact that some standard
UNIX header files, notably, `stat.h`, rely on a `struct` and a variable or function
having the same name. Such compatibility issues are important and a delight for language lawyers. Unfortunately, until a satisfactory – and usually trivially simple –
solution is found, such problems absorb an undesirable amount of time and energy.
Once a solution is found, a compatibility problem becomes indescribably boring
because it has no inherent intellectual value, only practical importance. The C++
solution to the C multiple namespace problem is that a name can denote a class and
also a function or a variable. If it does, the name denotes the non-class unless explicitly qualified by one of the keywords `struct`, `class`, and `union`.

Dealing with stubborn old-time C users, would-be C experts, and genuine C/C++
compatibility issues has been one of the most difficult and frustrating aspects of
developing C++. It still is.

2.8.3 The Importance of Syntax

I am of the opinion that most people focus on syntax issues to the detriment of type
issues. The critical issues in the design of C++ were always those of type, ambiguity,
and access control, not those of syntax.

It is not that syntax isn't important; it is immensely important because the syntax
is quite literally what people see. A well-chosen syntax significantly helps programmers learn new concepts and avoids silly errors by making them harder to express
than their correct alternatives. However, the syntax of a language should be designed
to follow the semantic notions of the language, not the other way around. This
implies that language discussions should focus on what can be expressed rather than
how it is expressed. An answer to the *what* often yields an answer to the *how*,
whereas a focus on syntax usually degenerates into an argument over personal taste.

A subtle aspect of C compatibility discussions is that old-time C programmers are
comfortable with the old ways of doing things and can therefore be quite intolerant of
the incompatibilities needed to support styles of programming that C wasn't designed
for. Conversely, non-C programmers usually underestimate the value that C programmers attribute to the C syntax.

2.9 Derived Classes

The derived class concept is C++'s version of Simula's prefixed class notion and thus
a sibling of Smalltalk's subclass concept. The names *derived* and *base* were chosen
because I never could remember what was *sub* and what was *super* and observed that
I was not the only one with this particular problem. I also noted that many people
found it counterintuitive that a subclass typically has *more* information than its superclass. In inventing the terms derived class and base class, I departed from my usual
principle of not inventing new names where old ones exist. In my defense, I note that
I have never observed any confusion about what is base and what is derived among
C++ programmers, and that the terms are trivially easy to learn even for people who
don't have a grounding in mathematics.

The C with Classes concept was provided without any form of run-time support.
In particular, the Simula (and later C++) concept of a virtual function was missing.
The reason for this was that I – with good reason, I think – doubted my ability to
teach people how to use them, and even more, my ability to convince people that a
virtual function is as efficient in time and space as an ordinary function as typically
used. Often, people with Simula and Smalltalk experience still don't quite believe
that until they have had the C++ implementation explained to them in detail – and
many still harbor irrational doubts after that.

Even without virtual functions, derived classes in C with Classes were useful for
building new data structures out of old ones and for associating operations with the
resulting types. In particular, they allowed list and task classes to be defined
[Stroustrup,1980,1982b].

2.9.1 Polymorphism without Virtual Functions

In the absence of virtual functions, a user could use objects of a derived class and treat
base classes as implementation details. For example, given a vector class with elements indexed from 0 and no range checking:

```
class vector {
    /* ... */
    int get_elem(int i);
};
```

one can build a range-checked vector with elements in a specified range:

```
class vec : vector {
    int hi, lo;
public:
    /* ... */
    new(int lo, int hi);
    get_elem(int i);
};
```

```
int vec.get_elem(int i)
{
    if (i<lo || hi<i) error("range error");
    return vector.get_elem(i-lo);
}
```

Alternatively, an explicit type field could be introduced in a base class and used together with explicit type casts. The former strategy was used where the user only sees specific derived classes and "the system" sees only the base classes. The latter strategy was used for various application classes where, in effect, a base class was used to implement a variant record for a set of derived classes.

For example, [Stroustrup,1982b] presents this ugly code for retrieving an object from a table and using it based on a type field:

```
class elem { /* properties to be put into a table */ };
class table { /* table data and lookup functions */ };

class cl_name * cl;    /* cl_name is derived from elem */
class po_name * po;    /* po_name is derived from elem */
class hashed * table; /* hashed is derived from table */

elem * p = table->look("carrot");

if (p) {
  switch (p->type) { /* type field in elem objects */
    case PO_NAME:
      po = (class po_name *) p; /* explicit type conversion */
      ...
      break;
    case CL_NAME:
      cl = (class cl_name *) p; /* explicit type conversion */
      ...
      break;
    default:
      error("unknown type of element");
  }
}
else
   error("carrot not defined");
```

Much of the effort in C with Classes and C++ has been to ensure that programmers needn't write such code.

2.9.2 Container Classes Without Templates

Most important in my thinking at the time and in my own code was the combination of base classes, explicit type conversions, and (occasionally) macros to provide generic container classes. For example, [Stroustrup,1982b] demonstrates how a list that holds objects of a single type can be built from a list of links:

```
class wordlink : link
{
    char word[SIZE];
public:
    void clear(void);
    class wordlink * get(void)
        { return (class wordlink *) link.get(); };
    void put(class wordlink * p) { link.put(p); };
};
```

Because every `link` that is `put()` onto a list through a `wordlink` must be a `wordlink`, it is safe to cast every `link` that is taken off the list using `get()` back to a `wordlink`. Note the use of private inheritance (the default in the absence of the keyword `public` in the specification of the base class `link`; §2.10). Allowing a `wordlink` to be used as a plain `link` would have compromised type safety.

Macros were used to provide generic types. Quoting from [Stroustrup,1982b]:

"The class `stack` example in the introduction explicitly defined the stack to be a stack of characters. That is sometimes too specific. What if a stack of long integers was also needed? What if a class `stack` was needed for a library so that the actual stack element type could not be known in advance? In these cases the class `stack` declaration and its associated function declarations should be written so that the element type can be provided as an argument when a stack is created in the same way as the size was.

There is no direct language support for this, but the effect can be achieved through the facilities of the standard C preprocessor. For example:

```
class ELEM_stack {
    ELEM * min, * top, * max;
    void new(int), delete(void);
public:
    void push(ELEM);
    ELEM pop(void);
};
```

This declaration can then be placed in a header file and macro-expanded once for each type `ELEM` for which it is used:

```
#define ELEM long
#define ELEM_stack long_stack
#include "stack.h"
#undef ELEM
#undef ELEM_stack

typedef class x X;
#define ELEM X
#define ELEM_stack X_stack
#include "stack.h"
```

```
#undef ELEM
#undef ELEM_stack

class long_stack ls(1024);
class long_stack ls2(512);
class X_stack xs(512);
```

  This is certainly not perfect, but it is simple.''

This was one of the earliest and crudest techniques. It proved too error-prone for real use, so I soon defined a few ''standard'' token-pasting macros and recommended a stylized macro usage based on them for generic classes [Stroustrup,1986,§7.3.5]. Eventually, these techniques matured into C++'s template facility and the techniques for using templates together with base classes to express commonality among instantiated templates (§15.5).

2.9.3 The Object Layout Model

The implementation of derived classes was simply concatenation of the members of the base and derived classes. For example, given:

```
class A {
     int a;
public:
     /* member functions */
};

class B : public A {
     int b;
public:
     /* member functions */
};
```

an object of class B will be represented by a structure:

```
struct B { /* generated C code */
     int a;
     int b;
};
```

that is

```
            int a
            int b
```

Name clashes between base members and derived members are handled by the compiler internally assigning suitably unambiguous names to the members. Calls are handled exactly as when no derivation is used. No added overhead in time or space is imposed relative to C.

2.9.4 Retrospective

Was it reasonable to avoid virtual functions in C with Classes? Yes, the language was useful without them, and their absence postponed time-consuming debates about their utility, proper use, and efficiency. Their absence led to development of language mechanisms and techniques that have proven useful even in the presence of more powerful inheritance mechanisms and provided a counterweight to the tendency of some programmers to use inheritance to the exclusion of all other techniques (see §14.2.3). In particular, classes were used to implement concrete types, such as `complex` and `string`, and interface classes became popular. A class `stack` used as an interface to a more general class `dequeue` is an example of inheritance without virtual functions.

Were virtual functions needed for C with Classes to serve the needs it aimed to serve? Yes, and therefore they were added as the first major extension to make C++.

2.10 The Protection Model

Before starting work on C with Classes, I worked with operating systems. The notions of protection from the Cambridge CAP computer and similar systems – rather than any work in programming languages – inspired the C++ protection mechanisms. The class is the unit of protection and the fundamental rule is that you cannot grant yourself access to a class; only the declarations placed in the class declaration (supposedly by its owner) can grant access. By default, all information is private.

Access is granted by declaring a member in the public part of a class declaration, or by specifying a function or a class as a `friend`. For example:

```
class X {
    /* representation */
public:
    void f();           /* member function with access */
                        /* to representation           */

    friend void g(); /* global function with access */
                        /* to representation           */
};
```

Initially, only classes could be friends, thus granting access to all member functions of the `friend` class, but later it was found convenient to be able to grant access (friendship) to individual functions. In particular, it was found useful to be able to grant access to global functions; see also §3.6.1.

A friendship declaration was seen as a mechanism similar to that of one protection domain granting a read-write capability to another. It is an explicit and specific part of a class declaration. Consequently, I have never been able to see the recurring assertions that a `friend` declaration "violates encapsulation" as anything but a combination of ignorance and confusion with non-C++ terminology.

Even in the first version of C with Classes, the protection model applied to base classes as well as members. Thus, a class could be either publicly or privately derived from another. The private/public distinction for base classes predates the debate on implementation inheritance vs. interface inheritance by about five years [Snyder,1986] [Liskov,1987]. If you want to inherit an implementation only, you use private derivation in C++. Public derivation gives users of the derived class access to the interface provided by the base class. Private derivation leaves the base as an implementation detail; even the public members of the private base class are inaccessible except through the interface explicitly provided for the derived class.

To provide ''semi-transparent scopes'' a mechanism was provided to allow individual public names from a private base class to be made public [Stroustrup,1982b]:

```
class vector {
    /* ... */
public:
    /* ... */
    void print(void);
};
```

```
class hashed : vector /* vector is private base of hashed */
{
    /* ... */
public:
    vector.print;   /* semi-transparent scope */
                    /* other vector functions cannot */
                    /* be applied to hashed objects */
    /* ... */
};
```

The syntax for making an otherwise inaccessible name accessible is simply naming it. This is an example of a perfectly logical, minimalistic, and unambiguous syntax. It is also unnecessarily obscure; almost any other syntax would have been an improvement. This syntax problem has now been solved by the introduction of *using-declarations* (see §17.5.2).

In the [ARM], the C++ notion of protection is summarized:

[1] Protection is provided by compile-time mechanisms against accident, not against fraud or explicit violation.

[2] Access is granted by a class, not unilaterally taken.

[3] Access control is done for *names* and does not depend on the type of what is named.

[4] The unit of protection is the class, not the individual object.

[5] Access is controlled, not visibility.

All of this was true in 1980, though some of the terminology was different then. The last point can be explained like this:

```
int a;        // global a

class X {
private:
    int a;    // member X::a
};

class XX : public X {
    void f() { a = 1; }   // which a?
};
```

Had visibility been controlled, X::a would have been invisible, and XX::f() would have referred to the global a. In fact, C with Classes and C++ deem the global a hidden by the inaccessible X::a and thus XX::f() gets a compile-time error for trying to access an inaccessible variable X::a. Why did I define it that way, and was it the right choice? My recollection on this point is vague, and the stored records are of no use. One point I do remember from the discussion at the time is that given the example above, the rule adopted ensures that f()'s reference to a refers to the same a independently of what access is declared for X::a. Making public/private control visibility, rather than access, would have a change from public to private quietly change the meaning of the program from one legal interpretation (access X::a) to another (access the global a). I no longer consider this argument conclusive (if I ever did), but the decision made has proven useful in that it allows programmers to add and remove public and private specifications during debugging without quietly changing the meaning of programs. I do wonder if this aspect of the C++ definition is the result of a genuine design decision. It could simply be a default outcome of the preprocessor technology used to implement C with Classes that didn't get reviewed when C++ was implemented with more appropriate compiler technology (§3.3).

Another aspect of C++'s protection mechanism that shows operating system influence is the attitude towards circumvention of the rules. I assume that any competent programmer can circumvent any rule that is not enforced by hardware so it is not worth even trying to protect against fraud [ARM]:

"The C++ access control mechanisms provide protection against accident – *not* against fraud. Any programming language that supports access to raw memory will leave data open to deliberate tampering in ways that violate the explicit type rules specified for a given data item."

The task of the protection system is to make sure that any such violation of the type system is explicit and to minimize the need for such violations.

The operating system notion of read/write protection grew into C++'s notion of const (§3.8).

Over the years, there have been many proposals for providing access to a unit smaller than a whole class. For example:

```
grant X::f(int) access to Y::a, Y::b, and Y::g(char);
```

I have resisted such suggestions on the grounds that such finer-grain control gives no
added protection: Any member function can modify any data member of a class, so a
function granted access to a function member can indirectly modify every member. I
considered, as I still do, the complications in specification, implementation, and use to
outweigh the benefits of more explicit control.

2.11   Run-Time Guarantees

The access-control mechanisms described above simply prevent unauthorized access.
A second kind of guarantee was provided by "special member functions," such as
constructors, that were recognized and implicitly invoked by the compiler. The idea
was to allow the programmer to establish guarantees, sometimes called *invariants*,
that other member functions could rely on (see also §16.10).

2.11.1 Constructors and Destructors

One way I often explained the concept at the time was that a "new function" (a constructor) created the environment in which the member functions would operate and
the "delete function" (a destructor) would destroy that environment and release all
resources acquired for it. For example:

```
class monitor : object {
    /* ... */
public:
    new()    { /* create the monitor's lock */ }
    delete() { /* release and delete lock */ }
    /* ... */
};
```

See also §3.9 and §13.2.4.

Where did the notion of constructors come from? I suspect I just invented it. I
was acquainted with Simula's class object initialization mechanism. However, I saw
a class declaration as primarily the definition of an interface so I wanted to avoid having to put code in there. Because C with Classes followed C in having three storage
classes, some form of initialization functions almost had to be recognized by the compiler (§2.11.2). The observation that several constructors would be useful was soon
made, and this became one of the major sources of the C++ overloading mechanisms
(§3.6).

2.11.2 Allocation and Constructors

Like in C, objects can be allocated in three ways: on the stack (automatic storage), at a
fixed address (static storage), and on the free store (on the heap, dynamic storage). In
each case, the constructor must be called for the created object. Allocating an object
on the free store in C involves only a call of an allocation function. For example:

```
monitor* p = (monitor*)malloc(sizeof(monitor));
```

This was clearly insufficient for C with Classes because there was no way of guaranteeing that a constructor was called. Consequently, I introduced an operator to ensure that both allocation and initialization was done:

```
monitor* p = new monitor;
```

The operator was called `new` because that was the name of the corresponding Simula operator. The `new` operator invokes some allocation function to obtain memory and then invokes a constructor to initialize that memory. The combined operation is often called instantiation or simply object creation; it creates an object out of raw memory.

The notational convenience offered by operator `new` is significant (§3.9). However, combining allocation and initialization in a single operation without an explicit error-reporting mechanism led to some practical problems. Handling and reporting errors in constructors was rarely critical, though, and the introduction of exceptions (§16.5) provided a general solution.

To minimize recompilation, Cfront implemented a use of operator `new` for a class with a constructor as simply a call of the constructor. The constructor then did both the allocation and the initialization. This implied that if a translation unit allocates all objects of class X using `new` and calls no inline functions from X then that translation unit need not be recompiled if the size and representation of X changes. *Translation unit* is the ANSI C term for a source file after preprocessing; that is, for the information given to a compiler at one time for separate compilation. I found it very useful to organize my simulation programs to minimize recompilation. However, the importance of such minimizing wasn't generally appreciated in the C with Classes and C++ community until much later (§13.2).

An operator `delete` was introduced to complement `new` in the same way as the deallocation function `free()` complements `malloc()` (§3.9, §10.7).

2.11.3 Call and Return Functions

Curiously enough, the initial implementation of C with Classes contained a feature that is not provided by C++, but is often requested. One could define a function that would implicitly be called before every call of every member function (except the constructor) and another that would be implicitly called before every return from every member function (except the destructor). They were called `call` and `return` functions. They were used to provide synchronization for the monitor class in the original task library [Stroustrup,1980b]:

```
class monitor : object {
    /* ... */
    call()   { /* grab lock */ }
    return() { /* release lock */ }
    /* ... */
};
```

These are similar in intent to the CLOS :before and :after methods. Call and return functions were removed from the language because nobody (but me) used them and because I seemed to have completely failed to convince people that call() and return() had important uses. In 1987 Mike Tiemann suggested an alternative solution called "wrappers" [Tiemann,1987], but at the USENIX implementers' workshop in Estes Park this idea was determined to have too many problems to be accepted into C++.

2.12 Minor Features

Two very minor features, overloading of assignment and default arguments were introduced into C with Classes. They were the precursors of C++'s overloading mechanisms (§3.6).

2.12.1 Overloading of Assignment

It was soon noticed that classes with a nontrivial representation such as string and vector couldn't be copied successfully because C's semantics of assignment (bit-wise copy) wasn't right for such types. This default copy semantics led to shared representations rather than true copies. My response was to allow the programmer to specify the meaning of assignment [Stroustrup,1980]:

"Unfortunately, this standard struct-like assignment is not always ideal. Typically a class object is only the root of a tree of information and a simple copy of that root without any notice taken of the branches is undesirable. Similarly, simply overwriting a class object can create chaos.

Changing the meaning of assignment for objects of a class provides a way of handling these problems. This is done by declaring a class member function called operator=. For example:

```
class x {
public:
    int    a;
    class y * p;
    void operator = (class x *);
};

void x.operator = (class x * from)
{
    a = from->a;
    delete p;
    p = from->p;
    from->p = 0;
}
```

This defines a destructive read for objects of class x, as opposed to the copy operation implied by the standard semantics."

The [Stroustrup,1982] version uses an example that checks for `this==from` to handle self-assignment correctly. Apparently, I learned that technique the hard way.

Where defined, an assignment operator was used to implement all explicit and implicit copy operations. Initialization was handled by first initializing to a default value using a `new`-function (constructor) taking no arguments and then assigning. This was found to be inefficient and led to the introduction of copy constructors in C++ (§11.4.1).

2.12.2 Default Arguments

The heavy use of default constructors implied by the user-defined assignment operators naturally led to the introduction of default arguments [Stroustrup,1980]:

"The default argument list was a very late addition to the class mechanism. It was added to curb the proliferation of identical "standard argument lists" for class objects passed as function arguments, for class objects that were members of other classes, and for base class arguments. Providing argument lists in these cases proved enough of a nuisance to overcome the aversion to include yet another "feature," and they can be used to make `class` object declarations less verbose and more similar to `struct` declarations."

Here is an example:

"It is possible to declare a default argument list for a `new()` function. This list is then used whenever an object of the class is declared without an argument. For example, the declaration:

```
class char_stack
{
        void new(int=512);
        ...
};
```

makes the declaration

```
class char_stack s3;
```

legal, and initializes `s3` by the call `s3.new(512)`."

Given general function overloading (§3.6, §11), default arguments are logically redundant and at best a minor notational convenience. However, C with Classes had default argument lists for years before general overloading became available in C++.

2.13   Features Considered, but not Provided

In the early days many features were considered that later appeared in C++ or are still discussed. These included virtual functions, `static` members, templates, and multiple inheritance. However,

"All of these generalizations have their uses, but every "feature" of a language takes time and effort to design, implement, document, and learn. ... The base class

concept is an engineering compromise, like the C class concept
[Stroustrup,1982b].''
I just wish I had explicitly mentioned the need for experience. With that, the case
against featurism and for a pragmatic approach would have been complete.

The possibility of automatic garbage collection was considered on several occasions before 1985 and deemed unsuitable for a language already in use for real-time
processing and hard-core systems tasks such as device drivers. In those days, garbage
collectors were less sophisticated than they are today, and the processing power and
memory capacity of the average computer were small fractions of what today's systems offer. My personal experience with Simula and reports on other garbage-
collection-based systems convinced me that garbage collection was unaffordable by
me and my colleagues for the kind of applications we were writing. Had C with
Classes (or even C++) been defined to require automatic garbage collection, it would
have been more elegant, but stillborn.

Direct support for concurrency was also considered, but I rejected that in favor of
a library-based approach (§2.1).

2.14 Work Environment

C with Classes was designed and implemented by me as a research project in the
Computing Science Research Center of Bell Labs. This center provided – and still
provides – a possibly unique environment for such work. When I joined, I was basically told to ''do something interesting,'' given suitable computer resources, encouraged to talk to interesting and competent people, and given a year before having to
formally present my work for evaluation.

There was a cultural bias against ''grand projects'' that required more than a couple of people, against ''grand plans'' like untested paper designs for others to implement, and against a class distinction between designers and implementers. If you
liked such things, Bell Labs and others have many places where you could indulge
such preferences. However, in the Computing Science Research Center it was almost
a requirement that you – if you were not into theory – personally implemented something embodying your ideas and found users that could benefit from what you built.
The environment was very supportive for such work and the Labs provided a large
pool of people with ideas and problems to challenge and test anything built. Thus, I
could write in [Stroustrup,1986]:

> ''There never was a C++ paper design; design, documentation, and implementa-
> tion went on simultaneously. Naturally, the C++ front-end is written in C++.
> There never was a ''C++ project'' either, or a ''C++ design committee''.
> Throughout, C++ evolved, and continues to evolve, to cope with problems
> encountered by users, and through discussions between the author and his friends
> and colleagues.''

Only after C++ was an established language did more conventional organizational
structures emerge and even then I was officially in charge of the reference manual and

had the final say over what went into it until that task was handed over to the ANSI C++ committee in early 1990. As the standards committee's chairman of the working group for extensions, I'm still directly responsible for every feature that enters C++ (§6.4). On the other hand, after the first few months I never had the freedom to design just for the sake of designing something beautiful or to make arbitrary changes in the language as it stood at any given time. Every language feature required an implementation to make it real, and any change or extension required the concurrence and usually enthusiasm of key C with Classes and later C++ users.

Since there was no guaranteed user population, the language and its implementations could only survive by serving the needs of its users well enough to counteract the organizational pull of established languages and the marketing hype of newer languages. In particular, introducing even a minor incompatibility required delivering some much larger benefit to the users, so major incompatibilities were not often introduced even in the early days. Since to a user almost any incompatibility can seem major, incompatibilities were as rare as I could manage. Only in the move from C with Classes to C++ were many programs deliberately broken.

The absence of a formal organizational structure, of larger-scale support in terms of money, people, "captive" users, and marketing was more than compensated for by the informal help and insights of my peers in the Computing Science Research Center and the protection from nontechnical demands from development organizations offered by the center management. Had it not been for the insights of members of the center and the insulation from political nonsense, the design of C++ would have been compromised by fashions and special interests and its implementation bogged down in a bureaucratic quagmire. It was also most important that Bell Labs provided an environment where there was no need to hoard ideas for personal advancement. Instead, discussion could, did, and still does flow freely, allowing people to benefit from the ideas and opinions of others. Unfortunately, the Computing Science Research Center is not typical even within Bell Labs.

C with Classes grew through discussions with people in the Computing Science Research Center and early users there and elsewhere in the Labs. Most of C with Classes and later C++ was designed on somebody else's blackboard and the rest on mine. Most such ideas were rejected as being too elaborate, too limited in usefulness, too hard to implement, too hard to teach for use in real projects, not efficient enough in time or space, too incompatible with C, or simply too weird. The few ideas that made it through this filter – invariably involving discussions with at least two people – I then implemented. Typically, the idea mutated through the effort of implementation, testing, and early use by me and a few others. The resulting version was tried on a larger audience and would often mutate a bit further before finding its way into the "official" version of C with Classes as shipped by me. Usually, a tutorial was written somewhere along the way. Writing a tutorial was considered an essential design tool, because if a feature cannot be explained simply, the burden of supporting it will be too great. This point was never far from my mind because during the early years I *was* the support organization.

In the early days Sandy Fraser, my department head at the time, was very influential. For example, I believe he was the one to encourage me to break from the Simula style of class definition where the complete function definition is included and adopt the style where function definitions are typically elsewhere thus emphasizing the class declaration's role as an interface. Much of C with Classes was designed to allow simulators to be built that could be used in Sandy Fraser's work in network design. The first real application of C with Classes was such network simulators. Sudhir Agrawal was another early user who influenced the development of C with Classes through his work with network simulations. Jonathan Shopiro provided much feedback on the C with Classes design and implementation based on his simulation of a "dataflow database machine."

For more general discussions on programming language issues, as opposed to looking at applications to determine which problems needed to be solved, I turned to Dennis Ritchie, Steve Johnson, and in particular Doug McIlroy. Doug's influence on the development of both C and C++ cannot be overestimated. I cannot remember a single critical design decision in C++ that I have not discussed at length with Doug. Naturally, we didn't always agree, but I still have a strong reluctance to make a decision that goes against Doug's opinion. He has a knack for being right and an apparently infinite amount of experience and patience.

Since the main design work for C with Classes and C++ was done on blackboards, the thinking tended to focus on solutions to "archetypical" problems: small examples that are considered characteristic for a large class of problems. Thus, a good solution to the small example will provide significant help in writing programs dealing with real problems of that class. Many of these problems have entered the C++ literature and folklore through my use of them as examples in my papers, books, and talks. For C with Classes, the example considered most critical was the `task` class that was the basis of the task-library supporting Simula-style simulation. Other key classes were `queue`, `list`, and `histogram` classes. The `queue` and `list` classes were based on the idea – borrowed from Simula – of providing a `link` class from which users derived their own classes.

The danger inherent in this approach is to create a language and tools that provide elegant solutions to small selected examples, yet don't scale to building complete systems or large programs. This was counteracted by the simple fact that C with Classes (and later C++) had to pay for itself during its early years. This ensured that C with Classes couldn't evolve into something that was elegant but useless.

Being an individual working closely with users also gave me the freedom to promise only what I could actually deliver, rather than having to inflate my promises to the point where it would appear to make economic sense for an organization to allocate significant resources to the development, support, and marketing of "a product." Like all languages that have worked for a living during childhood, C++ matured with a distinct practical and pragmatic bent and a number of scars. The simulations of networks, board layouts, chips, network protocols, etc., based on the task library were my bread and butter in those early years.

3

The Birth of C++

No ties bind so strongly
as the links of inheritance.
– Stephen Jay Gould

From C with Classes to C++ — Cfront, the initial implementation of C++ — virtual functions and object-oriented programming — operator overloading and references — constants — memory management — type checking — C++'s relationship to C — dynamic initialization — declaration syntax — description and evaluation of C++.

3.1 From C with Classes to C++

During 1982 it became clear to me that C with Classes was a "medium success" and would remain so until it died. I defined a medium success as something so useful that it easily paid for itself and its developer, but not so attractive and useful that it would pay for a support and development organization. Thus, continuing with C with Classes and its C preprocessor implementation would condemn me to support C with Classes indefinitely. I saw only two ways out of this dilemma:

[1] Stop supporting C with Classes so that the users would have to go elsewhere (freeing me to do something else).

[2] Develop a new and better language based on my experience with C with Classes that would serve a large enough set of users to pay for a support and development organization (thus freeing me to do something else). At the time I estimated that 5,000 industrial users was the necessary minimum.

The third alternative, increasing the user population through marketing (hype), never occurred to me. What actually happened was that the explosive growth of C++, as the new language was eventually named, kept me so busy that to this day I haven't managed to get sufficiently detached to do something else of significance.

The success of C with Classes was, I think, a simple consequence of meeting its design aim: C with Classes did help organize a large class of programs significantly better than C without the loss of run-time efficiency and without requiring enough cultural changes to make its use infeasible in organizations that were unwilling to undergo major changes. The factors limiting its success were partly the limited set of new facilities offered over C and partly the preprocessor technology used to implement C with Classes. There simply wasn't enough support in C with Classes for people who *were* willing to invest significant efforts to reap matching benefits: C with Classes was an important step in the right direction, but it was only one small step. As a result of this analysis, I began designing a cleaned-up and extended successor to C with Classes and implementing it using traditional compiler technology.

The resulting language was at first still called C with Classes, but after a polite request from management it was given the name C84. The reason for the naming was that people had taken to calling C with Classes "new C," and then C. This abbreviation led to C being called "plain C," "straight C," and "old C." The last name, in particular, was considered insulting, so common courtesy and a desire to avoid confusion led me to look for a new name.

The name C84 was used only for a few months, partly because it was ugly and institutional, partly because there would still be confusion if people dropped the "84." Also, Larry Rosler, the editor of the X3J11 ANSI committee for the standardization of C, asked me to find another name. He explained, "standardized languages are often referred to by their name followed by the year of the standard and it would be embarrassing and confusing to have a superset (C84, a.k.a. C with Classes, and later C++) with a lower number than its subset (C, possibly C85, and later ANSI C)." That seemed eminently reasonable – although Larry turned out to have been somewhat optimistic about the date of the C standard – and I started asking for ideas for a new name among the C with Classes user community.

I picked C++ because it was short, had nice interpretations, and wasn't of the form "adjective C." In C, ++ can, depending on context, be read as "next," "successor," or "increment," though it is always pronounced "plus plus." The name C++ and its runner up ++C are fertile sources for jokes and puns – almost all of which were known and appreciated before the name was chosen. The name C++ was suggested by Rick Mascitti. It was first used in December of 1983 when it was edited into the final copies of [Stroustrup,1984] and [Stroustrup,1984c].

The "C" in C++ has a long history. Naturally, it is the name of the language Dennis Ritchie designed. C's immediate ancestor was an interpreted descendant of BCPL class B designed by Ken Thompson. BCPL was designed and implemented by Martin Richards from Cambridge University while visiting MIT in the other Cambridge. BCPL in turn was Basic CPL, where CPL is the name of a rather large (for its time) and elegant programming language developed jointly by the universities of Cambridge and London. Before the London people joined the project "C" stood for Cambridge. Later, "C" officially stood for Combined. Unofficially, "C" stood for Christopher because Christopher Strachey was the main power behind CPL.

3.2 Aims

During the 1982 to 1984 period, the aims for C++ gradually became more ambitious and more definite. I had come to see C++ as a language separate from C, and libraries and tools had emerged as areas of work. Because of that, because tool developers within Bell Labs were beginning to show interest in C++, and because I had embarked on a completely new implementation that would become the C++ compiler front-end, Cfront, I had to answer several key questions:

[1] Who will the users be?

[2] What kind of systems will they use?

[3] How will I get out of the business of providing tools?

[4] How should the answers to [1], [2], and [3] affect the language definition?

My answer to [1], "Who will the users be?," was that first my friends within Bell Labs and I would use it, then more widespread use within AT&T would provide more experience, then some universities would pick up the ideas and the tools, and finally AT&T and others would be able to make some money by selling the set of tools that had evolved. At some point, the initial and somewhat experimental implementation done by me would be faded out in favor of more industrial-strength implementations by AT&T and others.

This made practical and economic sense; the initial (Cfront) implementation would be tool-poor, portable, and cheap because that was what I, my colleagues, and many university users needed and could afford. Later, there would be ample scope for better tools and more specialized environments. Such better tools aimed primarily at industrial users needn't be cheap either, and would thus be able to pay for the support organizations necessary for large-scale use of the language. That was my answer to [3], "How will I get out of the business of providing tools?" Basically, the strategy worked. However, just about every detail actually happened in an unforeseen way.

To get an answer to [2], "What kind of systems will they use?" I simply looked around to see what kind of systems the C with Classes users actually did use. They used everything from systems that were so small they couldn't run a compiler to mainframes and supercomputers. They used more operating systems than I had heard of. Consequently, I concluded that extreme portability and the ability to do cross compilation were necessities and that I could make no assumption about the size and speed of the machines running generated code. To build a compiler, however, I would have to make assumptions about the kind of system people would develop their programs on. I assumed that one MIPS plus one Mbyte would be available. That assumption, I considered a bit risky because most of my prospective users at the time had a shared PDP11 or some other relatively low-powered and/or timeshared system.

I did not predict the PC revolution, but by over-shooting my performance target for Cfront I happened to build a compiler that (barely) could run on an IBM PC/AT, thus providing an existence proof that C++ could be an effective language on a PC and thereby spurring commercial software developers to beat it.

As the answer to [4], "How does all this affect the language definition?" I concluded that no feature must require really sophisticated compiler or run-time support, that available linkers must be used, and that the code generated would have to be efficient (comparable to C) even initially.

3.3   Cfront

The Cfront compiler front-end for the C84 language was designed and implemented by me between the spring of 1982 and the summer of 1983. The first user outside the computer science research center, Jim Coplien, received his copy in July of 1983. Jim was in a group that had been doing experimental switching work using C with Classes in Bell Labs in Naperville, Illinois for some time.

In that same time period, I designed C84, drafted the reference manual published January 1, 1984 [Stroustrup,1984], designed the `complex` number library and implemented it together with Leonie Rose [Rose,1984], designed and implemented the first `string` class together with Jonathan Shopiro, maintained and ported the C with Classes implementation, supported the C with Classes users, and helped them become C84 users. That was a busy year and a half.

Cfront was (and is) a traditional compiler front-end that performs a complete check of the syntax and semantics of the language, builds an internal representation of its input, analyzes and rearranges that representation, and finally produces output suitable for some code generator. The internal representation is a graph with one symbol table per scope. The general strategy is to read a source file one global declaration at a time and produce output only when a complete global declaration has been completely analyzed.

In practice, this means that the compiler needs enough memory to hold the representation of all global names and types plus the complete graph of one function. A few years later, I measured Cfront and found that its memory usage leveled out at about 600 Kbytes on a DEC VAX just about independently of which real program I fed it. This fact was what made my initial port of Cfront to a PC/AT in 1986 feasible. At the time of Release 1.0 in 1985 Cfront was about 12,000 lines of C++.

The organization of Cfront is fairly traditional except maybe for the use of many symbol tables instead of just one. Cfront was originally written in C with Classes (what else?) and soon transcribed into C84 so that the very first working C++ compiler was done in C++. Even the first version of Cfront used classes and derived classes heavily. It did not use virtual functions, though, because they were not available at the start of the project.

Cfront is a compiler front-end (only) and can never be used for real programming by itself. It needs a driver to run a source file through the C preprocessor, Cpp, then run the output of Cpp through Cfront and the output from Cfront through a C compiler:

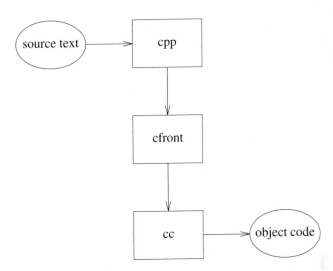

In addition, the driver must ensure that dynamic (run-time) initialization is done. In Cfront 3.0, the driver becomes yet more elaborate as automatic template instantiation (§15.2) is implemented [McCluskey,1992].

3.3.1 Generating C

The most unusual – for its time – aspect of Cfront was that it generated C code. This has caused no end of confusion. Cfront generated C because I needed extreme portability for an initial implementation and I considered C the most portable assembler around. I could easily have generated some internal back-end format or assembler from Cfront, but that was not what my users needed. No assembler or compiler back-end served more than maybe a quarter of my user community and there was no way that I could produce the, say, six backends needed to serve just 90% of that community. In response to this need, I concluded that using C as a common input format to a large number of code generators was the only reasonable choice. The strategy of building a compiler as a C generator later became popular. Languages such as Ada, Eiffel, Modula-3, Lisp, and Smalltalk have been implemented that way. I got a high degree of portability at a modest cost in compile-time overhead. The sources of overhead were

[1] The time needed for Cfront to write the intermediate C.
[2] The time needed for a C compiler to read the intermediate C.
[3] The time ''wasted'' by the C compiler analyzing the intermediate C.
[4] The time needed to control this process.

The size of this overhead depends critically on the time needed to read and write the intermediate C representation and that primarily depends on the disc read/write strategy of a system. Over the years I have measured this overhead on various systems and found it to be between 25% and 100% of the ''necessary'' parts of a compilation. I have also seen C++ compilers that didn't use intermediate C yet were slower than

Cfront plus a C compiler.

Please note that the C compiler is used as a code generator *only*. Any error message from the C compiler reflects an error in the C compiler or in Cfront, but not in the C++ source text. Every syntactic and semantic error is in principle caught by Cfront, the C++ compiler front-end. In this, C++ and its Cfront implementation differed from preprocessor-based languages such as Ratfor [Kernighan,1976] and Objective C [Cox,1986].

I stress this because there has been a long history of confusion about what Cfront is. It has been called a preprocessor because it generates C, and for people in the C community (and elsewhere) that has been taken as proof that Cfront was a rather simple program – something like a macro preprocessor. People have thus ''deduced'' (wrongly) that a line-for-line translation from C++ to C is possible, that symbolic debugging at the C++ level is impossible when Cfront is used, that code generated by Cfront must be inferior to code generated by ''real compilers,'' that C++ wasn't a ''real language,'' etc. Naturally, I have found such unfounded claims most annoying – especially when they were leveled as criticisms of the C++ language. Several C++ compilers now use Cfront together with local code generators without going through a C front end. To the user, the only obvious difference is faster compile times.

The irony is that I dislike most forms of preprocessors and macros. One of C++'s aims is to make C's preprocessor redundant (§4.4, §18) because I consider its actions inherently error prone. Cfront's primary aim was to allow C++ to have rational semantics that could not be implemented with the kind of compilers that were used for C at the time: Such compilers simply don't know enough about types and scopes to do the kind of resolution C++ requires. C++ was designed to rely heavily on traditional compiler technology, rather than on run-time support or detailed programmer resolution of expressions (as you need in languages without overloading). Consequently, C++ cannot be compiled with any traditional preprocessor technology. I considered and rejected such alternatives for language semantics and translator technology at the time. Cfront's immediate predecessor, Cpre, was a fairly traditional preprocessor that didn't understand every syntax, scope, and type rule of C. This had been a source of many problems both in the language definition and in actual use. I was determined not to see these problems repeated for my revised language and new implementation. C++ and Cfront were designed together and language definition and compiler technology definitely affected each other, but not in the simple-minded manner people sometimes assume.

3.3.2 Parsing C++

In 1982 when I first planned Cfront, I wanted to use a recursive descent parser because I had experience writing and maintaining such a beast, because I liked such parsers' ability to produce good error messages, and because I liked the idea of having the full power of a general-purpose programming language available when decisions had to be made in the parser. However, being a conscientious young computer scientist I asked the experts. Al Aho and Steve Johnson were in the Computer Science

Research Center and they, primarily Steve, convinced me that writing a parser by hand was most old-fashioned, would be an inefficient use of my time, would almost certainly result in a hard-to-understand and hard-to-maintain parser, and would be prone to unsystematic and therefore unreliable error recovery. The right way was to use an LALR(1) parser generator, so I used Al and Steve's YACC [Aho,1986].

For most projects, it would have been the right choice. For almost every project writing an experimental language from scratch, it would have been the right choice. For most people, it would have been the right choice. In retrospect, for me and C++ it was a bad mistake. C++ was not a new experimental language, it was an almost compatible superset of C – and at the time nobody had been able to write an LALR(1) grammar for C. The LALR(1) grammar used by ANSI C was constructed by Tom Pennello about a year and a half later – far too late to benefit me and C++. Even Steve Johnson's PCC, which was the preeminent C compiler at the time, cheated at details that were to prove troublesome to C++ parser writers. For example, PCC didn't handle redundant parentheses correctly so that `int(x);` wasn't accepted as a declaration of **x**. Worse, it seems that some people have a natural affinity to some parser strategies and others work much better with other strategies. My bias towards top-down parsing has shown itself many times over the years in the form of constructs that are hard to fit into a YACC grammar. To this day, Cfront has a YACC parser supplemented by much lexical trickery relying on recursive descent techniques. On the other hand, it *is* possible to write an efficient and reasonably nice recursive descent parser for C++. Several modern C++ compilers use recursive descent.

3.3.3 Linkage Problems

As mentioned, I decided to live within the constraints of traditional linkers. However, there was one constraint I found insufferable, yet so silly that I had a chance of fighting it if I had sufficient patience: Most traditional linkers had a very low limit on the number of characters that can be used in external names. A limit of eight characters was common, and six characters and one case only are guaranteed to work as external names in K&R C; ANSI/ISO C also accepts that limit. Given that the name of a member function includes the name of its class and that the type of an overloaded function has to be reflected in the linkage process somehow or other (see §11.3.1), I had little choice.

Consider:

```
void task::schedule() { /* ... */ }  // 4+8 characters

void hashed::print() { /* ... */ }  // 6+5 characters

complex sqrt(complex);  // 4 character plus 'complex'
double sqrt(double);    // 4 character plus 'double'
```

Representing these names with only six upper case characters would require some form of compression that would complicate tool building. It would probably also involve some form of hashing so that a rudimentary "program database" would be needed to resolve hash overflows. The former is a nuisance, and the latter could be a serious problem because there is no concept of a "program database" in the traditional C/Fortran linkage model.

Consequently, I started (in 1982) lobbying for longer names in linkers. I don't know if my efforts actually had any effect, but these days most linkers do give me the much larger number of characters I need. Cfront uses encodings to implement type-safe linkage in a way that makes a limit of 32 characters too low for comfort, and even 256 is a bit tight at times (see §11.3.2). In the interim, systems of hash coding of long identifiers have been used with archaic linkers, but that was never completely satisfactory.

3.3.4 Cfront Releases

The first C with Classes and C++ implementations to make their way out of Bell Labs were early versions that people in various university departments had requested directly from me. In that way, people in dozens of educational institutions got to use C with Classes. Examples are Stanford University (December 1981, first Cpre shipment), University of California at Berkeley, University of Wisconsin in Madison, Caltech, University of North Carolina at Chapel Hill, MIT, University of Sydney, Carnegie-Mellon University, University of Illinois at Urbana-Champaign, University of Copenhagen, Rutherford Labs (Oxford), IRCAM, INRIA. The shipments of implementations to individual educational institutions continued after the design and implementation of C++. Examples are University of California at Berkeley (August 1984, first Cfront shipment), Washington University (St. Louis), University of Texas in Austin, University of Copenhagen, and University of New South Wales. In addition, students showed their usual creativity in avoiding paperwork. Even then, handling individual releases soon became a burden for me and a source of annoyance for university people wanting C++. Consequently, my department head, Brian Kernighan, AT&T's C++ product manager, Dave Kallman, and I came up with the idea of having a more general release of Cfront. The idea was to avoid commercial problems such as determining prices, writing contracts, handling support, advertising, getting documentation to conform to corporate standards, etc., by basically giving Cfront and a few libraries to university people at the cost of the tapes used for shipping. This was called Release E, "E" for "Educational." The first tapes were shipped in January 1985 to organizations such as Rutherford Labs (Oxford).

Release E was an eye opener for me. In fact, Release E was a flop. I had expected interest in C++ in universities to surge. Instead, the growth of C++ users continued along its usual curve (§7.1) and what we saw instead of a flood of new users was a flood of complaints from professors because C++ wasn't commercially available. Again and again I was contacted and told "Yes, I want to use C++, and I know that I can get Cfront for free, but unfortunately I can't use it because I need something I can use in my consulting and something my students can use in industry." So much for the pure academic pursuit of learning. Steve Johnson, then the department head in charge of C and C++ development, Dave Kallman, and I went back to the drawing board and came back with the plan for a commercial Release 1.0. However, the policy of ''almost free'' C++ implementations (with source and libraries) to educational institutions that originated with Release E remains in place to this day.

Versions of C++ are often named by Cfront release numbers. Release 1.0 was the language as defined in *The C++ Programming Language* [Stroustrup,1986]. Releases 1.1 (June 1986) and 1.2 (February 1987) were primarily bug-fix releases, but also added pointers to members and protected members (§13.9).

Release 2.0 was a major cleanup that also introduced multiple inheritance (§12.1) in June 1989. It was widely perceived as a significant improvement both in functionality and quality. Release 2.1 (April 1990) was primarily a bug-fix release that brought Cfront (almost) into line with the definition in *The Annotated C++ Reference Manual* [ARM] (§5.3).

Release 3.0 (September 1991) added templates (§15) as specified in the ARM. A variant of 3.0 supporting exception handling (§16) as specified in the ARM was produced by Hewlett-Packard [Cameron,1992] and shipped starting late 1992.

I wrote the first versions of Cfront (1.0, 1.1, 1.2) and maintained them; Steve Dewhurst worked on it with me for a few months before Release 1.0 in 1985. Laura Eaves did much of the work on the Cfront parser for Release 1.0, 1.1, 2.1, and 3.0. I also did the lion's share of the programming for Release 1.2 and 2.0, but starting with Release 1.2, Stan Lippman also spent most of his time on Cfront. Laura Eaves, Stan Lippman, George Logothetis, Judy Ward, and Nancy Wilkinson did most of the work for Release 2.1 and 3.0. The work on 1.2, 2.0, 2.1, and 3.0 was managed by Barbara Moo. Andrew Koenig organized Cfront testing for 2.0. Sam Haradhvala from Object Design Inc. did an initial implementation of templates in 1989 that Stan Lippman extended and completed for Release 3.0 in 1991. The initial implementation of exception handling in Cfront was done by Hewlett-Packard in 1992. In addition to these people who have produced code that has found its way into the main version of Cfront, many people have built local C++ compilers from it. Over the years a wide variety of companies including Apple, Centerline (formerly Saber), Comeau Computing, Glockenspiel, ParcPlace, Sun, Hewlett-Packard, and others have shipped products that contain locally modified versions of Cfront.

3.4 Language Features

The major additions to C with Classes introduced to produce C++ were:

　　[1] Virtual functions (§3.5)
　　[2] Function name and operator overloading (§3.6)
　　[3] References (§3.7)
　　[4] Constants (§3.8)
　　[5] User-controlled free-store memory control (§3.9)
　　[6] Improved type checking (§3.10)

In addition, the notion of call and return functions (§2.11) was dropped due to lack of use and many minor details were changed to produce a cleaner language.

3.5   Virtual Functions

The most obvious new feature in C++ – and certainly the one that had the greatest impact on the style of programming one could use for the language – was virtual functions. The idea was borrowed from Simula and presented in a form that was intended to make a simple and efficient implementation easy. The rationale for virtual functions was presented in [Stroustrup,1986] and [Stroustrup,1986b]. To emphasize the central role of virtual functions in C++ programming, I will quote it in detail here [Stroustrup,1986]:

"An abstract data type defines a sort of black box. Once it has been defined, it does not really interact with the rest of the program. There is no way of adapting it to new uses except by modifying its definition. This can lead to severe inflexibility. Consider defining a type shape for use in a graphics system. Assume for the moment that the system has to support circles, triangles, and squares. Assume also that you have some classes:

```
class point{ /* ... */ };
class color{ /* ... */ };
```

You might define a shape like this:

```
enum kind { circle, triangle, square };

class shape {
    point center;
    color col;
    kind k;
    // representation of shape
public:
    point where()        { return center; }
    void move(point to) { center = to; draw(); }
    void draw();
    void rotate(int);
    // more operations
};
```

The "type field" k is necessary to allow operations such as draw() and rotate() to determine what kind of shape they are dealing with (in a Pascal-like language, one might use a variant record with tag k). The function draw() might be defined like this:

```
void shape::draw()
{
    switch (k) {
    case circle:
        // draw a circle
        break;
```

```
        case triangle:
            // draw a triangle
            break;
        case square:
            // draw a square
            break;
        }
    }
```

This is a mess. Functions such as draw() must "know about" all the kinds of shapes there are. Therefore the code for any such function grows each time a new shape is added to the system. If you define a new shape, every operation on a shape must be examined and (possibly) modified. You are not able to add a new shape to a system unless you have access to the source code for every operation. Since adding a new shape involves "touching" the code of every important operation on shapes, it requires great skill and potentially introduces bugs into the code handling other (older) shapes. The choice of representation of particular shapes can get severely cramped by the requirement that (at least some of) their representation must fit into the typically fixed sized framework presented by the definition of the general type shape.

The problem is that there is no distinction between the general properties of any shape (a shape has a color, it can be drawn, etc.) and the properties of a specific shape (a circle is a shape that has a radius, is drawn by a circle-drawing function, etc.). Expressing this distinction and taking advantage of it defines object-oriented programming. A language with constructs that allows this distinction to be expressed and used supports object-oriented programming. Other languages don't.

The Simula inheritance mechanism provides a solution that I adopted for C++. First, specify a class that defines the general properties of all shapes:

```
class shape {
    point center;
    color col;
    // ...
public:
    point where() { return center; }
    void move(point to) { center = to; draw(); }
    virtual void draw();
    virtual void rotate(int);
    // ...
};
```

The functions for which the calling interface can be defined, but where the implementation cannot be defined except for a specific shape, have been marked virtual (the Simula and C++ term for "may be redefined later in a class derived from this one"). Given this definition, we can write general functions manipulating shapes:

```
void rotate_all(shape** v, int size, int angle)
    // rotate all members of vector "v"
    // of size "size" "angle" degrees
{
    for (int i = 0; i < size; i++) v[i]->rotate(angle);
}
```

To define a particular shape, we must say that it is a shape and specify its particular properties (including the virtual functions).

```
class circle : public shape {
    int radius;
public:
    void draw() { /* ... */ };
    void rotate(int) {}     // yes, the null function
};
```

In C++, class `circle` is said to be *derived* from class `shape`, and class `shape` is said to be a *base* of class `circle`. An alternative terminology calls `circle` and `shape` subclass and superclass, respectively.''
For further discussion of virtual functions and object-oriented programming see §13.2, §12.3.1, §13.7, §13.8, and §14.2.3.

I don't remember much interest in virtual functions at the time. I probably didn't explain the concepts involved well, but the main reaction I received from people in my immediate vicinity was one of indifference and skepticism. A common opinion was that virtual functions were simply a kind of crippled pointer to function and thus redundant. Worse, it was sometimes argued that a well-designed program wouldn't need the extensibility and openness provided by virtual functions so that proper analysis would show which non-virtual functions could be called directly. Therefore, the argument went, virtual functions were simply a form of inefficiency. Clearly, I disagreed and added virtual functions anyway.

I deliberately did not provide a mechanism for explicit inquiry about the type of an object in C++:

"The Simula67 `INSPECT` statement was deliberately not introduced into C++. The reason for that is to encourage modularity through the use of virtual functions [Stroustrup,1986].''

The Simula `INSPECT` statement is a switch on a system-provided type field. I had seen enough misuses to be determined to rely on static type checking and virtual functions in C++ as long as possible. A mechanism for run-time type inquiry was eventually added to C++ (§14.2). I hope its form will make it less seductive than the Simula `INSPECT` was and is.

3.5.1 The Object Layout Model

The key implementation idea was that the set of virtual functions in a class defines an array of pointers to functions so that a call of a virtual function is simply an indirect function call through that array. There is one such array, usually called a virtual function table or `vtbl`, per class with virtual functions. Each object of such a class contains a hidden pointer, often called the `vptr`, to its class's virtual function table. Given:

```
class A {
    int a;
public:
    virtual void f();
    virtual void g(int);
    virtual void h(double);
};

class B : public A {
public:
    int b;
    void g(int);    // overrides A::g()
    virtual void m(B*);
};

class C : public B {
public:
    int c;
    void h(double); // overrides A::h()
    virtual void n(C*);
};
```

a class C object looked something like this:

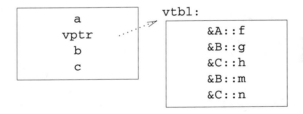

A call to a virtual function is transformed by the compiler into an indirect call. For example,

```
void f(C* p)
{
    p->g(2);
}
```

becomes something like

```
(*(p->vptr[1]))(p,2); /* generated code */
```

This implementation is not the only one possible. Its virtues are simplicity and run-time efficiency; its problem is that recompilation of user code is necessary if you change the set of virtual functions for a class.

At this point, the object model becomes real in the sense that an object is more than the simple aggregation of the data members of a class. An object of a C++ class with a virtual function is a fundamentally different beast from a simple C `struct`. Then why did I not at this point choose to make structs and classes different notions?

My intent was to have a single concept: a single set of layout rules, a single set of lookup rules, a single set of resolution rules, etc. Maybe we could have lived with two set of rules, but a single concept provides a smoother integration of features and simpler implementations. I was convinced that if `struct` came to mean "C and compatibility" to users and `class` to mean "C++ and advanced features," the community would fall into two distinct camps that would soon stop communicating. Being able to use as many or as few language features as needed when designing a class was an important idea to me. Only a single concept would support my ideas of a smooth and gradual transition from "traditional C-style programming," through data abstraction, to object-oriented programming. Only a single concept would support the notion of "you only pay for what you use" ideal.

In retrospect, I think these notions have been very important for C++'s success as a practical tool. Over the years, just about everybody has had some kind of expensive idea that could be implemented "for classes only," leaving low overhead and low features to `struct`s. I think the idea of keeping `struct` and `class` the same concept saved us from classes supporting an expensive, diverse, and rather different set of features than we have now. In other words, the "a `struct` is a `class`" notion is what has stopped C++ from drifting into becoming a much higher-level language with a disconnected low-level subset. Some would have preferred that to happen.

3.5.2 Overriding and Virtual Function Matching

A virtual function could only be overridden by a function in a derived class with the same name and exactly the same argument and return type. This avoided any form of run-time type checking of arguments and any need to keep more extensive type information around at run time. For example:

```
class Base {
public:
    virtual void f();
    virtual void g(int);
};


class Derived : public Base {
public:
    void f();       // overrides Base::f()
    void g(char); // doesn't override Base::g()
};
```

This opens an obvious trap for the unwary: The non-virtual `Derived::g()` is actually unrelated to the virtual `Base::g()` and hides it. This is a problem if you work with a compiler that doesn't warn you about the problem. However, the problem is trivial for a compiler to detect and is a non-problem given an implementation that does warn. Cfront 1.0 didn't warn, thus causing some grief, but Cfront 2.0 and higher do.

The rule requiring an exact type match for an overriding function was later relaxed for the return type; see §13.7.

3.5.3 Base Member Hiding

A name in a derived class hides any object or function of the same name in a base class. Whether this is a good design decision has been the subject of some debate over the years. The rule was first introduced in C with Classes. I saw it as a simple consequence of the usual scope rules. When arguing the point, I hold that the opposite rule – names from derived and base classes are merged into a single scope – gives at least as many problems. In particular, state-changing functions would occasionally be called for sub-objects by mistake:

```
class X {
    int x;
public:
    virtual void copy(X* p) { x = p->x; }
};

class XX: public X {
    int xx;
public:
    virtual void copy(XX* p) { xx = p->xx; X::copy(p); }
};

void f(X a, XX b)
{
    a.copy(&b); // ok: copy X part of b
    b.copy(&a); // error: copy(X*) is hidden by copy(XX*)
}
```

Allowing the second copy operation, as would happen if base and derived scopes were merged, would cause b's state to be partially updated. In most real cases, this would lead to very strange behavior of operations on XX objects. I have seen examples of people getting caught in exactly this way when using the GNU C++ compiler (§7.1.4), which allowed the overloading.

In the case where copy() is virtual, one might consider having XX::copy() override X::copy(), but then one would need run-time type checking to catch the problem with b.copy(&a) and programmers would have to code defensively to catch such errors at run time (§13.7.1). This was understood at the time, and I feared that there were further problems that I didn't understand, so I chose the current rules as the strictest, simplest, and most efficient.

In retrospect, I suspect that the overloading rules introduced in 2.0 (§11.2.2) might have been able to handle this case. Consider the call `b.copy(&a)`. The variable `b` is an exact type match for the implicit argument of `XX::copy`, but requires a standard conversion to match `X::copy`. The variable `a` on the other hand, is an exact match for the explicit argument of `X::copy`, but requires a standard conversion to match `XX::copy`. Thus, had the overloading been allowed, the call would have been an error because it was ambiguous.

See §17.5.2 for a way to explicitly request overloading of base and derived class functions.

3.6 Overloading

Several people had asked for the ability to overload operators. Operator overloading ''looked neat'' and I knew from experience with Algol68 how the idea could be made to work. However, I was reluctant to introduce the notion of overloading into C++ because:

[1] Overloading was reputed to be hard to implement and caused compilers to grow to monstrous size.

[2] Overloading was reputed to be hard to teach and hard to define precisely. Consequently, manuals and tutorials would grow to monstrous size.

[3] Code written using operator overloading was reputed to be inherently inefficient.

[4] Overloading was reputed to make code incomprehensible.

If [3] or [4] were true, C++ would be better off without overloading. If [1] or [2] were true, I didn't have the resources to provide overloading.

However, if all of these conjectures were false, overloading would solve some real problems for C++ users. There were people who would like to have complex numbers, matrices, and APL-like vectors in C++. There were people who would like range-checked arrays, multidimensional arrays, and strings. There were at least two separate applications for which people wanted to overload logical operators such as | (or), & (and), and ^ (exclusive or). The way I saw it, the list was long and would grow with the size and the diversity of the C++ user population. My answer to [4], ''overloading makes code obscure,'' was that several of my friends, whose opinion I valued and whose experience was measured in decades, claimed that their code would become cleaner if they had overloading. So what if one can write obscure code with overloading? It is possible to write obscure code in any language. It matters more how a feature can be used well than how it can be misused.

Next, I convinced myself that overloading wasn't inherently inefficient [Stroustrup,1984b] [ARM,§12.1c]. The details of the overloading mechanism were mostly worked out on my blackboard and those of Stu Feldman, Doug McIlroy, and Jonathan Shopiro.

Thus, having worked out an answer to [3], ''code written using overloading is inefficient,'' I needed to concern myself with [1] and [2], the issue of compiler and language complexity. I first observed that use of classes with overloaded operators, such as `complex` and `string`, was quite easy and didn't put a major burden on the programmer. Next, I wrote the manual sections to prove that the added complexity wasn't a serious issue; the manual needed less than a page and a half extra (out of a 42-page manual). Finally, I did the first implementation in two hours using only 18 lines of extra code in Cfront, and I felt I had demonstrated that the fears about definition and implementation complexity were somewhat exaggerated. Nevertheless, §11 will show that overloading problems did appear.

Naturally, all these issues were not really tackled in this strict sequential order, but the emphasis of the work did slowly shift from utility issues to implementation issues. The overloading mechanisms were described in detail in [Stroustrup,1984b], and examples of classes using the mechanisms were written up [Rose,1984] [Shopiro,1985].

In retrospect, I think that operator overloading has been a major asset to C++. In addition to the obvious use of overloaded arithmetic operators (+, *, +=, *=, etc.) for numerical applications, [ ] subscripting, ( ) application, and = assignment are often overloaded to control access, and << and >> have become the standard I/O operators (§8.3.1).

3.6.1 Basic Overloading

Here is an example that illustrates the basic techniques:

```
class complex {
    double re, im;
public:
    complex(double);
    complex(double,double);

    friend complex operator+(complex,complex);
    friend complex operator*(complex,complex);
    // ...
};
```

This allows simple complex expressions to be resolved into function calls:

```
void f(complex z1, complex z2)
{
    complex z3 = z1+z2; // operator+(z1,z2)
}
```

Assignment and initialization needn't be explicitly defined. They are by default defined as memberwise copy; see §11.4.1.

In my design of the overloading mechanism, I relied on conversions to decrease the number of overloading functions needed. For example:

```
void g(complex z1, complex z2, double d)
{
    complex z3 = z1+z2;  // operator+(z1,z2)
    complex z4 = z1+d;   // operator+(z1,complex(d))
    complex z5 = d+z2;   // operator+(complex(d),z2)
}
```

That is, I rely on the implicit conversion of `double` to `complex` to allow me to support "mixed-mode arithmetic" with a single complex add function. Additional functions can be introduced to improve efficiency or numerical accuracy.

In principle, we could do without implicit conversions altogether by either requiring explicit conversion or by providing the full set of complex add functions:

```
class complex {
public:
    friend complex operator+(complex,complex);
    friend complex operator+(complex,double);
    friend complex operator+(double,complex);
    // ...
};
```

Would we have been better off without implicit conversions? The language would have been simpler without them, implicit conversions can certainly be overused, and a call involving a conversion function is typically less efficient than a call of an exactly matching function.

Consider the four basic arithmetic operations. Defining the full set of mixed-mode operations for `complex` and `double` requires 12 arithmetic functions compared to 3 plus a conversion function when implicit conversion is used. Where the number of operations and the number of types involved are higher, the difference between the linear increase in the number of functions that we get from using conversions and the quadratic explosion we get from requiring all combinations becomes significant. I have seen examples in which the complete set of operators was provided because conversion operators couldn't be safely defined. The result was more than 100 functions defining operators. I consider that acceptable in special cases, but not as a standard practice.

Naturally, I realized that not all constructors defined meaningful and unsurprising implicit conversions. For example, a `vector` type usually has a constructor taking an integer argument indicating the number of elements. It was an unfortunate sideefect to have `v=7` construct a `vector` of seven elements and assign it to `v`. I didn't consider this problem urgent, though. Several members of the C++ standards committee (§6.2), notably Nathan Myers, suggested that a solution was necessary. In 1995, the problem was solved by allowing the prefix `explicit` to be added to the declaration of a constructor. A constructor declared `explicit` is used for explicit construction only and not for implicit conversions. For example, declaring `vector`'s constructor ''`explicit vector(int);`'' makes `v=7` an error while the more explicit `v=vector(7)` as ever constructs and assigns a `vector`.

3.6.2 Members and Friends

Note how a global `operator+`, a `friend` function, was used in preference to a member function to ensure that the operands of + are handled symmetrically. Had member functions been used, we would have needed a resolution like this:

```
void f(complex z1, complex z2, double d)
{
    complex z3 = z1+z2; // z1.operator+(z2);
    complex z4 = z1+d;  // z1.operator+(complex(d))
    complex z5 = d+z2;  // d.operator+(z2)
}
```

This would have required us to define how to add a `complex` to the built-in type `double`. This would not only require more functions, but also require modification of code in separate places (that is, the definition of class `complex` and the definition of the built-in type `double`). This was deemed undesirable. I considered allowing the definition of additional operations on built-in types. However, I rejected the idea because I did not want to change the rule that no type – built-in or user-defined – can have operations added after its definition is complete. Other reasons were that the definition of conversions between C's built-in types is too messy to allow additions, and that the member-function solution to provide mixed-mode arithmetic is intrinsically more messy than the global-function-plus-conversion-function solution adopted.

The use of a global function allows us to define operators so that their arguments are logically equivalent. Conversely, defining an operator as a member ensures that no conversions are invoked for the first (leftmost) operand. This allows us to mirror the rules for operands that require an lvalue as their leftmost operand, such as the assignment operators:

```
class String {
    // ...
public:
    String(const char*);
    String& operator=(const String&);
    String& operator+=(const String&); // add to end
    // ...
};

void f(String& s1, String& s2)
{
    s1 = s2;
    s1 = "asdf"; // fine: s1.operator=(String("asdf"));
    "asdf" = s2; // error: String assigned to char*
}
```

Later, Andrew Koenig observed that the assignment operators such as += are more fundamental and more efficient than their ordinary arithmetic cousins such as +. It is often best to define only assignment operator functions, such as += and *=, as members and define ordinary operator functions, such as + and *, as global functions later:

```
String& String::operator+=(const String& s)
{
    // add s onto the end of *this

    return *this;
}

String operator+(const String& s1, const String& s2)
{
    String sum = s1;
    sum+=s2;
    return sum;
}
```

Note that no friendship is required, and that the definition of the binary operator is trivial and stylized. No temporary variables are needed to implement the call of +=, and the local variable sum is all the temporary variable management that the user has to consider. The rest can be handled simply and efficiently by the compiler (see §3.6.4).

My original idea was to allow every operator to be either a member or a global function. In particular, I had found it convenient to provide simple access operations as member functions and then let users implement their own operators as global functions. For operators such as + and – my reasoning was sound, but for operator = itself we ran into problems. Consequently, Release 2.0 required operator = to be a member. This was an incompatible change that broke a few programs, so the decision wasn't taken lightly. The problem was that unless operator = is a member, a program can have two different interpretations of = dependent on the location in the source code. For example:

```
class X {
    // no operator=
};

void f(X a, X b)
{
    a = b; // predefined meaning of =
}

void operator=(X&,X); // disallowed by 2.0

void g(X a, X b)
{
    a = b; // user-defined meaning of =
}
```

This could be most confusing, especially where the two assignments appeared in separately compiled source files. Since there is no built-in meaning for += for a class that problem cannot occur for +=.

However, even in the original design of C++, I restricted operators [ ], ( ), and ->
to be members. It seemed a harmless restriction that eliminated the possibility of
some obscure errors because these operators invariably depend on and typically modify the state of their left-hand operand. However, it is probably a case of unnecessary
nannyism.

3.6.3 Operator Functions

Having decided to support implicit conversions and the model of mixed mode operations supported by them, I needed a way of specifying such conversions. Constructors of a single argument provide one such mechanism. Given

```
class complex {
    // ...
    complex(double); // converts a double to a complex
    // ...
};
```

we can explicitly or implicitly convert a `double` to a `complex`. However, this
allows the designer of a class to define conversions *to* that class only. It was not
uncommon to want to write a new class that had to fit into an existing framework.
For example, the C library has dozens of functions taking string arguments, that is,
arguments of type `char*`. When Jonathan Shopiro first wrote a full-blown `String`
class, he found that he would either have to replicate every C library function taking a
string argument:

```
int strlen(const char*);    // original C function
int strlen(const String&);  // new C++ function
```

or provide a `String` to `const char*` conversion operator.

Consequently, I added the notion of conversion operator functions to C++:

```
class String {
    // ...
    operator const char*();
    // ...
};

int strlen(const char*);    // original C function

void f(String& s)
{
    // ...
    strlen(s); // strlen(s.operator const char*())
    // ...
}
```

In real use, implicit conversion has sometimes proven tricky to use. However, providing the full set of mixed-mode operations isn't pretty either. I would like a better
solution, but of the solutions I know, implicit conversions is the least bad.

3.6.4 Efficiency and Overloading

Contrary to (frequently expressed) naive superstition there is no fundamental difference between operations expressed as function calls and operations expressed as operators. The efficiency issues for overloading were (and are) inlining and the avoidance
of spurious temporaries.

To convince myself of that, I first noted that code generated from something like
a+b or v[i] was identical to what one would get from function calls add(a,b)
and v.elem(i).

Next, I observed that by using inlining, a programmer could ensure that simple
operations would not carry function-call overhead (in time or space). Finally, I
observed that call-by-reference would be necessary to support this style of programming effectively for larger objects (more about that in §3.7). This left the problems of
how to avoid spurious copying in examples such as a=b+c. Generating

```
assign(add(b,c),t); assign(t,a);
```

would not compare well to the

```
add_and_assign(b,c,a);
```

that a compiler can generate for a built-in type and a programmer can write explicitly.
In the end, I demonstrated [Stroustrup,1984b] how to generate

```
add_and_initialize(b,c,t); assign(t,a);
```

That left one "spurious" copy operation that can be removed only where it can be
proved that the + and = operations don't actually depend on the value assigned to
(aliasing). For a more accessible reference for this optimization, see [ARM]. This
optimization did not become available in Cfront until Release 3.0. I believe the first
available C++ implementation using that technique was Zortech's compiler. Walter
Bright easily implemented the optimization after I explained it to him over an ice
cream sundae at the top of the Space Needle in Seattle after an ANSI C++ standards
meeting in 1990.

The reason I considered this slightly sub-optimal scheme acceptable was that more
explicit operators such as += are available for hand-optimization of the most common
operations, and also that the absence of aliasing can be assumed in initializations.
Borrowing the Algol68 notion that a declaration can be introduced wherever it is
needed (and not just at the top of some block), I could enable an "initialize-only" or
"single-assignment" style of programming that would be inherently efficient – and
also less error-prone than traditional styles where variables are assigned again and
again. For example, one can write

```
complex compute(complex z, int i)
{
    if ( /* ... */ ) {
        // ...
    }
    complex t = f(z,i);
    // ...
    z += t;
    // ...
    return t;
}
```

rather than the more verbose and less efficient:

```
complex compute(complex z, int i)
{
    complex t;
    if ( /* ... */ ) {
        // ...
    }
    t = f(z,i);
    // ...
    z = z + t;
    // ...
    return t;
}
```

For yet another idea for increasing run-time efficiency by eliminating temporaries, see §11.6.3.

3.6.5 Mutation and New Operators

I considered it important to provide overloading as a mechanism for extending the language and *not* for mutating it; that is, it is possible to define operators to work on user-defined types (classes), but not to change the meaning of operators on built-in types. In addition, I didn't want to allow programmers to introduce new operators. I feared cryptic notation and having to adopt complicated parsing strategies like those needed for Algol68. In this matter, I think my restraint was reasonable. See also §11.6.1 and §11.6.3.

3.7   References

References were introduced primarily to support operator overloading. Doug McIlroy recalls that once I was explaining some problems with a precursor to the current operator overloading scheme to him. He used the word *reference* with the startling effect that I muttered "Thank you," and left his office to reappear the next day with the current scheme essentially complete. Doug had reminded me of Algol68.

C passes every function argument by value, and where passing an object by value

would be inefficient or inappropriate the user can pass a pointer. This strategy
doesn't work where operator overloading is used. In that case, notational convenience
is essential because users cannot be expected to insert address-of operators if the
objects are large. For example:

```
a = b - c;
```

is acceptable (that is, conventional) notation, but

```
a = &b - &c;
```

is not. Anyway, &b-&c already has a meaning in C, and I didn't want to change that.

It is not possible to change what a reference refers to after initialization. That is,
once a C++ reference is initialized it cannot be made to refer to a different object later;
it cannot be re-bound. I had in the past been bitten by Algol68 references where
r1=r2 can either assign through r1 to the object referred to or assign a new reference value to r1 (re-binding r1) depending on the type of r2. I wanted to avoid
such problems in C++.

If you want to do more complicated pointer manipulation in C++, you can use
pointers. Because C++ has both pointers and references, it does not need operations
for distinguishing operations on the reference itself from operations on the object
referred to (like Simula) or the kind of deductive mechanism employed by Algol68.

I made one serious mistake, though, by allowing a non-const reference to be initialized by a non-lvalue. For example:

```
void incr(int& rr) { rr++; }

void g()
{
    double ss = 1;
    incr(ss);      // note: double passed, int expected
                   // (fixed: error in Release 2.0)
}
```

Because of the difference in type the int& cannot refer to the double passed so a
temporary was generated to hold an int initialized by ss's value. Thus, incr()
modified the temporary, and the result wasn't reflected back to the calling function.

The reason to allow references to be initialized by non-lvalues was to allow the
distinction between call-by-value and call-by-reference to be a detail specified by the
called function and of no interest to the caller. For const references, this is possible;
for non-const references it is not. For Release 2.0 the definition of C++ was
changed to reflect this.

It is important that const references can be initialized by non-lvalues and lvalues
of types that require conversion. In particular, this is what allows a Fortran function
to be called with a constant:

```
extern "Fortran" float sqrt(const float&);

void f()
{
    sqrt(2); // call by reference
}
```

In addition to the obvious uses of references, such as reference arguments, we considered the ability to use references as return types important. This allowed us to have a very simple index operator for a string class:

```
class String {
    // ...
    char& operator[](int index);   // subscript operator
                                   // return a reference
};

void f(String& s, int i)
{
    char c1 = s[i];    // assign operator[]'s result
    s[i] = c1;         // assign to operator[]'s result
    // ...
}
```

Returning a reference to the internal representation of a `String` assumes responsible behavior by the users. That assumption is reasonable in many situations.

3.7.1 Lvalue vs. Rvalue

Overloading `operator[]()` to return a reference doesn't allow the writer of `operator[]()` to provide different semantics for reading and writing an element identified by subscripting. For example,

```
s1[i] = s2[j];
```

we can't cause one action on the `String` written to, `s1`, and another on the string read, `s2`. Jonathan Shopiro and I considered it essential to provide separate semantics for read access and write access when we considered strings with shared representation and database accesses. In both cases, a read is a very simple and cheap operation, whereas a write is a potentially expensive and complicated operation involving replication of data structures.

We considered two alternatives:

[1] Specifying separate functions for lvalue use and rvalue use.

[2] Having the programmer use an auxiliary data structure.

The latter approach was chosen because it avoided a language extension and because we considered the technique of returning an object describing a location in a container class, such as a `String`, more general. The basic idea is to have a helper class that identifies a position in the container class much as a reference does, but has separate semantics for reading and writing. For example:

```
class char_ref { // identify a character in a String
friend class String;
    int i;
    String* s;
    char_ref(String* ss, int ii) { s=ss; i=ii; }
public:
    void operator=(char c);
    operator char();
};
```

Assigning to a `char_ref` is implemented as assignment to the character referenced. Reading from a `char_ref` is implemented as a conversion to `char` returning the value of the character identified:

```
void char_ref::operator=(char c) { s->r[i]=c; }
char_ref::operator char() { return s->r[i]; }
```

Note that only a `String` can create a `char_ref`. The actual assignment is implemented by the `String`:

```
class String {
friend class char_ref;
    char* r;
public:
    char_ref operator[](int i)
        { return char_ref(this,i); }
    // ...
};
```

Given these definitions,

```
s1[i] = s2[j];
```

means

```
s1.operator[](i) = s2.operator[](j)
```

where both `s1.operator[](i)` and `s2.operator[](j)` return temporary objects of class `char_ref`. That in turn means

```
s1.operator[](i).operator=(s2.operator[](j).operator char())
```

Inlining makes the performance of this technique acceptable in many cases, and the use of friendship to restrict the creation of `char_refs` ensures that we do not get lifetime temporary problems (§6.3.2). For example, this technique has been used in successful `String` classes. However, it does seem complicated and heavyweight for simple uses such as access to individual characters, so I have often considered alternatives. In particular, I have been looking for an alternative that would be both more efficient and not a special-purpose wart. Composite operators (§11.6.3) is one possibility.

3.8 Constants

In operating systems, it is common to have access to some piece of memory controlled directly or indirectly by two bits: one that indicates whether a user can write to
it and one that indicates whether a user can read it. This idea seemed to me directly
applicable to C++, and I considered allowing every type to be specified `readonly` or
`writeonly`. An internal memo dated January 1981 [Stroustrup,1981b] describes
the idea:

"Until now it has not been possible in C to specify that a data item should be *read
only*, that is, that its value must remain unchanged. Neither has there been any
way of restricting the use of arguments passed to a function. Dennis Ritchie
pointed out that if `readonly` was a type operator, both facilities could be
obtained easily, for example:

```
readonly char table[1024];    /* the chars in "table"
                                  cannot be updated */

int f(readonly int * p)
{
    /* "f" cannot update the data denoted by "p" */
    /* ... */
}
```

The `readonly` operator is used to prevent the update of some location. It specifies that out of the usually legal ways of accessing the location, only the ones that
do not change the value stored there are legal."
The memo goes on to point out that

"The `readonly` operator can be used on pointers, too. `*readonly` is interpreted as "readonly pointer to," for example:

```
readonly int * p;     /* pointer to read only int */
int * readonly pp;    /* read only pointer to int */
readonly int * readonly ppp;   /* read only pointer
                                  to read only int */
```

Here, it is legal to assign a new value to `p`, but not to `*p`. It is legal to assign to
`*pp`, but not to `pp`, and it is illegal to assign to `ppp`, or `*ppp`."
Finally, the memo introduces `writeonly`:

"There is the type operator `writeonly`, which is used like `readonly`, but
prevents reading rather than writing. For example:

```
struct device_registers {
    readonly int    input_reg, status_reg;
    writeonly int   output_reg, command_reg;
};
```

```
void f(readonly char * readonly from,
    writeonly char * readonly to)
/*
    "f" can obtain data through "from",
    deposit results through "to",
    but can change neither pointer
*/
{
    /* ... *.
}
```

```
int * writeonly p;
```

Here, ++p is illegal because it involves reading the old value of p, but p=0 is legal.''

The proposal focused on specifying interfaces rather than on providing symbolic constants for C. Clearly, a readonly value is a symbolic constant, but the scope of the proposal is far greater. Initially, I proposed pointers to readonly but not readonly pointers. A brief discussion with Dennis Ritchie evolved the idea into the readonly/writeonly mechanism that I implemented and proposed to an internal Bell Labs C standards group chaired by Larry Rosler. There, I had my first experience with standards work. I came away from a meeting with an agreement (that is, a vote) that readonly would be introduced into C – yes C, not C with Classes or C++ – provided it was renamed const. Unfortunately, a vote isn't executable, so nothing happened to our C compilers. Later, the ANSI C committee (X3J11) was formed and the const proposal resurfaced there and became part of ANSI/ISO C.

In the meantime, I had experimented further with const in C with Classes and found that const was a useful alternative to macros for representing constants only if global consts were implicitly local to their compilation unit. Only in that case could the compiler easily deduce that their value really didn't change. Knowing that allows us to use simple consts in constant expressions and to avoid allocating space for such constants. C did not adopt this rule. For example, in C++ we can write:

```
const int max = 14;

void f(int i)
{
    int a[max+1]; // const 'max' used in constant expression

    switch (i) {
    case max:      // const 'max' used in constant expression
        // ...
    }
}
```

whereas in C, even today we must write

```
#define max 14
// ...
```

because in C, `const`s may not be used in constant expressions. This makes `const`s far less useful in C than in C++ and leaves C dependent on the preprocessor while C++ programmers can use properly typed and scoped `const`s.

3.9 Memory Management

Long before the first C with Classes program was written, I knew that free store (dynamic memory) would be used more heavily in a language with classes than in most C programs. This was the reason for the introduction of the `new` and `delete` operators in C with Classes. The `new` operator that both allocates memory from the free store and invokes a constructor to ensure initialization was borrowed from Simula. The `delete` operator was a necessary complement because I did not want C with Classes to depend on a garbage collector (§2.13, §10.7). The argument for the `new` operator can be summarized like this. Would you rather write:

```
X* p = new X(2);
```

or

```
struct X * p = (struct X *) malloc(sizeof(struct X));
if (p == 0) error("memory exhausted");
p->init(2);
```

and which version are you most likely to make a mistake in? Note that the checking against memory exhaustion is done in both cases. Allocation using `new` involves an implicit check and may invoke a user-supplied `new_handler` function; see [2nd,§9.4.3]. The arguments against – which were voiced quite a lot at the time – were, "but we don't *really* need it," and, "but someone will have used `new` as an identifier." Both observations are correct, of course.

Introducing operator `new` thus made the use of free store more convenient and less error-prone. This increased its use even further so that the C free-store allocation routine `malloc()` used to implement `new` became the most common performance bottleneck in real systems. This was no surprise either; the only problem was what to do about it. Having real programs spend 50% or more of their time in `malloc()` wasn't acceptable.

I found per-class allocators and deallocators very effective. The fundamental idea is that free-store memory usage is dominated by the allocation and deallocation of lots of small objects from very few classes. Take over the allocation of those objects in a separate allocator and you can save both time and space for those objects and also reduce the amount of fragmentation of the general free store.

I don't remember the earliest discussions about how to provide such a mechanism to the users, but I do remember presenting the "assignment to `this`" technique (described below) to Brian Kernighan and Doug McIlroy and summing up, "This is ugly as sin, but it works, and if you can't think of a better way either then that's the way I'll do it,'' or words to that effect. They couldn't, so we had to wait until Release 2.0 for the cleaner solution now in C++ (see §10.2).

The idea was that, by default, memory for an object is allocated ''by the system'' without requiring any specific action from the user. To override this default behavior, a programmer simply assigns to the `this` pointer. By definition, `this` points to the object for which a member function is called. For example:

```
class X {
    // ...
public:
    X(int i);
    // ...
};


X::X(int i)
{
    this = my_alloc(sizeof(X));
    // initialize
}
```

Whenever the `X::X(int)` constructor is used, allocation will be done using `my_alloc()`. This mechanism was powerful enough to serve its purpose, and several others, but far too low level. It didn't interact well with stack allocation or with inheritance. It was error-prone and repetitive to use when – as is typical – an important class had many constructors.

Note that static and automatic (stack allocated) objects were always possible and that the most effective memory management techniques relied heavily on such objects. The string class was a typical example. `String` objects are typically on the stack, so they require no explicit memory management, and the free store they rely on is managed exclusively and invisibly to the user by the `String` member functions.

The constructor notation used here is discussed in §3.11.2 and §3.11.3.

3.10 Type Checking

The C++ type checking rules were the result of experience with C with Classes. All function calls are checked at compile time. The checking of trailing arguments can be suppressed by explicit specification in a function declaration. This is essential to allow C's `printf()`:

```
int printf(const char* ...); // accept any argument after
                             // the initial character string

// ...

printf("date: %s %d 19%d\n",month,day,year); // maybe right
```

Several mechanisms were provided to alleviate the withdrawal symptoms that many C programmers feel when they first experience strict checking. Overriding type checking using the ellipsis was the most drastic and least recommended of those. Function name overloading (§3.6.1) and default arguments [Stroustrup,1986] (§2.12.2) made it possible to give the appearance of a single function taking a variety of argument lists without compromising type safety.

In addition, I designed the stream I/O system to demonstrate that weak checking wasn't necessary even for I/O (see §8.3.1):

```
cout<<"date: "<<month<<' '<<day<<" 19"<<year<<'\n';
```

is a type-safe version of the example above.

I saw, and still see, type checking as a practical tool rather than a goal in itself. It is essential to realize that eliminating every type violation in a program doesn't imply that the resulting program is correct or even that the resulting program cannot crash because an object was used in a way that was inconsistent with its definition. For example, a stray electric pulse may cause a critical memory bit to change its value in a way that is impossible according to the language definition. Equating type insecurities with program crashes and program crashes with catastrophic failures such as airplane crashes, telephone system breakdowns, and nuclear power station meltdowns is irresponsible and misleading.

People who make statements to that effect fail to appreciate that the reliability of a system depends on all of its parts. Ascribing an error to a particular part of the total system is simply pin-pointing the error. We try to design life-critical systems so that a single error or even many errors will not lead to a ''crash.'' The responsibility for the integrity of the system is in the people who produce the system and not in any one part of the system. In particular, type safety is not a substitute for testing even though it can be a great help in getting a system ready for testing. Blaming programming language features for a specific system failure, even a purely software one, is confusing the issue; see also §16.2.

3.11 Minor Features

During the transition from C with Classes to C++, several minor features were added.

3.11.1 Comments

The most visible minor change was the introduction of BCPL-style comments:

```
int a; /* C-style explicitly terminated comment */
int b; // BCPL-style comment terminated by end-of-line
```

Since both styles of comments are allowed, people can use the style they like best. Personally, I like the BCPL-style for one-line comments. The immediate cause for introducing the // comments was that I sometimes made silly mistakes forgetting to terminate C comments and found that the three extra characters I used to terminate a

/* comment sometimes made my lines wrap around on my screen. I also noted that // comments were more convenient than /* comments for commenting out small sections of code.

The addition of // was soon discovered not to be 100% C compatible because of examples such as

```
x = a//* divide */b
```

which means x=a in C++ and x=a/b in C. At the time and also now, most C++ programmers considered such examples of little real importance.

3.11.2 Constructor Notation

The name "new-function" for constructors had been a source of confusion, so the named constructor was introduced. At the same time, the concept was extended to allow constructors to be used explicitly in expressions. For example,

```
complex i = complex(0,1);

complex operator+(complex a, complex b)
{
      return complex(a.re+b.re,a.im+b.im);
}
```

The expressions of the form complex(x,y) are explicit invocations of a constructor for class complex.

To minimize the number of new keywords, I didn't use an explicit syntax like this:

```
class X {
     constructor();
     destructor();
     // ...
};
```

Instead, I chose a declaration syntax that mirrored the use of constructors:

```
class X {
     X();  // constructor
     ~X(); // destructor (~ is the C complement operator)
     // ...
};
```

This may have been overly clever.

The explicit invocation of constructors in expressions proved very useful, but it is also a fertile source of C++ parsing problems. In C with Classes, new() and delete() functions had been public by default. This anomaly was eliminated so that C++ constructors and destructors obey the same access control rules as other functions. For example:

```
class Y {
    Y(); // private constructor
    // ...
};

Y a; // error:  cannot access Y::Y(): private member
```

This led to several useful techniques based on the idea of controlling operations by hiding the functions that perform them; see §11.4.

3.11.3 Qualification

In C with Classes, a dot was used to express membership of a class as well as to express selection of a member of a particular object. This had been the cause of some minor confusion and could also be used to construct ambiguous examples. Consider:

```
class X {
    int a;
public:
    void set(X);
};

void X.set(X arg) { a = arg.a; };    // so far so good

class X X; // common C practice:
           // class and object with the same name

void f()
{
    // ...
    X.a; // now, which X do I mean?
         // the class or the object?
    // ...
}
```

To alleviate this, : : was introduced to mean membership of class, and . was retained exclusively for membership of object. The example thus becomes:

```
void X::set(X arg) { a = arg.a; };

class X X;

void g()
{
    // ...
    X.a;  // object.member
    X::a; // class::member
    // ...
}
```

3.11.4 Initialization of Global Objects

It was my aim to make user-defined types usable wherever built-in types were, and I had experienced the lack of global variables of class type as a source of performance problems in Simula. Consequently, global variables of class type were allowed in C++. This had important and somewhat unexpected ramifications. Consider:

```
class Double {
    // ...
    Double(double);
};

Double s1 = 2;       // construct s1 from 2
Double s2 = sqrt(2); // construct s1 from sqrt(2)
```

Such initialization cannot in general be done completely at compile time or at link time. Dynamic (run-time) initialization is necessary. Dynamic initialization is done in declaration order within a translation unit. No order is defined for initialization of objects in different translation units except that all static initialization takes place before any dynamic initialization.

3.11.4.1 Problems with Dynamic Initialization

My assumption had been that global objects would be rather simple and therefore require relatively uncomplicated initialization. In particular, I had expected that global objects with initialization that depended on other global objects in other compilation units would be rare. I regarded such dependencies simply as poor design and therefore didn't feel obliged to provide specific language support to resolve them. For simple examples, such as the one above, I was right. Such examples are useful and cause no problems. Unfortunately, I found another and more interesting use of dynamically initialized global objects.

A library often has some actions that need to be performed before its individual parts can be used. Alternatively, a library may provide objects that are supposed to be pre-initialized so that users can use them directly without first having to initialize them. For example, you don't have to initialize C's stdin and stdout: the C startup routine does that for you. Similarly, C's exit() closes stdin and stdout. This is a very special treatment, and no equivalent facilities are offered for other libraries. When I designed the stream I/O library, I wanted to match the convenience of C's I/O without introducing special-purpose warts into C++. Thus, I simply relied on dynamic initialization of cout and cin.

That worked nicely, except that I had to rely on an implementation detail to ensure that cout and cin were constructed before user code was run and destroyed after the last user code had completed. Other implementers were less considerate and/or careful. People found their programs could dump core because cout was used before constructed, or some of their output could be lost because cout had been destroyed (and flushed) too soon. In other words, we had been bitten by the order dependency that I had considered "unlikely and poor design."

3.11.4.2 Workarounds for Order Dependencies

The problem wasn't insurmountable, though. There are two solutions: The obvious one is to add a first-time switch to every member function. This relies on global data being initialized to 0 by default. For example:

```
class Z {
    static int first_time;
    void init();
    // ...
public:
    void f1();
    // ...
    void fn();
};
```

Every member function would look like this:

```
void Z::f1()
{
    if (first_time == 0) {
        init();
        first_time = 1;
    }
    // ...
}
```

This is tedious and the overhead is potentially significant for simple functions such as a single character output operation.

In his redesign of stream I/O (§8.3.1), Jerry Schwarz used a clever variant of this [Schwarz,1989]. An <iostream.h> header contains something like this:

```
class io_counter {
    static int count;
public:
    io_counter()
    {
        if (count++ == 0) { /* initialize cin, cout, etc. */ }
    }

    ~io_counter()
    {
        if (--count == 0) { /* clean up cin, cout, etc. */ }
    }
};
```

```
static io_counter io_init;
```
Now every file that includes the iostream header also creates an `io_counter` object and initializes it with the effect of increasing `io_counter::count`. The first time this happens the library objects will be initialized. Since the library header appears before any use of the library facilities proper initialization is ensured. Since

destruction is done in reverse order of construction, this technique also ensures that cleanup is done after the last use of the library.

This technique solves the order dependency problem in general at the trivial cost of having the library provider add a few lines of highly stylized code. Unfortunately, the performance implications can be serious. Where such tricks are used, most C++ object files will contain dynamic initialization code and (assuming an ordinary linker) that means that these dynamic initialization routines are scattered throughout the address space of a process. On a virtual memory system, it means that most pages of a program will be brought into primary memory during the initial startup phase and during the final cleanup. This is not well-behaved virtual memory use and can lead to seconds of delays in the startup of significant applications.

A trivial solution for an implementer is to modify the linker to coalesce dynamic startup code in a single place. Also, the problem doesn't occur unless a system supports some form of dynamic loading of program into primary memory. However, that is cold comfort for a C++ user who suffers from the problem [Reiser,1992]. Fundamentally, this violates the dictum that a C++ feature not only has to be useful, it also has to be affordable (§4.3). Can the problem be solved by adding a feature? On the surface, it can't because neither a language design nor even an official standards committee can legislate efficiency. The proposals I have seen attack the ordering problem – which has already been solved by Jerry's initialization trick – rather than the efficiency problems they imply. I suspect that the real solution is to find some means to encourage implementers to avoid "virtual memory bashing" by dynamic initialization routines. Techniques for achieving that are known, but some explicit wording in the standard may be needed as encouragement.

3.11.4.3 Dynamic Initialization of Built-in Types

In C, a static object can only be initialized using a slightly extended form of constant expressions. For example:

```
double PI = 22/7;        /* ok */
double sqrt2 = sqrt(2); /* error in C */
```

However, C++ allows completely general expressions for the initialization of class objects. For example:

```
Double s2 = sqrt(2); // ok
```

Thus, the built-in types had been made "second-class citizens" because the support for classes had progressed beyond what was provided for the built-in types. The anomaly was easily removed, but the facility was not made generally available until Release 2.0:

```
double sqrt2 = sqrt(2); // ok in C++ (2.0 and higher)
```

3.11.5 Declaration Statements

I borrowed the Algol68 notion that a declaration can be introduced wherever it is needed (and not just at the top of some block). Thus, I enabled an "initialize-only" or "single-assignment" style of programming that is less error-prone than traditional styles. This style is essential for references and constants that cannot be assigned and inherently more efficient for types where default initialization is expensive. For example:

```
void f(int i, const char* p)
{
    if (i<=0) error("negative index");
    const int len = strlen(p);
    String s(p);
    // ...
}
```

Having constructors guarantee initialization (§2.11) is another part of the effort to minimize problems caused by uninitialized variables.

3.11.5.1 Declarations in for-statements

One of the most common reasons to introduce a new variable in the middle of a block is to get a variable for a loop. For example:

```
int i;
for (i=0; i<MAX; i++) // ...
```

To avoid separating the declaration of the variable from its initialization, I allowed the declaration to be moved after the `for`:

```
for (int i=0; i<MAX; i++) // ...
```

Unfortunately, I didn't take the opportunity to change the semantics to limit the scope of a variable introduced in this way to the scope of the *for-statement*. The reason for this omission was primarily to avoid adding a special case to the rule that says "the scope of a variable extends from its point of declaration to the end of its block."

This rule was the subject of much discussion and was eventually revised to match the rule for declarations in conditions (§3.11.5.2). That is, a name introduced in a *for-statement* initializer goes out of scope at the end of the *for-statement*.

3.11.5.2 Declarations in Conditions

Where people conscientiously try to avoid uninitialized variables, they are left with:
[1] Variables used for input:

```
    int i;
    cin>>i;
```

[2] Variables used in conditions:

```
Tok* ct;
if (ct = gettok()) { /* ... */ }
```

During the design of the run-time type identification mechanism in 1991 (§14.2.2.1), I realized that the latter cause of uninitialized variables could be eliminated by allowing declarations to be used as conditions. For example:

```
if (Tok* ct = gettok()) {
    // ct is in scope here
}

// ct is not in scope here
```

This feature is not merely a cute trick to save typing. It is a direct consequence of the ideal of locality. By joining the declaration of a variable, its initialization, and the test on the result of that initialization, we achieve a compactness of expression that helps eliminate errors arising from variables being used before they are initialized. By limiting their scope to the statement controlled by the condition, we also eliminate the problem of variables being ''reused'' for other purposes or accidentally used after they were supposed to have outlived their usefulness. This eliminated a further minor source of errors.

The inspiration for allowing declarations in expressions came from expression languages – in particular from Algol68. I ''remembered'' that Algol68 declarations yielded values and based my design on that. Later, I found my memory had failed me: declarations are one of the very few constructs in Algol68 that do not yield values! I asked Charles Lindsey about this and received the answer, ''Even Algol68 has a few blemishes where it isn't completely orthogonal.'' I guess this just proves that a language doesn't have to live up to its own ideals to provide inspiration.

If I were to design a language from scratch, I would follow the Algol68 path and make every statement and declaration an expression that yields a value. I would probably also ban uninitialized variables and abandon the idea of declaring more than one name in a declaration. However, these ideas are clearly far beyond what would be acceptable for C++.

3.12   Relationship to Classic C

With the introduction of the name C++ and the writing of a C++ reference manual [Stroustrup,1984], compatibility with C became an issue of major importance and a point of controversy.

Also, in late 1983 the branch of Bell Labs that developed and supported UNIX and produced AT&T's 3B series of computers became interested in C++ to the point where they were willing to put resources into the development of C++ tools. Such development was necessary for the evolution of C++ from a one-man show to a language that a corporation could base critical projects on. Unfortunately, it also implied that development management needed to consider C++.

The first demand to emerge from development management was that of 100% compatibility with C. The ideal of C compatibility is quite obvious and reasonable, but the reality of programming isn't that simple. For starters, which C should C++ be compatible with? C dialects abounded, and though ANSI C was emerging, it was still years from having a stable definition, and its definition allowed many dialects. I remember at the time calculating – partly in jest – that there were about 3^{42} strictly-conforming ANSI C dialects. That number was based on taking the number of undefined and implementation-defined aspects and using it as the exponent for the average number of alternatives.

Naturally, the average user who wanted C compatibility wanted C++ to be compatible with the local C dialect. This was an important practical problem and a great concern to me and my friends. It seemed far less of a concern to business-oriented managers and salesmen, who either didn't quite understand the technical details or would like to use C++ to tie users into their software and/or hardware. The Bell Labs C++ developers, on the other hand, independently of who they worked for, were "emotionally committed to portability as a concept [Johnson,1992]" and resisted management pressure to enshrine a particular C dialect in the C++ definition.

Another side of the compatibility issue was more critical: "In which ways must C++ differ from C to meet its fundamental goals?" Also, "In which ways must C++ be compatible with C to meet its fundamental goals?" Both sides of the issue are important, and revisions were made in both directions during the transition from C with Classes to Release 1.0 of C++. Slowly and painfully, an agreement emerged that there would be no gratuitous incompatibilities between C++ and ANSI C (when it became a standard) [Stroustrup,1986] but also that there was such a thing as an incompatibility that was not gratuitous. Naturally, the concept of "gratuitous incompatibilities" was a topic of much debate and it took up a disproportionate part of my time and effort. This principle has lately been known as "C++: As close to C as possible – but no closer," after the title of a paper by Andrew Koenig and me [Koenig,1989]. One measure of the success of this policy is that every example in K&R2 [Kernighan,1988] is written in the C subset of C++. Cfront was the compiler used for the primary testing of the K&R2 code examples.

Some conclusions about modularity and how a program is composed out of separately compiled parts were explicitly reflected in the original C++ reference manual [Stroustrup,1984]:

[a] Names are private unless they are explicitly declared public.
[b] Names are local to their file unless explicitly exported from it.
[c] Static type rules are checked unless the check is explicitly suppressed.
[d] A class is a scope (implying that classes nest properly).

Point [a] doesn't affect C compatibility, but [b], [c], [d] imply incompatibilities:

[1] The name of a non-local C function or object is by default accessible from other compilation units.
[2] C functions need not be declared before use and calls are by default not type checked.
[3] C structure names don't nest (even when they are lexically nested).

In addition,

[4] C++ has a single namespace, whereas C had a separate namespace for ''structure tags'' (§2.8.2).

The ''compatibility wars'' now seem petty and boring, but some of the underlying issues are still unresolved, and we are still struggling with them in the ANSI/ISO standards committee. I strongly suspect that the reason the compatibility wars were drawn out and curiously inconclusive was that we never quite faced the deeper issues related to the differing goals of C and C++ and saw compatibility as a set of separate issues to be resolved individually.

Typically, the least fundamental issue, [4] ''namespaces,'' took up the most effort, but was eventually resolved by a compromise in [ARM].

I had to compromise the notion of a class as a scope, [3], and accept the C ''solution'' to be allowed to ship Release 1.0. One practical problem was that I had never realized that a C struct didn't constitute a scope so that examples like this:

```
struct outer {
    struct inner {
        int i;
    };
    int j;
};


struct inner a = { 1 };
```

are legal C. Not only that, but such code was found in the standard UNIX header files. When the issue came up towards the end of the compatibility wars, I didn't have time to fathom the implications of the C ''solution,'' and it was much easier to agree than to fight the issue. Later, after many technical problems and much discontent from users, nested class scopes were reintroduced into C++ in 1989 [ARM] (§13.5).

After much hassle, C++'s stronger type checking of function calls was accepted (unmodified). An implicit violation of the static type system is the original example of a C/C++ incompatibility that is not gratuitous. The ANSI C committee adopted a slightly weaker version of C++'s rules and notation on this point and declared uses that don't conform to the C++ rules obsolete.

I had to accept the C rule that global names are by default accessible from other compilation units. There simply wasn't any support for the more restrictive C++ rule. This meant that C++, like C, lacked an effective mechanism for expressing modularity above the level of the class and the file. This led to a series of complaints until the ANSI/ISO committee accepted namespaces (§17) as the mechanisms to avoid name space pollution. However, Doug McIlroy and others argued that C programmers would not accept a language in which every object and function meant to be accessible from another compilation unit had to be explicitly declared as such. They were probably right at the time and saved me from making a serious mistake. I am now convinced that the original C++ solution wasn't elegant enough anyway.

One problem with compatibility issues is that there always seem to be two camps that are so sure of their views they hardly feel the need to argue their cases. The first camp demands 100% compatibility – often without having understood the implications. For example, many who demand 100% C compatibility are surprised to learn that this would imply incompatibilities with existing C++ that would cause tens of millions of lines of C++ code to stop compiling. In many cases, the demand for 100% compatibility is based on the assumption that C++ has few users. It is also not unusual for people to hide ignorance of C++ or dislike of newer features behind a demand for 100% compatibility.

The other camp can be equally annoying by declaring C compatibility a non-issue and arguing for new features that would seriously inconvenience people who want to mix C and C++ code. Naturally, the more extreme claims of each camp make the other camp even further entrenched out of fear of losing aspects of a language they care about. Where – as almost always – cooler heads prevail and the needs of the people involved and the actual facts of C and C++ usage are taken into account, the debates usually converge on the more constructive examination of the minutiae of the compromise. At the organizational meeting of the X3J16 ANSI committee, Larry Rosler, the original ANSI C committee editor, explained to a skeptical Tom Plum, "C++ is C as we tried to make it, but couldn't." This is probably an overstatement, but not too far from the truth for the common subset of C and C++.

3.13 Tools for Language Design

Theory and tools more advanced than a blackboard have not been given much space in the description of the design and evolution of C++. I tried to use YACC (an LALR(1) parser generator [Aho,1986]) for the grammar work, and was defeated by C's syntax (§2.8.1). I looked at denotational semantics, but was again defeated by quirks in C. Ravi Sethi had looked into that problem and found that he couldn't express the C semantics that way [Sethi,1980].

The main problem was the irregularity of C and the number of implementation-dependent and undefined aspects of a C implementation. Much later, the ANSI/ISO C++ committee had a stream of formal definition experts explain their techniques and tools and give their opinions of the extent to which a genuine formal approach to the definition of C++ would help us in the standards effort. I also looked at the formal specifications of ML and Modula-2 to see if a formal approach was likely to lead to a shorter and more elegant description than traditional English text would. I don't think that such a description of C++ would be less likely to be misinterpreted by implementers and expert users. My conclusion is that a formal definition of a language that is not designed together with a formal definition method is beyond the ability of all but a handful of experts in formal definition. This confirms my conclusion at the time.

However, abandoning hope of a formal specification left us at the mercy of imprecise and insufficient terminology. Given that, what could I do to compensate? I tried to reason about new features both on my own and with others to check my logic.

However, I soon developed a healthy disrespect for arguments (definitely including my own) because I found that it is possible to construct a plausible logical argument for just about any feature. On the other hand, you simply don't get a useful language by accepting every feature that makes life better for someone. There are far too many reasonable features and no language could provide them all and stay coherent. Consequently, wherever possible, I tried to experiment.

Unfortunately, you usually cannot conduct proper experiments either. It is not possible to provide full-scale systems with implementation, tools, and education and have some people use the one and some people use the other and measure the differences. People are too different, projects are too different, and suggested features mutate during the effort to define, implement, and explain them. So I used the effort to define, implement, and explain features as a design aid. Once a feature was implemented, I and a few others used it and I tried as best I could to be highly suspicious of any positive claims made. As far as possible, I relied on the opinions of experienced programmers considering real applications only. Thus, I tried to compensate for the fundamental limitations of my ''experiments.'' These experiments were usually only comparisons of implementations, examinations of quality of source code for small examples, together with run-time and space measurements on those examples. At least I had feedback in the design process so I could rely on experience rather than on pure thought alone. I firmly believe that language design isn't an exercise in pure thought, but a very practical exercise in balancing needs, ideals, techniques, and constraints. A good language is not merely designed, it is grown. The exercise has more to do with engineering, sociology, and philosophy than with mathematics.

In retrospect, I wish I had known a way of formalizing the rules for type conversion and argument matching. This topic has proven very hard to get right and to document unambiguously. Unfortunately, I suspect that no rational and general formalism would be able to deal with the very irregular C rules governing the built-in types and operators in a convenient manner.

There is a great temptation for a language designer to provide features and services where the alternative is for users to use a workaround. The screams when an addition is rejected are usually far louder than the complaints that ''yet another useless feature has been added.'' This is also a serious problem for standards committees (§6.4). The worst variant of this argument is the cult of orthogonality. Many people feel that if the language would be more orthogonal if it provided a feature, then that is a conclusive argument for accepting that feature. I agree that orthogonality is a good thing in principle, but note that it also carries costs. Usually, despite all good intentions about orthogonality, the definition of a combination of features does require extra work on the manual and the tutorial material. Most often, implementation of combinations prescribed by the ideal of orthogonality is harder than people realize. In the case of C++, I always considered the run-time and space cost of orthogonality for people who did not use a combination. If that cost couldn't at least in principle be made zero, I was most reluctant to admit the feature – however orthogonal. Thus orthogonality is a secondary principle – after the primary but subjective concerns of utility and efficiency.

My impression was and is that many programming languages and tools represent solutions looking for problems, and I was determined that my work should not fall into that category. Thus, I follow the literature on programming languages and the debates about programming languages primarily looking for ideas for solutions to problems my colleagues and I have encountered in real applications. Other programming languages constitute a mountain of ideas and inspiration – but it has to be mined carefully to avoid featurism and inconsistencies. The main sources for ideas for C++ were Simula, Algol68, and later Clu, Ada, and ML. The key to good design is insight into problems, not the provision of the most advanced features.

3.14   The C++ Programming Language (1st edition)

In the autumn of 1984, my next-door neighbor at work, Al Aho, suggested that I write a book on C++ structured along the lines of Brian Kernighan and Dennis Ritchie's *The C Programming Language* [Kernighan,1978] based on my published papers, internal memoranda, and the C++ reference manual. Completing the book took nine months. I completed the book mid-August 1985 and the first copies appeared mid-October. Thanks to a curiosity in the US publishing industry the book has a 1986 copyright.

The preface mentions the people who had by then contributed the most to C++: Tom Cargill, Jim Coplien, Stu Feldman, Sandy Fraser, Steve Johnson, Brian Kernighan, Bart Locanthi, Doug McIlroy, Dennis Ritchie, Larry Rosler, Jerry Schwarz, and Jonathan Shopiro. My criterion for adding a person to that list was that I was able to identify a specific C++ feature that the person has caused to be added.

The book's opening line, ''C++ is a general-purpose programming language designed to make programming more enjoyable for the serious programmer,'' was deleted twice by reviewers who refused to believe that the purpose of programming-language design could be anything but some serious mutterings about productivity, management, and software engineering. However,

> ''C++ was designed primarily so that the author and his friends would not have to program in assembler, C, or various modern high-level languages. Its main purpose is to make writing good programs easier and more pleasant for the individual programmer.''

This was the case whether those reviewers were willing to believe it or not. The focus of my work is the person, the individual (whether part of a group or not), the programmer. This line of reasoning has been strengthened over the years and is even more prominent in second edition [2nd] where design and software development issues are discussed in greater depth.

The C++ Programming Language was the definition of C++ and the introduction to C++ for an unknown number of programmers, and its presentation techniques and organization (borrowed with acknowledgments if not always sufficient skill from *The C Programming Language*) have become the basis for an almost embarrassing number of articles and books. It was written with a fierce determination not to preach any particular programming technique. In the same way I feared to build limitations into the language out of ignorance and misguided paternalism, I didn't want the book to turn into a manifesto for my personal preferences.

3.15 The Whatis? Paper

Having shipped Release 1.0 and sent the camera-ready copy of the book to the printers, I finally found time to reconsider larger issues and to document overall design issues. Just then, Karel Babcisky (the chairman of the Association of Simula Users) phoned from Oslo with an invitation to give a talk on C++ at the 1986 ASU conference in Stockholm. Naturally, I wanted to go, but I was worried that presenting C++ at a Simula conference would be seen as a vulgar example of self-advertisement and an attempt to steal users away from Simula. After all, I said, "C++ is not Simula so why would Simula-users want to hear about it." Karel replied, "Ah, we are not hung up on syntax." This provided me with an opportunity to write not only about what C++ was but also what it was supposed to be and where it didn't measure up to those ideals. The result was the paper *What is "Object-Oriented Programming?"* [Stroustrup,1986b]. An extended version was presented to the first ECOOP conference in June 1987 in Paris.

The significance of this paper is that it is the first exposition of the set of techniques that C++ was aiming to provide support for. All previous presentations, to avoid dishonesty and hype, had been restricted to describe what features were already implemented and in use. The "whatis paper" defined the set of problems I thought a language supporting data abstraction and object-oriented programming ought to solve and gave examples of language features needed.

The result was a reaffirmation of the importance of the "multi-paradigm" nature of C++:

"Object-oriented programming is programming using inheritance. Data abstraction is programming using user-defined types. With few exceptions, object-oriented programming can and ought to be a superset of data abstraction. These techniques need proper support to be effective. Data abstraction primarily needs support in the form of language features, and object-oriented programming needs further support from a programming environment. To be general purpose, a language supporting data abstraction or object-oriented programming must enable effective use of traditional hardware."

The importance of static type checking was also strongly emphasized. In other words, C++ follows the Simula rather than the Smalltalk model of inheritance and type checking:

"A Simula or C++ class specifies a fixed interface to a set of objects (of any derived class), whereas a Smalltalk class specifies an initial set of operations for objects (of any subclass). In other words, a Smalltalk class is a minimal specification and the user is free to try operations not specified, whereas a C++ class is an exact specification and the user is guaranteed that only operations specified in the

class declaration will be accepted by the compiler.''
This has deep implications for the way one designs systems and for what language
facilities are needed. A dynamically typed language such as Smalltalk simplifies the
design and implementation of libraries by postponing type checking to run time. For
example (using C++ syntax):

```
void f()    // dynamic checking only, not C++
{
    stack cs;
    cs.push(new Saab900);
    cs.pop()->takeoff();    // Oops! Run-time error:
                            // a car does not have a
                            // takeoff method.
}
```

This delayed type-error detection was considered unacceptable for C++, yet there had
to be a way of matching the notational convenience and the standard libraries of a
dynamically typed language. The notion of parameterized types was presented as the
(future) solution for that problem in C++:

```
void g()
{
    stack(plane*) cs;

    cs.push(new Saab37b);    // ok a Saab37b is a plane
    cs.push(new Saab900);    // error, type mismatch:
                             // car passed, plane* expected.

    cs.pop()->takeoff();    // no run-time check needed
    cs.pop()->takeoff();    // no run-time check needed
}
```

The key reason for considering compile-time detection of such problems essential was
the observation that C++ is often used for programs executing where no programmer
is present. Fundamentally, the notion of static type checking was seen as the best way
of providing as strong guarantees as possible for a program rather than merely a way
of gaining run-time efficiency.

This is partly a special case of the general notion that what can be guaranteed by
machine and from general rules shouldn't be done by people and by debugging. Naturally, it also helps debugging. However, the most fundamental reason for relying on
statically checked interfaces was that I was – as I still am – firmly convinced that a
program composed out of statically type-checked parts is more likely to faithfully
express a well-thought-out design than a program relying on weakly-typed interfaces
or dynamically-checked interfaces. Please remember though, that not every interface
can be exclusively statically checked and that static checking doesn't imply the
absence of errors.

The ''whatis'' paper lists three aspects in which C++ was deficient:

[1] ''Ada, Clu, and ML support parameterized types. C++ does not; the syntax

used here is simply devised as an illustration. Where needed, parameterized classes are "faked" using macros. Parameterized classes would clearly be extremely useful in C++. They could easily be handled by the compiler, but the current C++ programming environment is not sophisticated enough to support them without significant overhead and/or inconvenience. There need not be any run-time overheads compared with a type specified directly.''

[2] "As programs grow, and especially when libraries are used extensively, standards for handling errors (or more generally: "exceptional circumstances") become important. Ada, Algol68, and Clu each support a standard way of handling exceptions. Unfortunately, C++ does not. Where needed, exceptions are "faked" using pointers to functions, "exception objects," "error states," and the C library `signal` and `longjmp` facilities. This is not satisfactory in general and fails even to provide a standard framework for error handling.''

[3] "Given this explanation, it seems obvious that it might be useful to have a class B inherit from two base classes A1 and A2. This is called multiple inheritance.''

All three facilities were linked to the need to provide better (that is, more general and more flexible) libraries. All are now available in C++ (templates, §15; exceptions, §16; multiple inheritance, §12). Note that adding multiple inheritance and templates was considered plausible directions for further evolution as early as [Stroustrup,1982b]. That paper also mentions exception handling as a possibility, but I was worried rather than positive about the possible need to move in that direction.

As usual, I pointed out that demands on run-time and space efficiency, and of the ability to coexist with other languages on traditional systems provided "limits to perfection" that could not be violated by a language claiming to be "general purpose."

4

C++ Language Design Rules

If the map and the terrain disagree,
trust the terrain.
– Swiss army aphorism

Rules for the design of C++ — overall design aims — sociological rules — C++ as a language supporting design — language-technical rules — C++ as a language for low-level programming.

4.1 Rules and Principles

To be genuinely useful and pleasant to work with, a programming language must be designed according to an overall view that guides the design of its individual language features. For C++, this overall view takes the form of a set of rules and constraints. I call them *rules* because I find the term *principles* pretentious in a field as poor in genuine scientific principles as programming language design. Also, to many people the term principle implies the unrealistic implication that no exceptions are acceptable. My rules for the design of C++ most certainly have exceptions. In fact, if a rule and practical experience are in conflict, the rule gives way. This may sound crude, but it is a variant of the principle that theory must account for experimental data or be replaced by a better theory.

These rules cannot be brainlessly applied; nor can they be replaced by a few glib slogans. I saw my job as language designer as deciding which problems needed to be addressed, deciding which problems could be addressed within the framework of C++, and then maintaining balance between the various rules of design for the actual language feature.

The rules guided the working out of features. However, the framework for improvements was provided by the fundamental aims of C++:

Aims:
C++ makes programming more enjoyable for serious programmers.
C++ is a general-purpose programming language that
— is a better C
— supports data abstraction
— supports object-oriented programming

I have organized the rules into four broad sections. The first contains overall ideals for the whole language. These are so general that individual language features don't enter directly into the picture. The second set of rules primarily addresses C++'s role in supporting design. The third addresses technicalities related to the form of the language, and the fourth focuses on C++'s role as a language for low-level systems programming.

The formulation of the rules here has the benefit of hindsight, but the rules and sentiments expressed dominated my thinking from before the completion of the first C++ release in 1985, and – as described in the previous chapters – many of these rules were part of the original conception of C with Classes.

4.2 General Rules

The most general and most important C++ rules have little to do with language-technical issues. They are almost sociological in their focus on the community C++ serves. The nature of the C++ language is largely determined by my choice to serve the current generation of systems programmers solving current problems on current computer systems. Importantly, because the meaning and nature of *current* changes with time, C++ had to evolve to meet the needs of its users; it could not be defined once and for all.

General rules:
C++'s evolution must be driven by real problems.
Don't get involved in a sterile quest for perfection.
C++ must be useful *now*.
Every feature must have a reasonably obvious implementation.
Always provide a transition path.
C++ is a language, not a complete system.
Provide comprehensive support for each supported style.
Don't try to force people.

C++'s evolution must be driven by real problems: In computer science, as in many other fields, we see too many people searching for a problem to apply their pet solution to. I don't know any foolproof way of keeping fads from distorting my view of what is important, but I am acutely aware that many of the language features presented to me as essential are infeasible within the framework of C++ and often irrelevant to real-world programmers.

The right motivation for a change to C++ is for several independent programmers to demonstrate how the language is insufficiently expressive for their projects. I prefer input from non-research projects. Whenever possible, I involve real users in the effort to find and complete a solution. I read the programming language literature avidly looking for solutions to such problems and also for general techniques that might help. However, I find the literature wholly unreliable on the subject of what is a genuine problem. Theory itself is never sufficient justification for adding or removing a feature.

Don't get involved in a sterile quest for perfection: No programming language is perfect, and none will ever be as long as problems and systems keep changing. Polishing a language for years trying to reach some notion of perfection simply deprives programmers of benefits from the progress made thus far. It also deprives the language designer of genuine feedback. Without appropriate feedback, a language can be evolved into irrelevance. Problems, computer systems, and – most importantly – people differ radically between environments so that a ''perfect fit'' to some small environment is almost certainly too specialized to thrive in the larger real world. On the other hand, programmers spend most of their time modifying or interfacing to old code. They need stability to get real work done. Once a language is in real use, radical changes are infeasible, and even small changes are difficult without harming users. Consequently, the necessary quest for significant improvement must rely on genuine feedback and must be accompanied by a serious concern for compatibility, transition, and education. As the language matures, one must increasingly prefer alternatives based on tools, techniques, and libraries over language changes.

Not every problem needs to be solved by C++, and not every problem in C++ is significant enough to warrant a solution. For example, C++ need not be extended to cope directly with pattern matching or theorem proving, and the well-known C operator precedence pitfalls (§2.6.2) are better left alone or addressed through warning messages.

C++ must be useful now: Most programming is relatively mundane, done on relatively low-powered computers, running relatively dated operating systems and tools. Most programmers have less formal training than they would have liked and most have insufficient time to upgrade their knowledge. To serve these programmers, C++ must be useful to someone with average skills, using an average computer.

Though tempted at times, I had no real desire to abandon these people to gain the freedom to adjust my designs to top-of-the-line systems and the tastes of computer science researchers.

The meaning of this rule – like most of the others – changes with time and partly as a result of C++'s success. More powerful computers are now available, and more programmers are now acquainted with the basic concepts and techniques that C++ relies on. Further, as people's ambitions and expectations grow, the problems faced by programmers change. This implies that features requiring more computer resources and more maturity from programmers can and must be considered. Exception handling (§16) and run-time type identification (§14.2) are examples of this.

Every feature must have a reasonably obvious implementation: No feature should require complicated algorithms for correct or efficient implementation. Ideally, obvious analysis and code-generation strategies should exist, and these should be good enough for real use. If added thought can produce even better results, so much the better. Most features were implemented, used experimentally, and revised before being accepted. Where this pattern was not followed, as in the case of the template instantiation mechanism (§15.10), problems surfaced.

However, there are *many* more users than there are compiler writers, so where there is a real tradeoff between compiler complexity and complexity of use, the resolution must favor the users. I have earned the right to this opinion through years of compiler maintenance.

Always provide a transition path: C++ must grow gradually to serve its users and to benefit from feedback. This implies that great care must be taken to ensure that older code continues to work. When an incompatibility is unavoidable, great care must be taken to help users update their programs. Similarly, there has to be a path from the use of error-prone C-like techniques to a more effective use of C++.

The general strategy for eliminating an unsafe, error-prone, or simply awkward language feature is first to provide a better alternative, then recommend that people avoid the old feature or technique, and only years later – if at all – remove the offending feature. This strategy can be effectively supported by warning messages from the compilers. Often, it is not feasible to eliminate a feature or correct a mistake (the reason is typically the need for C compatibility); the alternative is warnings (§2.6.2). Thus, a C++ implementation can be safer than it appears from the language definition.

C++ is a language, not a complete system: A programming environment has many components. One approach has been to merge all parts into a single, "integrated" system. Another approach has been to maintain the classical distinctions between parts of a system such as compilers, linkers, language run-time support libraries, I/O libraries, editors, file systems, databases, etc. C++ follows the latter approach. Through libraries, calling conventions, etc., C++ adapts to the system conventions guiding interoperability of language and tools on each system. This is key for easy portability of implementations and – more importantly – the key to cooperation between code written in different languages. This also allows sharing of tools, eases the cooperation between programmers with different preferences in programming languages, and eases the use of many languages by an individual programmer.

C++ is designed to be one language among many. C++ enables tool development, but does not mandate particular forms. The programmer retains freedom of choice. A key idea is that C++ and its associated tools should "feel" right for a given system rather than impose some particular view of what a system and an environment is. This is especially important for large systems and systems with unusual constraints. Such systems are not usually well supported because "standard" systems tend to be specialized to serve individuals or small groups doing fairly "average" work.

Provide comprehensive support for each supported style: C++ must grow to meet the needs of serious developers. Simplicity is essential, but it is considered relative to the complexity of the projects in which C++ is used. Maintainability and run-time performance of systems written in C++ is considered more important than keeping the language definition short. This implies a relatively large language.

It also implies – as experience showed – that many hybrid styles of programming must be supported. People don't just write classes that fit a narrowly defined abstract data type or object-oriented style; they also – often for perfectly good reasons – write classes that take on aspects of both. They also write programs in which different parts use different styles to match needs and taste.

Consequently, features must be designed to be used in combination. This leads to a degree of orthogonality in the design of C++. The opportunity for ''unusual'' uses is an important source of flexibility and has repeatedly allowed C++ to be used in areas where a more restricted and narrowly focused language would have failed. For example, the C++ rules for access protection, name lookup, `virtual/non-virtual` binding, and type are orthogonal. This opens the possibility for a variety of techniques relying on information hiding and derived classes. Some who would prefer to see only a few narrowly defined styles of programming supported deem this ''hackery.'' On the other hand, orthogonality is not a first-order principle; it is applied wherever it doesn't conflict with one of the rules and whenever it provides some benefit without complicating implementations.

Having a relatively large language implies that some of the effort to manage complexity moves from the understanding of libraries and individual programs to learning the language and its basic design techniques. For most people, this change in emphasis, the adoption of new programming techniques, and the application of ''advanced'' features must be gradual. Few can completely absorb the new techniques ''in one sitting'' or apply all of their new skills to their work at once (§7.2). C++ is designed to make such a gradual approach feasible and natural. The ideal is: What you don't know won't hurt you. The static type system and compiler warning messages help.

Don't try to force people: Programmers are smart people. They are engaged in challenging tasks and need all the help they can get from a programming language as well as from other supporting tools and techniques. Trying to seriously constrain programmers to do ''only what is right'' is inherently wrongheaded and will fail. Programmers will find a way around rules and restrictions they find unacceptable. The language should support a range of reasonable design and programming styles rather than try to force people into adopting a single notion.

This does not imply that all ways of programming are equally good or that C++ should try to support every kind of programming style. C++ was designed to directly support styles of design relying on extensive static type checking, data abstraction, and inheritance. However, moralizing over how to use the features is kept to a minimum, language mechanisms are as far as possible kept policy free, and no feature is added to or subtracted from C++ exclusively to prevent a coherent style of programming.

I am well aware that not everyone appreciates choice and variety. However, people who prefer a more restrictive environment can impose one through style rules in C++ or choose a language designed to provide the programmer with a smaller set of alternatives.

Many programmers particularly dislike being told that something might be an error when it happens not to be. Consequently, "potential errors" are not errors in C++. For example, it is not an error to write declarations that will allow an ambiguous use. The error is an ambiguous use, not the mere possibility of such an error. In my experience, most "potential errors" never manifest themselves so to defer the error message is to avoid giving it. Much convenience and flexibility result from such deferrals.

4.3 Design Support Rules

The rules listed here relate primarily to C++'s role in supporting design based on notions of data abstraction and object-oriented programming. That is, they are more concerned with the language's role as a support for thinking and expression of high-level ideas than its role as a "high-level assembler" along the lines of C or Pascal.

Design support rules:
Support sound design notions.
Provide facilities for program organization.
Say what you mean.
All features must be affordable.
It is more important to allow a useful feature than to prevent every misuse.
Support composition of software from separately developed parts.

Support sound design notions: Each individual language feature must fit into an overall pattern. That overall pattern must help answer questions of what abilities are desirable. The language itself cannot provide that; the guiding pattern must come from a different conceptual level. For C++, that level is provided by ideas of how programs can be designed.

My aim is to raise the level of abstraction in systems programming in a way similar to what C did by replacing assembler as the mainstay of systems work. Ideas for new features are considered in light of how they might enhance C++ as a language for expressing designs. In particular, individual features are considered in light of how they can make the notion that a concept is represented by a class effective. This is the key to C++'s support for data abstraction and object-oriented programming.

A programming language is not and should not be a complete design language. A design language should be richer and less concerned with details than a language suitable for systems programming must be. However, the programming language should support some notions of design as directly as possible to ease communication between designers and programmers (who are often the same people "wearing different hats") and to simplify tool building.

Viewing the programming language in terms of design techniques allows suggested language features to be accepted or excluded based on their relationship to the design styles supported. No language can support every style, and a language supporting only one narrowly defined design philosophy will fail for lack of adaptability. Enhancing C++ to support the continuum of design techniques that map into the ''better C'' / data abstraction / object-oriented programming spectrum helped avoid the temptation to try to make C++ everything to all people while providing a constant stimulus to improvements.

Provide facilities for program organization: Compared to C, C++ helps organize programs to be easier to write, read, and maintain. I considered computation a problem solved by C. Like just about everybody else, I have ideas of how the expression and statement part of C could be improved, but I decided to focus my efforts elsewhere. Whenever a new kind of expression or statement has been suggested, it has been evaluated based on whether it affected the structure of the program or merely made the expression of some local computation easier. With few exceptions, such as allowing declarations to appear where a variable is first needed (§3.11.5), the C expressions and statements have been left unchanged.

Say what you mean: The fundamental problem with lower-level languages is the gap between what people can express when they talk to each other and what they can express directly in the programming language. The basic structure of a program disappears in a mess of bits, bytes, pointers, loops, etc.

The primary means of narrowing this semantic gap is to make a language more declarative. Almost every facility provided by C++ hinges on making something declarative and then exploiting the added structure in consistency checking, detection of silly errors, and improved code generation.

Where a declarative structure cannot be employed, a more explicit notation can often help. The allocation/deallocation operators (§10.2) and the new cast syntax (§14.3) are examples. An early expression of the ideal of direct and explicit expression of intent was ''to allow expression of all important things in the language itself rather than in the comments or through macro hackery.'' This implies that the language in general, and its type system in particular, must be more expressive and flexible than earlier general-purpose languages.

All features must be affordable: It is not enough to provide a user with a language feature or recommend a technique for some problem. The solution offered must also be affordable. Otherwise, the advice is almost an insult: ''Rent an executive jet,'' may be a valid response to, ''What is the best way of getting to Memphis?'' but to all but millionaires, it is not a very helpful answer.

A feature was added to C++ only when there was no way of achieving similar functionality at significantly lesser cost. My experience is that if programmers are given the choice of doing something efficiently or elegantly, most will choose efficiency unless there is an obvious major reason not to. For example, inline functions were provided to allow cost-free crossing of protection boundaries and to be a better-behaved alternative to many uses of macros. The ideal is of course for facilities to be elegant and efficient. Where that is not feasible, the facility either isn't provided or – if it is deemed essential – it is provided efficiently.

It is more important to allow a useful feature than to prevent every misuse: You can write bad programs in *any* language. It is important to minimize the chance of accidental misuse of features, and much effort has been spent trying to ensure that the default behavior of C++ constructs is either sensible or leads to compile-time errors. For example, by default all function argument types are checked – even across separate compilation boundaries – and by default, all class members are private. However, a systems programming language cannot prevent a determined programmer from breaking the system so design effort is better expended providing facilities for writing good programs than preventing the inevitable bad ones. In the longer run, programmers seem to learn. This is a variant of the old C "trust the programmer" slogan. The various type checking and access control rules exist to allow a class provider to state clearly what is expected from users, to protect against accidents. Those rules are not intended as protection against deliberate violation (§2.10).

Support composition of software from separately developed parts: Programmers need more support for complex applications than simple ones, more support for large programs than small ones, and more support for applications under efficiency constraints than applications with ample resources. Much of the effort in the design of C++ was spent addressing the first two of those observations under the constraints of the third. As applications get larger and more complex, they must be composed out of semi-independent parts to be manageable.

Anything that allows a component of a larger system to be developed independently and then used without modification in a larger system serves this purpose. Much of the evolution of C++ has been driven by that idea. Classes themselves are the original such C++ feature, and abstract classes (§13.2.2) explicitly support separation between interfaces and implementations. In fact, classes can be used to express a continuum of coupling strategies [Stroustrup,1990b]. Exceptions allow error handling to be decoupled from a library (§16.1), templates allow composition based on types (§15.3, §15.6, §15.8), namespaces solve the namespace pollution problem (§17.2), and run-time type identification addresses the problem of what to do when the exact type of an object has been "lost" by passing it through a library (§14.2.1).

The notion that programmers need more support when developing larger systems implies that efficiency mustn't be compromised by reliance on optimization techniques that work best for small programs. Consequently, object layout can be determined given a single compilation unit in isolation, and virtual function calls can be compiled into efficient code without relying on cross-compilation-unit optimizations. This is true even when *efficient* means efficiently compared to C. Further optimizations are possible when information about a complete program is available. For example, looking at a complete program and a call of a virtual function, one can – in the absence of dynamic linking – sometimes determine the actual function called. In that case, one can replace the virtual function call with an ordinary function call or even inline. C++ implementations that can do that exist. However, such optimizations are not necessary for generating efficient code; they are simply an added benefit when run-time efficiency is preferred to compile-time efficiency and dynamic linking of new derived classes. When such global optimization is not deemed reasonable, a virtual function call can still be optimized away when the virtual function is applied to an object of known type; even Cfront Release 1.0 did that.

Support for larger systems is often discussed under the heading "support for libraries" (§8).

4.4 Language-Technical Rules

The following rules address questions of how things are expressed in C++ rather than questions of what can be expressed.

Language-technical rules:
No implicit violations of the static type system.
Provide as good support for user-defined types as for built-in types.
Locality is good.
Avoid order dependencies.
If in doubt, pick the variant of a feature that is easiest to teach.
Syntax matters (often in perverse ways).
Preprocessor usage should be eliminated.

No implicit violations of the static type system: Every object is created with a specific type such as `double`, `char*`, or `dial_buffer`. If an object is used in a way that is inconsistent with its given type the type system has been violated. A language where such violation can never happen is strongly typed. A language where every such violation is detected at compile time is strongly statically typed.

C++ inherits features from C, such as unions, casts, and arrays, that make it impossible to detect every violation at compile time. Currently, C++ does not admit implicit violation of the type system. That is, you need to explicitly use a union, cast, array, an explicitly unchecked function argument, or explicitly unsafe C linkage to break the system. Any use of the unsafe features can be made to cause a (compile time) warning. More importantly, C++ now possesses language features that make it more convenient and equally efficient to avoid the unsafe features than to use them. Examples are derived classes (§2.9), a standard array template (§8.5), type-safe linkage (§11.3), and dynamically checked casts (§14.2). Because of C compatibility requirements and common practice, the path to this state of affairs has been long and hard; most programmers have yet to adopt the safer practices.

Wherever possible, checking is done at compile time. Wherever possible, things that cannot be checked given only the information in a single compilation unit are checked at link time. Finally, run-time type information (§14.2) and exceptions (§16) are provided to help the programmer cope with error conditions that a compiler and a linker cannot catch. Where applicable, compile-time checking is cheaper and more dependable, though.

Provide as good support for user-defined types as for built-in types: Since user-defined types are intended to be central to C++ programs, they need as much support as possible from the language. Therefore, restrictions such as "class objects can be allocated only on the free store" were not acceptable. The need to provide genuine local variables for arithmetic types such as `complex` led to support for value-oriented types (concrete types) comparable to or even superior to the built-in types.

Locality is good: When writing a piece of code, one would prefer it to be self-contained except where it needs a service from elsewhere. One would also prefer such services to be available without too much fuss and bother. Conversely, one would like to supply functions, classes, etc., to others without fear of interference between implementation details and other people's code.

C is about as far from these ideals as one can get. Every global function and variable name is visible to the linker and will clash with other uses of the same name unless explicitly declared `static`. Every name can be used as a function name without previous declaration. As a relic of the days when the names of structure members were global, the names of structures declared within structures are global. In addition, the preprocessor's macro processing doesn't respect scope, so any sequence of characters in the program text just might be changed into something different if a change is made to a header file or a compiler option (§18.1). All this adds up to very powerful stuff if you want to affect the meaning of some apparently local code or want to affect the rest of the world by a small "local" change. On average, I consider this most disruptive to my comprehension of complex software and to maintenance. Consequently, I set out to provide better insulation against disruptions from "elsewhere" and better control over what is "exported" from my code.

Classes provide the first and most important mechanisms for localizing code and channeling access through a well-defined interface. Nested classes (§3.12, §13.5) and namespaces (§17) extend notions of local scope and explicit granting of access further. In each case, the amount of global information in a system decreases significantly.

Access control localizes access without imposing run-time or space overheads needed for complete decoupling (§2.10). Abstract classes allow a greater degree of decoupling at minimal cost (§13.2).

Within classes and namespaces, it is important that people can separate the declarations from the implementations, thus making it easier to see what a class does without having to skip past function bodies specifying how it is done. Inline functions in class declarations are allowed so that locality can be achieved when this separation is not helpful.

Finally, code is easier to understand and manipulate if significant chunks fit on a screen. C's traditional terseness helps here, and the C++ rules that allow new variables to be introduced where they are first needed (§3.11.5) is a further step in this direction.

Avoid order dependencies: An order dependence is an opportunity for confusion and for errors when code is reorganized. People are aware that statements are executed in a definite order, but dependencies between global declarations and between class member declarations are often overlooked. The overloading rules (§11.2) and the rules for the use of base classes (§12.2) were specifically crafted to avoid order dependencies. Ideally, it should be an error if the reversal of the order of two declarations could cause a different meaning. That is the rule for class members (§6.3.1), but it cannot be imposed for global declarations. The C preprocessor can wreak havoc by introducing unexpected and ill-behaved dependencies through macro processing (§18.1).

I sometime express my desire to avoid subtle resolutions by saying, "It is not the compiler's job to make up your mind for you." In other words, a compile-time error is more acceptable than an obscure resolution. The ambiguity rules for multiple inheritance are a good example of this (§12.2). The ambiguity rules for overloaded functions are an example of how hard this is to achieve under constraints of compatibility and flexibility (§11.2.2).

If in doubt, pick the variant of a feature that is easiest to teach: This is a secondary rule for choosing between alternatives. It is tricky to apply because it can be an argument for logical beauty and also for sticking to the familiar. Writing tutorials and reference manual descriptions to see how easy they are for people to understand is a practical application of this rule. One intent is to ease the task for educators and support personnel. It is important to remember that programmers are not stupid; simplicity mustn't be achieved at the expense of important functionality.

Syntax matters (often in perverse ways): It is essential to have the type system coherent and in general to have the semantics of the language clean and well defined. Syntax is a secondary issue, and it appears that programmers can learn to love absolutely any syntax.

However, syntax is what people see. Syntax is the language's primary user interface. People are devoted to certain forms of syntax and express their opinions with curious fanaticism. I see no hope of changing this or introducing new semantic notions and design ideas in the face of emotional opposition to a particular syntax. Consequently, the C++ syntax is crafted with care to avoid offending programmers' prejudices, while aiming to make the syntax more rational and regular over time. My aim is to fade out warts such as implicit `int` (§2.8.1) and old-style casts (§14.3.1), while minimizing the use of the more complicated forms of the declarator syntax (§2.8.1).

My experience is that people are addicted to keywords for introducing concepts to the point where a concept that doesn't have its own keyword is surprisingly hard to teach. This effect is more important and deep-rooted than people's vocally expressed dislike for new keywords. Given a choice and time to consider, people invariably choose the new keyword over a clever workaround.

I try to make significant operations highly visible. For example, one significant problem with old-style casts is that they are almost invisible. In addition, I prefer to make semantically ugly operations, such as ill-behaved casts, syntactically ugly to match (§14.3.3). In general, verbosity is avoided.

Preprocessor usage should be eliminated: Without the C preprocessor, C itself and later C++ would have been stillborn. Without Cpp, they simply weren't sufficiently expressive and flexible to handle every task needed in significant projects. On the other hand, the ugly and low-level semantics of Cpp are the primary reason more advanced and elegant C programming environments have been too difficult and expensive to build and use.

Consequently, alternatives that fit with the syntax and semantics of C++ must be found for every essential Cpp feature. That done, we'll get cheaper and much improved C++ programming environments. Along the way, we'll root out the sources of many difficult bugs. Templates (§15), inline functions (§2.4.1), `const` (§3.8), and namespaces (§17) are steps on the way.

4.5 Low-Level Programming Support Rules

Naturally, the rules mentioned above apply to essentially all language features. The rules below also affect C++ as a language for expressing high-level designs.

Low-level programming support rules:
Use traditional (dumb) linkers.
No gratuitous incompatibilities with C.
Leave no room for a lower-level language below C++ (except assembler).
What you don't use, you don't pay for (zero-overhead rule).
If in doubt, provide means for manual control.

Use traditional (dumb) linkers: Ease of porting and ease of cooperation with software written in other languages were early goals. Insisting that C++ should be implementable with traditional linkers ensures that. Having to manage with linker technology that dates from early Fortran days can be painful, though. Several features of C++, notably type-safe linkage (§11.3) and templates (§15), can be implemented using traditional linkers, but they can be implemented better with more linker support. A secondary aim has been for C++ to provide a stimulus to improved linker design.

Using traditional linkers makes it relatively easy to maintain link compatibility with C. This is essential for smooth use of operating system facilities, for using C, Fortran, etc., libraries, and for writing code to be used as libraries from other languages. Using traditional linkers is also essential for writing code intended to be part of the lower levels of a system, such as device drivers.

No gratuitous incompatibilities with C: C is the most successful systems programming language ever. Hundreds of thousands of programmers know C well, billions of lines of C exist, and a tools and services industry focused on C exists. C++ is based on C. The question is, "How closely should the C++ definition match that of C?" C++ doesn't aim at 100% compatibility with C because that would have compromised the aims of type safety and support for design. However, where these aims are not interfered with incompatibilities are avoided – even at the cost of inelegance. In most cases, C incompatibilities have been accepted only when a C rule left a gaping hole in the type system.

Over the years, C++'s greatest strength and its greatest weakness has been its C compatibility. This came as no surprise. The degree of C compatibility will be a major issue in the future. Over the coming years, C compatibility will become less and less of an advantage and more and more of a liability. A path of evolution must be provided (§9).

Leave no room for a lower-level language below C++ (except assembler): If a language aims at being truly high level – that is, it completely protects its programmers from the ugly and boring details of the underlying computer – it must relinquish the dirtier tasks of systems programming to some other language. Typically, that language has been C. Typically, C has then replaced the higher-level language in most areas where control or speed were deemed essential. Often, this has led to a system programmed completely in C or to one that could only be mastered by someone who knows both languages well. In the latter case, a programmer is too often left with a difficult choice of which level of programming is most suitable for a given task and has to keep the primitives and principles of both in mind. C++ tried another path by providing low-level features, abstraction mechanisms, and support for creating hybrid systems out of both.

To remain a viable systems programming language, C++ must maintain C's ability to access hardware directly, to control data structure layout, and to have primitive operation and data types that map on to hardware in a one-to-one fashion. The alternative is to use C or assembler. The language design task is to isolate the low-level features and render them unnecessary for code that doesn't deal directly with system details. The aim is to protect programmers against accidental misuse without imposing undue burdens.

What you don't use, you don't pay for (zero-overhead rule): Large languages have a well-earned reputation for generating large and slow code. The usual reason is that the overhead of supporting supposedly advanced features is distributed over all the features in the language. For example, all objects are large to hold information needed for various kinds of housekeeping, indirect access is imposed on all data because some features are best managed through indirections, or control structures are elaborated to accommodate "advanced control abstractions." This kind of "distributed fat" was deemed unsuitable for C++. Accepting it would leave room for a lower-level language below C++ and make C a better choice than C++ for low-level and high-performance work.

This rule has repeatedly been crucial for C++ design decisions. Virtual functions (§3.5), multiple inheritance (§12.4.2), run-time type identification (§14.2.2.2), exception handling, and templates are all features that owe part of their design to this rule. In each case, the feature was accepted only after I convinced myself that an implementation that obeyed the zero-overhead rule could be constructed. Naturally, an implementer can decide to make a tradeoff between the zero-overhead rule and some other desirable property of a system, but this has to be done very carefully. Many programmers react harshly and emotionally to distributed fat.

Of all the rules, the zero-overhead rule is probably the one that has the sharpest edge when it comes to rejecting a suggested feature.

If in doubt, provide means for manual control: I am reluctant to trust "advanced technology" and particularly loath to assume that something really sophisticated will be universally and cheaply available. Inline functions are a good example of this (§2.4.1). Template instantiation is an example where I should have been more careful and later had to add a mechanism for explicit control (§15.10). The detailed control of memory management is an example of where important gains were made through manual control, yet only time will tell if these gains were made at the expense of getting in the way of automated techniques (§10.7).

4.6   A Final Word

All of these rules must be taken into account for a major language feature. Leaving one out would most likely lead to an imbalance that could hurt a group of users. Similarly, letting one rule dominate at the expense of others would cause similar problems.

I have tried to keep my rules positive and prescriptive rather than building up a list of prohibitions. This makes it inherently more difficult to exclude new ideas. My view of C++ as a language for production software and a focus on facilities that affect program structure counteracts the natural tendency to make minor adjustments.

A more specific and detailed list of issues considered for a language feature is the checklist suggested by the ANSI/ISO committee's working group for extensions (§6.4.1).

5

Chronology 1985-1993

Remember, things take time.
– Piet Hein

Post-Release-1.0 chronology — Release 2.0 — 2.0 feature overview —
The Annotated C++ Reference Manual and informal standardization —
ARM feature overview — ANSI and ISO standardization — standard feature overview.

5.1 Introduction

Part II presents features added to complete C++. The presentation is organized around language features rather than chronologically. This chapter provides the chronology.

The reason to depart from the chronological organization is that the actual time order was not important to the final definition of C++. I knew in general terms where the language was going, what problems needed to be addressed, and what kind of features might be needed to address them. However, there was no way I could just sit down and do it all in one major revision of the language. That would have taken too long and would have left me working in a vacuum without essential feedback. Consequently, extensions were developed and added to the language piecemeal. The actual order was of crucial importance to the users at the time and essential for keeping the language coherent at all times. It was, however, not of major importance to the final shape of C++. Presenting the extensions in chronological order would therefore obscure the logical structure of the language.

This chapter presents the work leading to Release 2.0 of Cfront, the work leading to *The Annotated C++ Reference Manual*, and the standards effort:

1986-1989:   Release 2.0 rounded off C++ with features such as abstract classes, type-safe linkage, and multiple inheritance, but didn't add anything radically new.

1988-1990:   *The Annotated C++ Reference Manual* added templates and exception handling, and in doing so presented a major challenge to implementers and opened the way to radical changes in the way C++ programs could be written.

1989-1993:   The standards effort added namespaces, run-time type identification, and many minor features to the C++ programmer's toolset.

In all three cases, significant work was done to make the definition of C++ more precise and to clean up the language by minor changes. From my perspective, it was all one continuing effort.

5.2 Release 2.0

By mid-1986, the course for C++ was set for all who cared to see. The key design decisions were made. The direction of the future evolution was set with the aim for parameterized types, multiple inheritance, and exception handling. Much experimentation and adjustment based on experience was needed, but the glory days were over. C++ had never been silly putty, but there was now no real possibility for radical change. For good and bad, what was done was done. What was left was an incredible amount of solid work. At this point, C++ had about 2,000 users worldwide.

This was the point where the plan – as originally conceived by Steve Johnson and me – was for a development and support organization to take over the day-to-day work on tools (primarily Cfront), thus freeing me to work on the new features and the libraries that were expected to depend on them. This was also the point where I expected first AT&T and then others to start building compilers and other tools that eventually would make Cfront redundant.

Actually, they had already started, but the good plan was soon derailed due to development management indecisiveness, ineptness, and lack of focus. A project to develop a brand new C++ compiler diverted attention and resources from Cfront maintenance and development. A plan to ship a Release 1.3 in early 1988 completely fell through the cracks. The net effect was that we had to wait until June 1989 for Release 2.0 and that even though 2.0 was significantly better than Release 1.2 in almost all ways, 2.0 did not provide the language features outlined in the "whatis paper" (§3.15) and – partly as a consequence – a significantly improved and extended library wasn't part of it. Shipping such a library would have been feasible because much of what became the USL† Standard Components library had by then been in internal AT&T production use for some time. However, my wish for direct support

---

† USL started out as an AT&T organization supporting and distributing Unix and related tools; later, it became a separate company called Unix System Laboratories; later it was bought by Novell.

for templates still blinded me to alternatives. There was also a misguided belief among some development managers that the library might become both a standard and a significant source of income.

Release 2.0 was the work of a group consisting of Andrew Koenig, Barbara Moo, Stan Lippman, Pat Philip, and me. Barbara coordinated; Pat integrated; Stan and I coded; Andy and I evaluated bug reports and discussed language details; Andy and Barbara did the testing. In all, I implemented all of the new features and something like 80% of the bug fixes for 2.0. In addition, I wrote most of the documentation. As ever, language design issues and the maintenance of the reference manual were my responsibility. Barbara Moo and Stan Lippman became the nucleus of the team that eventually produced Release 2.1 and 3.0.

Many of the people who influenced C with Classes and the original C++ continued to help with the evolution in various ways. Phil Brown, Tom Cargill, Jim Coplien, Steve Dewhurst, Keith Gorlen, Laura Eaves, Bob Kelley, Brian Kernighan, Andy Koenig, Archie Lachner, Stan Lippman, Larry Mayka, Doug McIlroy, Pat Philip, Dave Prosser, Peggy Quinn, Roger Scott, Jerry Schwarz, Jonathan Shopiro, and Kathy Stark were explicitly acknowledged in [Stroustrup,1989b]. The most active in language discussion during this period were Doug McIlroy, Andy Koenig, Jonathan Shopiro, and I.

Stability of the language definition and its implementation was considered essential [Stroustrup,1987c]:

"It is emphasized that these language modifications are extensions; C++ has been and will remain a stable language suitable for long term software development."

And so was C++'s role as a general-purpose language for industrial use [Stroustrup,1987c]:

"Portability of at least some C++ implementations is a key design goal. Consequently, extensions that would add significantly to the porting time or to the demands on resources for a C++ compiler have been avoided. This ideal of language evolution can be contrasted with plausible alternative directions such as making programming convenient
- at the expense of efficiency or structure;
- for novices at the expense of generality;
- in a specific application area by adding special purpose features to the language;
- by adding language features to increase integration into a specific C++ environment."

Release 2.0 was a major improvement, but not by providing anything radically new. At the time, I liked to explain that "all of the 2.0 features – including multiple inheritance – are simply removal of restrictions that we had come to see as too constraining; so we removed them." This was an exaggeration, but a prudent counter to the general tendency to overrate every new feature. From a language design point of view, the most important aspect of Release 2.0 was that it increased the generality of the individual language features and improved their integration into the language. From a user's point of view, I suspect that the most important aspects of Release 2.0 were the more solid implementation and the improved support.

5.2.1 Feature Overview

The main features of 2.0 were first presented in [Stroustrup,1987c] and summarized in the revised version of that paper [Stroustrup,1989b] that accompanied 2.0 as part of its documentation:

[1]   Multiple inheritance (§12.1)

[2]   Type-safe linkage (§11.3)

[3]   Better resolution of overloaded functions (§11.2)

[4]   Recursive definition of assignment and initialization (§11.4.4)

[5]   Better facilities for user-defined memory management (§10.2, §10.4)

[6]   Abstract classes (§13.2)

[7]   Static member functions (§13.4)

[8]   `const` member functions (§13.3)

[9]   `protected` members (first provided in Release 1.2) (§13.9)

[10] Generalized initializers (§3.11.4)

[11] Base and member initializers (§12.9)

[12] Overloading of operator `->` (§11.5.4)

[13] Pointers to members (first provided in Release 1.2) (§13.11)

Most of these extensions and refinements represented experience gained with C++ and couldn't have been added earlier without more foresight than I possessed. Naturally, integrating these features involved significant work, but it was most unfortunate that this was allowed to take priority over the completion of the language as outlined in the ''whatis'' paper (§3.15).

Most features enhanced the safety of the language in some way or other. Cfront 2.0 checked the consistency of function types across separate compilation units (type-safe linkage), made the overload resolution rules order-independent, and ensured that more calls were considered ambiguous. The notion of `const` was made more comprehensive, pointers to members closed a loophole in the type system, and explicit class-specific memory allocation and deallocation operations were provided to make the error-prone ''assignment to `this`'' technique (§3.9) redundant.

Of these features, [1], [3], [4], [5], [9], [10], [11], [12], and [13] were in use within Bell Labs at the time of my 1987 USENIX presentation (§7.1.2).

5.3   The Annotated Reference Manual

Sometime in 1988 it became clear that C++ would eventually have to be standardized [Stroustrup,1989]. There were now a handful of independent implementations being produced. Clearly, an effort had to be made to write a more precise and comprehensive definition of the language. Further, it would be necessary to gain wide acceptance for that definition. At first, formal standardization wasn't considered an option. Many people involved with C++ considered – and still consider – standardization before genuine experience has been gained abhorrent. However, making an improved reference manual wasn't something that could be done by one person (me) in private. Input and feedback from the C++ community was needed. Thus I came upon the idea of rewriting the C++ reference manual and circulating its draft among important and insightful members of the C++ community worldwide.

At about the same time, the part of AT&T that sold C++ commercially (USL) wanted a new and improved C++ reference manual and gave one of its employees, Margaret Ellis, the task of writing it. It seemed only reasonable to combine the efforts and produce a single, externally reviewed reference manual. It also seemed obvious to me that publishing this manual with some additional information would help the acceptance of the new definition and make C++ more widely understood. Thus, *The Annotated C++ Reference Manual* was written [ARM]:

> "to provide a firm basis for the further evolution of C++ ... [and] to serve as a starting point for the formal standardization of C++. ... The C++ reference manual alone provides a complete definition of C++, but the terse reference manual style leaves many reasonable questions unanswered. Discussions of what is *not* in the language, *why* certain features are defined as they are, and *how* one might implement some particular feature have no place in a reference manual but are nevertheless of interest to most users. Such discussions are presented as annotations and in the commentary sections.
>
> The commentary also helps the reader appreciate the relationships among different parts of the language and emphasizes points and implications that might have been overlooked in the reference manual itself. Examples and comparisons with C also make this book more approachable than the bare reference manual"

After some minor squabbling with the product people it was agreed that we'd write the ARM (as *The Annotated C++ Reference Manual* is commonly called) describing the whole of C++, that is, with templates and exception handling, rather than as a manual for the subset implemented by the most recent AT&T release. This was important because it clearly established the language itself as different from any one implementation of it. This principle had been present from the very beginning, but it needs to be restated often because users, implementers, and salesmen seem to have difficulty remembering it.

Of the ARM, I wrote every word of the reference manual proper except the section on the preprocessor (§18) that Margaret Ellis adapted from the ANSI C Standard. The annotations and the commentary sections were jointly written and partly based on my earlier papers [Stroustrup,1984b,1987,1988,1988b,1989b].

The reference manual proper of the ARM was reviewed by about a hundred people from two dozen organizations. Most are named in the acknowledgment section of the ARM. In addition, many contributed to the whole of the ARM. The contributions of Brian Kernighan, Andrew Koenig, and Doug McIlroy were specifically noted. The reference manual proper from the ARM was accepted as the basis for the ANSI standardization of C++ in March 1990.

The ARM doesn't explain the techniques that the language features support: "this book does not attempt to teach C++ programming; it explains what the language is – not how to use it [ARM]." That job was left for the second edition of *The C++*

Programming Language [2nd]. Unfortunately, some people discard the advice. The result is often a view of C++ as a mere collection of obscure details and a consequential inability to write elegant and maintainable C++ code; see §7.2.

5.3.1 Feature Overview

The ARM presented a few minor features that were not implemented until Release 2.1 from AT&T and other C++ compiler vendors. The most obvious of these were nested classes. I was strongly encouraged to revert to the original definition of nested class scopes by comments from external reviewers of the reference manual. I also despaired over ever making the scope rules of C++ coherent while the C rule was in place (§2.8.1).

The major new features presented in the ARM were templates (§15) and exception handling (§16). In addition, the ARM allows people to overload prefix and postfix increment (++) independently (§11.5.3).

To match ANSI C, initialization of local static arrays was allowed.

To match ANSI C, the `volatile` modifier was introduced to help optimizer implementers. I am not at all sure that the syntactic parallel with `const` is warranted by semantic similarities. However, I never had strong feelings about `volatile` and see no reason to try to improve on the ANSI C committee's decisions in this area.

To sum up, the features presented in the ARM were:
–   The 2.0 features (§5.2.1)
–   Templates (§15)
–   Exceptions (§16)
–   Nested classes (§13.5)
–   Separate overloading of prefix and suffix ++ and -- (§11.5.3)
–   `volatile`
–   Local static arrays

The ARM features, excluding exceptions, first became widely available in Release 3.0 of Cfront in September 1991. The complete set of ARM features were first made available in the DEC and IBM C++ compilers in early 1992.

5.4 ANSI and ISO Standardization

From 1990 onward, the ANSI/ISO C++ standards committee has been the primary forum for the effort to complete C++.

The initiative to formal (ANSI) standardization of C++ was taken by Hewlett-Packard in conjunction with AT&T, DEC, and IBM. Larry Rosler from Hewlett-Packard was important in this initiative. In particular, Larry approached me sometime near the end of 1988, and we had a discussion about the need for formal standardization. The key problem was one of timing. Larry presented the case for urgency on behalf of major users, and I presented the case for delay to allow for further experimentation and experience before standardization. After weighing the multitude of nebulous technical and commercial issues, we agreed that there was a window of about a year during which formal standardization had to begin for us to have a fair chance of success. As I remember it, the first technical meeting of the ANSI committee took place three days before our one-year window opened (March 1990).

The proposal for ANSI standardization was written by Dmitry Lenkov [Lenkov,1989] from Hewlett-Packard. Dmitry's proposal cites several reasons for immediate standardization of C++:

– C++ is going through a much faster public acceptance than most other languages.
– Delay ... will lead to dialects.
– C++ requires a careful and detailed definition providing full semantics ... for each language feature.
– C++ lacks some important features ... [including] exception handling, aspects of multiple inheritance, features supporting parametric polymorphism, and standard libraries.

The proposal also stressed the need for compatibility with ANSI C. The organizational meeting of the ANSI C++ committee, X3J16, took place in December 1989 in Washington, DC, and was attended by about 40 people, including people who took part in the C standardization, people who by now were "old-time C++ programmers," and others. Dmitry Lenkov became its chairman, and Jonathan Shopiro became its editor.

The first technical meeting was hosted by AT&T in Somerset, New Jersey, in March 1990. AT&T gained that honor not because of any judgement about the company's contribution to C++, but because we (the members of X3J16 present at the Washington, DC meeting) decided to schedule the first years' meetings based on the weather. Thus, Microsoft hosted the second meeting in Seattle in July, and Hewlett-Packard hosted the third meeting in Palo Alto in November. This way, we had splendid weather for all three meetings and defused jockeying for status among the corporations represented.

The committee now has more than 250 members out of which something like 70 turn up at meetings. The original aim of the committee was a draft standard for public review in late 1993 or early 1994 with the hope of an official standard about two years later. This was an ambitious schedule for the standardization of a general-purpose programming language. To compare, the standardization of C took seven years. The current schedule, which I think we have a good chance of meeting, calls for delivery of a draft standard for public review in April 1995†.

Naturally, standardization of C++ isn't just an American concern. From the start, representatives from other countries attended the ANSI C++ meetings. In Lund, Sweden, in June 1991 the ISO C++ committee WG21 was convened, and the two C++ standards committees decided to hold joint meetings – starting immediately in Lund.

---

† In July 1994, the committee voted for "CD registration" as the first step of the completion the ISO process is now called. Scheduling a standard isn't easy. In particular, "details" such as what a standard is and how you must make one aren't standardized and seems to change every year.

Representatives from Canada, Denmark, France, Japan, Sweden, the UK, and USA were present. Notably, the vast majority of these national representatives were actually long-time C++ programmers.

The C++ committee had a difficult charter:

- The definition of the language must be precise and comprehensive.
- C/C++ compatibility had to be addressed.
- Extensions beyond current C++ practice had to be considered.
- Libraries had to be considered.

On top of that, the C++ community was already *very* diverse and totally unorganized so that the standards committee naturally became an important focal point of the community. In the short run, that is actually the most important role for the committee:

"The C++ committee is a place where compiler writers, tools writers, their friends and representatives can meet and discuss language definition and – as far as commercial rivalries allow – implementation issues. Thus, the C++ committee has already served the C++ community by helping the implementations to become more similar (more ''correct'') by providing a forum where issues can be aired. The alternative is a compiler writer alone or together with a few friends finding questions that they see no answer to in the ARM and having to make a guess. Maybe they would mail me – many do – but I can't cope with every problem that arises and some people do feel that dealing with an individual on such issues isn't quite proper. Lack of communication inevitably leads to dialects. The committee counteracts such trends. I don't see how someone who is not directly or indirectly represented on the committee could currently hope to build a tool that was in line with the assumptions made by the major players in the C++ market [Stroustrup,1992b].''

Standardization isn't easy. There are people on the committee who are there to preserve status quo, there are people with an idea of status quo that makes them want to turn the clock back several years, there are people who want to make a clean break from the past and design a completely new language, there are people who care only about a single issue, there are people who care only about a single class of systems, there are people whose votes are tied by their employers, there are people who represent only themselves, there are people with a primarily theoretical view of programming and programming languages, there are people who want a standard *now!* even if it means some details left unresolved, there are people who want nothing short of a *perfect* definition, there are people who come thinking that C++ is a brand new language with hardly any users, there are people who represent users with many millions of lines of code built over a decade, etc. Under the rules of standardization, we all have to more or less agree. We have to reach ''consensus'' (usually defined as a large voting majority). These are reasonable rules – and even if they were not, they would still be the national and international rules the committee would have to follow. All the interests are legitimate and having a majority squelch significant minority interests would yield a standard that was useful only to an unnecessarily narrowly defined user community. Thus, every member of the committee must learn to respect points of view that seem alien and learn to compromise. That is actually very much in the spirit of C++.

C compatibility was the first major controversial issue we had to face. After some occasionally heated debate, it was decided that 100% C/C++ compatibility wasn't an option. Neither was significantly decreasing C compatibility. C++ is a separate language and not a strict superset of ANSI C and can't be changed to be such a superset without seriously weakening the guarantees provided by the C++ type system – and without breaking millions of lines of C++ code. Similarly, any significant decrease in C compatibility would break code, complicate the creation and maintenance of mixed C and C++ systems, and complicate a transition from C to C++. This decision, often referred to as ''As close to C as possible – but no closer'' after a paper written by Andrew Koenig and me [Koenig,1989], is the same conclusion that has been reached over and over again by individuals and groups considering C++ and the direction of its evolution (§3.12). Working out all the details of ''As close to C as possible – but no closer'' after the independent changes C++ and ANSI C made to the original C manual takes a major part of the standards committee's effort. Thomas Plum has been a major contributor to this effort.

5.4.1 Feature Overview

The features provided by C++ after the November 1994 meeting in Valley Forge specified by the standard committee's working paper can be summarized as:
 – Features specified in the ARM (§5.3)
 – European character set representation of C++ (§6.5.3.1)
 – Relaxing rule for return types for overriding functions (§13.7)
 – Run-time type identification (§14.2)
 – Declarations in conditions (§3.11.5.2)
 – Overloading based on enumerations (§11.7.1)
 – User-defined allocation and deallocation operators for arrays (§10.3)
 – Forward declaration of nested classes (§13.5)
 – Namespaces (§17)
 – Mutable (§13.3.3)
 – New casts (§14.3)
 – A Boolean type (§11.7.2)
 – Explicit template instantiation (§15.10.4)
 – Explicit template argument specification in template function calls (§15.6.2)
 – Member templates (§15.9.3)
 – Class templates as template arguments (§15.3.1)
 – A `const static` member of integral type can be initialized by a *constant-expression* within a class declaration.
 – Explicit constructors (§3.6.1)
 – Static checking of exception specifications (§16.9).
For more details, see §6.4.2.

6

Standardization

*Don't you try to outweird me,
I get stranger things than you
free with my breakfast cereal.*
– Zaphod Beeblebrox

What is a standard? — aims of the C++ standards effort — how does the committee operate? — who is on the committee? — language clarifications — name lookup rules — lifetime of temporaries — criteria for language extension — list of proposed extensions — keyword arguments — an exponentiation operator — restricted pointers — character sets.

6.1 What is a Standard?

There is much confusion in the minds of programmers about what a standard is and what it ought to be. One ideal for a standard is to completely specify exactly which programs are legal and exactly what the meaning of every such program is. For C and C++ at least, that is not the whole story. In fact, it can't and shouldn't be the ideal for languages designed to exploit the diverse world of hardware architectures and gadgets. For such languages, it is essential to have some behavior implementation-dependent. Thus, a standard is often described as ''a contract between the programmer and the implementer.'' It describes not only what is ''legal'' source text, but also what a programmer can rely on in general and what behavior is implementation-dependent. For example, in C and C++ one can declare variables of type int, but the standard doesn't specify how large an int is, only that it has at least 16 bits.

It is possible to have long and somewhat learned debates about what the standard really is and what terminology can best be employed to express it. However, the key points are to sharply distinguish what is and what is not a valid program, and further to specify what behavior should be the same in all implementations and what is implementation-dependent. Exactly how those distinctions are drawn is important, but not very interesting to practical programmers. Most committee members focus on the more language-technical aspects of standardization so the main burden of tackling the thorny issues of what the standard standardizes falls on the committee's project editor. Fortunately, our original project editor Jonathan Shopiro has an interest in such matters. Jonathan has now retired as editor in favor of Andrew Koenig, but Jonathan is still a member of the committee.

Another interesting (that is, very difficult) question is to which extent an implementation with features not specified in the standard is acceptable. It seems unreasonable to ban all such extensions. After all, some extensions are necessary to important sub-sections of the C++ community. For example, some machines have hardware that supports specific concurrency mechanisms, special addressing constraints, or special vector hardware. We can't burden every C++ user with features to support all these incompatible special-purpose extensions. They will be incompatible and will often impose a cost even on non-users. However, it would be unfortunate to discourage implementers serving such communities from trying to be perfectly conforming except for their essential extensions. On the other hand, I was once presented with an ''extension'' that allowed access to private members of a class from every function in the program; that is, the implementer had not bothered to implement access control. I didn't consider that a reasonable extension. Wordsmithing the standard to allow the former and not the latter is a nontrivial task.

An important point is to ensure that nonstandard extensions are detectable; otherwise, a programmer might wake up some morning and find significant code dependent on a supplier's unique extensions and thus without the option to change suppliers with reasonable ease. As a naive student, I remember being surprised and pleased to find that the Fortran on our university mainframe was an ''extended Fortran'' with some neat features. My surprise turned to dismay when I realized that this implied that my programs would be useless except on CDC6000 series machines.

Thus, 100% portability of standards-conforming programs is not in general an achievable or desirable ideal for C++. A program that conforms to a standard is not necessarily 100% portable because it may display implementation-dependent behavior. Actually, most do. For example, a perfectly legal C or C++ program may change its meaning if it happens to depend on the results of the built-in remainder operator % applied to a negative number.

Further, real programs tend to have dependencies on libraries providing services not offered on every system. For example, a Microsoft Windows program is unlikely to run unchanged under X, and a program using the Borland foundation classes will not trivially be ported to run under MacApp. Portability of real programs comes from design that encapsulates implementation and environment dependencies, not just from adherence to a few simple rules in a standards document.

Knowing what a standard doesn't guarantee is at least as important as knowing what it does promise.

6.1.1 Implementation Details

Every week, there seems to be a new request for standardizing things like the virtual table layout, the type-safe linkage name encoding scheme, or the debugger. However, these are quality-of-implementation issues or implementation details that are beyond the scope of the standard. Users would like libraries compiled with one compiler to work with code compiled with another, would like binaries to be transferable from one machine architecture to another, and would like debuggers to be independent of the implementation used to compile the code being examined.

However, standardization of instruction sets, operating-system interfaces, debugger formats, calling sequences, and object layouts is far beyond the ability of the standards group for a programming language that is merely one little cog in a much bigger system. Such universal standardization probably isn't even desirable because it would stifle progress in machine architectures and operating systems. If a user needs total independence from hardware the system/environment must be built as an interpreter with its own standard environment for applications. That approach has its own problems; in particular, specialized hardware becomes hard to exploit and local style guides cannot be followed. If those problems are overcome by interfacing to code written in another language that allows nonportable code, such as C++, the problem recurs.

For a language suitable for serious systems work, we must live with the fact that every now and again a naive user posts a message to the net: "I moved my object code from my Mac to my SPARC and now it won't work." Like portability, interoperability is a matter of design and understanding of the constraints imposed by the environments. I often meet C programmers who are unaware that code compiled with two different C compilers for the same system is not guaranteed to link and in fact is unlikely to do so – yet express horror that C++ doesn't guarantee such interoperability. As usual, we have a major task in educating users.

6.1.2 Reality Check

In addition to the many formal constraints on a standards committee, there is an informal and practical one: Many standards are simply ignored by their intended users. For example, the Pascal and Pascal2 standards are almost completely forgotten. For most Pascal programmers, "Pascal" means Borland's greatly extended Pascal dialect. The language defined by the Pascal standard didn't provide features users considered essential and the Pascal2 standard didn't appear until a different informal "industry standard" had established itself. Another cautionary observation is that on UNIX most work is still done in K&R C; ANSI C is struggling in that community. The reason seems to be that some users don't see the technical benefits of ANSI/ISO C compared to K&R C outweighing the short-term costs of a transition. Even an unchallenged standard can be slow finding its way into use. To become accepted, a standard must be timely and relevant to users' needs. In my opinion, delivering a good standard for a good language in a timely manner is essential. Trying to change C++ into a "perfect" language or to produce a standard that cannot be misread by anyone –

however devious or ill-educated – is far beyond the abilities of the committee (§3.13).
In fact, it is beyond anyone working under the time constraint provided by a large user
community (§7.1).

6.2 How does the Committee Operate?

There are actually several committees formed to standardize C++. The first and largest is the American National Standards Institute's ANSI-X3J16 committee. That
committee is the responsibility of the Computer and Business Equipment Manufac-
tures Association, CBEMA, and operates under its rules. In particular, this means
one-company-one-vote voting and a person who doesn't work for a company counts
as a company. A member can start voting at the second meeting attended. Officially,
the most important committee is the International Standards Organization's ISO-
WG-21. That committee operates under international rules and is the one that will
finally make the result an international standard. In particular, this means one-
country-one-vote voting. Other countries, including Britain, Denmark, France, Ger-
many, Japan, Russia, and Sweden now have their own national committees for standardizing C++. These national committees send requests, recommendations, and representatives to the joint ANSI/ISO meetings.

Basically, we have decided not to accept anything that doesn't pass under both
ANSI and ISO voting rules. This implies that the committee operates rather like a
bicameral parliament with a ''lower house'' (ANSI) doing most of the arguing and an
''upper house'' (ISO) ratifying the decisions of the lower house provided they make
sense and duly respect the interests of the international community.

On one occasion, this procedure led to the rejection of a proposal that would otherwise have passed by a small majority. Thus, I think the national representatives
saved us from a mistake that could have caused dissension. I couldn't interpret that
majority as reflecting a consensus and I therefore think that – independently of the
technical merit of the proposal – the national representatives gave the committee an
important reminder of their responsibilities under their charter. The issue in question
was that of whether C++ should have a specific form of defined minimum translation
limits. A significantly improved proposal was accepted at a later meeting.

The ANSI and ISO committees meet jointly three times a year. To avoid confusion I will refer to them using the singular *committee*. A meeting lasts a week out of
which many hours are taken up with legally mandated procedural stuff. Yet more
hours are taken up by the kind of confusion you might expect when 70 people try to
understand what the issues really are. Some daytime hours and several evenings are
taken up by technical sessions where major C++ issues, such as international character
handling and run-time type identification, and issues relevant to standards work, such
as formal methods and organizations of international standardization bodies, are presented and discussed. The rest of the time is mostly taken up by working group meetings and discussions based on the reports from those working groups.

The current working groups are:
- – C compatibility
- – Core language
- – Editorial
- – Environment
- – Extensions
- – International issues
- – Libraries
- – Syntax

Clearly, there is too much work for the committee to handle in only three weeks of meetings a year, so much of the actual work goes on between meetings. To aid communication, we use email a lot. Every meeting involves something like three inches of double-sided paper memos. These memos are sent in two packages: one arrives a couple of weeks before a meeting to help members prepare, and one a couple of weeks after to reflect work done between the first mailing and the end of the meeting.

6.2.1 Who is on the C++ Standards Committee?

The C++ committee consists of individuals of diverse interests, concerns, and backgrounds. Some represent themselves, some represent giant corporations. Some use PCs, some use UNIX boxes, some use mainframes, etc. Some use C++, some don't. Some want C++ to be more of an object-oriented language (according to a variety of definitions of "object-oriented"), others would have been more comfortable had ANSI C been the end-point of C's evolution. Many have a background in C, some don't. Some have a background in standards work, many don't. Some have a computer science background, some don't. Some are programmers, some are not. Some are language lawyers, some are not. Some serve end-users, some are tools suppliers. Some are interested in large projects, some are not. Some are interested in C compatibility, some are not.

Except that all are officially unpaid volunteers (though most represent companies), it is hard to find a generalization that covers all. This is good; only a very diverse group could ensure that the diverse interests of the C++ community are represented. It does make constructive discussion difficult and slow at times. In particular, this very open process is vulnerable to disruption by individuals whose technical or personal level of maturity doesn't allow them to understand or respect the views of others. I also worry that the voice of C++ users (that is, programmers and designers of C++ applications) can be drowned by the voices of language lawyers, would-be language designers, standards bureaucrats, implementers, etc.

Usually about 70 people attend a meeting, and of those, about half attend almost all meetings. The number of voting, alternate, and observing members is more than 250. I'm an alternate member, meaning that I represent my company, but someone else from my company votes. Let me give you an idea about who is represented here by simply glancing over a list of members and copying out some of the better-known names chosen from the membership list in 1990: Amdahl, Apple, AT&T, Bellcore,

Borland, British Aerospace, CDC, Data General, DEC, Fujitsu, Hewlett-Packard, IBM, Los Alamos National Labs, Lucid, Mentor Graphics, Microsoft, MIPS, NEC, NIH, Object Design, Ontologics, Prime Computer, SAS Institute, Siemens Nixdorf, Silicon Graphics, Sun, Tandem Computers, Tektronix, Texas Instruments, Unisys, US WEST, Wang, and Zortech. This list is of course biased towards companies I know of and towards large companies, but I hope you get the idea that the industry is well represented. Naturally, the individuals involved are as important as the companies they represent, but I will refrain from turning this into an advertisement for my friends by naming them.

6.3 Clarifications

Much of the best standards work is invisible to the average programmer and appears quite esoteric and often boring when presented. The reason is that a lot of effort is expended in finding ways of expressing clearly and completely ''what everyone already knows, but just happens not to be spelled out in the manual'' and in resolving obscure issues that – at least in theory – don't affect most programmers. Naturally, these issues are essential to implementers trying to ensure that a given language use is correctly handled. In turn, these issues become essential to programmers because even the most carefully written large program will deliberately or accidentally depend on some feature that would appear obscure or esoteric to some. Unless implementers agree, the programmer has little choice between implementations and becomes the hostage of a single compiler purveyor – and *that* would be contrary to my view of what C++ is supposed to be (see §2.1).

I will present two issues, name lookup and lifetime of temporaries, to illustrate the difficult and detailed work done. The majority of the committee's efforts are expended on such issues.

6.3.1 Lookup Issues

The most stubborn problems in the definition of C++ relate to name lookup: *exactly* which uses of a name refer to which declarations? Here, I'll describe just one kind of lookup problem: the ones that relate to order dependencies between class member declarations. Consider:

```
int x;

class X {
    int f() { return x; }
    int x;
};
```

Which x does X::f() refer to? Also:

```
typedef char* T;

class Y {
    T f() { T a = 0; return a; }
    typedef int T;
};
```

Which T does Y::f() use?

The ARM gives the answers: The x referred to in X::f() is X::x, and the definition of class Y is an error because the meaning of the type T changes after its use in Y::f().

Andrew Koenig, Scott Turner, Tom Pennello, Bill Gibbons, and several others devoted hours to finding precise, complete, useful, logical, and compatible (with the C standard and existing C++ code) answers to this kind of question at several consecutive meetings and weeks of work in between meetings. My involvement in these discussions was limited by my need to focus on extension-related issues.

Difficulties arise because of conflicts between goals:

[1] We want to be able to do syntax analysis reading the source text once only.

[2] Reordering the members of a class should not change the meaning of the class.

[3] A member function body explicitly written inline should mean the same thing when written out of line.

[4] Names from an outer scope should be usable from an inner scope (in the same way as they are in C).

[5] The rules for name lookup should be independent of what a name refers to.

If all of these rules hold, the language will be reasonably fast to parse, and users won't have to worry about these rules because the compiler will catch the ambiguous and near ambiguous cases. The current rules come very close to this ideal.

6.3.1.1 The ARM Name Lookup Rules

In the ARM, I addressed the problems with moderate success. Names from outer scopes can be used directly, and I tried to minimize the resulting order dependencies by two rules:

[1] The type redefinition rule: A type name may not be redefined in a class after it has been used there.

[2] The rewrite rule: Member functions defined inline are analyzed as if they were defined immediately after the end of their class declarations.

The redefinition rule makes class Y an error:

```
typedef char* T;

class Y {
    T f() { T a = 0; return a; }
    typedef int T; // error T redefined after use
};
```

The rewrite rule says that class X should be understood as

```
int x;

class X {
    int f();
    int x;
};

inline int X::f() { return x; } // returns X::x
```

Unfortunately, not all examples are this simple. Consider:

```
const int i = 99;

class Z {
    int a[i];
    int f() { return i; }
    enum { i = 7 };
};
```

According to the ARM rules and (clearly?) contrary to their intent, this example is legal, and the two uses of i refer to different definitions and yield different values. The rewrite rule ensures that the i used in Z::f() is Z::i with the value 7. However, there is no rewrite rule for the i used as an index, so it refers to the global i with the value 99. Even though i is used to determine a type, it is not itself a type name, so it is not covered by the type redefinition rule. The ANSI/ISO rules ensure that the example is illegal because i is redefined after it has been used.

Also:

```
class T {
    A f();
    void g() { A a; /* ... */ }
    typedef int A;
};
```

Assume that no type A was defined outside T. Is the declaration of T::f() legal? Is the definition of T::g() legal? The ARM deems the declaration of T::f() illegal because A is undefined at that point; the ANSI/ISO rules agree. On the other hand, the ARM deems the definition of g() legal if you interpret the rewrite rule to say that "rewriting" takes place before syntax analysis and illegal if you interpret it to allow syntax analysis first and rewrite afterward. The issue is whether A is a type name when the syntax analysis is done. I think that the ARM supports the first view (that is, the declaration of T::g() is legal), but I wouldn't claim that to be indisputably obvious. The ANSI/ISO rules agree with my interpretation of the ARM rules.

6.3.1.2 Why Allow Forward References?

In principle, these problems could be avoided by insisting on strict one-pass analysis: You can use a name if and only if it has been declared "above/before" and what happens "below/after" can't affect a declaration. This is, after all, the rule in C and elsewhere in C++. For example:

```
int x;

void f()
{
    int y = x;   // global x
    int x = 7;
    int z = x;        // local x
}
```

However, when I first designed classes and inline functions, Doug McIlroy argued convincingly that serious confusion would result from applying that rule to class declarations. For example:

```
int x;

class X {
    void f() { int y = x; } // ::x or X::x ?
    void g();
    int x;
    void h() { int y = x; } // X::x
};

void X::g() { int y = x; }   // X::x
```

When the declaration of X is large, the fact that different xs are present will often be unnoticed. Worse, unless the member x was used consistently, a silent change of meaning would result from a reordering of members. Taking a function body out of the class declaration into a separate member function declaration could also quietly change its meaning. The rewrite and redefinition rules provided protection against subtle errors and some freedom to reorganize classes.

These arguments apply to nonclass examples also, but only for classes is the compiler overhead of this protection affordable – and only for classes could C compatibility problems be avoided. In addition, class declarations are exactly where reorderings are most frequent and most likely to have undesirable side effects.

6.3.1.3 The ANSI/ISO Name Lookup Rules

Over the years, we found many examples that weren't covered by the explicit ARM rules, were order-dependent in obscure and potentially dangerous ways, or the interpretation of the rules were uncertain. Some were pathological. One favorite was found by Scott Turner:

```
typedef int P();
typedef int Q();
```

```
class X {
  static P(Q);  // define Q to be a P.
                // equivalent to ''static int Q()''
                // the parentheses around Q are redundant

                // Q is no longer a type in this scope

  static Q(P);  // define Q to be a function
                // taking an argument of type P
                // and returning an int.
                // equivalent to ''static int Q(int())''
};
```

Declaring two functions with the same name in the same scope is fine as long as their argument types differ sufficiently. Reverse the order of member declarations, and we define two functions called P instead. Remove the typedef for either P or Q from the context, and we get yet other meanings.

This example ought to convince anybody that standards work is dangerous to your mental health. The rules we finally adopted makes this example undefined.

Note that this example – like many others – is based on the unfortunate "implicit int" rule inherited from C. I tried to get rid of that rule more than ten years ago (§2.8.1). Unfortunately, not all sick examples rely on the implicit int rule. For example:

```
int b;

class Z {
    static int a[sizeof(b)];
    static int b[sizeof(a)];
};
```

This example is an error because b changes meaning after it has been used. Fortunately, this kind of error is easy for a compiler to catch – unlike the P(Q) example.

At the Portland meeting in March 1993 the committee adopted these rules:

[1] The scope of a name declared in a class consists not only of the text following the name's declarator but also of all function bodies, default arguments, and constructor initializers in that class (including such things in nested classes). It excludes the name's own declarator.

[2] A name used in a class S must refer to the same declaration when reevaluated in its context and in the completed scope of S. The completed scope of S consists of the class S, S's base classes, and all classes enclosing S. This is often called "the reconsideration rule."

[3] If reordering member declarations in a class yields an alternate valid program under [1] and [2], the program's meaning is undefined. This is often called "the reordering rule."

Note that very few programs are affected by this change of rules. The new rules are primarily a clearer statement of the original intent. At first glance, these rules seem to require a multi-pass algorithm in a C++ implementation. However, they can be implemented by a single pass followed by one or more passes over information gathered during the first pass, and are not a performance bottleneck.

6.3.2 Lifetime of Temporaries

Many operations in C++ require the use of temporary values. For example:

```
void f(X a1, X a2)
{
    extern void g(const X&);
    X z;
    // ...
    z = a1+a2;
    g(a1+a2);
    // ...
}
```

In general, an object (probably of type X) is needed to hold the result of a1+a2 before assigning it to z. Similarly, an object is needed to hold the result of a1+a2 passed to g(). Assume that X is a class with a destructor. Where, then, is the destructor for this temporary invoked? My original answer to that question was "at the end of the block just like every other local variable." There proved to be two problems with this answer:

[1] Sometimes, that doesn't leave a temporary around for long enough. For example, g() might push a pointer to its argument (the temporary resulting from a1+a2) onto a stack, and someone might pop that pointer and try to use it after f() has returned, that is, after the temporary has been destroyed.

[2] Sometimes, that leaves a temporary around for too long. For example, X might be a 1,000 by 1,000 matrix type and dozens of temporary matrixes might be created before the end of block is reached. This will exhaust even large real memories and can send a virtual memory mechanism into spasms of paging.

In my experience, the former problem is rare in real programs, and its general solution is the use of automatic garbage collection (§10.7). The latter problem, however, is common and serious. In practice, it forced some people to enclose each statement suspected of generating temporaries in its own block:

```
void f(X a1, X a2)
{
    extern void g(const X&);
    X z;
    // ...
    {z = a1+a2;}
    {g(a1+a2);}
    // ...
}
```

With the point of destruction at the end of the block – as implemented by Cfront –

users could at least explicitly work around the problem. However, a better resolution was loudly demanded by some users. Consequently, in the ARM, I relaxed the rule to allow destruction at any point after the temporary value was first used and the end of the block. This was a misguided act of intended kindness. It caused confusion and helped nobody because as different implementers chose different lifetimes of temporaries, nobody could write code that was guaranteed to be portable except by assuming immediate destruction – and that was quickly shown to be unacceptable by breaking code using common and well-liked C++ idioms. For example:

```
class String {
    // ...
public:
    friend String operator+(const String&, const String&);
    // ...
    operator const char*(); // C-style string
};

void f(String s1, String s2)
{
    printf("%s", (const char*)(s1+s2));
    // ...
}
```

The idea is that `String`'s conversion operator is invoked to produce a C-style string for `printf` to print. In the typical (naive and efficient) implementation, the conversion operator simply returns a pointer to part of the `String` object.

Given this simple implementation of the conversion operator, this example wouldn't work under an "immediate destruction of temporaries" implementation: A temporary is created for `s1+s2`, the conversion to a C-style string obtains a pointer to the internals of this temporary, the temporary is destroyed, and *then* the pointer to the internals of the now-destroyed temporary is passed to `printf()`. The destructor for the `String` temporary holding `s1+s2` would have freed the memory holding the C-style string.

Such code is common and even implementations that generally follow an immediate destruction strategy, such as GNU's G++, tended to delay destruction in such cases. This kind of thinking led to the idea of destroying temporaries at the end of the statement in which they were constructed. This would make the example above not only legal, but guaranteed portable across implementations. However, other "almost equivalent" examples would break. For example:

```
void g(String s1, String s2)
{
    const char* p = s1+s2;
    printf("%s",p);
    // ...
}
```

Given the "destroy temporaries at the end of statement" strategy the C-string pointed to by p would reside in the temporary representing s1+s2 and be freed at the end of the statement initializing p.

Discussions of the lifetime of temporaries festered in the standards committee for about two years until Dag Brück successfully brought it to a close. Before that, the committee spent much time discussing the relative merits of solutions that all were good enough. Everyone also agreed that no solution was perfect. My opinion – somewhat loudly expressed – was that users were hurting for lack of a resolution and that the time had come to just pick one. I think the best alternative was chosen.

Dag's summary of the issues in July 1993 was primarily based on work by Andrew Koenig, Scott Turner, and Tom Pennello. It identified seven main alternative points of destruction of a temporary:

[1] Just after the first use.
[2] At the end of statement.
[3] At the next branching point.
[4] At the end of block (original C++ rule, like Cfront).
[5] At the end of function.
[6] After the last use (implies garbage collection).
[7] Leave undefined between first use and end of block (ARM rule).

I leave it as an exercise to the reader to construct valid arguments in favor of each alternative. It can be done. However, serious, valid objections can also be made for each. Consequently, the real problem is picking an alternative with a good balance of benefits and problems.

In addition, we considered the possibility of having a temporary destroyed after its last use in a block, but that requires flow analysis, and we didn't feel we could require every compiler to do a flow analysis well enough to ensure that "after the last use in a block" was a well-defined point in the computation in every implementation. Please note that local flow analysis would not be sufficient to provide reliable warning against "too early destruction;" conversion functions returning a pointer to the internals of an object are often defined in a compilation unit different from the ones in which they are used. Trying to ban such functions would be pointless because a ban would break much existing code and couldn't be enforced anyway.

From about 1991, the committee focused on "end of statement," and naturally that alternative was colloquially known as EOS. The problem was to decide precisely what EOS should mean. For example:

```
void h(String s1, String s2)
{
    const char* p;

    if (p = s1+s2) {
        // ...
    }
}
```

Should the value of p be useful within the statement block? That is, does the destruction of the object holding s1+s2 take place at the end of the condition or at the end of the whole `if` statement? The answer is that the object holding `s1+s2` will be destroyed at the end of the condition. It would be absurd to guarantee this:

```
if (p = s1+s2) printf("%s",p);
```

while making this

```
p = s1+s2;
printf("%s",p);
```

implementation-dependent.

How should branching within an expression be handled? For example, should this be guaranteed to work?:

```
if ((p=s1+s2) && p[0]) {
    // ...
}
```

The answer is yes. It is much easier to explain this answer than to explain special rules for `&&`, `||`, and `?:`. There was some opposition to this, though, because this rule cannot be implemented in general without introducing flags to ensure that temporary objects are destroyed only if they appeared on a branch actually taken. However, the compiler writers on the committee rose to the challenge and demonstrated that the overhead imposed was vanishingly small and basically irrelevant.

Thus, EOS came to mean ''end of full expression,'' where a full expression is an expression that is not a sub-expression of another expression.

Note that the resolution to destroy temporaries at the end of full expression will break some Cfront code, but it will not break any code guaranteed to work by the ARM. The resolution addresses the desire for a well-defined and easy-to-explain point of destruction. It also satisfies the desire not to have temporaries hanging around for too long. Objects that need to stay around for longer must be named. Alternatively, one can use techniques that don't require long-lived objects. For example:

```
void f(String s1, String s2)
{
    printf("%s",s1+s2);   // ok

    const char* p = s1+s2;
    printf("%s",p);   // won't work, temporary destroyed

    String s3 = s1+s2;
    printf("%s",(const char*)s3);   // ok

    cout << s3;   // ok

    cout << s1+s2;   // ok
}
```

6.4　Extensions

A critical issue was – and is – how to handle the constant stream of proposals for language changes and extensions. The focus of that effort is the extensions working group of which I'm chairman. It is much easier to accept a proposal than to reject it. You win friends that way, and people praise the language for having so many ''neat features.'' However, a language made as a shopping list of features without coherence will die, so there is no way we could accept even most of the features that would be of genuine help to some section of the C++ community.

At the Lund (Sweden) meeting this cautionary tale became popular:

''We often remind ourselves of the good ship Vasa. It was to be the pride of the Swedish navy and was built to be the biggest and most beautiful battleship ever. Unfortunately, to accommodate enough statues and guns, it underwent major redesigns and extension during construction. The result was that it only made it half way across Stockholm harbor before a gust of wind blew it over, and it sank killing about 50 people. It has been raised and you can now see it in a museum in Stockholm. It is a beauty to behold – far more beautiful at the time than its unextended first design and far more beautiful today than if it had suffered the usual fate of a 17th century battle ship – but that is no consolation to its designer, builders, and intended users [Stroustrup,1992b].''

But why consider extensions at all? After all, X3J16 is a standards group, not a language design group chartered to design ''C++++.'' Worse, a group of more than 250 people with its members changing over time isn't a promising forum for language design.

First of all, the group was mandated to deal with templates and exception handling. Even before the committee had time to work on those, suggestions for extensions and even for incompatible changes were being sent to committee members. The user community, even most users who didn't personally submit proposals, clearly expected the committee to consider these suggestions. If the committee takes such suggestions seriously, as it does, it provides a focus for discussion of C++'s future. If it does not, the activity will simply go elsewhere and incompatible extensions will appear.

Also, despite paying lip service to minimalism and stability, many people *like* new features. Language design is intrinsically interesting, the debates about new features are stimulating, and they provide a good excuse for new articles and releases. Some features might even help programmers, but for many that seems to be a secondary motivation. If ignored, these factors can disrupt progress. I prefer them to have a constructive outlet.

Thus, the committee has a choice between discussing extensions, discussing dialects after they have come into use, and ignoring reality. Every one of these alternatives have been chosen by various standards committees over the years. Most – including the Ada, C, Cobol, Fortran, Modula-2, and Pascal-2 committees – have chosen to consider extensions.

My personal opinion is that extension activity of various sorts is inevitable, and it is better to have it out in the open and conducted in a semi-civilized manner in a public forum under somewhat formal rules. The alternative is a scramble to get ideas accepted through the mechanism of attracting users in the marketplace. That mechanism isn't conducive to calm deliberation, open discussion, and attempts to serve *all* users. The result would be the language fracturing into dialects.

I consider the obvious dangers inherent in dealing with extensions preferable to the certain chaos that would result from not dealing with them. A slowly eroding majority of the committee has agreed, and we are approaching the point where extensions work as conducted until now must cease because standards documents will start appearing, and all activity must be directed towards responding to comments on those.

Only time will tell where the energy thus left without an outlet will go to. Some will go to other languages, some will go into experimental work, some will go into library building (the traditional C++ alternative to language changes). It is interesting to note that standards groups, like all other organizations, find it hard to disband themselves. Often, a standards group reconstitutes itself as a forum for revisions or as the bureaucratic mechanism for the creation of a next-level standard, that is, as a design committee for a new language or dialect. The Algol, Fortran, and Pascal committees, and even the ANSI C committee, provide examples of this phenomenon. Usually, the redirection of effort from standardizing an established language to the design of a would-be successor is accompanied by a major change in personnel and also of ideals.

In the meantime, I try to guard against the dangers of design by committee by spending significant time on every proposed extension. This strategy isn't foolproof, but it does provide a degree of protection against the acceptance of mutually inconsistent features and against the loss of a coherent view of the language.

The danger of design by committee is the danger of losing a coherent view of what the language is and ought to evolve into in favor of political deals over individual features and resolutions.

A committee can easily fall into the trap of approving a feature just because someone insists that it is essential. It is always easier to argue for a feature than to argue that the advantage of the feature – which will be very plausible in all interesting cases – is outweighed by nebulous concerns of coherence, simplicity, stability, difficulties of transition, etc. Also, the way language committees work does not seem to lend itself well to arguments based on experimentation and experience-based reasoning. I'm not quite sure why this is, but maybe the committee format and resolution by voting favor arguments that are more easily digested by exhausted members. It also appears that logical arguments (and sometimes even illogical arguments) are more persuasive than reports on other people's experience and experiments.

Thus, "standardization" can become a force for instability. The results of such instability can be a change for the better, but there is always the danger that it might become random change or change for the worse. To avoid this, standardization has to be done at the right stage of a language's evolution: after its path of evolution has been clearly outlined and before divergent dialects supported by powerful commercial interests has emerged. I hope this is the case for C++, and that the committee will continue to show the necessary restraint in innovation.

It is worth remembering that people will manage even without extensions. Proponents of language features tend to forget that it is quite feasible to build good software without fancy language support. No individual language feature is *necessary* for good software design, not even the ones we would hate to be without. Good software can be and often is written in C or in a small subset of C++. The benefits of language features are the convenience of expressing ideas, the time needed to get a program right, the clarity of the resulting code, and the maintainability of the resulting code. It is not an absolute either/or. More *good* code has been written in languages denounced as "bad" than in languages proclaimed "wonderful" – much more.

6.4.1 Criteria

To help people understand what was involved in proposing an extension or a change to C++, the extensions working group formulated a set of questions that is likely to be asked about every proposed feature [Stroustrup,1992b]:

"The list presents criteria that have been used to evaluate features for C++.

[1] Is it precise? (Can we understand what you are suggesting?) Make a clear, precise statement of the change as it affects the current draft of the language reference standard.

[a] What changes to the grammar are needed?

[b] What changes to the description of the language semantics are needed?

[c] Does it fit with the rest of the language?

[2] What is the rationale for the extension? (Why do *you* want it, and why would *we* also want it?)

[a] Why is the extension needed?

[b] Who is the audience for the change?

[c] Is this a general-purpose change?

[d] Does it affect one group of C++ language users more than others?

[e] Is it implementable on all reasonable hardware and systems?

[f] Is it useful on all reasonable hardware and systems?

[g] What kinds of programming and design styles does it support?

[h] What kinds of programming and design styles does it prevent?

[i] What other languages (if any) provide such features?

[j] Does it ease the design, implementation, or use of libraries?

[3] Has it been implemented? (If so, has it been implemented in the exact form that you are suggesting; and if not, why can you assume that experience from "similar" implementations or other languages will carry over to the feature as proposed?)

[a] What effect does it have on a C++ implementation?

[x] on compiler organization?

[y] on run-time support?

[b] Was the implementation complete?

[c] Was the implementation used by anyone other than the implementer(s)?
[4] What difference does the feature have on code?
    [a] What does the code look like without the change?
    [b] What is the effect of not doing the change?
    [c] Does use of the new feature lead to demands for new support tools?
[5] What impact does the change have on efficiency and compatibility with C and existing C++?
    [a] How does the change affect run-time efficiency?
      [x] of code that uses the new feature?
      [y] of code that does not use the new feature?
    [b] How does the change affect compile and link times?
    [c] Does the change affect existing programs?
      [x] Must C++ code that does not use the feature be recompiled?
      [y] Does the change affect linkage to languages such as C and Fortran?
    [d] Does the change affect the degree of static or dynamic checking possible for C++ programs?
[6] How easy is the change to document and teach?
    [a] to novices?
    [b] to experts?
[7] What reasons could there be for *not* making the extension? There will be counter-arguments and part of our job is to find and evaluate them, so you can just as well save time by presenting a discussion.
    [a] Does it affect old code that does not use the construct?
    [b] Is it hard to learn?
    [c] Does it lead to demands for further extensions?
    [d] Does it lead to larger compilers?
    [e] Does it require extensive run-time support?
[8] Are there
    [a] Alternative ways of providing a feature to serve the need?
    [b] Alternative ways of using the syntax suggested?
    [c] Attractive generalizations of the suggested scheme?
Naturally, this list is not exhaustive. Please expand it to cover points relevant to your specific proposal and leave out points that are irrelevant.''
These questions are of course a collection of the kinds of questions practical language designers have always asked.

6.4.2 Status

So how is the committee doing? We won't really know until the standard appears because there is no way of knowing how new proposals will fare. This summary is based on the state of affairs after the November 1994 meeting in Valley Forge. Proposing extensions for C++ seems to be popular. For example:
- Extended (international) character sets (§6.5.3.2)
- Various template extensions (§15.3.1,§15.4 , §15.8.2)

- Garbage collection (§10.7)
- NCEG proposals (for example, §6.5.2)
- Discriminated unions
- User-defined operators (§11.6.2)
- Evolvable/indirect classes
- Enumerations with predefined ++, <<, etc., operators
- Overloading based on return type
- Composite Operators (§11.6.3)
- Keyword for the null pointer (NULL, nil, etc.) (§11.2.3)
- Pre- and post-conditions
- Improvements to the Cpp macros
- Rebinding of references
- Continuations
- Currying.

There is some hope of restraint and that accepted features will be properly integrated into the language. Only a few new features have been accepted so far:

- Exception handling (''mandated'') (§16)
- Templates (''mandated'') (§15)
- European character set representation of C++ (§6.5.3.1)
- Relaxing rule for return types for overriding functions (§13.7)
- Run-time type identification (§14.2)
- Declarations in conditions (§3.11.5.2)
- Overloading based on enumerations (§11.7.1)
- User-defined allocation and deallocation operators for arrays (§10.3)
- Forward declaration of nested classes (§13.5)
- Namespaces (§17)
- Mutable (§13.3.3)
- Boolean type (§11.7.2)
- A new syntax for type conversion (§14.3)
- An explicit template instantiation operator (§15.10.4)
- Explicit template arguments in template function calls (§15.6.2)
- Member templates (§15.9.3)
- Class templates as template arguments (§15.3.1)
- A const static member of integral type can be initialized by a *constant-expression* within a class declaration
- Explicit constructors (§3.6.1)
- Static checking of exception specifications (§16.9).

Exceptions and templates stand out among the extensions as being mandated by the original proposal and described in the ARM, and also by being a couple of orders of magnitudes more difficult to define and to implement than any of the other proposals.

To contrast, the committee has rejected many proposals. For examples:

- Several proposals for direct support for concurrency
- Renaming of inherited names (§12.8)
- Keyword arguments (§6.5.1)

- Several proposals for slight modifications of the data hiding rules
- Restricted pointers ("son of `noalias`") (§6.5.2)
- Exponentiation operator (§11.5.2)
- Automatically generated composite operators
- User-defined `operator.()` (§11.5.2)
- Nested functions
- Binary literals
- General initialization of members within a class declaration.

Please note that a rejection doesn't imply that the proposal was deemed bad or even useless. In fact, most proposals that reach the committee are technically sound and would help at least some subset of the C++ user community. The reason is that most ideas never make it through the initial scrutiny and effort to make it into a proposal.

6.4.3 Problems with Good Extensions

Even good extensions cause problems. Assume for a moment that we have an extension everybody likes so that no time is wasted discussing its validity. It will still divert implementer efforts from tasks that some people will consider more important. For example, an implementer may have a choice of implementing the new feature or implementing an optimization in the code generator. Often, the feature will win out because it is more visible to users.

An extension can be perfect when viewed in isolation, yet flawed from a wider perspective. Most work on an extension focuses on its integration into the language and its interactions with other language features. The difficulty of this kind of work and the time needed to do it well is invariably underestimated.

Any new feature makes existing implementations outdated. They don't handle the new feature. Thus, users will have to upgrade, live without the feature for a while, or manage two versions of a system (one for the latest implementations and one for the old one). This last option is typically the one library and tool builders must choose.

Teaching material will have to be updated to reflect the new feature – and maybe simultaneously reflect how the language used to be for the benefit of users that haven't yet upgraded.

These are the negative effects of a "perfect" extension. If a proposed extension is controversial, it will in addition soak up effort from the committee members and from the community at large. If the extension has incompatible aspects, these may have to be addressed when upgrading from an older implementation to a new one – sometimes even when the new feature isn't used. The classical example is the introduction of a new keyword. For example, this innocent looking function

```
void using(Table* namespace) { /* ... */ }
```

ceased to be legal when namespaces were introduced because `using` and `namespace` are new keywords. In my experience, though, the introduction of new keywords creates few technical problems, and those are easily fixed. Proposing a new keyword, on the other hand, never fails to cause a howl of outrage. The practical problems with new keywords can be minimized by choosing names that aren't too likely to clash with existing identifiers. For this reason, `using` was preferred to `use`, and `namespace` was chosen over `scope`. When, as an experiment, we introduced `using` and `namespace` into a local implementation without any announcement, nobody actually noticed their presence for two months.

In addition to the very real problems of getting a new feature accepted and into use, the mere discussion of extensions can have negative effects by creating an impression of instability in the minds of some users. Many users and would-be users do not understand that changes are carefully screened to minimize effects on existing code. Idealistic proponents of new features often find the constraints of stability and compatibility with both C and existing C++ hard to accept and rarely do much to allay fears of instability. Also, enthusiastic proponents of "improvements" tend to overstate the weaknesses of the language to make their extensions look more attractive.

6.4.4 Coherence

I see the main challenge of extension proposals as maintaining the coherence of C++ and communicating a view of this coherence to the user community. Features accepted into C++ must work in combination, must support each other, must compensate for serious real problems in C++ as it stood without them, must fit syntactically and semantically into the language, and must support a manageable style of programming. A programming language cannot be just a set of neat features, and the primary effort involved in evaluating and developing extensions is to refine them so that they become an integral part of the language. For an extension that I consider seriously, I estimate that about 95% of my personal effort goes into finding a form of the original idea/proposal that can be smoothly integrated into C++. Typically, much of this effort involves working out a clear transition path for implementers and users. Even the best new feature must be rejected if there is no way users can adopt it without throwing away most of their old code and old tools. See Chapter 4 for a more extensive discussion of acceptance criteria.

6.5 Examples of Proposed Extensions

Generally in this book, I discuss a proposed language feature in the context of related features. A few, however, don't seem to fit anywhere, so I use them as examples here. Not surprisingly, the features that don't naturally fit anywhere have a tendency to get rejected. A feature, however reasonable when considered in isolation, should be considered with great suspicion unless it can be seen as part of a general effort to evolve the language in some definite direction.

6.5.1 Keyword Arguments

Roland Hartinger's proposal for keyword arguments, that is, for a mechanism for specifying function arguments by name in a call, was close to technically perfect. The reason the proposal was withdrawn rather than accepted is therefore particularly interesting. It was withdrawn because the extensions group reached a consensus that the proposal was close to redundant, would cause compatibility problems with existing C++ code, and would encourage programming styles that ought not to be encouraged. The discussion here reflects the discussions in the extensions working group. As usual, hundreds of relevant remarks must remain unmentioned for lack of space.

Consider an ugly, but unfortunately not unrealistic, example borrowed from an analysis paper written by Bruce Eckel:

```
class window {
    // ...
public:
    window(
        wintype=standard,
        int ul_corner_x=0,
        int ul_corner_y=0,
        int xsize=100,
        int ysize=100,
        color Color=black,
        border Border=single,
        color Border_color=blue,
        WSTATE window_state=open);
    // ...
};
```

If you want to define a default `window`, all is well. If you want to define a `window` that is "almost default," the specification can get tedious and error-prone. The proposal was simply to introduce a new operator, `:=`, to be used in calls to specify a value for a named argument. For example:

```
new window(Color:=green,ysize:=150);
```

would be equivalent to

```
new window(standard,0,0,100,150,green);
```

which, thanks to the default arguments, is equivalent to

```
new window(standard,0,0,100,150,green,single,blue,open);
```

This seems to be a useful bit of syntactic sugar that might make programs more readable and more robust. The proposal was implemented to be sure that all conceptual and integration problems were ironed out; no significant or difficult problems were found. In addition, the proposed mechanism was based on experience from other languages, such as Ada.

On the other hand, there is no doubt that we can live without keyword arguments; they do not provide any new fundamental facility, don't support a significant new programming paradigm, and don't close a hole in the type system. This leaves questions with answers that depend more on taste and impression of the state of the C++ user community:

[1] Will keyword arguments lead to better code?

[2] Will keyword arguments lead to confusion or teaching problems?

[3] Will keyword arguments cause compatibility problems?

[4] Should keyword arguments be one of the few extensions we can accept?

The first serious problem discovered with the proposal was that keyword arguments would introduce a new form of binding between a calling interface and an implementation:

[1] An argument must have the same name in a function declaration as in the function definition.

[2] Once a keyword argument is used, the name of that argument cannot be changed in the function definition without breaking user code.

Because of the cost of recompilation, many people are worried about any increase in the degree of binding between interfaces and implementations. Worse, this turned out to be a compatibility problem of significant magnitude. Some organizations recommend a style with ''long, informative'' argument names in header files, and ''short, convenient'' names in the definitions. For example:

```
void reverse(int* elements, int length_of_element_array);

// ...

void reverse(int* v, int n)
{
    // ...
}
```

Naturally, some people find that style abhorrent, whereas others (including me) find it quite reasonable. Apparently, significant amounts of such code exist. Further, an implication of keyword arguments would be that no name in a commonly distributed header file could be changed without risking breaking code. Different suppliers of header files for common services (for example, Posix or X) would also have to agree on argument names. This could easily become a bureaucratic nightmare.

Alternatively, the language shouldn't require declarations to have the same name for the same argument. That seemed viable to me. However, people didn't seem to like that variant either.

There could be a noticeable impact on link times if the rule that argument names must match across compilation units is checked. If it isn't checked, the facility would not be type safe and could become a source of subtle errors.

Both the potential linking cost and the very real binding problem could be easily avoided by omitting argument names in header files. A cautious user might therefore avoid specifying argument names in header files. Thus, to quote Bill Gibbons, ''The net impact on readability of C++ might actually be negative.''

My main worry about keyword arguments was actually that keyword arguments might slow the gradual transition from traditional programming techniques to data abstraction and object-oriented programming in C++. In code that I find best written and easiest to maintain, long argument lists are very rare. In fact, it is a common observation that a transition to a more object-oriented style leads to a significant decrease in the length of argument lists; what used to be arguments or global values become local state. Based on experience, I expect the average number of arguments to drop to less than two and that functions with more than two arguments will become rare. This implies that keyword arguments would be most useful in code we deemed poorly written. Would it be sensible to introduce a new feature that primarily supported programming styles that we would prefer to see decline? The consensus, based on this argument, the compatibility issues, and a few minor details, was no.

6.5.1.1 Alternatives to Keyword Arguments

Given that we don't have keyword arguments, how would I reduce the length of the argument list in the `window` example to something convenient? First of all, the apparent complexity is already reduced by the default arguments. Adding extra types to represent common variants is another common technique:

```
class colored_window : public window {
public:
    colored_window(color c=black)
        :window(standard,0,0,100,100,c) { }
};
```

```
class bordered_window : public window {
public:
    bordered_window(border b=single, color bc=blue)
        :window(standard,0,0,100,100,black,b,bc) { }
};
```

This technique has the advantage of channeling usage into a few common forms and can therefore be used to make code and behavior more regular. Another technique is to provide explicit operations for changing settings from the defaults:

```
class w_args {
    wintype wt;
    int ulcx, ulcy, xz, yz;
    color wc, bc;
    border b;
    WSTATE ws;
public:
    w_args()   // set defaults
      : wt(standard), ulcx(0), ulcy(0), xz(100), yz(100),
      wc(black), b(single), bc(blue), ws(open) { }
```

```
// override defaults:

w_args& ysize(int s) { yz=s; return *this; }
w_args& Color(color c) { wc=c; return *this; }
w_args& Border(border bb) { b = bb; return *this; }
w_args& Border_color(color c) { bc=c; return *this; }
// ...
};

class window {
    // ...
    window(w_args wa); // set options from wa
    // ...
};
```

From this, we get a notational convenience that is roughly equivalent to what key-word arguments provide:

```
window w; // default window
window w( w_args().Color(green).ysize(150) );
```

This technique has the significant advantage that it becomes easy to pass objects representing arguments around in a program.

Naturally, these techniques can be used in combination. The net effect of such techniques is to shorten argument lists and thereby decrease the need for keyword arguments.

A further reduction in the number of arguments could be obtained by using a Point type rather than expressing interfaces directly in terms of coordinates.

6.5.2 Restricted Pointers

A Fortran compiler is allowed to assume that if a function is given two arrays as arguments, then those arrays don't overlap. A C++ function is not allowed to assume that. The result is an advantage in speed for the Fortran routine of between 15% and 30 times dependent on the quality of the compiler and the machine architecture. The spectacular savings come from vectorizing operations for machines with special vector hardware such as Crays.

Given C's emphasis on efficiency, this was considered an affront and the ANSI C committee proposed to solve the problem by a mechanism called noalias to specify that a C pointer should be considered alias-free. Unfortunately, the proposal was late and so half-baked that it provoked Dennis Ritchie to his only intervention in the C standards process. He wrote a public letter stating, "noalias must go; this is non-negotiable."

After that, the C and C++ community was understandably reluctant to tackle aliasing problems, but the issue is of key importance to C users on Crays so Mike Holly from Cray grasped the nettle and presented an improved anti-aliasing proposal to the Numerical C Extensions Group (NCEG) and to the C++ committee. The idea was to allow a programmer to state that a pointer should be considered alias-free by declaring it `restricted`. For example:

```
void* memcopy(void*restrict s1, const void* s2, size_t n);
```

Since `s1` is specified to have no alias, there is no need to declare `s2` `restricted`, also. The keyword `restrict` would syntactically apply to `*` in the same way that `const` and `volatile` do. This proposal would solve the C/Fortran efficiency discrepancy by selectively adopting the Fortran rule.

The C++ committee was naturally sympathetic to any proposal that improves efficiency and discussed the proposal at some length, but finally decided to reject it with hardly a dissenting voice. The key reasons for the rejection were:

[1] The extension is not safe. Declaring a pointer `restricted` allows the compiler to assume that the pointer has no aliases. However, a user wouldn't necessarily be aware of this, and the compiler can't ensure it. Because of the extensive use of pointers and references in C++, more errors are likely to arise from this source than Fortran experience might suggest.

[2] Alternatives to the extension have not been sufficiently explored. In many cases, alternatives such as an initial check for overlap combined with special code for non-overlapping arrays is an option. In other cases, direct calls to specialized math libraries, such as BLAS, can be used to tune vector operations for efficiency. Promising alternatives for optimization have yet to be explored. For example, global optimization of relatively small and stylized vector and matrix operations appears feasible and worthwhile for C++ compilers for high-performance machines.

[3] The extension is architecture-specific. High-performance numerical computation is a specialized field using specialized techniques and often specialized hardware. Because of this, it may be more appropriate to introduce a nonstandard architecture specific extension or pragma. Should the need for the utility of this kind of optimization prove useful beyond a narrow community using specialized machine architectures, the extension must be reevaluated.

One way of looking at this decision is as a reconfirmation of the idea that C++ supports abstraction through general mechanisms rather than specialized application areas through special-purpose mechanisms. I would certainly like to help the numerical computation community. The question is how? Following closely in Fortran's footsteps for the classical vector and matrix algorithms may not be the best approach. It would be nice if every kind of numeric software could be written in C++ without loss of efficiency, but unless something can be found that achieves this without compromising the C++ type system it may be preferable to rely on Fortran, assembler, or architecture-specific extensions.

6.5.3 Character Sets

C relies on the American variant of the international 7-bit character set ISO 646-1983 called ASCII (ANSI3.4-1968). This causes two problems:

[1] ASCII contains punctuation characters and operator symbols, such as] and {, that are not available in many national character sets.

[2] ASCII doesn't contain characters, such as Å and æ, used in languages other than English.

6.5.3.1 Restricted Character Sets

The ASCII (ANSI3.4-1968) special characters [,], {, }, |, and \ occupy character set positions designated as alphabetic by ISO. In most European national ISO-646 character sets, these positions are occupied by letters not found in the English alphabet. For example, the Danish national character set uses these values for the vowels Æ, Å, æ, å, ø, and Ø. No significant amount of text can be written in Danish without them. This leaves Danish programmers with the unpleasant choice of acquiring computer systems that handle full 8-bit character sets, such as ISO-8859/1/2, not using three vowels of their native language, or not using C++. Speakers of French, German, Spanish, Italian, etc., face the same alternatives. This has been a notable barrier to the use of C in Europe, especially in commercial settings (such as banking) where the use of 7-bit national character sets is pervasive in many countries.

For example, consider this innocent-looking ANSI C and C++ program:

```
int main(int argc, char* argv[])
{
    if (argc<1 || *argv[1]=='\0') return 0;
    printf("Hello, %s\n",argv[1]);
}
```

On a standard Danish terminal or printer this program will appear like this:

```
int main(int argc, char* argvÆÅ)
æ
    if (argc<1 øø *argvÆ1Å=='Ø0') return 0;
    printf("Hello, %sØn",argvÆ1Å);
å
```

It is amazing to realize that some people read and write this with ease. I don't think that is a skill anyone should have to acquire.

The ANSI C committee adopted a partial solution to this problem by defining a set of trigraphs that allows national characters to be expressed:

#	[	{	\	]	}	^	|	~
??=	??(	??<	??/	??)	??>	??'	??!	??-

This can be useful for interchange of programs, but doesn't make programs readable:

```
int main(int argc, char* arg??(??))
??<
    if (argc<1 ??!??! *argv??(1??)=='??/0') return 0;
    printf("Hello, %s??/n",argv??(1??));
??>
```

Naturally, the real solution to this problem is for C and C++ programmers to buy equipment that supports both their native language and the characters needed by C and C++ well. Unfortunately, this appears to be infeasible for some, and the introduction of new equipment can be a very slow process. To help programmers stuck with such equipment and thereby help C++, the C++ standards committee decided to provide a more readable alternative.

The following keywords and digraphs are provided as equivalents to operators containing national characters:

keywords		digraphs	
and	&&	<%	{
and_eq	&=	%>	}
bitand	&	<:	[
bitor	|	:>	]
compl	~	%:	#
not	!	%:%:	##
or	||		
or_eq	|=		
xor	^		
xor_eq	^=		
not_eq	!=		

I would have preferred `%%` for `#` and `<>` for `!=` but `%:` and `not_eq` were the best that the C and C++ committees could compromise on.

We can now write the example like this:

```
int main(int argc, char* argv<: :>)
<%
    if (argc<1 or *argv<:1:>=='??/0') return 0;
    printf("Hello, %s??/n",argv<:1:>);
%>
```

Note that trigraphs are still necessary for putting "missing" characters such as \ into strings and character constants.

The introduction of the digraphs and the new keywords was most controversial. A large number of people – mostly people with English as their native language and with a strong C background – saw no reason to complicate and corrupt C++ for the benefit of people who were "unwilling to buy decent equipment." I sympathize with that position because the digraphs and trigraphs are not pretty, and new keywords are always a source of incompatibilities. On the other hand, I have had to work on equipment that didn't support my native language, and I have seen people drop C as a possible programming language in favor of "a language that doesn't use funny characters." In support of this observation, the IBM representative reported that the absence of ! in the EBCDIC character set used on IBM mainframes causes frequent and repeated complaints. I found it interesting to note that even where extended character sets are available, systems administration issues sometimes force their disuse.

My guess is that for a transition period of maybe a decade, keywords, digraphs, and trigraphs is the least bad solution. My hope is that it will help C++ become accepted in areas that C failed to penetrate, and thus support programmers who have not been represented in the C and C++ culture.

6.5.3.2 Extended Character Sets

Support for a restricted character set representation for C++ is essentially backward-looking. A more interesting and difficult problem is how to support extended character sets; that is, how to take advantage of character sets with more characters than ASCII. There are two distinct problems:

[1] How to support manipulation of extended character sets?

[2] How to allow extended character sets in the source text of a C++ program?

The C standards committee approached the former problem by defining a type `wchar_t` to represent multi-byte characters. In addition, a multi-byte string type `wchar_t[]` and `printf`-family I/O for `wchar_t` were provided. C++ continues in this direction by making `wchar_t` a proper type (rather than merely a synonym for another type defined using `typedef` as it is in C), by providing a standard string of `wchar_t` class called `wstring`, and by supporting these types in stream I/O.

This supports only a single "wide character" type. If a programmer needs more types, say a Japanese character, a string of Japanese characters, a Hebrew character, or a string of Hebrew characters, there are at least two alternative approaches. One can map these characters into a common character set large enough to hold both, say, Unicode, and write code that handles that using `wchar_t`. Alternatively one can define classes for each kind of character and string, say, `Jchar`, `Jstring`, `Hchar`, and `Hstring`, and have these classes supply the correct behavior for each. Such classes ought to be generated from a common template. My experience is that either approach can work, but that any decision that touches internationalization and multiple character sets becomes controversial and emotional faster than any other kind of problem.

The question of if and how to allow extended character sets to be used in C++ program text is no less tricky. Naturally, I would like to use the Danish words for apple, tree, boat, and island in programs dealing with such concepts. Allowing æble, træ, båd, and ø in comments is not difficult, and comments in languages other than English are indeed not uncommon. Allowing extended character sets in identifiers is more problematic. In principle, I'd like to allow identifiers written in Danish, Japanese, and Korean in a C or C++ program. There are no serious technical problems in doing that. In fact, a local C compiler written by Ken Thompson allows all unicode characters with no special meaning in C in identifiers.

I worry about portability and comprehension, though. The technical portability problem can be handled. However, English has an important role as a common language for programmers, and I suspect that it would be unwise to abandon that without serious consideration. To most programmers, a systematic use of Hebrew, Chinese, Korean, etc., would be a significant barrier to comprehension. Even my native Danish could cause some headaches for the average English-speaking programmer.

The C++ committee hasn't made any decisions on this issue so far, but I suspect it will have to and that every possible resolution will be controversial.

7

Interest and Use

Some languages are designed to solve a problem;
others are designed to prove a point.
– Dennis M. Ritchie

C++ usage — compilers — conferences, books, and journals — tools and environments — ways of learning C++ — users and applications — commercial competition — alternatives to C++ — expectations and attitudes.

7.1 The Explosion in Interest and Use

C++ was designed to serve users. It was not an academic experiment to design the perfect programming language, nor was it a commercial product meant to enrich its developers. Thus, to fulfill its purpose C++ had to have users – and it has:

Date	Estimated number of C++ users
Oct 1979	1
Oct 1980	16
Oct 1981	38
Oct 1982	85
Oct 1983	??+2 (no Cpre count)
Oct 1984	??+50 (no Cpre count)
Oct 1985	500
Oct 1986	2,000
Oct 1987	4,000
Oct 1988	15,000
Oct 1989	50,000

| Oct 1990 | 150,000 |
| Oct 1991 | 400,000 |

In other words, the C++ user population on average doubled every seven and a half months during these twelve years. These are conservative figures. C++ users have never been easy to count. First, there are implementations such as GNU's G++ and Cfront shipped to universities for which no meaningful records can be kept. Second, many companies – both tools suppliers and end-users – consider the number of their users and the kind of work they do secret. However, I always had many friends, colleagues, contacts, and compiler suppliers who were willing to trust me with figures as long as I used them in a responsible manner. This enabled me to estimate the number of C++ users. These estimates were created by taking the number of users reported to me or estimated based on personal experience, rounding them all down, adding them, and then rounding down again. These numbers are the estimates made at the time and are not adjusted in any way. To support the claim that these figures are conservative, I can mention that Borland, the largest single C++ compiler supplier, publicly stated that it had shipped 500,000 compilers by October 1991. That figure is plausible and also credible because Borland is a public company.

The number of C++ users has now reached the point where I have no reasonable way of counting them. I don't think I could determine the current number of C++ users to the nearest 100,000. Public figures show that well over 1,000,000 C++ compilers had been sold by late 1992.

7.1.1 Lack of C++ Marketing

To me, the most surprising thing about these numbers is that early users were gained without the benefit of traditional marketing (§7.4). Instead, various forms of electronic communication played a crucial role in this. In the early years, most distribution and all support was done using email. Relatively early on, newsgroups dedicated to C++ were created by users. This intensive use of networks allowed a wide dissemination of information about the language, techniques, and the current state of tools. These days this is fairly ordinary, but in 1981 it was relatively new. I suspect C++ was the first major language to take this path.

Later, more conventional forms of communication and marketing arose. After AT&T released Cfront 1.0, some resellers, notably John Carolan's Glockenspiel in Ireland and their US distributor Oasys (later part of Green Hills), started some minimal advertising in 1986. When independently developed C++ compilers such as Oregon Software's C++ Compiler and Zortech's C++ Compiler appeared, C++ became a common sight in ads (from about 1988).

7.1.2 Conferences

In 1987, David Yost of USENIX, the UNIX Users' association, took the initiative to hold the first conference specifically devoted to C++. Because David wasn't quite sure if enough people were interested, the conference was called a ''workshop'' and

David told me privately that "if not enough people sign up, we have to cancel." He wouldn't tell me what "enough people" meant, but I suspect a number in the region of 30. David Yost selected Keith Gorlen from the National Institutes of Health as the program chairman and Keith contacted me and others, collected email addresses of interesting projects we had heard about and emailed calls for papers. In the end, 30 papers were accepted, and 214 people turned up in Santa Fe, NM in November 1987.

The Santa Fe conference set a good example for future conferences with a mix of papers on applications, programming and teaching techniques, ideas for improvements to the language, libraries, and implementation techniques. Notably for a USENIX conference, there were papers on C++ on the Apple Macintosh, OS/2, the Connection machine, and for implementing non-UNIX operating systems (for example, CLAM [Call,1987] and Choices [Campbell,1987]). The NIH library [Gorlen,1987] and the Interviews library [Linton,1987] also made their public debuts in Santa Fe. An early version of what became Cfront 2.0 was demonstrated and I gave the first public presentation of its features [Stroustrup,1987c]. The USENIX C++ conferences continue to be the primary technically and academically oriented C++ conference. The proceedings from these conferences are among the best readings about C++ and its use.

The Santa Fe conference was meant to be a workshop and because of the intensity of the discussions, it actually was a workshop despite the 200 participants. It was obvious, however, that at the next conference the experts would be drowned by the novices and by people trying to figure out what C++ was. That would make a deep and open technical discussion quite difficult to achieve; tutorial and commercial concerns would dominate. At the suggestion of Andrew Koenig, an "implementers workshop" was tagged on to the 1988 USENIX C++ conference in Denver. After the conference, a busload of conference speakers, C++ implementers, etc., set off from Denver to Estes Park for a day's animated discussion. In particular, the ideas of `static` member functions (§13.4) and `const` member functions (§13.3) were so positively accepted that I decided to make these features part of Cfront 2.0, which was still delayed due to internal AT&T politics (§3.3.4). At my urging, Mike Miller presented a paper [Miller,1988] that led to the first serious public discussion of exception handling in C++.

In addition to the USENIX C++ conferences, there are now many commercial and semi-commercial conferences devoted to C++, to C including C++, and to object-oriented programming including C++. In Europe, the Association of C and C++ Users (ACCU) also arranges conferences.

7.1.3 Journals and Books

By mid-1992 there were more than 100 books on C++ available in English alone and both translations and locally written books available in Chinese, Danish, French, German, Italian, Japanese, Russian, etc. Naturally, the quality varies enormously. I am pleased to find my books translated into ten languages so far.

The first journal devoted to C++, *The C++ Report*, started appearing in January

1989 with Rob Murray as its editor. A larger and glossier quarterly *The C++ Journal* appeared in the spring of 1991 with Livleen Singh as editor. In addition, there are several newsletters controlled by C++ tools suppliers, and many journals such as *Computer Language, The Journal of Object-Oriented Programming* (JOOP), *Dr. Dobbs Journal, The C Users' Journal,* and *.EXE* run regular columns or features on C++. Andrew Koenig's column in JOOP is particularly consistent in its quality and lack of hype. The set of publications that discuss C++-related issues and their editorial policies change relatively fast. My purpose in mentioning journals, conferences, compilers, tools, etc., is not to give an up-to-date "consumer survey," but to illustrate the breadth of the early C++ community.

Newsgroups and bulletin boards such as comp.lang.c++ on usenet and c.plus.plus on BIX also produced tens of thousands of messages over the years to the delight and despair of their readers. Keeping up with what is written about C++ is currently more than a full-time job.

7.1.4 Compilers

The Santa Fe conference (§7.1.2) marked the announcement of the second wave of C++ implementations. Steve Dewhurst described the architecture of a compiler he and others were building in AT&T's Summit facility. Mike Ball presented some ideas for what became the TauMetric C++ compiler (more often known as the Oregon Software C++ compiler) that he and Steve Clamage were writing in San Diego. Mike Tiemann gave a most animated and interesting presentation of how the GNU C++ compiler he was building would do just about everything and put all other C++ compiler writers out of business. The new AT&T C++ compiler never materialized; GNU C++ version 1.13 was first released in December 1987; and TauMetric C++ first shipped in January 1988.

Until June 1988, all C++ compilers on PCs were Cfront ports. Then Zortech started shipping their compiler developed by Walter Bright in Seattle. The appearance of the Zortech compiler made C++ "real" for many PC-oriented people for the first time. More conservative people reserved judgment until the Borland C++ compiler was released in May 1990 or even until Microsoft's C++ compiler emerged in March 1992. DEC released their first independently developed C++ compiler in February 1992, and IBM released their first independently developed C++ compiler in May 1992. There are now more than a dozen independently developed C++ compilers.

In addition to these compilers, Cfront ports seems to be everywhere. In particular, Sun, Hewlett-Packard, Centerline, ParcPlace, Glockenspiel, and Comeau Computing have shipped Cfront-based products on just about every platform.

7.1.5 Tools and Environments

C++ was designed to be a viable language in a tool-poor environment. This was partly a necessity because of the almost complete lack of resources in the early years and the relative poverty later on. It was also a conscious decision to allow simple implementations and, in particular, simple porting of implementations.

C++ programming environments that are a match for the environments routinely supplied with other object-oriented languages are now emerging. For example, ObjectWorks for C++ from ParcPlace is essentially a Smalltalk program development environment adapted for C++, and Centerline C++ (formerly Saber C++) is an interpreter-based C++ environment inspired by the Interlisp environment. This gives C++ programmers the option of using the more whizzy, more expensive, and often more productive environments that have previously only been available for other languages, as research toys, or both. An environment is a framework in which tools can cooperate. There is now a host of such environments for C++. Most C++ implementations on PCs are compilers embedded in a framework of editors, tools, file systems, standard libraries, etc. MacApp and the Mac MPW is the Apple Mac version of that, ET++ is a public domain version in the style of the MacApp. Lucid's Energize and Hewlett-Packard's Softbench are yet other examples.

Though sophisticated beyond what has been generally used for C, these environments are only primitive forerunners of much more advanced systems. A well-written C++ program is a vast reservoir of information waiting to be used. Current tools tend to focus on syntactic aspects of the language, on the run-time properties of an execution, and on a textual view of the program. To deliver the full benefits of the C++ language, a programming environment must understand and use the full type system and escape the simple files-and-characters view of the static program representation. It must also be able to associate run-time information with the static structure of a program in a coherent manner. Naturally, such an environment must also scale to handle the large programs (for example, 500,000 lines of C++) where tools are of the greatest importance.

Several such systems are under development. I'm personally deeply involved with one such project [Murray,1992] [Koenig,1992]. I think a caveat is in place, though. A programming environment can be used by a supplier to lock users into a closed world of features, libraries, tools, and work patterns that cannot be easily transferred to other systems. Thus a user can become overly dependent on a single supplier and deprived of the opportunity to use machine architectures, libraries, databases, etc., that that supplier is disinclined to support. One of my major aims for C++ was to give users a choice of a variety of systems; a program development environment can be designed to compromise that aim, but it doesn't have to [Stroustrup,1987d]:

"Care must be taken to ensure that program source can be cost-effectively transferred between different such environments."

In the same way as I see no hope for a single, grand, standard library, I see no hope for a single standard C++ software development environment [Stroustrup,1987d]:

"For C++ at least, there will always be several different development and execution environments, and there will be radical differences between such environments. It would be unrealistic to expect a common execution environment for, say, an Intel 80286 and a Cray XMP, and equally unrealistic to expect a common program development environment for an individual researcher and for a team of

200 programmers engaged in large-scale development. It is also clear, however, that many techniques can be used to enhance both kinds of environments and that one must strive to exploit commonality wherever it makes sense.''

A multiplicity of libraries, run-time environments, and development environments are essential to support the range of C++ applications. This view guided the design of C++ as early as 1987; in fact, it is older yet. Its roots are in the view of C++ as a general-purpose language (§1.1, §4.2).

7.2 Teaching and Learning C++

The growth and nature of C++ use have been strongly influenced by the way C++ is learned. It follows that it can be hard to understand C++ without some insight into the way it can be taught and learned. Aspects of C++'s rapid growth can be incomprehensible without such insight.

Thoughts about how C++ could be taught and used effectively by relative novices influenced the design of C++ from the earliest days. I did a lot of teaching – at least I did a lot of teaching for someone who is a researcher rather than a professional educator. My successes and failures in getting my ideas across and in seeing the real programs written by people I and others had taught strongly influenced the design of C++.

After a few years, an approach that emphasized concepts up front followed by an emphasis on the relationship between the concepts and the main language features emerged. Details of individual language features were left for people to learn if and when they needed to know them. Where that approach was found not to work, the language was modified to support it. The net effect was that the language grew to be a better tool for design.

The people I worked with and the people I taught tended to be professional programmers and designers who needed to learn on the job rather than taking weeks or months out of their lives to learn the new techniques. From this came much of the desire to design C++ so that it can be learned and its features adopted gradually. C++ is organized such that you can learn its concepts in a roughly linear order and gain practical benefits along the way. Importantly, you can gain benefits roughly in proportion to the effort expended.

I think the practical concern underlying many discussions about programming languages, language features, styles of programming, etc., has more to do with education than with programming language features as such. For many, the key question is:

> Given that I don't have much time to learn new techniques
> and concepts, how do I start using C++ effectively?

If the answer for some other language is more satisfactory than for C++, that language will often be chosen because at this stage programmers usually have a choice (as they ought to have). In early 1993, I answered the question on comp.lang.c++ like this:

"It is clear that to use C++ "best" in an arbitrary situation you need a deep understanding of many concepts and techniques, but that can only be achieved through years of study and experiment. It is little help to tell a novice (a novice with C++, typically not a novice with programming in general), first to gain a thorough understanding of C, Smalltalk, CLOS, Pascal, ML, Eiffel, assembler, capability-based systems, OODBMSs, program verification techniques, etc., and then apply the lessons learned to C++ on his or her next project. All of those topics are worthy of study and would - in the long run - help, but practical programmers (and students) cannot take years off from whatever they are doing for a comprehensive study of programming languages and techniques.

On the other hand, most novices understand that ''a little knowledge is a dangerous thing'' and would like some assurance that the little they can afford time to learn before/while starting their next project will be of help and not a distraction or a hindrance to the success of that project. They would also like to be confident that the little new they can absorb immediately can be part of a path that can lead to the more comprehensive understanding actually desired rather than an isolated skill leading nowhere further.

Naturally, more than one approach can fulfill these criteria and exactly which to choose depends on the individual's background, immediate needs, and the time available. I think many educators, trainers, and posters to the net underestimate the importance of this: after all, it appears so much more cost effective - and easier - to ''educate'' people in large batches rather than bothering with individuals.

Consider a few common questions:

> I don't know C or C++, should I learn C first?
> I want to do OOP, should I learn Smalltalk before C++?
> Should I start using C++ as an OOPL or as a better C?
> How long does it take to learn C++?

I don't claim to have the only answers to these questions. As I said, the ''right'' answer depends on the circumstances. Most C++ textbook writers, teachers, and programmers have their own answers. My answers are based on years of programming in C++ and other languages, teaching short C++ design and programming courses (mainly to professional programmers), consulting about the introduction of and use of C++, discussing C++, and generally thinking about programming, design, and C++.

I don't know C or C++, should I learn C first? No. Learn C++ first. The C subset of C++ is easier to learn for C/C++ novices and easier to use than C itself. The reason is that C++ provides better guarantees than C (through stronger type checking). In addition, C++ provides many minor features, such as operator new, that are notationally more convenient and less error-prone than their C alternatives. Thus, if you plan to learn C and C++ (or just C++), you shouldn't take the detour through C. To use C well, you need to know tricks and techniques that aren't anywhere near as important or common in C++ as they are in C. Good C textbooks tend (reasonably enough) to emphasize the techniques that you will need for completing major projects in C. Good C++ textbooks, on the other hand, emphasize techniques and features that lead to the use of C++ for data abstraction and object-oriented programming. Knowing the C++ constructs, their (lower-level) C alternatives are trivially learned (if necessary).

To show my inclinations: to learn C, use [Kernighan,1988] as the primary text-book; to learn C++, use [2nd]. Both books have the advantage of combining a tutorial presentation of language features and techniques with a complete refer-ence manual. Both describe their respective languages rather than particular implementations and neither attempts to describe particular libraries shipped with particular implementations.

There are many other good textbooks and many other styles of presentation, but these are my favorites for comprehension of concepts and styles. It is always wise to look carefully at at least two sources of information to compensate for bias and possible shortcomings.

I want to do OOP, should I learn Smalltalk before C++? No. If you plan to use C++, learn C++. Languages such as C++, Smalltalk, Simula, CLOS, Eiffel, etc., each have their own view of the key notions of abstraction and inheritance and each supports them in slightly different ways to support different notions of design. Learning Smalltalk will certainly teach you valuable lessons, but it will not teach you how to write programs in C++. In fact, unless you have the time to learn and digest both the Smalltalk and the C++ concepts and techniques, using Smalltalk as a learning tool can lead to poor C++ designs.

Naturally, learning both C++ and Smalltalk so that you can draw from a wider field of experience and examples is the ideal, but people who haven't taken the time to digest all the new ideas often end up ''writing Smalltalk in C++,'' that is, applying Smalltalk design notions that don't fit well in C++. This can be as sub-optimal as writing C or Fortran in C++.

One reason often given for learning Smalltalk is that it is ''pure'' and thus forces people to think and program ''object-oriented.'' I will not go into the dis-cussion of ''purity'' beyond mentioning that I think that a general-purpose pro-gramming language ought to and can support more than one programming style (paradigm).

The point here is that styles that are appropriate and well supported in Smalltalk are not necessarily appropriate for C++. In particular, a slavish follow-ing of Smalltalk style in C++ leads to inefficient, ugly, and hard-to-maintain C++ programs. The reason is that good C++ requires design that takes advantage of C++'s static type system rather than fights it. Smalltalk supports a dynamic type system (only) and that view translated into C++ leads to extensive unsafe and ugly casting.

I consider most casts in C++ programs signs of poor design. Some casts are essential, but most aren't. In my experience, old-time C programmers using C++ and C++ programmers introduced to OOP through Smalltalk are among the heavi-est users of casts of the kind that could have been avoided by more careful design.

In addition, Smalltalk encourages people to see inheritance as the sole or at least the primary way of organizing programs and to organize classes into single-rooted hierarchies. In C++, classes are types and inheritance is by no means the only means of organizing programs. In particular, templates are the primary means for representing container classes.

I am also deeply suspicious of arguments proclaiming the need to *force* people to write in an object-oriented style. People who don't want to learn usually cannot be taught with reasonable effort. In my experience there is no shortage of people who *do* want to learn, and time and effort are better spent on those. Unless you manage to demonstrate the principle behind data abstraction and object-oriented programming, all you'll get is inappropriate ''baroque'' misuses of the language features that support these notions – in C++, Smalltalk, or any other language.

See *The C++ Programming (2nd Edition)* [2nd] and in particular Chapter 12 for a more thorough discussion of the relationship between C++ language features and design.

Should I start using C++ as an OOPL or as a better C? That depends. Why do you want to start using C++? The answer to that question ought to determine the way you approach C++, not some one-size-fits-all philosophy. In my experience, the safest bet is to learn C++ bottom-up, that is, first learn the features C++ provides for traditional procedural programming, the better-C subset, then learn to use and appreciate the data abstraction features, and then learn to use class hierarchies to organize sets of related classes.

It is – in my opinion – dangerous to rush through the earlier stages because there is too high a probability of missing some key point.

For example, an experienced C programmer might consider the better-C subset of C ''well-known'' and skip the 100 pages or so of a textbook that describes it. However, in doing so the C programmer might miss the ability to overload functions, the difference between initialization and assignment, the use of operator new for allocation, the explanation of references, or some other minor feature in such a way that it will come back to haunt at a later stage where sufficient new concepts are in play to complicate matters. If the concepts used in the better-C subset are known the 100 pages will only take a couple of hours to read and some details will be interesting and useful. If not, the time spent is essential.

Some people have expressed fear that this ''gradual approach'' leads people to write in C-style forever. This is of course a possible outcome, but nowhere as likely as proponents of ''pure'' languages and proponents of the use of force in teaching programming like to believe. The key thing to realize is that using C++ well as a data abstraction and/or object-oriented language requires the understanding of a few new concepts that have no direct counterpart in languages such as C and Pascal.

C++ isn't just a new syntax for expressing the same old ideas - at least not for most programmers. This implies a need for education, rather than mere training. New concepts have to be learned and mastered through practice. Old and well-tried habits of work have to be reevaluated. Rather than dashing off and doing things ''the good old way'' one must consider new ways - often doing things a new way will be harder and more time-consuming than the old way when tried for the first time.

The overwhelming experience is that taking the time and making the effort to learn the key data abstraction and object-oriented techniques is worthwhile for almost all programmers and yields benefits not just in the very long run but also within three to twelve months. There are benefits in using C++ without making this effort, but most benefits require the extra effort to learn new concepts – I wonder why anyone not willing to make that effort would switch to C++.

When approaching C++ for the first time or for the first time after some time, take the time to read a good textbook or a few well-chosen articles (*The C++ Report* and *The C++ Journal* contain many). You may also want to look at the definition or the source code of some major library and consider the techniques and concepts used. This is also a good idea for people who have used C++ for some time. Many could do with a review of the concepts and techniques. Much has happened to C++ and its associated programming and design techniques since C++ first appeared. A quick comparison of the first and the second edition of *The C++ Programming Language* should convince anyone of that.

How long does it take to learn C++? Again, that depends. It depends both on your experience and on what you mean by "learning C++." The syntax and basics for writing C++ in the better-C style plus defining and using a few simple classes takes a week or two for most programmers. That's the easy part. The main difficulty, and the most fun and gain, comes from mastering new design and programming techniques. Most experienced programmers I have talked with quote times from a half year to one and a half years before becoming really comfortable with C++ and the key data abstraction and object-oriented techniques it supports. That assumes that they learn on the job and stay productive – usually by programming in a "less adventurous" style of C++ during that period. If you could devote full time to learning C++, you would be comfortable faster, but without actual application of the new ideas on real projects that degree of comfort could be misleading. Object-oriented programming and object-oriented design are essentially practical rather than theoretical disciplines. Unapplied or applied only to toy examples, these ideas can become dangerous "religions."

Note that learning C++ is then primarily learning programming and design techniques, not language details. Having worked through a good textbook I would suggest a book on design such as [Booch,1991], which has nice longish examples in five different languages (Ada, CLOS, C++, Smalltalk, and Object Pascal) and is therefore somewhat immune to the language bigotry that mars some design discussions†. The parts of the book I like best are the presentation of the design concepts and the example chapters.

Looking at design contrasts sharply with the approach of looking very carefully at the details of the definition of C++ - usually using the ARM which

---

† Booch's second edition [Booch,1993] uses C++ examples throughout.

contains much useful information, but no information about how to write C++ programs. A focus on details can be very distracting and lead to poor use of the language. You wouldn't try to learn a foreign language from a dictionary and grammar, would you?

When learning C++, it is essential to keep the key design notions in mind so that you don't get lost in the language-technical details. That done, learning and using C++ can be both fun and productive. A little C++ can lead to significant benefits compared to C; further efforts to understand data abstraction and object-oriented techniques yield further benefits.''

This view is biased by the current state of affairs in tools and libraries. Given a more protective environment (for example, including extensive default run-time checks) and a small well-defined foundation library, you can move to the more adventurous uses of C++ earlier. This would allow a greater shift of the focus from C++ language features to the design and programming techniques C++ supports.

It is important to divert interest from syntax and the minute language-technical details where some long-time programmers like to poke around. Often, such interest is indistinguishable from an unwillingness to learn new programming techniques.

Similarly, in every course and on every project there is someone who just cannot believe that C++ features can be affordable and therefore sticks to the familiar and trusted C subset for future work. Only some actual numbers on performance of individual C++ features and of systems written in C++ (for example, [Russo,1988] [Russo,1990] [Keffer,1992]) have any hope of overcoming strongly held opinions to the effect that facilities more convenient than C's must be unaffordable. Given the amount of hype and the number of unfulfilled promises in the languages and tools area people ought to be skeptical and demand evidence.

Every course and project also has someone who is convinced that efficiency doesn't matter and proceeds to design systems of a generality that implies visible delays on even the most up-to-date hardware. Unfortunately, such delays are rarely noticeable for the toy programs people write while learning C++, so the problems with that attitude tend to be postponed until real projects. I'm still looking for a simple, yet realistic, problem that'll bring a good workstation to its knees when solved in an overly general way. Such a problem would allow me to demonstrate the value of lean designs and thus counteract excess enthusiasm and wishful thinking in the way performance figures counteract excess caution and conservatism.

7.3 Users and Applications

My view of what C++ was used for and what else it might be applied to affected its evolution. The growth of C++ features is primarily a response to such real and imagined needs.

One aspect of C++ usage has repeatedly reasserted itself in my mind: a disproportionate number of C++ applications seemed to be odd in some way. This may of course simply reflect that unusual applications are more interesting to discuss, but I suspect a more fundamental reason. C++'s strength is in its flexibility, efficiency, and portability. This makes it a strong candidate for projects involving unusual hardware, unusual operating environments, or interfacing with several different languages. An example of such a project is a Wall Street system that needed to run on mainframes cooperating with COBOL code, on workstations cooperating with Fortran code, on PCs cooperating with C code, and on the network connecting all of them.

I think this reflects that C++ has been at the leading edge of industrial production code. In this, C++'s focus differs from languages with a bias towards experimental use – be it industrial or academic – or teaching. Naturally, C++ has been extensively used for experimental and exploratory work as well as for educational uses. However, its role in production code has typically been the deciding factor in design decisions.

7.3.1 Early Users

The early world of C with Classes and C++ was a small one characterized by a high degree of personal contacts that allowed a thorough exchange of ideas and a rapid response to problems. Thus, I could directly examine the problems of the users and respond with bug fixes to Cfront or the basic libraries and occasionally even with a language change. As mentioned in §2.14 and §3.3.4 these users where mainly, though not exclusively, researchers and developers at Bell Labs.

7.3.2 Later Users

Unfortunately, many users don't bother to document their experiences. Worse yet, many organizations treat experience data as state secrets. Consequently, much myth and misinformation – and in cases even disinformation – about programming languages and programming techniques compete with genuine data for the attention of programmers and managers. This leads to widespread replication of effort and repetition of known mistakes. The purpose of this section is to present a few areas in which C++ has been used and to encourage developers to document their efforts in a way that will benefit the C++ community as a whole. My hope is that this will give an impression of the breadth of use that has influenced the growth of C++. Each of the areas mentioned represents at least two people's efforts over two years. The largest project that I have seen documented consists of 5,000,000 lines of C++ developed and maintained by 200 people over seven years:

Animation, autonomous submersible, billing systems (telecom), bowling alley control, circuit routing (telecom), CAD/CAM, chemical engineering process simulations, car dealership management, CASE, compilers, control panel software, cyclotron simulation and data processing, database systems, debuggers, decision support systems, digital photography processing, digital signal processing, electronic mail, embroidery machine control, expert systems, factory automation, financial reporting, flight mission telemetry, foreign exchange dealing (banking), funds transfer (banking), genealogy search software, gas station pump control and billing, graphics, hardware description, hospital records management, industrial robot control, instruction set simulation, interactive multi-media, magnetohydrodynamics, medical imaging, medical monitoring, missile guidance, mortgage company management (banking), networking, network management and maintenance systems (telecom), network monitoring (telecom), operating systems (real-time, distributed, workstation, mainframe, "fully object-oriented"), programming environments, superannuation (insurance), shock-wave physics simulation, slaughterhouse management, SLR camera software, switching software, test tools, trading systems (banking), transaction processing, transmissions systems (telecom), transport system fleet management, user-interfaces, video games, and virtual reality.

7.4 Commercial Competition

Commercial competitors were largely ignored, and the C++ language was developed according to the original plan, its own internal logic, and the experience of its users. There was (and is) always much discussion among programmers, in the press, at conferences, and on the electronic bulletin boards about which language "is best" and which language "will win" in some sort of competition for users. Personally, I consider much of that debate to be misguided and uninformed, but that doesn't make the issues less real to a programmer, manager, or professor who has to choose a programming language for his or her next project. For good and bad, people debate programming languages with an almost religious fervor and often consider the choice of programming language the most important choice of a project or organization.

Ideally, people would choose the best language for each project and use many languages in the course of a year. In reality, most people don't have the time to learn a new language to the point where it is an effective tool often enough to build up expertise in many languages. Because of that, even evaluating a programming language for an individual programmer or organization becomes a challenging task that is only rarely done well – and even less often documented in a dispassionate way that would be useful to others. In addition, organizations (for good and bad reasons) find it extraordinarily hard to manage mixed-language software development. This problem is exacerbated by language designers and implementers who don't consider cooperation between code written in their language and other languages important.

To make matters worse, practical programmers need to evaluate a language as a tool rather than as simply an intellectual achievement. This implies looking at implementations, tools, various forms of performance, support organizations, libraries, educational support (books, journals, conferences, teachers, consultants), etc., both at their current state and their likely short-term development. Looking at the longer term is usually too hazardous because of the overpowering amount of commercial hype and wishful thinking.

In the early years, Modula-2 was by many considered a competitor to C++. However, until the commercial release of C++ in 1985, C++ could hardly be considered a competitor to any language, and by then Modula-2 seemed to me to have been largely outcompeted by C in the US. Later, it was popular to speculate about whether C++ or Objective C [Cox,1986] was to be *the* object-oriented C. Ada was often a possible choice for organizations who might use C++. In addition, Smalltalk [Goldberg,1983] and some object-oriented variant of Lisp [Kiczales,1992] would often be considered for applications that did not require hard-core systems work or maximum perfor-mance. Lately, some people have been comparing C++ with Eiffel [Meyer,1988] and Modula-3 [Nelson,1991] for some uses.

7.4.1 Traditional Languages

My personal view is different. The main competitor to C++ was C. The reason that C++ is the most widely used object-oriented language today is that it was and is the only language that can consistently match C on C's own turf – and at the same time offer significant improvements. C++ provides transition paths from C to styles of sys-tem design and implementation based on a more direct mapping between application-level concepts and language concepts (usually called *data abstraction* or *object-oriented programming*). Secondarily, many organizations that consider a new pro-gramming language have a tradition for the use of an in-house language (usually a Pascal variant) or Fortran. Except for serious scientific computation, these languages can be considered roughly equivalent to C when compared with C++.

I have a deep respect for the strengths of C that most language experts don't share. In my opinion, they are too blinded by C's obvious flaws to see its strengths (§2.7). My strategy for dealing with C is simple: Do everything C does, do it as well as C or better in every way and everywhere C does it; in addition, provide significant services to real programmers that C doesn't.

Fortran is harder to compete with. It has a dedicated following who – like a large fraction of C programmers – care little for programming languages or the finer points of computer science. They simply want to get their work done. That is often a rea-sonable attitude; their intellectual interests are focused elsewhere. Many Fortran com-pilers are excellent at generating efficient code for high-performance machines and that is often of crucial importance to Fortran users. The reason is partly Fortran's lax anti-aliasing rules, partly that inlining of key mathematical subroutines is the norm on the machines that really matter, and partly the amount of raw effort and talent expended on the compilers. C++ has occasionally managed to compete successfully against Fortran, but rarely head-on in the crucial areas of high-performance scientific and engineering computation. This will happen. C++ compilers are becoming more mature and more aggressive in areas such as inlining. Fortran's mature libraries are also being used directly from C++ programs.

C++ is increasingly being used for numerical and scientific work [Forslund,1990] [Budge,1992] [Barton,1994]. This has given rise to a number of extension proposals. Generally, these have been inspired by Fortran and haven't been too successful. This reflects a desire to focus on abstraction mechanisms rather than specific language fea-tures. My hope is that focusing on higher-level features and optimization techniques will in the long run serve the scientific and numeric community better than simple addition of low-level Fortran features. I see C++ as a language for scientific computation and would like to support such work better than what is currently provided. The real question is not "if?" but "how?"

7.4.2 Newer Languages

In the secondary competition between C++ and languages supporting abstraction mechanisms (that is, object-oriented programming languages and languages supporting data abstraction) C++ was during the early years (1984 to 1989) consistently the underdog as far as marketing was concerned. In particular, AT&T's marketing budget during that period was usually empty and AT&T's total spending on C++ advertising was about $3,000. Of that, $1,000 were spent to send a plain letter to UNIX licensees telling them that C++ existed and was for sale. It apparently had no effect. Another $2,000 was spent on a reception for the attendees at the very first C++ conference in Santa Fe in 1987. That didn't help C++ much either, but at least we enjoyed the party. At the first OOPSLA conference, the AT&T C++ people could afford only the smallest booth available. This booth was staffed by volunteers using a blackboard as an affordable alternative to computers and a sign-up sheet for copies of technical papers as an alternative to glossy handouts. We thought of making some C++ buttons, but couldn't find funds.

To this day, most of AT&T's visibility in the C++ arena relies on Bell Labs' traditional policy of encouraging developers and researchers to give talks, write papers, and attend conferences rather than on any deliberate policy to promote C++. Within AT&T, C++ was also a grass-roots movement without money or management clout. Naturally, coming from AT&T Bell Labs helps C++, but that help is earned the hard way by surviving in a large-company environment.

In competition with newer languages, C++'s fundamental strength is its ability to operate in a traditional environment (social and computer-wise), its run-time and space efficiency, the flexibility of its class concept, its low price, and its non-proprietary nature. Its weaknesses are some of the uglier parts inherited from C, its lack of spectacular new features (such as built-in database support), its lack of spectacular program development environments (only lately have the kind of environments that people take for granted with Smalltalk and Lisp become available for C++; see §7.1.5), its lack of standard libraries (only lately have major libraries become widely available for C++ – and they are not "standard;" see §8.4), and its lack of salesmen to balance the efforts of richer competitors. With C++'s recent dominance in the market the last factor has disappeared. Some C++ salesmen will undoubtedly embarrass the C++ community by emulating some of the sleazy tricks and unscrupulous practices that salesmen and admen have used to attempt to derail C++'s progress.

In competition with traditional languages, C++'s inheritance mechanism was a major plus. In competition with languages with inheritance, C++'s static type checking was a major plus. Of the languages mentioned, only Eiffel and Modula-3 combine the two in a way similar to C++. The revision of Ada, Ada9X, also provides inheritance.

C++ was designed to be a systems programming language and a language for applications that had a large systems-like component. This was the area my friends and I knew well. The decision not to compromise C++'s strengths in this area to broaden its appeal has been crucial in its success. Only time will tell if this has also compromised its ability to appeal to an even larger audience. I would not consider that a tragedy because I am not among those who think that a single language should be all things to all people. C++ already serves the community it was designed for well. However, I suspect that through the design of libraries, C++'s appeal will be very wide (§9.3).

7.4.3 Expectations and Attitudes

People often express surprise that AT&T allows others to implement C++. That shows ignorance of both law and AT&T's aims. Once the C++ reference manual [Stroustrup,1984] was published, nothing could prevent anyone from writing an implementation. Further, AT&T didn't just allow others to enter the growing market for C++ implementations, tools, education, etc., it welcomed and encouraged them. The fact that most people miss is simply that AT&T is a much larger consumer of programming products than it is a producer. Consequently, AT&T greatly benefits from the efforts of "competitors" in the C++ field.

No company language could succeed on the scale AT&T would like C++ to succeed. A proper implementation, tools, library, and education infrastructure is simply too costly for a single organization – however large – to afford. A company language would also tend to reflect company policy and politics, which could impede its ability to survive in a larger, more open, and freer world. In all, I suspect that any language that can survive both the internal strains of Bell Labs politics and the viciousness of the open market can't be all bad – even if it is unlikely to follow the dictates of academic fashion.

Naturally, faceless corporations don't just magically produce policies. Policy is formulated by people and agreement over policy is reached among people. The policy for C++ stemmed from ideas prevalent in Bell Lab's Computer Science Research Center and elsewhere in AT&T. I was active in formulating the ideas as they related to C++, but I would have had no chance of getting C++ made widely available had notions of generally available software not been widely accepted.

Obviously, not everybody agreed all of the time. I was told that one manager once had the obvious idea of keeping C++ secret as a "competitive advantage" for AT&T. He was dissuaded by another manager who added, "Anyway, the issue is moot because Bjarne has already shipped 700 copies of the reference manual out of the company." Those manuals were of course shipped with all proper permissions and at the encouragement of my management.

An important factor, both for and against C++, was the willingness of the C++ community to acknowledge C++'s many imperfections. This openness is reassuring to many who have become cynics from years of experience with the people and products of the software tools industry, but it is also infuriating to perfectionists and a fertile source for fair and not-so-fair criticism of C++. On balance, I think that tradition of throwing rocks at C++ within the C++ community has been a major advantage. It kept us honest, kept us busy improving the language and its tools, and kept the expectations of C++ users and would-be users realistic.

Some have expressed surprise that I discuss "commercial competition" without reference to specific language features, specific tools, release dates, marketing strategies, surveys, or commercial organizations. Partly, this is a result of being burned in language wars where proponents of various languages argue with religious fervor and by marketing campaigns where cynics rule. In both cases, intellectual honesty and facts are not at a premium and "debating" techniques I thought belonged only in fringe politics abound. Sadly, people often forget that there always will be a need for a variety of languages, for genuine niche languages, and for experimental languages. Praise for one language, say for C++, doesn't imply a criticism of all other languages.

More importantly, my discussion of language choices is based on a belief that individual language features and individual tools are of little importance in the greater picture and serve only as a focus for pseudo-scientific skirmishes. Some variant of the law of large numbers is in effect.

All of the languages mentioned here can do the easy part of a project; so can C. All of the languages mentioned here can do the easy parts of a project more elegantly than C. Often, that doesn't matter. What matters in the long run is whether all of a project can be done well in a language and whether all of the main projects that an organization – be it a company or a university department – encounters over a period of time can be handled well by that organization using that language.

The real competition is not a beauty contest between individual language features or even between complete language specifications, but a contest between user communities in all their aspects, all their diversity, and all their inventiveness. A well-organized user community united by a grand idea has a local advantage, but is in the longer run and in the larger picture at a severe disadvantage.

Elegance can be achieved at an unacceptable cost. The "elegant" language will eventually be discarded if the elegance is bought at the cost of restricting the application domain, at the expense of run-time or space efficiency, at the cost of restricting the range of systems a language can be used on, at the cost of techniques too alien for an organization to absorb, at the cost of dependence on a particular commercial organization, etc., The wide range of C++'s features, the diversity of its user community, and its ability to handle mundane details well is its real edge. The fact that C++ matches C in run-time efficiency rather than being two, three, or ten times slower also helps.

8

Libraries

Life can only be understood backwards,
but it must be lived forwards.
– Sø ren Kierkegaard

Library design tradeoffs — aims of library design — language support for
libraries — early C++ libraries — the stream I/O library — concurrency
support — foundation libraries — persistence and databases — numeric
libraries — specialized libraries — a standard C++ library.

8.1 Introduction

More often than people realize, designing a library is better than adding a language
feature. Classes can represent almost all the concepts we need. Libraries generally
can't help with syntax, but constructors and operator overloading occasionally come
in handy. Where needed, special semantics or exceptional performance can be implemented by coding functions in languages other than C++. An example is libraries that
provide high-performance vector operations through (inlined) operator functions that
expand into code tuned to vector-processing hardware.

Since no language can support every desirable feature and because even accepted
extensions take time to implement and deploy, people ought to always consider
libraries as a first choice. Designing libraries is more often than not the most constructive outlet for enthusiasm for new facilities. Only if the library route is genuinely
infeasible should the language extension route be followed.

8.2 C++ Library Design

A Fortran library is a collection of subroutines, a C library is a collection of functions
with some associated data structures, and a Smalltalk library is a hierarchy rooted
somewhere in the standard Smalltalk class hierarchy. What is a C++ library? Clearly,
a C++ library can be very much like a Fortran, C, or Smalltalk library. It might also
be a set of abstract types with several implementations (§13.2.2), a set of templates
(§15), or a hybrid. You can imagine further alternatives. The designer of a C++
library has several choices for the basic structure of a library and can even provide
more than one interface style for a single library. For example, a library organized as
a set of abstract types might be presented as a set of functions to a C program, and a
library organized as a hierarchy might be presented to clients as a set of handles.

   We are obviously faced with an opportunity, but can we manage the resulting
diversity? I think we can. The diversity reflects the diversity of needs in the C++
community. A library supporting high-performance scientific computation has different constraints from a library supporting interactive graphics, and both have different
needs from a library that supplies low-level data structures to builders of other
libraries.

   C++ evolved to enable this diversity of library architectures and some of the newer
C++ features are designed to ease the coexistence of libraries.

8.2.1 Library Design Tradeoffs

Early C++ libraries often show a tendency to mimic design styles found in other languages. For example, my original task library [Stroustrup,1980b] [Stroustrup,1987b]
– the very first C++ library – provided facilities similar to the Simula67 mechanisms
for simulation, the complex arithmetic library [Rose,1984] provided functions like
those found for floating point arithmetic in the C math library, and Keith Gorlen's
NIH library [Gorlen,1990] provides a C++ analog to the Smalltalk library. New
''early C++'' libraries still appear as programmers migrate from other languages and
produce libraries before they have fully absorbed C++ design techniques and appreciate the design tradeoffs possible in C++.

   What tradeoffs are there? When answering that question people often focus on
language features: Should I use inline functions? virtual functions? multiple inheri-
tance? single-rooted hierarchies? abstract classes? overloaded operators? That is the
wrong focus. These language features exist to support more fundamental tradeoffs:
Should the design
   – Emphasize run-time efficiency?
   – Minimize recompilation after a change?
   – Maximize portability across platforms?
   – Enable users to extend the basic library?
   – Allow use without source code available?
   – Blend in with existing notations and styles?
   – Be usable from code not written in C++?
   – Be usable by novices?

Given answers to these kinds of questions, the answers to the language-level questions will follow. Modern libraries often provide a variety of classes to allow users to make such tradeoffs. For example, a library may provide a very simple and efficient string class. In addition, it can also supply a higher-level string class with more facilities and more opportunities for user-modification of its behavior (§8.3).

8.2.2 Language Features and Library Building

The C++ class concept and type system is the primary focus for all C++ library design. Its strengths and weaknesses determine the shape of C++ libraries. My main recommendation to library builders and users is simple: Don't fight the type system. Against the basic mechanisms of a language, a user can win Pyrrhic victories only. Elegance, ease of use, and efficiency can only be achieved within the basic framework of a language. If that framework isn't viable for what you want to do, it is time to consider another programming language.

The basic structure of C++ encourages a strongly-typed style of programming. In C++, a class is a type. The rules of inheritance, the abstract class mechanism, and the template mechanism combine to encourage users to manipulate objects strictly in accordance with the interfaces they present to their users. To put it more crudely: Don't break the type system with casts. Casts are necessary for many low-level activities and occasionally for mapping from higher-level to lower-level interfaces, but a library that requires its end users to do extensive casting is imposing an undue and usually unnecessary burden on them. C's `printf` family of functions, `void*` pointers, unions, and other low-level features are best kept out of library interfaces because they imply holes in the library's type system.

8.2.3 Managing Library Diversity

You can't just take two libraries and expect them to work together. Many do, but in general quite a few concerns must be addressed for successful joint use. Some issues must be addressed by the programmer, some by the library builder, and a few fall to the language designer.

For years, C++ has been evolving towards a situation where the language provides sufficient facilities to cope with the basic problems that arise when a user tries to use two independently-designed libraries. To complement, library providers are beginning to consider multiple library use when they design libraries.

Namespaces address the basic problem of different libraries using the same name (§17.2). Exception handling provides the basis for a common model of error handling (§16). Templates (§15) provide a mechanism for defining containers and algorithms independent of individual types; such types can then be supplied by users or by other libraries. Constructors and destructors provide a common model for initialization and cleanup of objects (§2.11). Abstract classes provide a mechanism for defining interfaces independently of the classes they interface to (§13.2.2). Run-time type information provides a mechanism for recovering type information that was lost when an object was passed to a library and passed back with less specific type information (as a base class) (§14.2.1). Naturally, this is just one use of these language facilities, but viewing them as supports for composition of programs out of independently developed libraries can be enlightening.

Consider multiple inheritance (§12.1) in this light: Smalltalk-inspired libraries often rely on a single "universal" root class. If you have two of those you could be out of luck, but if the libraries were written for distinct application domains, the simplest form of multiple inheritance sometimes helps:

```
class GDB_root :
    public GraphicsObject,
    public DataBaseObject {};
```

A problem that cannot be solved that easily arises when the two "universal" base classes both provide some basic service. For example, both may provide a run-time type identification mechanism and an object I/O mechanism. Some such problems are best solved by factoring out the common facility into a standard library or a language feature. Others can be handled by providing functionality in the new common root. However, merging "universal" libraries will never be easy. The best solution is for library providers to realize that they don't own the whole world and never will, and that it is in their interest to design their libraries accordingly.

Memory management presents yet another set of problems for library designers in general and users of multiple libraries in particular (§10.7).

8.3 Early Libraries

The very first real code to be written in C with Classes was the task library [Stroustrup,1980b] (§8.3.2.1), which provides Simula-like concurrency for simulation. The first real programs were simulations of network traffic, circuit board layout, etc., using the task library. The task library is still heavily used today. The standard C library was available from C++ – without additional overhead or complication – from day one. So are all other C libraries. Classical data types such as character strings, range-checked arrays, dynamic arrays, and lists were among the examples used to design C++ and test its early implementations (§2.14).

The early work with container classes such as list and array was severely hampered by the lack of support for a way of expressing parameterized types (§9.2.3). In the absence of proper language support, we had to make do with macros. The best that can be said for the C preprocessor's macro facilities is that they allowed us to gain experience with parameterized types and support individual and small group use.

Much of the work on designing classes was done in cooperation with Jonathan Shopiro who in 1983 produced list and string classes that saw wide use within AT&T and are the basis for the classes currently found in the "Standard Components" library that was developed in Bell Labs and sold by USL. The design of these early libraries interacted directly with the design of the language and in particular with the design of the overloading mechanisms.

The key aim of these early string and list libraries was to provide relatively simple classes that could be used as building blocks in applications and in more ambitious libraries. Typically, the alternative was hand-written code using C and C++ language facilities directly, so efficiency in time and space was considered crucial. For this reason, there was a premium on self-contained classes rather than hierarchies, on the inlining of time-critical operations, and on classes that could be used in traditional programs without major redesign or retraining of programmers. In particular, no attempts were made to enable users to modify the operation of these classes by overriding virtual functions in derived classes. If a user wanted a more general and modifiable class, it could be written with the "standard" class as a building block. For example:

```
class String { // simple and efficient
    // ...
};

class My_string { // general and adaptable
    String rep;
    // ...
public:
    // ...
    virtual void append(const String&);
    virtual void append(const My_string&);
    // ...
};
```

8.3.1 The Stream I/O Library

C's `printf` family of functions is an effective and often convenient I/O mechanism. It is not, however, type-safe or extensible to user-defined types (classes and enumerations). Consequently, I started looking for a type-safe, terse, extensible, and efficient alternative to the `printf` family. Part of the inspiration came from the last page and a half of the Ada Rationale [Ichbiah,1979], which argues that you cannot have a terse and type-safe I/O library without special language features to support it. I took that as a challenge. The result was the stream I/O library that was first implemented in 1984 and presented in [Stroustrup,1985]. Soon after, Dave Presotto reimplemented the stream library to improve performance by bypassing the standard C I/O functions I had used in the initial implementation and using operating systems facilities directly. He did this without changing the stream interfaces; in fact, I only learned about the change from Dave after having used the new implementation for a morning or so.

To introduce stream I/O, this example was considered:

```
fprintf(stderr,"x = %s\n",x);
```

Because `fprintf()` relies on unchecked arguments that are handled according to the format string at run time this is not type safe and [Stroustrup,1985]

"had x been a user-defined type like `complex` there would have been no way of specifying the output format of x in the convenient way used for types "known to `printf()`'' (for example, `%s` and `%d`). The programmer would typically have defined a separate function for printing complex numbers and then written something like this:

```
fprintf(stderr,"x = ");
put_complex(stderr,x);
fprintf(stderr,"\n");
```

This is inelegant. It would have been a major annoyance in C++ programs that use many user-defined types to represent entities that are interesting/critical to an application.

Type-security and uniform treatment can be achieved by using a single overloaded function name for a set of output functions. For example:

```
put(stderr,"x = ");
put(stderr,x);
put(stderr,"\n");
```

The type of the argument determines which "put function" will be invoked for each argument. However, this is too verbose. The C++ solution, using an output stream for which `<<` has been defined as a "put to" operator, looks like this:

```
cerr << "x = " << x << "\n";
```

where `cerr` is the standard error output stream (equivalent to the C `stderr`). So, if `x` is an `int` with the value `123`, this statement would print

```
x = 123
```

followed by a newline onto the standard error output stream.

This style can be used as long as `x` is of a type for which operator `<<` is defined, and a user can trivially define operator `<<` for a new type. So, if `x` is of the user-defined type `complex` with the value `(1,2.4)`, the statement above will print

```
x = (1,2.4)
```

on `cerr`.

The stream I/O facility is implemented exclusively using language features available to every C++ programmer. Like C, C++ does not have any I/O facilities built into the language. The stream I/O facility is provided in a library and contains no extra-linguistic magic.''

The idea of providing an output operator rather than a named output function was suggested by Doug McIlroy by analogy with the I/O redirection operators in the UNIX shell (`>`, `>>`, `|`, etc.). This requires operators that return their left-hand operand for use by further operations:

''An `operator<<` function returns a reference to the `ostream` it was called for so that another `ostream` can be applied to it. For example:

```
cerr << "x = " << x;
```

where x is an int, will be interpreted as

```
(cerr.operator<<("x = ")).operator<<(x);
```

In particular, this implies that when several items are printed by a single output statement, they will be printed in the expected order: left to right.''

Had an ordinary, named function been chosen the user would have been forced to write code like that last example. Several operators were considered for input and output operations:

''The assignment operator was a candidate for both input and output, but it binds the wrong way. That is, cout=a=b would be interpreted as cout=(a=b), and most people seemed to prefer the input operator to be different from the output operator.

The operators < and > were tried, but the meanings ''less than'' and ''greater than'' were so firmly implanted in people's minds that the new I/O statements were for all practical purposes unreadable (this does not appear to be the case for << and >>). Apart from that, '<' is just above ',' on most keyboards and people were writing expressions like this:

```
cout < x , y , z;
```

It is not easy to give good error messages for this.''

Actually, now we could overload comma (§11.5.5) to give the desired meaning, but that was not possible in C++ as defined in 1984 and would require messy duplication of output operators.

The c in the names of the standard I/O streams cout, cin, etc., stands for *character*; they were designed for character-oriented I/O.

In connection with Release 2.0, Jerry Schwarz reimplemented and partially redesigned the streams library to serve a larger class of applications and to be more efficient for file I/O [Schwarz,1989]. A significant improvement was the use of Andrew Koenig's idea of manipulators [Koenig,1991] [Stroustrup,1991] to control formatting details such as the precision used for floating point output and the base of integers. For example:

```
int i = 1234;

cout << i << ' '               // decimal by default: 1234
     << hex << i << ' '        // hexadecimal: 4d2
     << oct << i << '\n';      // octal: 2322
```

Experience with streams was a major reason for the change to the basic type system and to the overloading rules to allow char values to be treated as characters rather than small integers the way they are in C (§11.2.1). For example:

```
char ch = 'b';
cout << 'a' << ch;
```

would in Release 1.0 output a string of digits reflecting the integer values of the characters a and b, whereas Release 2.0 outputs ab as one would expect.

The iostreams shipped with Release 2.0 of Cfront became the model for iostream implementations shipped by other suppliers and for the iostream library that is part of the upcoming standard (§8.5).

8.3.2 Concurrency Support

Concurrency support has always been a fertile source for libraries and extensions. One reason has been the firm conviction by pundits that multi-processor systems will soon be much more common. As far as I can judge, this has been the current wisdom for at least 20 years.

Multi-processor systems are becoming more common, but so are amazingly fast single-processors. This implies the need for at least two forms of concurrency: multi-threading within a single processor, and multi-processing with several processors. In addition, networking (both WAN and LAN) imposes its own demands and special-purpose architectures abound. Because of this diversity, I recommend parallelism be represented by libraries within C++ rather than as a general language feature. Such a feature, say something like Ada's tasks, would be inconvenient for almost all users.

It is possible to design concurrency support libraries that approach built-in concurrency support both in convenience and efficiency. By relying on libraries, you can support a variety of concurrency models, though, and thus serve the users that need those different models better than can be done by a single built-in concurrency model. I expect this will be the direction taken by most people and that the portability problems that arise when several concurrency-support libraries are used within the community can be dealt with by a thin layer of interface classes.

Examples of concurrency support libraries can be found in [Stroustrup,1980b], [Shopiro,1987], [Faust,1990], and [Parrington,1990]. Examples of language extensions supporting some form of concurrency are Concurrent C++ [Gehani,1988], Compositional C++ [Chandy,1993], and Micro C++ [Buhr,1992]. In addition, proprietary threads and lightweight process packages abound.

8.3.2.1 A Task Example

As an example of a concurrent program expressed using mechanisms presented through a library, let me show Eratosthenes' sieve for finding prime numbers using one task per prime number. The example uses the queues from the task library [Stroustrup,1980b] to carry integers to the filters defined as tasks:

```
#include <task.h>
#include <iostream.h>
```

```
class Int_message : public object {
    int i;
public:
    Int_message(int n) : i(n) {}
    int val() { return i; }
};
```

The task system queues carry messages of classes derived from class `object`. The
use of the name `object` proves that this is a very old library. In a modern program,
I would also have wrapped the queues in templates to provide type safety, but here I
retained the style of the early task library uses. Using the task library queues for car-
rying single integers is a bit overblown, but it is easy and the queues ensure proper
synchronizations of `put()`s and `get()`s from different tasks. The use of the queues
illustrates how information can be carried around in a simulation or in a system that
doesn't rely on shared memory.

```
class sieve : public task {
    qtail* dest;
public:
    sieve(int prime, qhead* source);
};
```

A class derived from `task` will run in parallel with other such tasks. The real work
is done in the task's constructors or in code called from those. In this example, each
sieve is a task. A sieve gets a number from an input queue and checks if that number
is divisible by the prime number represented by the sieve. If not, the sieve passes the
number along to the next sieve. If there isn't a next sieve, we have found a new prime
number and can create a new sieve to represent it:

```
sieve::sieve(int prime, qhead* source) : dest(0)
{
    cout << "prime\t" << prime << '\n';
    for(;;) {
        Int_message* p = (Int_message*) source->get();
        int n = p->val();
        if (n%prime) {
            if (dest) {
                dest->put(p);
                continue;
            }

            // prime found: make new sieve
            dest = new qtail;
            new sieve(n,dest->head());
        }
        delete p;
    }
}
```

A message is created on the free store and deleted by whichever sieve consumes that message. The tasks run under the control of a scheduler; that is, the task system differs from a pure co-routine system in which the transfer of control between co-routines is explicit.

To complete the program we need a `main()` to create the first sieve:

```
int main()
{
    int n = 2;
    qtail* q = new qtail;
    new sieve(n,q->head());   // make first sieve
    for(;;) {
        q->put(new Int_message(++n));
        thistask->delay(1);   // give sieves a chance to run
    }
}
```

This program will run until it has completely consumed some system resource. I have not bothered to program it to die gracefully. This is not an efficient way of calculating primes. It consumes one task and many task context switches per prime. This program could be run as a simulation using a single processor and address space shared between all tasks or as a genuine concurrent program using many processors. I tested it as a simulation with 10,000 primes/tasks on a DEC VAX. For an even more amazing variant of Eratosthenes' sieve in C++ see [Sethi,1989].

8.3.2.2 Locking

When dealing with concurrency, the concept of locking is often more fundamental than the concept of a task. If a programmer can say when exclusive access to some data is required, there often isn't a need to know exactly what a process, task, thread, etc., actually is. Some libraries take advantage of this observation by providing a standard interface to locking mechanisms. Porting the library to a new architecture involves implementing this interface correctly for whatever notion of concurrency is found there. For example:

```
class Lock {
    // ...
public:
    Lock(Real_lock&);   // grab lock
    ~Lock();            // release lock
};

void my_fct()
{
    Lock lck(q2lock); // grab lock associated with q2
    // use q2
}
```

Releasing the lock in the destructor simplifies code and makes it more reliable. In

particular, this style interacts nicely with exceptions (§16.5). Using this style of locking, key data structures and policies can be made independent of concurrency details.

8.4 Other Libraries

Here, I will present only a very short list of other libraries to indicate the diversity of
C++ libraries. Many more libraries exist and several new C++ libraries appear every
month. It seems that one form of the software-components industry that pundits have
promised for years – and bemoaned the lack of – has finally come into existence.

The libraries mentioned here are classified as ''other libraries'' because they did
not affect the development of C++ significantly. This is not a judgment on their technical merit or importance to users. In fact, a library builder can often serve users best
by being careful and conservative with the set of language features used. This is one
way of maximizing library portability.

8.4.1 Foundation Libraries

There are two almost orthogonal views of what constitutes a foundation library. What
has been called a *horizontal* foundation library provides a set of basic classes that supposedly helps every programmer in every application. Typically, the list of such
classes includes basic data structures such as dynamic and checked arrays, lists, associative arrays, AVL trees, etc., and also common utility classes such as strings, regular
expressions, date-and-time. Typically, a horizontal foundation library tries hard to be
portable across execution environments.

A *vertical* foundation library, on the other hand, aims at providing a complete set
of services for a given environment such as the X Window System, MS Windows,
MacApp, or a set of such environments. Vertical foundation libraries typically provide the basic classes found in a horizontal foundation library, but their emphasis is
on classes for exploiting key features of the chosen environment. To this end, classes
supporting interactive user-interfaces and graphics often dominate. Interfaces to specific databases can also be an integral part of such a library. Often, the classes of a
vertical library are welded into a common framework in such a way that it becomes
difficult to use part of the library in isolation.

My personal preference is to keep the horizontal and vertical aspects of a foundation library independent to maintain simplicity and choice. Other concerns, both technical and commercial, tug in the direction of integration.

The most significant early foundation libraries were Keith Gorlen's NIH class
library [Gorlen,1990], which provided a Smalltalk-like set of classes, and Mark
Linton's Interviews library [Linton,1987], which made using the X Window System
convenient from C++. GNU C++ (G++) comes with a library designed by Doug Lea
that is distinguished by effective use of abstract base classes [Lea,1993]. The USL
Standards Components [Carroll,1993] provide a set of efficient concrete types for data
structures and Unix support used mainly in industry. Rogue Wave sells a library
called Tools++, which originated in a set of foundation classes written by Thomas

Keffer and Bruce Eckel at the University of Washington starting in 1987 [Keffer,1993]. Glockenspiel has for years supplied libraries for various commercial uses [Dearle,1990]. Rational ships a C++ version of The Booch Components that was originally designed for and implemented in Ada by Grady Booch. Grady Booch and Mike Vilot designed and implemented the C++ version. The Ada version is 125,000 non-commented source lines compared to the C++ version's 10,000 lines – inheritance combined with templates can be a very powerful mechanism for organizing libraries without loss of performance or clarity [Booch,1993].

8.4.2 Persistence and Databases

Persistence is many different things to different people. Some just want an object-I/O package as provided by many libraries, others want a seamless migration of objects from file to main memory and back, others want versioning and transaction logging, and others will settle for nothing less than a distributed system with proper concurrency control and full support for schema migration. For that reason, I think that persistence must be provided by special libraries, non-standard extensions, and/or third-party products. I see no hope of standardizing persistence, but the C++ run-time type identification mechanism contains a few "hooks" deemed useful by people dealing with persistence (§14.2.5).

Both the NIH library and the GNU library provide basic object I/O mechanisms. POET is an example of a commercial C++ persistence library. There are about a dozen object-oriented databases intended for use with C++ and also implemented in C++. ObjectStore , ONTOS [Cattell,1991], and Versant are examples.

8.4.3 Numeric Libraries

Rogue Wave [Keffer,1992] and Dyad supply large sets of classes primarily aimed at scientific users. The basic aim of such libraries is to make nontrivial mathematics available in a form that is convenient and natural to experts in some scientific or engineering field. Here is an example using the RHALE++ library from Sandia National Labs which supports mathematical physics:

```
void Decompose(const double delt, SymTensor& V,
                      Tensor& R, const Tensor& L)
{
  Symtensor D = Sym(L);
  AntiTensor W = Anti(L);
  Vector z = Dual(V*D);
  Vector omega = Dual(W) - 2.0*Inverse(V-Tr(V)*One)*z;
  AntiTensor Omega = 0.5*Dual(omega);

  R = Inverse(One-0.5*delt*Omega) * (One+0.5*delt*Omega)*R;
  V += delt*Sym(L*V-V*Omega);
}
```

According to [Budge,1992], "This code is transparent and its underlying class libraries are versatile and easy to maintain. A physicist familiar with the polar decomposition algorithm can make immediate sense of this code fragment without the need for additional documentation.''

8.4.4 Specialized Libraries

The libraries mentioned above exist primarily to support some general form of programming. Libraries that support a specific application area are at least as important to users. For example, one can find public domain, commercial, and company libraries that support application areas such as hydrodynamics, molecular biology, communication network analysis, telephone operator consoles, etc. To many C++ programmers, such libraries are where the real value of C++ manifests itself in terms of easier programming, fewer programming errors, reduced maintenance, etc. End users tend never to hear of such libraries; they simply benefit.

Here is an example of a simulation of a circuit switched network [Eick,1991]:

```
#include <simlib.h>

int trunks[] = { /* ... */ };
double load[] = { /* ... */ };
class LBA : public Policy { /* ... */ };


main()
{
   Sim sim;                              // event scheduler

   sim.network(new Network(trunks));     // create the network
   sim.traffic(new Traffic(load,3.0));   // traffic matrix
   sim.policy(new LBA);                  // Lba routing policy

   sim.run(180);   // simulate 180 minutes

   cout<<sim;      // output results
}
```

The classes involved are either SIMLIB library classes or classes that the user has derived from SIMLIB to define the network, load, and policy for this particular analysis.

As in the physics example in the previous section, the code makes perfect sense if and only if you are an expert in the field. In this case, however, the field is so narrow that the library serves only people in a highly specialized application area.

Many specialized libraries, such as libraries that support graphics and visualization, are actually quite general, but this book is not the place to try to enumerate C++ libraries or even to try for a complete classification. The variety of C++ libraries is mind-boggling.

8.5 A Standard Library

Given the bewildering variety of C++ libraries, the question arises: ''Which libraries should be standard?'' That is, which libraries should be specified in the C++ standard as required for every C++ implementation?

First of all, the key libraries now in almost universal use must be standardized. This means that the exact interface between C++ and the C standard libraries must be specified and the iostreams library must be specified. In addition, the basic language support must be specified. That is, we must specify functions such as `::operator new(size_t)` and `set_new_handler()`, which support the `new` operator (§10.6), `terminate()` and `unexpected()`, which support exception handling (§16.9), and classes `type_info`, `bad_cast`, and `bad_typeid`, which support run-time type information (§14.2).

Next, the committee must see if it can respond to the common demand for ''more useful and standard classes,'' such as `string` without getting into a mess of design by committee and without competing with the C++ library industry. Any libraries beyond the C libraries and iostreams accepted by the committee must be in the nature of building blocks rather than more ambitious frameworks. The key role of a standard library is to ease communication between separately-developed, more ambitious libraries.

With this in mind, the committee has accepted a `string` class and a wide charac-ter `wstring` class and is trying to unify these into a general string of anything tem-plate. It also accepted an array class, `dynarray` [Stal,1993], a template class `bits<N>` for fixed-sized sets of bits, and a class `bitstring` for sets of bits for which the size can be changed. In addition, the committee has accepted complex number classes (grandchildren of my original `complex` class; see §3.3) and looked at vector classes intended to support numeric/scientific computation. Because the set of standard classes, their specifications, and even their names are still vigorously debated, I'll refrain from giving details and examples.

I would like to see list and associative array (map) templates in the standard library (§9.2.3). However, as with Release 1.0, these classes may be lost to the urgency of completing the core language in a timely fashion†.

---

† Here, I have the great pleasure of eating my words! The committee did raise to the occation and approved a splendid library of containers, iterators, and fundamental algorithms designed by Alex Stepanov. This li-brary, often called the STL, is an elegant, efficient, formally sound, and well-tested framework for contain-ers and their use (Alexander Stepanov and Meng Lee: *The Standard Template Library*, HP Labs Techinical Report HPL-94-34 (R. 1), August, 1994. Mike Vilot: , The C++ Report, October 94). Naturally, the STL includes map and list classes, and subsumes the `dynarray`, `bits`, and `bitstring` classes mentioned above. In addition, the committee approved vector classes to support numeric/scientific computation based on a proposal from Ken Budge from Sandia Labs.

9

Looking Ahead

You cannot bathe in the same river twice.
– Heraclitus

Did C++ succeed at what it was designed for? — is C++ a coherent language? — what should have been different? — what should have been added? — what was the biggest mistake? — is C++ only a bridge? — what is C++ good for? — what will make C++ much more effective?

9.1 Introduction

This chapter is more speculative and relies more on personal opinions and generalizations than I like; I much prefer to present completed work and experience. However, this chapter answers common questions and presents issues that invariably come up when the design of C++ is discussed. The chapter consists of three related parts:

- A retrospective trying to assess where C++ currently is relative to its aims and relative to where it might have been (§9.2).
- A look at probable future problems for software development and programming languages to see how C++ might address them and fit into a changed world (§9.3).
- A look at some areas where C++ and its use can be significantly improved to make C++ a better tool (§9.4).

Discussing future developments is always hazardous, but it is a necessary hazard: Language design must in part anticipate future problems.

9.2 Retrospective

It is often claimed that hindsight is an exact science. It is not. The claim is based on the false assumptions that we know all relevant facts about the past, that we know the current state of affairs, and that we have a suitably detached point of view from which to judge. Typically, none of these conditions hold. Thus, a retrospective on something as large, complex, and dynamic as a programming language in large-scale use is not just a statement of fact. Anyway, let me try to stand back and answer some hard questions:

[1] Did C++ succeed at what it was designed for?

[2] Is C++ a coherent language?

[3] What was the biggest mistake?

Naturally, the replies to these questions are related. My basic answers are ''yes,'' ''yes,'' and ''not shipping a larger library with Release 1.0.''

9.2.1 Did C++ succeed at what it was designed for?

''C++ is a general-purpose programming language designed to make programming more enjoyable for the serious programmer'' [Stroustrup,1986b]. In this goal, C++ clearly succeeded. More specifically, it succeeded by enabling reasonably educated and experienced programmers to write programs at a higher level of abstraction (''just like in Simula'') without loss of efficiency compared to C. It allowed this for applications that were simultaneously demanding in time, space, inherent complexity, and constraints from the execution environment.

More generally, C++ made object-oriented programming and data abstraction available to the community of software developers that until then had considered such techniques and the languages that supported them such as Smalltalk, Clu, Simula, Ada, OO Lisp dialects, etc., with disdain and even scorn: ''expensive toys unfit for real problems.'' C++ did three things to overcome this formidable barrier:

[1] C++ produced code with run-time and space characteristics that competed head-on with the perceived leader in that field: C. Anything that matches or beats C *must* be fast enough. Anything that doesn't, can and will – out of necessity or mere prejudice – be ignored. It produced such performance from code relying on data abstraction and object-oriented techniques as well as for traditionally organized code.

[2] C++ allowed such code to be integrated into conventional systems and to be produced on traditional systems. A conventional degree of portability was essential. So was the ability to coexist with existing code and with traditional tools, such as debuggers and editors.

[3] C++ allowed a gradual transition to these new programming techniques. It takes time to learn new techniques. Companies simply cannot afford to have significant numbers of programmers unproductive while they are learning. Nor can they afford projects that fail because programmers overenthusiastically misapply partially-mastered new ideas.

C++ made object-oriented programming and data abstraction cheap and accessible.

In succeeding, C++ didn't just help its own user community. It also provided a major impetus to languages that support different aspects of object-oriented programming and data abstraction. C++ isn't everything to all people and doesn't deliver on every promise ever made about some language or other. It wasn't meant to, and I didn't make extravagant promises. However, C++ did deliver on its own promises often enough to break down the wall of disbelief that stood in the way of all languages that allowed programmers to work at a higher level of abstraction. By doing so, C++ opened many doors for itself and also for languages whose supporters tend to see C++ as a competitor only. In addition, C++ helped users of other languages by providing a strong incentive to implementers to improve the performance and flexibility of those languages.

9.2.2 Is C++ a Coherent Language?

Basically, I am happy with the language, and quite a few users agree. There are many details I'd like to improve if I could. However, the fundamental concept of a statically-typed language relying on classes with virtual functions and providing facilities for low-level programming is sound. Also, the major features work together in a mutually supportive fashion.

9.2.2.1 What Should and Could Have Been Different?

What would be a better language than C++ for the things C++ is meant for? Consider the first-order decisions (§1.1, §2.3, §2.7):
   – Use of static type checking and Simula-like classes.
   – Clean separation between language and environment.
   – C source compatibility ("as close as possible").
   – C link and layout compatibility ("genuine local variables").
   – No reliance on garbage collection.
I still consider static type checking essential for good design and run-time efficiency. Were I to design a new language for the kind of work done in C++ today, I would again follow the Simula model of type checking and inheritance, *not* the Smalltalk or Lisp models. As I have said many times, "Had I wanted an imitation Smalltalk, I would have built a much better imitation. Smalltalk is the best Smalltalk around. If you want Smalltalk, use it" [Stroustrup,1990]. Having both static type checking and dynamic type identification (for example, in the form of virtual function calls) implies some difficult tradeoffs compared to languages with only static or only dynamic type checking. The static and dynamic type models cannot be identical, and there will therefore be some complexity and inelegance that could be avoided by supporting only one type model. However, I wouldn't want to write programs with only one model.

I also still consider a separation between the environment and the language essential. I do not want to use only one language, one set of tools, and one operating system. To offer a choice, separation is necessary. However, once the separation exists, one can provide different environments to suit different tastes and different requirements for supportiveness, resource consumption, and portability.

We never have a clean slate. It is not enough to provide something new; we must also make it possible for people to make a transition from old tools and ideas to new. Thus, if C hadn't been there for C++ to be almost compatible with, I would have chosen to be almost compatible with some other language. However, any compatibility requirements imply some ugliness. By building on C, C++ inherited some syntactic oddities, some rather messy conversion rules for built-in types, etc. These imperfections have been a continuing hassle, but the alternatives – significant incompatibilities with C in a C-based language or getting a language built completely from scratch into widespread use – would have been *much* more troublesome. In particular, the link and library compatibility with C has been essential. Link compatibility with C implies that C++ can link with most other languages because they provide a binding to code written in C.

Should a language have reference semantics for variables (that is, a name is really a pointer to an object allocated elsewhere), such as in Smalltalk or Modula-3, or true local variables, such as in C and Pascal? This question is critical. It relates to several issues such as coexistence with other languages, run-time efficiency, memory management, and the use of polymorphic types. Simula dodged the question by having references to class objects (only) and true local variables for objects of built-in types (only). I consider it an open issue whether a language can be designed that provides the benefits of both references and true local variables without ugliness. Given a choice between elegance and the benefits of having both references and true local variables, I'll take the two kinds of variables.

Should a new language support garbage collection directly, say, as Modula-3 does? If so, could C++ have met its goals had it provided garbage collection? Garbage collection is great when you can afford it. Therefore, the option of having garbage collection is clearly desirable. However, garbage collection can be costly in terms of run time, real-time response, and porting effort (exactly how costly is the topic of much confused debate). Therefore, being forced to pay for garbage collection at *all* times isn't a blessing. C++ allows *optional* garbage collection [2nd,pp466-468]. Several experiments with garbage-collecting C++ implementations are in progress. I expect to rely on garbage collection in some, but not all, of my C++ programs within a couple of years (§10.7). However, I am convinced (after reviewing the issue many times over the years) that had C++ depended on garbage collection, it would have been stillborn.

9.2.2.2 What Should Have Been Left Out?

Even [Stroustrup,1980] voiced concern that C with Classes might have become too large. I think "a smaller language" is number one on any wish list for C++, yet people deluge me and the standards committee with extension proposals. I see no major part of C++ that could be removed without leaving important techniques unsupported. Even if we could completely disregard compatibility issues, only a few simplifications of C++'s fundamental mechanisms would be possible. These would primarily be in the C subset of C++ – sometimes we forget that C itself is a rather large and complicated language.

The fundamental reason for the size of C++ is that it supports more than one way of writing programs, more than one programming paradigm. From one point of view, C++ is really three languages in one:

- – A C-like language (supporting low-level programming)
- – An Ada-like language (supporting abstract data type techniques)
- – A Simula-like language (supporting object-oriented programming)
- – What it takes to integrate those features into a coherent whole.

One can write programs in those styles in a language like C also, but C provides no direct support for data abstraction or object-oriented programming. C++, on the other hand, supports several alternatives directly.

There always is a design choice but in most languages the language designer has made the choice for you. For C++ I did not; the choice is yours. This flexibility is naturally distasteful to people who believe that there is exactly one right way of doing things. It can also scare beginners and teachers who feel that a good language is one that you can completely understand in a week. C++ is not such a language. It was designed to provide a toolset for professionals, and complaining that there are too many features is like the ''layman'' looking into an upholsterer's tool chest and exclaiming that there couldn't possibly be a need for all those little hammers.

Every language in nontrivial use grows to meet the needs of its user community. This invariably implies an increase of complexity. C++ is part of a trend towards greater language complexity to deal with the even greater complexity of the programming tasks attempted. If the complexity doesn't appear in the language itself, it appears in libraries or tools. Examples of languages/systems that have grown enormously compared to their simpler origins are Ada, Eiffel, Lisp (CLOS), and Smalltalk. Because of C++'s emphasis on static type checking, much of the increase in complexity has appeared in the form of language extensions.

C++ was designed for serious programmers and grew to serve them in the increasing large and complex tasks they face. The result can be overwhelming for newcomers, even experienced newcomers. I have tried to minimize the practical effects of C++'s size by making it possible to learn and use C++ in stages (§7.2). The traditional negative performance impact of a large language has also been minimized by avoiding ''distributed fat'' (§4.5).

9.2.2.3 What Should Have Been Added?

As ever, the principle is to add as little as possible. A letter published on behalf of the extensions working group of the C++ standards committee puts it this way [Stroustrup,1992b]:

"First, let us try to dissuade you from proposing an extension to the C++ language. C++ is already too large and complicated for our taste and there are millions of lines of C++ code ''out there'' that we endeavor not to break. All changes to the language must undergo tremendous consideration. Additions to it are undertaken with great trepidation. Wherever possible we prefer to see programming techniques and library functions used as alternatives to language extensions.

Many communities of programmers want to see their favorite language construct or library class propagated into C++. Unfortunately, adding useful features from diverse communities could turn C++ into a set of incoherent features. C++ is not perfect, but adding features could easily make it worse instead of better.''

So, given that, what features have caused trouble by their absence and which are under debate so that they might make it into C++ over the next few years? Basically, the features described in this book (including the ones in Part II such as templates, exceptions, namespaces, and run-time type identification) are enough features for me. I'd like optional garbage collection too, but I classify that as a quality of implementation issue rather than a language feature.

9.2.3 What Was The Biggest Mistake?

To my mind, there really is only one contender for the title of *Worst Mistake*. Release 1.0 and my first edition [Stroustrup,1986] should have been delayed until a larger library including some fundamental classes such as singly and doubly linked lists, an associative array class, a range-checked array class, and a simple string class could have been included. The absence of those led to everybody reinventing the wheel and to an unnecessary diversity in the most fundamental classes. It also led to a serious diversion of effort. In an attempt to build such fundamental classes themselves, far too many new programmers started dabbling with the ''advanced'' features necessary to construct good foundation classes before they had mastered the basics of C++. Also, much effort went into techniques and tools to deal with libraries inherently flawed by the lack of template support.

Could I have avoided that? In a sense, I obviously could have. The original plan for my book included three library chapters, one on the stream library, one on the container classes, and one on the task library. I knew roughly what I wanted. Unfortunately, I was too tired and couldn't do container classes without some form of templates. The idea of ''faking'' templates by a preprocessor or an incomplete compiler hack unfortunately didn't occur to me.

9.3 Only a Bridge?

I built C++ as a bridge over which people could pass from traditional programming to styles relying on data abstraction and object-oriented programming. Does C++ have a future beyond that? Is C++ *only* a bridge? Once across to a world where data abstraction and object-oriented programming are second nature, are the features provided by C++ valuable by themselves or does its inheritance from C become a fatal liability? Also, assuming a positive answer, can anything be done for C++ users who don't care about C compatibility without causing damage to the people who will continue to care for at least the next decade?

A language exists to help solve problems. If a language is initially successful, it

will survive as long as people face the kinds of problems it helps them to solve. In addition, it ought to thrive provided no other language provides significantly better solutions for that set of problems. Thus, the questions become
- Will the problems C++ helps solve remain real?
- Will significantly better solutions emerge?
- Will C++ provide good solutions for new problems?

My basic answers are "many will," "slowly," and "yes."

9.3.1 We Need the Bridge for a Long Time

It will take people a long time to reach the level of sophistication and maturity with object-oriented programming, object-oriented design, etc., that I envisioned. The migration to C++ will not be complete five years from now. C++'s role as a bridge and as a vehicle for hybrid design and development will outlast this century. Its role as a vehicle for maintenance and upgrading of old code will last longer still.

It is sobering to realize that in places the move from assembler to C isn't yet complete. In the same way, the move from C to C++ may last for a long time. However, in this lies part of C++'s strength. To those who really need some pure C style, those styles are readily available and efficient in C++. Supporting those styles – both during a transition and where they simply are the most appropriate style – is part of C++'s fundamental aims.

9.3.2 If C++ is the Answer, What is the Question?

There is no *one* such question. C++ is a general-purpose language – or at least a multi-purpose one. This implies that for every single specific question, you can construct a language or system that is a better answer than C++. C++'s strength comes from being a good answer to many questions rather than being the best answer to one specific question. For example, like C, C++ is an excellent language for low-level systems work and typically outperforms any other high-level language for this kind of work. However, for most machine architectures, a good assembly programmer can produce code that is significantly smaller and faster than a good C++ compiler can. Usually, this is not significant because the fraction of a complete system where that difference is important is small, and the system would be unaffordable and unmaintainable if written completely in assembler.

I find it hard to imagine an application area for which one couldn't construct a specialized language better than C++ – and better than any other general-purpose language. Thus, the most a general-purpose language can hope for is to be "everybody's second choice."

That said, I'll examine some areas where C++ has fundamental strengths:
- Low-level systems programming
- Higher-level systems programming
- Embedded code
- Numeric/scientific computing
- General application programming

These categories are not distinct, nor do they have universally agreed-upon definitions. C++ will remain a good choice in all of these areas; further, any language that is a good choice will look a lot like C++ at the level of the fundamental services offered – though probably not at the syntactic or detailed semantic level. These areas don't exhaust the kinds of applications in which C++ has been used with success, but they represent key problems that C++ must address to continue to prosper.

9.3.2.1 Low-level Systems Programming

C++ is the best language available for low-level programming. It combines C's strengths in this area with the ability to do simple data abstraction at no cost in runtime and space and to manage larger programs of this sort. No new language is going to be sufficiently better in this area to replace C++. Systems programming involving a low-level component will remain an area of strength for C++. In this area, C++ fills its role as a better C. For years, the only real competitor to C++ in this area will remain C, and here C++ is the better choice exactly because it *is* a better C. I expect low-level systems programming to slowly – only slowly – decrease in importance and remain a significant area of strength for C++. For this reason, care must be taken not to "improve" the C++ language or C++ implementations to the point where it is *only* a higher-level language.

9.3.2.2 Higher-level Systems Programming

The size and complexity of traditional systems programs are growing rapidly. Examples are operating system kernels, network managers, compilers, email systems, typesetting programs, picture and sound manipulation systems, communication systems, user interfaces, and database systems. Consequently, the traditional emphasis on low-level efficiency gives way to a concern about overall structure. Efficiency still matters, but it becomes secondary in that it is irrelevant unless the larger systems can be economically constructed and maintained.

C++'s facilities for data abstraction and object-oriented programming directly address this concern. Templates, namespaces, and exceptions will become increasingly important to C++ programmers working on these kinds of applications. Isolating necessary violations of the type system in low-level functions, subsystems, and libraries will also become more critical. This technique keeps the main application code type safe and therefore easier to maintain. I expect higher-level systems programming to continue to grow in importance for many years and to be an area of strength for C++.

Many other languages can also serve higher-level systems programming well. Examples are Ada9X, Eiffel, and Modula-3. Except for support for garbage collection and concurrency, these languages are roughly equivalent to C++ in the fundamental mechanisms they offer. Naturally, the quality of individual features and their integration into a language can be discussed forever. Most programmers will have strong preferences. However, if implementations of sufficient quality become available, each of these languages can support a wide variety of systems applications. Problems unrelated to programming language-technical details, such as management, design techniques, and programmer education, will dominate development. C++ tends to have an advantage in run-time efficiency, flexibility, availability, and user community that gives it a competitive edge.

For some larger systems applications, garbage collection is a major advantage; for others, it is a hindrance. Unless C++ implementations provide optional garbage collection, C++ will suffer a systematic disadvantage in some areas, but I'm confident that C++ implementations supporting optional garbage collection will become common.

9.3.2.3 Embedded Systems

One area of systems programming that deserves special mention is embedded code; that is, programs running on computerized devices such as cameras, cars, rockets, and telephone switches. I expect this kind of work to increase in importance and to consist of a mixture of low-level and higher-level systems programming for which C++ is most suitable. Different applications and different organizations will create a variety of demands that a specialized language will be hard-pressed to meet. Some designs will rely heavily on exceptions; others will ban them as being too unpredictable. Similarly, the requirements for memory management will range from ''no dynamic memory allowed'' to ''automatic garbage collection must be used.'' In addition, a variety of different concurrency models will be used. It is important that C++ is a language rather than a complete system. This allows C++ to fit into specialized systems and to produce code for specialized execution environments. Being able to run C++ in separate development environments and in simulators on stock hardware can be essential for a project. The fact that C++ programs can be put into ROM has also been important in the past. I have high expectations for C++ in the area of programming computerized gadgets of all sorts. In this area, C++ can again build on C's traditional strengths.

9.3.2.4 Numeric/Scientific Computing

Numeric/scientific computing is a relatively small area in terms of number of programmers, but it is a very interesting and important one. I see a drift towards advanced algorithms that favor languages capable of expressing a variety of data structures and using them efficiently. This increased emphasis on flexibility compensates for Fortran's advantage in basic vector computation. Importantly, C++ programs can call basic Fortran and assembler routines where necessary or simply convenient. The integration of numeric programs into larger applications creates demands that suit C++. For example, Fortran's advantages in low-level computation are minimized when the emphasis is on nonnumeric concerns such as visualization, simulation, database access, and real-time data gathering.

9.3.2.5 General Application Programming

C++ is not ideally suited for applications that do not have major systems-programming components and where the run-time and space efficiency requirements are not demanding. However, when supported by libraries and possibly by a garbage collector C++ often is a viable tool.

I expect specialized languages, program generators, and direct manipulation tools to dominate many such application areas. For example, why write program text to generate a user interface when you can have the code generated by a program given an example screen layout composed from a menu? Similarly, why write Fortran or C++ to do advanced math when you can use much higher-level specialized languages? In such cases, however, the higher-level language, tool, or generator needs to be implemented in some suitable language and will often need to generate code in some lower-level language to actually perform the actions. The requirements for an implementation language and a target language usually fit C++ very well so I predict a major role for C++ as the implementation language for higher-level languages and tools. These are other roles that C++ inherits from C. C++ details such as the ability to declare variables almost anywhere combine with major program organization features such as namespaces to make C++ even better suited as a target language than C.

Higher-level tools and languages tend to be specialized. Consequently, good ones provide facilities for users to extend and modify the default behavior by adding code written in a lower-level language. C++'s abstraction mechanisms can be used to smoothly fit C++ code into a framework provided by a higher-level tool.

9.3.2.6 Mixed Systems

C++'s most significant strength comes from its ability to function in systems and organizations that combine aspects of several of these kinds of applications. My conjecture is that most significant systems and organizations need such combinations. User interfaces often need graphics; specific applications often rely on specialized languages and program generators; simulators and analytical subsystems require computation; communications subsystems require extensive systems programming; most large systems rely on some database; special hardware requires low-level work. In all these areas – and others – C++ will be at least the second choice. Overall, it will be the first choice often enough to be considered a major language.

All languages die or mutate to meet new challenges. A language with a large and vigorous user community will mutate rather than die. This is what happened to C yielding C++ and that is what some day will happen to C++. C++ is a relatively young language, but it is worthwhile considering its strengths and weaknesses to build on the former and compensate for the latter.

C++ isn't perfect; it wasn't designed to be and neither is any other general-purpose language. However, C++ is good enough not to be replaced by a similar language. Only a fundamentally different language could provide significant enough benefits to make it clearly superior. Just being a better C++ will not be sufficient to cause a change. That is why C++ isn't just a better C: Had C++ not provided significant new ways of writing programs it wouldn't have been worthwhile for programmers to upgrade from C. That is why Pascal and Modula-2 failed as alternatives to C even though a solid section of the academic community was pushing these languages for years: they were not sufficiently different from C to be significantly better. Also, if something better but not radically different appears, a lively and diverse community will simply absorb the new ideas and features. The initial design of C++ and its evolution into the current language provides ample examples of this.

I don't see a fundamentally different language that in the near future could replace C++ across its application areas – just languages that provide essentially similar feature sets in different ways, niche languages, and experimental languages. I expect that some of these experimental languages will in time grow to provide significant improvements over what C++ is now and will evolve into over the next few years.

9.4 What Will Make C++ Much More Effective?

There is no room for complacency in the world of software development. Over the years, the growth of expectations has consistently outstripped even the fantastic improvements of both hardware and software, and I see no reason for this to change soon. Much can be done to make C++ implementations more helpful to their users, and much can be learned by programmers and designers to make themselves more effective. Here, I will hazard a few comments about what I think should be done to make C++ programming more effective.

9.4.1 Stability and Standards

Stability of the language definition and of key libraries and interfaces comes high on the list of requirements for further progress. The ANSI/ISO C++ standard should provide the former, and various organizations and companies are working on the latter in areas such as operating system interfaces, dynamically linked libraries, database interfaces, etc. I am looking forward to the day – not too far in the future – when C++ as described in this book is generally available on all major platforms. This will be of great help to the libraries and tools industry.

People will of course keep asking for new features, but I can live with C++ as described here. I conjecture that so can most programmers of production code. It is worth remembering that no single feature is essential for producing good code – for any definition of "good."

9.4.2 Education and Technique

Of all the areas of C++ and its use, I see the greatest potential for improvement from simply learning new design and programming techniques. In principle, the easiest and cheapest improvements can be had by using C++ more effectively. No expensive tools are necessary. On the other hand, changing habits of thinking isn't easy. For most programmers, what is needed is not simply training in a new syntax, but an education in new concepts. Have a look at §7.2 and read a textbook that touches upon design issues such as [2nd] or [Booch,1993]. I expect to see significant improvements in design and programming technique over the next few years, but that is no reason for delay. Most of us are far enough behind the current state of the art in one or more areas that we can reap significant benefits from some reading and experimentation right now. That's also more fun than struggling at the bleeding edge of standards and tools.

9.4.3 Systems Issues

C++ is a language rather than a complete system. In most contexts that has been a strength, and tools are provided to make up a complete software development and execution environment. However, the interface between the language and the environment falls through the cracks of this classification. This has led to disappointingly slow progress in areas such as incremental linking and dynamic loading. By and large, people have done nothing, relied on mechanisms designed for C, or worked on mechanisms intended to be general enough to support ''all object-oriented programming languages.'' The results have been rather poor from the point of view of a C++ programmer.

Early experiments integrating C++ and dynamic linking were promising so I had expected dynamic linking of classes to be common years ago. For example, we had a technique for efficient and type-safe incremental linking based on abstract types running by 1990 [Stroustrup,1987d] [Dorward,1990]. The technique wasn't much used in real systems, but abstract classes became important in maintaining firewalls, minimizing recompilation after change, and in general to ease the use of software components from multiple sources (§13.2.2).

Another important issue that languished because it didn't fit well with the separation of the programmer's world into distinct areas of concern was support for evolution of software. Fundamentally, the problem is that once a library is in use, you can change its implementation only if its users either don't depend on implementation details such as the size of an object or are willing and able to recompile their code with the new version of the library. Object models such as Microsoft's OLE2, IBM's SOM, and the Object Management Group's CORBA address this problem by providing an interface that hides implementation details and is supposedly language independent. The language independence imposes some awkwardness on the C++ programmer and typically some time or space overhead as well. In addition, each major section of the software industry seems to have its own ''standard'' for addressing this problem. Only time will tell to what extent these techniques help and hinder C++ programmers. The namespace mechanism provides an approach to interface evolution within the C++ language itself (§17.4.4).

I have reluctantly come to accept that some system-related issues would have been better handled within C++. System-related issues, such as dynamic linking of classes and interface evolution do not logically belong in a language and language-based solutions are not preferable on technical grounds. However, the language provides the only common forum in which a truly standard solution can become accepted. For example, the Fortran and C calling interfaces have become a de facto standard for inter-language calls. They are a standard because C and Fortran are popular and because their calling interfaces are simple and efficient – the lowest common denominator. I dislike this conclusion because it implies a barrier to the use of multiple languages in a system unless the mechanism supplied by a single language becomes accepted as a standard by other languages.

9.4.4 Beyond Files and Syntax

Let me outline the program development environment I'd like for C++. First of all, I want incremental compilation. When I make a minor change, I want ''the system'' to note that the change was minor and have the new version compiled and ready to run in a second. Similarly, I want simple requests, such as ''Show me the declaration of this f?'' ''What fs are in scope here?'' ''What is the resolution of this use of +?'' ''Which classes are derived from class Shape?'' and ''What destructors are called at the end of this block?'' answered in a second.

A C++ program contains a wealth of information that in a typical environment is available only to a compiler. I want that information at the programmer's fingertips. However, most people look at a C++ program as a set of source files or as a string of characters. That is to confuse the representation with what is represented. A program is a collection of types, functions, statements, etc. To fit into traditional programming environments, these concepts are represented as characters in files.

Basing C++ implementations on character-oriented tools has been a major impediment to progress. If you have to preprocess and recompile every header file directly or indirectly included in the file containing a function in which you made a minor change, one-second recompilation is not going to happen. Several techniques exist for avoiding redundant recompilation, but dispensing with traditional source text and basing tools on an abstract internal representation seems to me the most promising and interesting approach. An early version of such a representation can be found in [Murray,1992] [Koenig,1992]. Naturally, we need text as input and for people to look at, but such text is easily absorbed into the system and easily reconstructed upon request. It need not be fundamental. Text in the C++ syntax formatted according to some indentation preference is just one of many alternative ways of looking at a program. The simplest application of this notion is to allow you to look at a program using your preferred layout style while I at the same time can look at the same program using my preferences.

A significant use of a non-textual representation would be as a target for code generation from higher-level languages, program generators, direct manipulation tools, etc. It would allow such tools to bypass the traditional C++ syntax. It might even become a tool for migrating C++ away from some of the more contorted aspects of its syntax. I maintain that C++'s type system and semantics are cleaner than its syntax. Within C++, there is a much smaller and cleaner language struggling to get out. An environment like the one I'm envisioning might be a way of proving that. Providing direct support for various forms for design are obvious applications.

From the notion of the syntax being the user interface of a language follows that alternative user interfaces are possible. The only really important constant in the system is the basic semantics of the language. That must be maintained at all times, and as long as that is the case, traditional C++ code in the familiar text form can always be produced on request.

An environment based on an abstract representation of C++ allows alternative ways of producing C++ and alternative ways of looking at C++. It would also provide alternative ways of linking, compiling, and executing code. For example, linking could be done before code generation because there would be no need to produce object code to gain access to linking information. The difference between an interpreter and a compiler would become somewhat academic because both would rely on the same information in roughly the same format.

9.4.5 Putting It All Together

C++'s main strength isn't being great at a single thing, but being good at a great variety of things. Similarly, progress isn't going to come primarily from a single improvement, but from a great variety of improvements in different areas. Better libraries, better design techniques, better-educated programmers and designers, a language standard, optional garbage collection, object-communication standards, databases, non-text-based environments, better tools, faster compilers, etc., will all contribute.

I think that we have barely begun to see what benefits we can reap from C++. The base has been constructed, but just the base. In the future, I expect to see the major activity and progress shift from the language proper – which is that base – to the tools, environments, libraries, applications, etc., that depend on it and build on it.

Part II

Part II describes C++ features developed after Release 1.0. The individual features are grouped into chapters based on their logical relationships. The chronology of their introduction into C++ is unimportant for the language as a whole and is not reflected here. The ordering of the chapters is of little importance; they can be read in any order. The features presented here represent the completion of C++ as envisioned in 1985 tempered by experience.

Chapters

Part II

10

Memory Management

No amount of genius can
overcome obsession with detail.
– traditional

The need for fine-grain control of allocation and deallocation — separating
allocation and initialization — array allocation — placement —
deallocation problems — memory exhaustion — handling memory exhaustion — automatic garbage collection.

10.1 Introduction

C++ provides the operator new to allocate memory on the free store and the operator
delete to release store allocated this way (§2.11.2). Occasionally, a user needs a
finer-grained control of allocation and deallocation.

An important case is a per-class allocator for a frequently used class (see
[2nd,pg177]). Many programs create and delete large numbers of small objects of a
few important classes such as tree nodes, linked lists links, points, lines, messages,
etc. The allocation and deallocation of such objects with a general-purpose allocator
can easily dominate the run time and sometimes also the storage requirements of the
programs. Two factors are at play: the simple run-time and space overhead of a
general-purpose allocation operation and the fragmentation of the free store caused by
a mix of object sizes. I found that the introduction of a per-class allocator typically
doubles the speed of a simulator, compiler, or similar program that hasn't previously
had its memory management tuned. I have seen factors of ten improvements where
fragmentation problems were severe. Inserting a per-class allocator (either handwrit-
ten or from a standard library) became a five-minute operation with the 2.0 features.

Another example of a need for fine-grain control was programs that had to run without interruption for a long time with very limited resources. Hard real-time systems often need guaranteed and predictable memory acquisition with minimal overhead that leads to similar requirements. Traditionally, such programs have avoided dynamic allocation altogether. A special-purpose allocator can be used to manage these limited resources.

Finally, I encountered several cases where an object had to be placed at a specific location or in a specific memory area because of hardware or system requirements.

The revision of C++'s memory management mechanisms (§2.11.2) for Release 2.0 was a response to such demands. The improvements consist primarily of mechanisms for control of allocation and rely on the programmer's understanding of the issues involved. They were intended to be used together with other language features and techniques to encapsulate the areas where control is exercised in delicate ways. These mechanisms were completed in 1992 with the introduction of `operator new[]` and `operator delete[]` to deal with arrays.

On several occasions, suggestions came from friends at Mentor Graphics where a very large and complex CAD/CAM system was being built in C++. In this system, most of the known programming problems had to be faced on the scale of hundreds of programmers, millions of lines of code, under severe performance requirements, with resource limitations, and market deadlines. In particular, Archie Lachner from Mentor provided insights on memory management issues that became significant in the 2.0 overhaul of C++.

10.2 Separating Allocation and Initialization

The pre-2.0 way of controlling allocation and deallocation on a per-class basis, using assignment to `this` (§3.9), proved error-prone and was declared obsolete. Release 2.0 allowed separate specification of allocation and initialization as an alternative. In principle, initialization is done by the constructor after allocation has been done by some independent mechanism. This allows a variety of allocation mechanisms – some user-provided – to be used. Static objects are allocated at link time, local objects on the stack, and objects created by the `new` operator by an appropriate `operator new()`. Deallocation is handled similarly. For example:

```
class X {
    // ...
public:
    void* operator new(size_t sz); // allocate sz bytes
    void operator delete(void* p); // free p

    X();        // initialize
    X(int i);   // initialize

    ~X();       // cleanup
    // ...
};
```

The type `size_t` is an implementation-defined integral type used to hold object sizes; it is borrowed from the ANSI C standard.

It is the `new` operator's job to ensure that the separately specified allocation and initialization are correctly used together. For example, it is the compiler's job to generate a call of the allocator `X::operator new()` and a call of an X constructor from a use of `new` for X. Logically, `X::operator new()` is called before the constructor. It must therefore return a `void*` rather than an `X*`. The constructor makes an X object out of the memory allocated for it.

Conversely, the destructor ''deconstructs'' an object leaving raw memory only for `operator delete()` to free. Therefore, `X::operator delete()` takes a `void*` argument, rather than an `X*`.

The usual rules for inheritance apply, so objects of a derived class will be allocated using a base class' `operator new()`:

```
class Y : public X {   // objects of class Y are also
                       // allocated using X::operator new
    // ...
};
```

For this, `X::operator new()` needs an argument specifying the amount of store to be allocated: `sizeof(Y)` is typically different from `sizeof(X)`. Unfortunately, novice users often get confused when they have to declare that argument, but don't have to supply it explicitly in calls. The notion of a user-declared function with an argument that is ''magically'' supplied by ''the system'' seems hard to grasp for some. In exchange for this added complexity, however, we get the ability to have a base class provide allocation and deallocation services for a set of derived classes – and more regular inheritance rules.

10.3 Array Allocation

A class specific `X::operator new()` is used for individual objects of class X only (including objects of classes derived from class X that do not have their own `operator new()`). It follows that

```
X* p = new X[10];
```

does not involve `X::operator new()` because `X[10]` is an array rather than an object of type X.

This caused some complaints because it didn't allow users to take control of allocations of arrays of X. However, I was adamant that an ''array of X'' wasn't an X and therefore the X allocator couldn't be used. If used for arrays, the writer of `X::operator new()` would have to deal with the problems of array allocation ''just in case,'' thus complicating the critical common case. If that case wasn't critical, why bother with a special allocator? Also, I pointed out, controlling the allocation of single-dimension arrays such as `X[d]` isn't sufficient: what about multiple-dimension arrays such as `X[d1][d2]`?

However, the lack of a mechanism for controlling array allocation caused a certain amount of grief in real cases and eventually the standards committee provided a solution. The most critical problem was that there was no way to prevent users from allocating arrays on the free store, yet no way of controlling such allocation. In systems relying on logically different storage management schemes, this can cause serious problems as users naively place large dynamic arrays in the default allocation area. I had not fully appreciated the implications of this.

The solution adopted is simply to provide a pair of functions specifically for array allocation/deallocation:

```
class X {
    // ...
    void* operator new(size_t sz);    // allocate objects
    void operator delete(void* p);

    void* operator new[](size_t sz); // allocate arrays
    void operator delete[](void* p);
};
```

The array allocator is used to obtain space for arrays of any dimension. As for all allocators, the job of `operator new[]` is to provide the number of bytes asked for; it does not concern itself about how that memory is used. In particular, it does not need to know the dimensions of the array or its number of elements. Laura Yaker from Mentor Graphics was the prime mover in the introduction of the array allocation and deallocation operators.

10.4 Placement

Two related problems were solved by a common mechanism:

[1] We needed a mechanism for placing an object at a specific address, for example, placing an object representing a process at the address required by special-purpose hardware.

[2] We needed a mechanism for allocating objects from a specific arena, for example, for allocating an object in the shared memory of a multi-processor or from an arena controlled by a persistent object manager.

The solution was to allow overloading of `operator new()` and to provide a syntax for supplying extra arguments to the `new` operator. For example, an `operator new()` that places an object at a particular address can be defined like this:

```
void* operator new(size_t, void* p)
{
    return p;    // place object at 'p'
}
```

and invoked like this:

```
void* buf = (void*)0xF00F;   // significant address

X* p2 = new(buf)X;   // construct an X at 'buf'
                     // invokes: operator new(sizeof(X),buf)
```

Because of this usage, the "`new(buf)X`" syntax for supplying extra arguments to `operator new()` is known as *the placement syntax*. Note that every `operator new()` takes a size as its first argument and that the size of the object allocated is implicitly supplied.

If anything, I underestimated the importance of placement at the time. With placement, operator `new` ceases to be simply a memory allocation mechanism. Because one can associate all kinds of logical properties with specific memory locations, `new` takes on aspects of general resource management.

An `operator new()` for a specific allocation arena might be defined like this:

```
void* operator new(size_t s, fast_arena& a)
{
    return a.alloc(s);
}
```

and used like this:

```
void f(fast_arena& arena)
{
    X* p = new(arena)X;   // allocate X in arena
    // ...
}
```

Here, a `fast_arena` is assumed to be a class with a member function `alloc()` that can be used to obtain memory. For example:

```
class fast_arena {
    // ...
    char* maxp;
    char* freep;
    char* expand(size_t s); // get more memory from
                            // general purpose allocator
public:
    void* alloc(size_t s) {
        char* p = freep;
        return ((freep+=s)<maxp) ? p : expand(s);
    }
    void free(void*) {}  // ignore
    clear(); // free all allocated memory
};
```

This would be an arena specialized for fast allocation and almost instant freeing. One important use of arenas is to provide specialized memory management semantics.

10.5 Deallocation Problems

There is an obvious and deliberate asymmetry between `operator new()` and `operator delete()`. The former can be overloaded, the latter can't. This matches the similar asymmetry between constructors and destructors. Consequently, you may be able to choose between four allocators and five constructors when creating an object, but when it comes time to destroy it, there is basically only one choice:

```
delete p;
```

The reason is that in principle you know everything at the point where you create an object, but when it comes to deleting it, all you have left is a pointer that may or may not be of the exact type of the object.

   The use of a virtual destructor is crucial for getting destruction right in cases in which a user deletes an object of a derived class through a pointer to the base class:

```
class  X {
    // ...
    virtual ~X();
};

class Y : public X {
    // ...
    ~Y();
};

void f(X* p1)
{
    X* p2 = new Y;
    delete p2;      // Y::~Y correctly invoked
    delete p1;      // correct destructor
                    // (whichever that may be) invoked
}
```

This will also ensure that if there are local `operator delete()` functions in the hierarchy, the right one will be called. Had a virtual destructor not been used, the cleanup specified in `Y`'s destructor would not have been performed.

   However, there is no language feature for selecting between deallocation functions to match the mechanism for selecting between allocation functions:

```
class X {
    // ...
    void* operator new(size_t); // ordinary allocation
    void* operator new(size_t, Arena&); // in Arena

    void operator delete(void*);
    // can't define void operator delete(void*, Arena&);
};
```

The reason is again that at the point of deletion, the user can't be expected to know how the object was allocated. Ideally, of course, a user should not have to deallocate an object at all. That is one use of special arenas. An arena can be defined to be deallocated as a unit at some well-defined point in a program, or one can write a special-purpose garbage collector for an arena. The former is quite common, the latter isn't and needs to be done very well to be able to compete with a standard conservative plug-in garbage collector [Boehm,1993].

More frequently, the `operator new()` functions are programmed to leave an indicator of how they want to be deallocated for `operator delete()` to find. Note that this is memory management and therefore at a conceptual level below that of the objects created by the constructors and destroyed by the destructors. Consequently the memory containing this information is not in the object as such but somewhere related to it. For example, an `operator new()` may place memory management information in the word ahead of the one pointed to by its return value. Alternatively, an `operator new()` can leave information in a place where constructors or other functions can find them to determine whether an object is allocated on a free store.

Was it a mistake not to allow users to overload `delete`? If so, it would be a misguided attempt to protect people against themselves. I'm undecided, but I'm pretty certain that this is one of the nasty cases where either solution would cause problems.

The possibility of calling a destructor explicitly was introduced in 2.0 to cater to rare cases where allocation and deallocation have been completely separated from each other. An example is a container that does all memory management for its contained objects.

10.5.1 Deallocating Arrays

From C, C++ inherited the problem that a pointer points to an individual object but that object may actually be the initial element of an array. In general, the compiler cannot tell. An object pointing to the first element of an array is typically said to point to the array and allocation and deallocation of arrays is handled through such pointers. For example:

```
void f(X* p1)    // p1 may point to an individual object
                 // or to an array
{
    X* p2 = new X[10]; // p2 points to the array
    // ...
}
```

How do we ensure that an array is correctly deleted? In particular, how do we ensure that the destructor is called for all elements of an array? Release 1.0 didn't have a satisfactory answer. Release 2.0 introduced an explicit delete-array operator `delete[]`:

```
void f(X* p1)    // p1 may point to an individual object
                 // or to an array
{
    X* p2 = new X[10]; // p2 points to the array
    // ...
    delete p2;      // error: p2 points to an array
    delete[] p2;    // ok
    delete p1;      // maybe ok, trust the programmer
    delete[] p1;    // maybe ok, trust the programmer
}
```

Plain delete isn't required to handle both individual objects and arrays. This avoids complicating the common case of allocating and deallocating individual objects. It also avoids encumbering individual objects with information necessary for array deallocation.

An intermediate version of delete[] required the programmer to specify the number of elements of the array. For example:

```
delete[10] p2;
```

That proved too error-prone, so the burden of keeping track of the number of elements was placed on the implementation instead.

10.6 Memory Exhaustion

Finding that a requested resource cannot be obtained is a general and nasty problem. I had decided (pre-2.0) that exception handling was the direction in which to look for general solutions to this kind of problem (§3.15). However, exception handling (§16) was then still far in the future, and the particular problem of free store exhaustion couldn't wait. Some solution, however ugly, was needed for an interim period of several years.

Two problems needed immediate solutions:
  [1] It must be possible for a user to gain control in all cases in which a library call fails due to memory exhaustion (more generally, in all cases in which a library call fails). This was an absolute requirement from important internal AT&T users.
  [2] The average user mustn't be required to test for memory exhaustion after each allocation operation. In any case, experience from C shows that users don't test consistently even when they are supposed to.

The first requirement was met by specifying that a constructor isn't executed if operator new() returns 0. In that case, the new expression also yields 0. This enables critical software to defend itself against allocation problems. For example:

```
void f()
{
    X* p = new X;
    if (p == 0) {
        // handle allocation error
        // constructor not called
    }
    // use p
}
```

The second requirement was met by what was known as a `new_handler`, that is, a user-supplied function guaranteed to be called if memory can't be found by operator new. For example:

```
void my_handler() { /* ... */ }

void f()
{
    set_new_handler(&my_handler);  // my_handler used for
                                   // memory exhaustion
                                   // from here on
    // ...
}
```

This technique was presented in [Stroustrup,1986] and is a general pattern for dealing with resource acquisition that occasionally fails. Basically, a `new_handler` can:

 – find more resources (that is, find free memory to allocate), or
 – produce an error message and exit (somehow).

With exception handling, "exit" can be less drastic than terminating the program (§16.5).

10.7 Automatic Garbage Collection

I deliberately designed C++ not to rely on automatic garbage collection (usually just called *garbage collection*). I feared the very significant space and time overheads I had experienced with garbage collectors. I feared the added complexity of implementation and porting that a garbage collector would impose. Also, garbage collection would make C++ unsuitable for many of the low-level tasks for which it was intended. I like the idea of garbage collection as a mechanism that simplifies design and eliminates a source of errors. However, I am fully convinced that had garbage collection been an integral part of C++ originally, C++ would have been stillborn.

My opinion was that if you needed garbage collection, you could either implement some automated memory management scheme yourself or use a language that supported it directly, say, my old favorite Simula. Today, the issue is not so clear cut. More resources are available for implementation and porting. Much C++ software exists that can't just be rewritten in other languages. Garbage collectors have improved, and many of the techniques for "home brew" garbage collection that I had envisioned or used don't scale up from individual projects to general-purpose libraries. Most importantly, more ambitious projects are now done in C++. Some of these could benefit from garbage collection and could afford it.

10.7.1 Optional Garbage Collection

Optional garbage collection is, I think, the right approach for C++. Exactly how that can best be done is not yet known, but we are going to get the option in several forms over the next couple of years. Implementations already exist, so it is just a matter of time before they make it out of research and into production code.

The fundamental reasons why garbage collection is desirable are easily stated:

[1] Garbage collection is the easiest for the user. In particular, it simplifies the building and use of some libraries.

[2] Garbage collection is more reliable than user-supplied memory management schemes for some applications.

The reasons against are more numerous, but less fundamental in that they are implementation and efficiency issues:

[1] Garbage collection causes run-time and space overheads that are not affordable for many current C++ applications running on current hardware.

[2] Many garbage collection techniques imply service interruptions that are not acceptable for important classes of applications, such as hard real-time applications, device drivers, control applications, human interface code on slow hardware, and operating system kernels.

[3] Some applications do not have the hardware resources of a traditional general-purpose computer.

[4] Some garbage collection schemes require banning several basic C facilities such as pointer arithmetic, unchecked arrays, and unchecked function arguments as used by `printf()`.

[5] Some garbage collection schemes impose constraints on object layout or object creation that complicates interfacing with other languages.

I know that there are more reasons for and against, but no further reasons are needed. These are sufficient arguments against the view that *every* application would be better done with garbage collection. Similarly, these are sufficient arguments against the view that *no* application would be better done with garbage collection.

When comparing garbage collection and non-garbage-collection systems, remember that not every program needs to run forever, not every piece of code is a foundation library, memory leaks are quite acceptable in many applications, and many applications can manage their memory without garbage collection or related techniques such as reference counting. C++ does not need garbage collection the way a language without genuine local variables (§2.3) needs garbage collection. When memory management is well-enough behaved to be handled by less general methods (for example, special purpose allocators (§10.2, §10.4, §15.3.1 [2nd,§5.5.6,§13.10.3]) automatic and static store (§2.4)), very significant speed and space advantages can be obtained compared with both manual and automatic general garbage collection. For many applications, those advantages are critical and the benefits of automatic garbage collection to other applications irrelevant. In an ideal implementation, this advantage would not be compromised by the presence of a garbage collector; that collector would simply not be invoked, or invoked infrequently enough to be unimportant to the overall efficiency of most applications.

My conclusion is that garbage collection is desirable in principle and feasible, but for current users, uses, and hardware we can't afford to have the semantics of C++ and of its most basic standard libraries depend on garbage collection.

The real problem is therefore whether *optional* garbage collection is a viable option for C++. When (not if) garbage collection becomes available, we will have two ways of writing C++ programs. This, in principle, is no more difficult than managing with several different libraries, several different application platforms, etc., that we already handle. Having to make such choices is a simple consequence of having a widely used general-purpose programming language. It would not make sense to require that the execution environment of a C++ program should be the same whether it is running in a missile head, a SLR camera, a PC, a telephone switch, a UNIX clone, an IBM mainframe, a Mac, a supercomputer, or something else. If provided in a reasonable way, garbage collection will simply become another option for someone choosing a run-time environment for an application.

Can optional garbage collection be legal and useful if it is not specified as part of the C++ standard? I think so, and anyway, we don't have the option of specifying garbage collection in the standard because we don't have a scheme that is anywhere near ready for standardization. An experimental scheme must be demonstrated to be good enough for a wide range of real applications. In addition, it must not have unavoidable drawbacks that would make C++ an unacceptable choice for significant applications. Given one such successful experiment, implementers will scramble to provide the best implementations. We can only hope that they don't choose mutually incompatible schemes.

10.7.2 What should optional garbage collection look like?

There are several options because there are several solutions to the basic problems. An ideal is to maximize the number of programs that can run in both garbage collection and non-garbage collection environments. This is an important and elusive goal for implementers, library designers, and application programmers.

Ideally, a garbage collection implementation would simply be as good as a non-garbage-collection implementation in time and space if you didn't use garbage collection. This is easy to achieve if the programmer has to say "no part of this program uses garbage collection," but very hard to do if the implementation is obliged to do garbage collection and tries to achieve the performance of a non-garbage-collection implementation through adaptive behavior.

Conversely, a garbage-collection implementer might need some "hints" from a user to make performance acceptable. For example, a scheme might require the user to state which objects require garbage collection and which do not (for example, because they originate in non-garbage-collected C or Fortran libraries). If at all possible, a non-garbage-collection implementation should be able to ignore such hints. Alternatively they should be trivial to remove from the source text.

Some C++ operations, such as ill-behaved casts, unions of pointers and non-pointers, pointer arithmetic, etc., are seriously detrimental to garbage collectors. These operations are generally infrequent in well-written C++ code, so it is tempting to ban them. Thus, two ideals clash:

[1] Ban any unsafe operation: that makes programming safer and garbage collection more efficient.

[2] Don't ban any currently legal C++ program.

I think a compromise can be reached. I suspect that a garbage collection scheme can be concocted that will work with (almost) every legal C++ program, but work even better when no unsafe operations are used.

When implementing a garbage collection scheme one must decide whether to invoke the destructor for a collected object or not. Deciding which is the right thing to do is not easy. In [2nd], I wrote:

"Garbage collection can be seen as a way of simulating an infinite memory in a limited memory. With this in mind, we can answer a common question: Should a garbage collector call the destructor for an object it recycles? The answer is no, because an object placed on free store and never deleted is never destroyed. Seen in this light, using `delete` is simply a way of requesting the destructor to be called (together with a notification to the system that the object's memory may be recycled). But what if we actually do want an action performed for an object allocated on the free store but never deleted? Note that this problem does not arise for static and automatic objects; their destructors are always called implicitly. Note also that actions performed "at garbage-collection time" are unpredictable because they may happen at essentially any time between the last use of the object and "the end of the program." This implies that the state of the program at the time of their execution is unknown. This again makes such actions hard to program correctly and less useful than is sometimes imagined.

Where such actions are needed, the problem of performing an action at some unspecified "destruction time" can be solved by providing a registration server. An object that needs a service performed "at the end of the program" places its address and a pointer to a "cleanup" function in a global associative array."

I am now less certain. This model would certainly work, but maybe having the garbage collector call the destructors would be sufficiently simple to use to be worthwhile. That depends on exactly what objects are collected and what actions their destructors perform. This is a question that can't be decided by armchair philosophy, and there doesn't seem to be much relevant experience from other languages. Unfortunately, it is also a problem for which it is hard to conduct real experiments.

I am under no illusion that building an acceptable garbage collection mechanism for C++ will be easy – I just don't think it is impossible. Consequently, given the number of people looking at the problem several solutions will soon emerge.

Overloading

The Devil is in the details.
– traditional

Fine-grain overload resolution — ambiguity control — the null pointer — type-safe linkage — name mangling — controlling copying, allocation, derivation, etc. — smart pointers — smart references — increment and decrement — an exponentiation operator — user-defined operators — composite operators — enumerations — a Boolean type.

11.1 Introduction

Operators are used to provide notational convenience. Consider a simple formula F=M*A. No basic physics textbook states that as `assign(F,multiply(M,A))`†. When variables can be of different types, we must decide whether to allow mixed-mode arithmetic or to require explicit conversion of operands to a common type. For example, if M is an `int` and A is a `double` we can either accept M*A and deduce that M must be promoted to a `double` before the multiplication, or we can require the programmer to write something like `double(M)*A`.

By choosing the former – as C, Fortran, and every other language used extensively for computation have – C++ entered a difficult area without perfect solutions. On the one hand, people want "natural" conversions without any fuss from the compiler, but on the other, they don't want surprises. What is considered natural differs radically among people, and so do the kinds of surprises people are willing to tolerate. This,

---

† Some may even prefer F=MA, but the explanation of how to make that work ("overloading missing whitespace") is beyond the scope of this book.

together with the constraint of compatibility with C's rather chaotic built-in types and conversions, results in a fundamentally difficult problem.

The desire for flexibility and freedom of expression clashes with wishes for safety, predictability, and simplicity. This chapter looks at the refinements to the overloading mechanisms that resulted from this clash.

11.2 Overload Resolution

Overloading of function names and operators, as originally introduced into C++ (§3.6) [Stroustrup,1984b] proved popular, but problems with the overload mechanism had surfaced. The improvements provided by Release 2.0 were summarized [Stroustrup,1989b]:

> "The C++ overloading mechanism was revised to allow resolution of types that used to be "too similar" and to gain independence of declaration order. The resulting scheme is more expressive and catches more ambiguity errors."

The work on fine-grain resolution gave us the ability to overload based on the int/char, float/double, const/non-const, and base/derived distinctions. Order independence eliminated a source of nasty bugs. I will examine these two aspects of overloading in turn. Finally, I'll explain why the overload keyword was made obsolete.

11.2.1 Fine-Grain Resolution

As first defined, the C++ overloading rules accepted the limitations of C's built-in types [Kernighan,1978]. That is, there were no values of type float (technically, no rvalues) because in computation a float is immediately widened to a double. Similarly there were no values of type char because in every use a char is widened to an int. This led to complaints that single-precision floating point libraries couldn't be provided naturally and that character manipulation functions were unnecessarily error-prone.

Consider an output function. If we can't overload based on the char/int distinction, we have to use two names. In fact, the original stream library (§8.3.1) used:

```
ostream& operator<<(int);  // output ints (incl. promoted
                           // chars) as sequence of digits.
ostream& put(char c);      // output chars as characters.
```

However, many people wrote

```
cout<<'X';
```

and were (naturally) surprised to find 88 (the numeric value of ASCII 'X') in their output instead of the character X.

To overcome this, the type rules of C++ were changed to allow types such as char and float to be considered in their unpromoted form by the overload resolution mechanism. In addition, the type of a literal character, such as 'X', was defined to be char. At the same time, the then recently invented ANSI C notation for expressing unsigned and float literals was adopted so that we could write:

```
float abs(float);
double abs(double);
int abs(int);
unsigned abs(unsigned);
char abs(char);


void f()
{
    abs(1);        // abs(int)
    abs(1U);       // abs(unsigned)
    abs(1.0);      // abs(double)
    abs(1.0F);     // abs(float)
    abs('a');      // abs(char)
}
```

In C, the type of a character literal such as 'a' is int. Surprisingly, giving 'a' type char in C++ doesn't cause compatibility problems. Except for the pathological example sizeof('a'), every construct that can be expressed in both C and C++ gives the same result.

In defining the type of a character literal as char, I relied partly on reports from Mike Tiemann on experience with a compiler option providing that interpretation in the GNU C++ compiler.

Similarly, it had been discovered that the difference between const and non-const could be used to good effect. An important use of overloading based on const was to provide a pair of functions

```
char* strtok(char*, const char*);
const char* strtok(const char*, const char*);
```

as an alternative to the ANSI C standard function

```
char* strtok(const char*, const char*);
```

The C strtok() returns a substring of the const string passed as its first argument. Having that substring non-const couldn't be allowed for a C++ standard library because an implicit violation of the type system is not acceptable. On the other hand, incompatibilities with C had to be minimized, and providing two strtok functions allows most reasonable uses of strtok.

Allowing overloading based on const was part of a general tightening up of the rules for const and a trend towards enforcing those rules (§13.3).

Experience showed that hierarchies established by public class derivations should be taken into account in function matching so that the conversion to the "most derived" class is chosen if there is a choice. A void* argument is chosen only if no other pointer argument matches. For example:

```
class B { /* ... */ };
class BB : public B { /* ... */ };
class BBB : public BB { /* ... */ };

void f(B*);
void f(BB*);
void f(void*);

void g(BBB* pbbb, BB* pbb, B* pb, int* pi)
{
    f(pbbb);    // f(BB*)
    f(pbb);     // f(BB*)
    f(pb);      // f(B*)
    f(pi);      // f(void*)
}
```

This ambiguity resolution rule matches the rule for virtual function calls where the member from the most derived class is chosen. Its introduction eliminated a source of errors. This change was so obvious that people greeted it with a yawn ("you mean it wasn't that way before?"). The bugs disappeared and that was all.

The rule has one interesting property, though. It establishes void* as the root of the tree of class conversions. This fits with the view that construction makes an object out of raw memory and a destructor reverses that process by making raw memory out of an object (§2.11.1, §10.2). A conversion such as B* to void* allows an object to be seen as raw memory where no other property is of interest.

11.2.2 Ambiguity Control

The original C++ overloading mechanism resolved ambiguities by relying on the order of declaration. Declarations were tried in order and the first match "won." To make this tolerable, only non-narrowing conversions were accepted in a match. For example:

```
overload void print(int);    // original (pre 2.0) rules:
void print(double);

void g()
{
    print(2.0);    // print(double): print(2.0)
                   // double->int conversion not accepted.
    print(2.0F);   // print(double): print(double(2.0F))
                   // float->int conversion not accepted
                   // float->double conversion accepted.
    print(2);      // print(int): print(2).
}
```

This rule was simple to express, simple for users to understand, efficient at compile time, trivial for implementers to get right, and was a constant source of errors and

confusion. Reversing the declaration order could completely change the meaning of a
piece of code:

```
overload void print(double);   // original rules:
void print(int);

void g()
{
    print(2.0);   // print(double): print(2.0).
    print(2.0F);  // print(double): print(double(2.0F))
                  // float->double conversion accepted.
    print(2);     // print(double): print(double(2))
                  // int->double conversion accepted.
}
```

Basically, order dependence was too error-prone. It also became a serious obstacle to
the effort to evolve C++ programming towards a greater use of libraries. My aim was
to move to a view of programming as the composition of programs out of independent
program fragments (see also §11.3) and order dependence was one of many obstacles.

The snag is that order-independent overloading rules complicate C++'s definition
and implementation because a significant degree of compatibility with C and with the
original C++ must be maintained. In particular, the simple rule "if an expression has
two possible legal interpretations, it is ambiguous and thus illegal," wasn't a real
option. For example, under that rule all of the calls of print() in the example
above would be ambiguous and illegal.

I concluded we needed some notion of a "better match" rule so that we would
prefer an exact type match to a match involving a conversion and prefer a safe conversion such as float to double over an unsafe (narrowing, value destroying, etc.)
conversion such as float to int. The resulting series of discussions, refinements,
and reconsiderations lasted for years. Some details are still being discussed in the
standards committee. The main participants were Doug McIlroy, Andy Koenig,
Jonathan Shopiro, and me. Early on, Doug pointed out that we were perilously close
to trying to design a "natural" system for implicit conversions. He considered PL/I's
rules, which he had helped design, proof that such a "natural" system cannot be
designed for a rich set of common data types – and C++ provides a rich set of built-in
types with anarchic conversions plus the ability to define conversions between arbitrary user-defined types. My stated reason for entering this swamp was that we didn't
have any option but to try.

C compatibility, people's expectations, and the aim to allow users to define types
that can be used exactly as built-in types prevented us from banning implicit conversions. In retrospect, I agree with the decision to proceed with implicit conversions. I
also agree with Doug's observation that the task of minimizing surprises caused by
implicit conversions is inherently difficult and that (at least given the requirement of
C compatibility) surprises cannot be completely eliminated. Different programmers
simply have differing expectations so whatever rule you choose, someone is going to
be surprised sometime.

A fundamental problem is that the graph of built-in implicit conversions contains cycles. For example, implicit conversions exist not only from `char` to `int`, but also from `int` to `char`. This has the potential for endless subtle errors and prevented us from adopting a scheme for implicit conversions based on a lattice of conversions. Instead we devised a system of "matches" between types found in function declarations and the types of actual arguments. Matches involving conversions we considered less error-prone and less surprising were preferred over others. This allowed us to accommodate C's standard promotion and standard conversion rules. I described the 2.0 version of this scheme like this [Stroustrup,1989b]:

"Here is a slightly simplified explanation of the new rules. Note that with the exception of a few cases where the older rules allowed order dependence the new rules are compatible and old programs produce identical results under the new rules. For the last two years or so C++ implementations have issued warnings for the now "outlawed" order-dependent resolutions.

C++ distinguishes 5 kinds of "matches":

[1] Match using no or only unavoidable conversions (for example, array name to pointer, function name to pointer to function, and T to `const T`).

[2] Match using integral promotions (as defined in the proposed ANSI C standard; that is, `char` to `int`, `short` to `int` and their `unsigned` counterparts) and `float` to `double`.

[3] Match using standard conversions (for example, `int` to `double`, `derived*` to `base*`, `unsigned int` to `int`).

[4] Match using user-defined conversions (both constructors and conversion operators).

[5] Match using the ellipsis `. . .` in a function declaration.

Consider first functions of a single argument. The idea is always to choose the "best" match, that is the one highest on the list above. If there are two best matches, the call is ambiguous and thus a compile-time error."

The examples above illustrate this rule. A more precise version of the rules can be found in the ARM.

A further rule is needed to cope with functions of more than one argument [ARM]:

"For calls involving more than one argument, a function is chosen provided it has a better match than every other function for at least one argument and at least as good a match as every other function for every argument. For example:

```
class complex {
    // ...
    complex(double);
};


void f(int,double);
void f(double,int);
void f(complex,int);
```

```
void f(int ...);
void f(complex ...);

void g(complex z)
{
    f(1,2.0);      // f(int,double)
    f(1.0,2);      // f(double,int)
    f(z,1.2);      // f(complex,int)
    f(z,1,3);      // f(complex ...)
    f(2.0,z);      // f(int ...)
    f(1,1);        // error: ambiguous,
                   // f(int,double) or f(double,int) ?

}
```

The unfortunate narrowing from double to int in the third and the second to last calls causes warnings. Such narrowings are allowed to preserve compatibility with C. In this particular case, the narrowing is harmless, but in many cases double to int conversions are value destroying and they should never be used thoughtlessly.''

Elaboration and formalization of this rule for multiple arguments led to the ''intersect rule'' found in [ARM,pp312-314]. The intersect rule was first formulated by Andrew Koenig during discussions with Doug McIlroy, Jonathan Shopiro, and me. I believe Jonathan was the one who found the truly bizarre examples that proved it necessary [ARM,pg313].

Please note how seriously the compatibility concerns were taken. My view is that anything less would have been taken quite badly by the vast majority of existing and future C++ users. A simpler, stricter, and more easily understood language would have attracted more adventurous programmers as well as programmers who are permanently discontented with existing languages. Had design decisions systematically favored simplicity and elegance over compatibility, C++ would today have been much smaller and cleaner. It would also have been an unimportant cult language.

11.2.3 The Null Pointer

Nothing seems to create more heat than a discussion of the proper way to express a pointer that doesn't point to an object, the null pointer. C++ inherited its definition of the null pointer from Classic C [Kernighan,1978]:

''A constant expression that evaluates to zero is converted to a pointer, commonly called the null pointer. It is guaranteed that this value will produce a pointer distinguishable from a pointer to any object or function.''

The ARM further warns:

''Note that the null pointer need not be represented by the same bit pattern as the integer 0.''

The warning reflects the common misapprehension that if p=0 assigns the null pointer to the pointer p, then the representation of the null pointer must be the same as the integer zero, that is, a bit pattern of all-zeros. This is not so. C++ is sufficiently strongly typed that a concept such as the null pointer can be represented in whichever way the implementer chooses, independently of how that concept is represented in the source text. The one exception is when people use the ellipsis to suppress function argument checking:

```
int printf(const char* ...); // C style unchecked calls

printf(fmt, 0, (char)0, (void*)0, (int*)0, (int(*)())0);
```

Here, the casts are needed to specify exactly which kind of 0 is wanted. In this example, five different values could conceivably be passed.

In K&R C, function arguments were never checked and even in ANSI C you still can't rely on argument checking because it is optional. For this reason, because 0 is not easy to spot in a C or C++ program and because people are used to a symbolic constant representing the null pointer in other languages, C programmers tend to use a macro called NULL to represent the null pointer. Unfortunately, there is no portable correct definition of NULL in K&R C. In ANSI C, (void*)0 is a reasonable and increasingly popular definition for NULL.

However, (void*)0 is not a good choice for the null pointer in C++:

```
char* p = (void*)0;   /* legal C, illegal C++ */
```

A void* cannot be assigned to anything without a cast. Allowing implicit conversions of void* to other pointer types would open a serious hole in the type system. One might make a special case for (void*)0, but special cases should only be admitted in dire need. Also, C++ usage was determined long before there was an ANSI C standard, and I do not want to have any critical part of C++ rely on a macro (§18). Consequently, I used plain 0, and that has worked very well over the years. People who insist on a symbolic constant usually define one of

```
const int NULL = 0; // or
#define NULL 0
```

As far as the compiler is concerned, NULL and 0 are then synonymous. Unfortunately, so many people have added definitions NULL, NIL, Null, null, etc., to their code that providing yet another definition can be hazardous.

There is one kind of mistake that is not caught when 0 (however spelled) is used for the null pointer. Consider:

```
void f(char*);

void g() { f(0); } // calls f(char*)
```

Now add another f() and the meaning of g() silently changes:

```
void f(char*);
void f(int);

void g() { f(0); } // calls f(int)
```

This is an unfortunate side effect of 0 being an int that can be promoted to the null pointer, rather than a direct specification of the null pointer. I think a good compiler should warn, but I didn't think of that in time for Cfront. Making the call f(0) ambiguous rather than resolving it in favor of f(int) would be feasible, but would probably not satisfy the people who want NULL or nil to be magical.

After one of the regular flame wars on comp.lang.c++ and comp.lang.c, one of my friends observed, "If 0 is their worst problem, then they are truly lucky." In my experience, using 0 for the null pointer is not a problem in practice. I am still amazed, though, by the rule that accepts the result of any constant expression evaluating to 0 as the null pointer. This rule makes 2-2 and ~-1 null pointers. Assigning 2+2 or -1 to a pointer is a type error, of course. That is not a rule that I like as an implementer either.

11.2.4 The overload Keyword

Originally, C++ allowed a name to be used for more than one name (that is, "to be overloaded") only after an explicit overload declaration. For example:

```
overload max;            // ``overload'' - obsolete in 2.0
int max(int,int);
double max(double,double);
```

I considered it too dangerous to use the same name for two functions without explicitly declaring an intent to overload. For example:

```
int abs(int);            // no ``overload abs''
double abs(double);      // used to be an error
```

This fear of overloading had two sources:
  [1] Concern that undetected ambiguities could occur.
  [2] Concern that a program could not be properly linked unless the programmer explicitly declared which functions were supposed to be overloaded.
The former fear proved largely groundless. The few problems found in actual use are dealt with by the order-independent overloading resolution rules. The latter fear proved to have a basis in a general problem with C separate compilation rules that had nothing to do with overloading (see §11.3).

On the other hand, the overload declarations themselves became a serious problem. One couldn't merge pieces of software using the same function name for different functions unless both pieces had declared that name overloaded. This wasn't usually the case. Typically, the name one wants to overload is the name of a C library function declared in a C header. For example:

```
/* Header for C standard math library, math.h: */
     double sqrt(double);
     /* ... */
```

```
// header for C++ complex arithmetic library, complex.h:
  overload sqrt;
  complex sqrt(complex);
  // ...
```

Now we could write

```
#include <complex.h>
#include <math.h>
```

but not

```
#include <math.h>
#include <complex.h>
```

because it was an error to use `overload` for `sqrt()` on its second declaration only. There were ways of alleviating this: rearranging declarations, putting constraints on the use of header files, and sprinkling `overload` declarations everywhere "just in case." However, we found such tricks unmanageable in all but the simplest cases. Abolishing `overload` declarations and getting rid of the `overload` keyword worked much better.

11.3 Type-Safe Linkage

C linkage is very simple and completely unsafe. You declare a function

```
extern void f(char);
```

and the linker will merrily link that `f` to any `f` in its universe. The `f` linked to may be a function taking completely different arguments or even a non-function. This usually causes a run-time error of some sort (core dump, segment violation, etc.). Linkage problems are especially nasty because they increase disproportionately with the size of programs and with the amount of library use. C programmers have learned to live with this problem. However, the needs of the overloading mechanism caused a sense of urgency. Any solution for this linkage problem for C++ had to leave it possible to call C functions without added complication or overhead.

11.3.1 Overloading and Linkage

The solution to the C/C++ linkage problem in pre-2.0 implementations was to let the name generated for a C++ function be the same as would be generated for a C function of the same name whenever possible. Thus `open()` gets the name `open` on systems where C doesn't modify its names on output, the name `_open` on systems where C adds a prefix underscore, etc.

This simple scheme clearly isn't sufficient to cope with overloaded functions. The keyword `overload` was introduced partly to distinguish the hard case from the easy ones (see also §3.6).

The initial solution, like the subsequent ones, was based on the idea of encoding type information into names given to the linker (§3.3.3). To allow linkage to C functions, only the second and subsequent versions of an overloaded function had their names encoded. Thus the programmer would write:

```
overload sqrt;
double sqrt(double);     // a linker sees: sqrt
complex sqrt(complex);   // a linker sees: sqrt__F7complex
```

The C++ compiler generated code referring to `sqrt` and `sqrt__F7complex`. Fortunately, I documented this trick only in the BUGS section of the C++ manual page.

The overloading scheme used for C++ before 2.0 interacted with the traditional C linkage scheme in ways that brought out the worst aspects of both. We had to solve three problems:

[1] Lack of type checking in the linker.

[2] Use of the `overload` keyword.

[3] Linking C++ and C program fragments.

A solution to 1 is to augment the name of *every* function with an encoding of its type. A solution to 2 is to abolish the `overload` keyword. A solution to 3 is for a C++ programmer to state explicitly when a function is supposed to have C-style linkage. Consequently, [Stroustrup,1988a]:

"The question is whether a solution based on these three premises can be implemented without noticeable overhead and with only minimal inconvenience to C++ programmers. The ideal solution would

– Require no C++ language changes.

– Provide type-safe linkage.

– Allow for simple and convenient linkage to C.

– Break no existing C++ code.

– Allow use of (ANSI-style) C headers.

– Provide good error detection and error reporting.

– Be a good tool for library building.

– Impose no run-time overhead.

– Impose no compile-time overhead.

– Impose no link-time overhead.

We have not been able to devise a scheme that fulfills all of these criteria strictly, but the adopted scheme is a good approximation."

Clearly, the solution was to type check all linkage. The problem then became how to do that without having to write a new linker for every system.

11.3.2 An Implementation of C++ Linkage

First of all, every C++ function name is encoded by appending its argument types. This ensures that a program will link only if every function called has a definition and that the argument types specified in declarations are the same as the types specified in the function definition. For example, given:

```
f(int i) { /* ... */ }              // defines f__Fi
f(int i, char* j) { /* ... */ }    // defines f__FiPc
```

These examples can be correctly handled:

```
extern f(int);              // refers to f__Fi
extern f(int,char*);        // refers to f__FiPc
extern f(double,double);    // refers to f__Fdd

void g()
{
    f(1);              // links to f__Fi
    f(1,"asdf");       // links to f__FiPc
    f(1,1);            // tries to link to f__Fdd
                       // link-time error: no f__Fdd defined
}
```

This leaves the problem of how to call a C function or a C++ function "masquerading" as a C function. To do this, a programmer must state that a function has C linkage. Otherwise, a function is assumed to be a C++ function and its name is encoded. To express this, an extension of the *linkage-specification* was introduced into C++:

```
extern "C" {
    double sqrt(double);   // sqrt(double) has C linkage
}
```

The linkage specification does not affect the semantics of the program using sqrt() but simply tells the compiler to use the C naming conventions for the name used for sqrt() in the object code. This means that the linkage name of *this* sqrt() is sqrt or _sqrt or whatever is required by the C linkage conventions in a given system. One could also imagine a system in which the C linkage rules were the type-safe C++ linkage rules as described above so that the linkage name of the C function sqrt() was sqrt__Fd.

Naturally, suffixing with an encoding of the type is only an example of an implementation technique. It is, however, the technique we successfully used for Cfront, and it has been widely copied. It has the important properties of being simple and working with existing linkers. This implementation of the idea of type-safe linkage is not 100% safe, but then, again, in general, very few useful systems are 100% safe. A more complete description of the encoding ("name mangling") scheme used by Cfront can be found in [ARM,§7.2c].

11.3.3 Retrospective

I think the combination of requiring type-safe linkage, providing a reasonable implementation, and providing an explicit escape for linking to other languages was the right one. As expected, the new linkage system eliminated problems without imposing burdens that users found hard to live with. In addition, a surprising number of linkage errors were found in old C and C++ code converted to the new style. My observation at the time was "switching to type-safe linkage feels like running lint on a C program for the first time – somewhat embarrassing." Lint is a popular tool for checking separately compiled units of C programs for consistent use of types [Kernighan,1984]. During the initial introduction period, I tried to keep track of experiences. Type-safe linkage detected a hitherto undiscovered error in every significant C or C++ program we compiled and linked.

One surprise was that several programmers had acquired the nasty habit of supplying wrong function declarations simply to shut up the compiler. For example, a call `f(1,a)` causes an error if `f()` isn't declared. When that happens, I had naively expected the programmer to either add the right declaration for the function or to add a header file containing that declaration. It turned out that there was a third alternative – just supply *some* declaration that fits the call:

```
void g()
{
    void f(int ...); // added to suppress error message
    // ...
    f(1,a);
}
```

Type-safe linkage detects such sloppiness and reports an error whenever a declaration doesn't match a definition.

We also discovered a portability problem. People declared library functions directly rather than including the proper header file. I suppose the aim was to minimize compilation time, but the effect was that when the code was ported to another system, the declaration became wrong. Type-safe linkage helped us catch quite a few porting problems (mainly between UNIX System V and BSD UNIX) of this kind.

We considered several alternatives to the type-safe linkage schemes before deciding on the one actually added to the language [Stroustrup,1988]:

– Provide no escape and rely on tools for C linkage
– Provide type-safe linkage and overloading for functions explicitly marked `overload` only
– Provide type-safe linkage only for functions that couldn't be C functions because they had types that couldn't be expressed in C

Experience with the way the adopted scheme has been used convinced me that the problems I conjectured for the alternatives were genuine. In particular, extending the checking to all functions by default has been a boon and mixed C/C++ has been so popular that any complication of C/C++ linkage would have been most painful.

Two details prompted complaints from users and are causes for concern still. In one case, I think we made the right choice. In the other, I'm not so sure.

A function declared to have C linkage still has C++ calling semantics. That is, the formal arguments must be declared, and the actual arguments must match under the C++ matching and ambiguity control rules. Some users wanted functions with C linkage to obey the C calling rules. Allowing that would have allowed more direct use of C header files. It would also have allowed sloppy programmers to revert to C's weaker type checking. Another argument against introducing special rules for C, however, is that programmers also asked for Pascal, Fortran, and PL/I linkage complete with support for the function-calling rules from those languages, such as implicit conversion of C-style strings to Pascal-type strings for functions with Pascal linkage, call by reference and added array-type information for functions with Fortran linkage, etc. Had we provided special services for C, we would have been obliged to add knowledge of an unbounded set of language calling conventions to C++ compilers. Resisting that pressure was right, though a significant added service could have been rendered to individual users of mixed language programming systems. Given the C++ semantics (only), people have found references (§3.7) useful to provide interfaces to languages such as Fortran and Pascal that support pass-by-reference arguments.

On the other hand, focusing only on linkage led to a problem. The solution doesn't directly address the problems of an environment that supports mixed-language programming and pointers to functions with different calling conventions. Using the C++ linkage rules, we can directly express that a function obeys C++ or C calling conventions. Specifying that the function itself obeys C++ conventions but its argument obeys C conventions cannot be expressed directly. One solution is to express this indirectly [ARM,pg118]. For example:

```
typedef void (*PV)(void*,void*);

void* sort1(void*, unsigned, PV);
extern "C" void* sort2(void*, unsigned, PV);
```

Here, sort1() has C++ linkage and takes a pointer to a function with C++ linkage; sort2() has C linkage and takes a pointer to a function with C++ linkage. These are the clear-cut cases. On the other hand, consider:

```
extern "C" typedef void (*CPV)(void*,void*);

void* sort3(void*, unsigned, CPV);
extern "C" void* sort4(void*, unsigned, CPV);
```

Here, sort3() has C++ linkage and takes a pointer to a function with C linkage; sort4() has C linkage and takes a pointer to a function with C linkage. That pushes the limits of what the language specifies and is ugly. The alternatives don't seem to be attractive either: You could introduce calling conventions into the type system or use calling stubs extensively to handle such mixtures of calling conventions.

Linkage, inter-language calls, and inter-language object passing are inherently difficult problems and have many implementation-dependent aspects. It is also an area where the ground rules change as new languages, hardware architectures, and implementation techniques are developed. I expect that we haven't heard the last of this matter.

11.4 Object Creation and Copying

Over the years, I have been asked for language features to disallow various operations regularly (say, twice a week for ten years). The reasons vary. Some want to optimize the implementation of a class in ways that can only be done if operations such as copying, derivation, or stack allocation are never performed on objects of that class. In other cases, such as objects representing real-world objects, the required semantics simply don't include all of the operations C++ supplies by default.

The answer to most such requests was discovered during the work on 2.0: If you want to prohibit something, make the operation that does it a private member function (§2.10).

11.4.1 Control of Copying

To prohibit copying of objects of class X, simply make the copy constructor and the assignment operator private:

```
class X {
    X& operator=(const X&);   // assignment
    X(const X&);              // copy constructor
    // ...
public:
    X(int);
    // ...
};


void f()
{
    X a(1);     // fine: can create Xs
    X b = a;    // error: X::X(const X&) private
    b = a;      // error: X::operator=(const X&) private
}
```

Naturally, the implementer of class X can still copy X objects, but in real cases that is typically acceptable or even required. Unfortunately, I don't remember who thought of this first; I doubt it was me, see [Stroustrup,1986,pg172].

I personally consider it unfortunate that copy operations are defined by default and I prohibit copying of objects of many of my classes. However, C++ inherited its default assignment and copy constructors from C, and they are frequently used.

11.4.2 Control of Allocation

Other useful effects can be achieved by declaring operations private. For example, declaring a destructor private prevents stack and global allocation. It also prevents random use of `delete`:

```
class On_free_store {
    ~On_free_store();  // private destructor
    // ...
public:
    static void free(On_free_store* p) { delete p; }
    // ...
};


On_free_store glob1;  // error: private destructor


void f()
{
    On_free_store loc;  // error: private destructor
    On_free_store* p = new On_free_store; // fine
    // ...
    delete p;  // error: private destructor
    On_free_store::free(p); // fine
}
```

Naturally, such a class will typically be used with a highly optimized free store allocator or other semantics taking advantage of objects being on the free store.

The opposite effect – allowing global and local variables, but disallowing free
store allocation – is obtained by declaring only an unusual operator new():

```
class No_free_store {
    class Dummy { };
    void* operator new(size_t,Dummy);
    // ...
};


No_free_store glob2;  // fine


void g()
{
    No_free_store loc;  // fine
    No_free_store* p = new No_free_store; // error:
            // no No_free_store::operator new(size_t)
}
```

11.4.3 Control of Derivation

A private destructor also prevents derivation. For example:

```
class D : public On_free_store {
    // ...
};


D d; // error: cannot call private base class destructor
```

This makes a class with a private destructor the logical complement to an abstract class. It is impossible to derive from `On_free_store`, so calls of `On_free_store` virtual functions need not use the virtual function mechanism. However, I don't think any current compilers optimize based on that.

Later, Andrew Koenig discovered that it was even possible to prevent derivation without imposing restrictions on the kind of allocation that could be done:

```
class Usable_lock {
    friend Usable;
private:
    Usable_lock() {}
};

class Usable : public virtual Usable_lock {
    // ...
public:
    Usable();
    Usable(char*);
    // ...
};

Usable a;

class DD : public Usable { };

DD dd;  // error: DD::DD() cannot access
        // Usable_lock::Usable_lock(): private  member
```

this relies on the rule that a derived class must call the constructor of a virtual base class (implicitly or explicitly).

Such examples are usually more of an intellectual delight than techniques of real importance. Maybe that's why discussing them is so popular.

11.4.4 Memberwise Copy

Originally, assignment and initialization were by default defined as bitwise copy. This caused problems when an object of a class with assignment was used as a member of a class that did not have assignment defined:

```
class X { /* ... */ X& operator=(const X&); };

struct Y { X a; };

void f(Y y1, Y y2)
{
    y1 = y2;
}
```

Here, `y2.a` was copied into `y1.a` with a bitwise copy. This is clearly wrong and simply the result of an oversight when assignment and copy constructors were introduced. After some discussion and at the urging of Andrew Koenig, the obvious solution was adopted: Copying of objects is defined as the memberwise copy of non-static members and base class objects.

This definition states that the meaning of x=y is x.operator=(y). This has an interesting (though not always desirable) implication. Consider:

```
class X { /* ... */ };
class Y : public X { /* ... */ };

void g(X x, Y y)
{
    x = y;   // x.operator=(y): fine
    y = x;   // y.operator=(x): error x is not a Y
}
```

By default, assignment to X is X& X::operator=(const X&) so x=y is legal because Y is publicly derived from X. This is usually called *slicing* because a "slice" of y is assigned to x. Copy constructors are handled in a similar manner.

I'm leery about slicing from a practical point of view, but I don't see any way of preventing it except by adding a very special rule. Also, at the time, I had an independent request for exactly these "slicing semantics" from Ravi Sethi who wanted it from a theoretical and pedagogical point of view: Unless you can assign an object of a derived class to an object of its public base class, then that would be the only point in C++ where a derived object couldn't be used in place of a base object.

This leaves one problem with default copy operations: pointer members are copied, but what they point to isn't. This is almost always wrong, but can't be disallowed because of C compatibility. However, a compiler can easily provide a warning whenever a class with a pointer member is copied using a default copy constructor or assignment. For example:

```
class String {
    char* p;
    int sz;
public:
    // no copy defined here (sloppy)
};

void f(const String& s)
{
    String s2 = s; // warning: pointer copied
    s2 = s;        // warning: pointer copied
}
```

By default, assignment and copy construction in C++ defines what is sometimes called *shallow copy*; that is, it copies the members of a class, but not objects pointed to by those members. The alternative that recursively copies objects pointed to (often called *deep copy*) must be explicitly defined. Given the possibility of self-referential objects things could hardly be otherwise. In general, it is unwise to try to define assignment to do deep copy; defining a (virtual) copy function is usually a much better idea (see [2nd,pp217-220] and §13.7).

11.5 Notational Convenience

My aim was to allow the user to specify the meaning of every operator as long as it made sense and as long as it didn't interfere seriously with predefined semantics. It would have been easier if I could have allowed overloading of all operators without exception, or disallowed overloading of every operator that had a predefined meaning for class objects. The resulting compromise doesn't please everybody.

Almost all discussion and most problems encountered relate to operators that don't fit the usual pattern of binary or prefix arithmetic operators.

11.5.1 Smart Pointers

Before 2.0, the pointer dereference operator -> couldn't be defined by users. This made it hard to create classes of objects intended to behave like "smart pointers." The reason was simply that when I defined operator overloading, I saw -> as a binary operator with very special rules for the right-hand operand (the member name). I remember a meeting at Mentor Graphics in Oregon where Jim Howard jumped up, marched round a rather large conference table to the blackboard, and disabused me of this misconception. Operator ->, he pointed out, could be seen as a unary postfix operator where the result was reapplied to the member name. When I reworked the overloading mechanism, I used that idea.

It follows that if the return type of an `operator->()` function is used, it must be a pointer to a class or an object of a class for which `operator->()` is defined. For example:

```
struct Y { int m; };

class Ptr {
    Y* p;
    // ...
public:
    Ptr(Symbolic_ref);
    ~Ptr();

    Y* operator->()
    {
        // check p
        return p;
    }
};
```

Here, `Ptr` is defined so that `Ptr`s act as pointers to objects of class `Y`, except that some suitable computation is performed on each access.

```
void f(Ptr x, Ptr& xr, Ptr* xp)
{
    x->m;    // x.operator->()->m; that is, x.p->m
    xr->m;   // xr.operator->()->m; that is, xr.p->m
    xp->m;   // error: Ptr does not have a member m
}
```

Such classes are especially useful when defined as templates (§15.9.1) [2nd]:

```
template<class Y> class Ptr { /* ... */ };

void f(Ptr<complex> pc, Ptr<Shape> ps) { /* ... */ }
```

This was understood when overloading of -> was first implemented in 1986. Unfortunately, it was years before templates became available so that such code could actually be written.

For ordinary pointers, use of -> is synonymous with some uses of unary * and []. For example, for a Y* p it holds that:

```
p->m == (*p).m == p[0].m
```

As usual, no such guarantee is provided for user-defined operators. The equivalence can be provided where desired:

```
class Ptr {
    Y* p;
public:
    Y* operator->() { return p; }
    Y& operator*() { return *p; }
    Y& operator[](int i) { return p[i]; }
    // ...
};
```

The overloading of -> is important to a class of interesting programs and not just a minor curiosity. The reason is that *indirection* is a key concept and that overloading -> provides a clean, direct, and efficient way of representing it in a program. Another way of looking at operator -> is to consider it a way of providing C++ with a limited, but very useful, form of *delegation* (§12.7).

11.5.2 Smart References

When I decided to allow overloading of operator ->, I naturally considered whether operator . could be similarly overloaded.

At the time, I considered the following arguments conclusive: If obj is a class object then obj.m has a meaning for every member m of that object's class. We try not to make the language mutable by redefining built-in operations (though that rule is violated for = out of dire need, and for unary &).

If we allowed overloading of . for a class X, we would be unable to access members of X by normal means; we would have to use a pointer and ->, but -> and &

might also have been re-defined. I wanted an extensible language, not a mutable one.

These arguments are weighty, but not conclusive. In particular, in 1990 Jim Adcock proposed to allow overloading of operator . *exactly* the way operator -> is.

Why do people want to overload `operator.()`? To provide a class that acts as a "handle" or a "proxy" for another class in which the real work is done. As an example, here is a multi-precision integer class used in the early discussions of overloading of `operator.()`:

```
class Num {
    // ...
public:
    Num& operator=(const Num&);
    int operator[](int);         // extract digit
    Num operator+(const Num&);
    void truncateNdigits(int);   // truncate
    // ...
};
```

I'd like to define a class `RefNum` that behaves like a `Num&` except for performing some added actions. For example, if I can write:

```
void f(Num a, Num b, Num c, int i)
{
    // ...
    c = a+b;
    int digit = c[i];
    c.truncateNdigits(i);
    // ...
}
```

then also I want to be able to write:

```
void g(RefNum a, RefNum b, RefNum c, int i)
{
    // ...
    c = a+b;
    int digits = c[i];
    c.truncateNdigits(i);
    // ...
}
```

Assume that `operator.()` is defined in exact parallel to `operator->()`. We first try the obvious definition of `RefNum`:

```
class RefNum {
    Num* p;
```

```
public:
    RefNum(Num& a) { p = &a; }
    Num& operator.() { do_something(p); return *p; }
    void bind(Num& q) { p = &q; }
};
```

Unfortunately, this doesn't have the right effect because . isn't explicitly mentioned in all cases:

```
c = a+b;                 // no dot
int digits = c[i];       // no dot
c.truncateNdigits(i);    // call operator.()
```

We would have to write forwarding functions to ensure the right action is performed when operators are applied to a RefNum:

```
class RefNum {
    Num* p;
public:
    RefNum(Num& a) { p = &a; }
    Num& operator.() { do_something(p); return *p; }
    void bind(Num& q) { p = &q; }

    // forwarding functions:

    RefNum& operator=(const RefNum& a)
        { do_something(p); *p=*a.p; return *this; }
    int operator[](int i)
        { do_something(p); return (*p)[i]; }
    RefNum operator+(const RefNum& a)
        { do_something(p); return RefNum(*p+*a.p); }
};
```

This is clearly tedious. Consequently, many people, including Andrew Koenig and me, considered the effect of applying operator.() to every operation on a RefNum. That way, the original definition of RefNum would make the original example work as desired (and initially expected).

However, applying operator.() this way implies that to access a member of RefNum itself you must use a pointer:

```
void h(RefNum r, Num& x)
{
    r.bind(x);        // error: no Num::bind
    (&r)->bind(x);    // ok: call RefNum::bind
}
```

The C++ community seems split over the issue of which interpretation of operator.() is best. I lean towards the view that if operator.() should be allowed then it should be invoked for implicit uses as well as explicit ones. After all, the reason for defining operator.() is to avoid writing forwarding functions. Unless implicit uses of . are interpreted by operator.(), we'll still have to write a lot of forwarding functions, or we would have to eschew operator overloading.

If we can define `operator.()`, the equivalence of `a.m` and `(&a)->m` would no longer hold by definition. It could be made to hold by defining both `operator&()` and `operator->()` to match `operator.()`, though, so I personally don't see that as a significant problem. However, if we did that there would be no way of accessing members of the smart reference class. For example, `RefNum::bind()` would become completely inaccessible.

Is that important? Some people have answered, "No, like ordinary references, smart references shouldn't ever be re-bound to a new object." However, my experience is that smart references often need a re-bind operation or some other operation to make them genuinely useful. Most people seem to agree.

We are thus left in a quandary: We can either maintain the `a.m` and `(&a)->m` equivalence or have access to members of the smart reference, but not both.

One way out of the dilemma would be to forward using `operator.()` for `a.m` only if the reference class doesn't itself have a member called `m`. This happens to be my favorite resolution.

However, there is no consensus on the importance of overloading `operator.()` either. Consequently, `operator.()` isn't part of C++ and the debates rage on.

11.5.3 Overloading Increment and Decrement

The increment operator `++` and the decrement operator `--` were among the operators that users could define. However, Release 1.0 did not provide a mechanism for distinguishing prefix from postfix application. Given

```
class Ptr {
    // ...
    void operator++();
};
```

the single `Ptr::operator++()` will be used for both:

```
void f(Ptr& p)
{
    p++; // p.operator++()
    ++p; // p.operator++()
}
```

Several people, notably Brian Kernighan, pointed out that this restriction was unnatural from a C perspective and prevented users from defining a class that could be used as a replacement for an ordinary pointer.

I had of course considered separate overloading or prefix and postfix increment when I designed the C++ operator overloading mechanism, but I had decided that adding syntax to express it wouldn't be worthwhile. The number of suggestions I received over the years convinced me that I was wrong, provided I could find some minimal change to express the prefix/postfix distinction.

I considered the obvious solution, adding the keywords `prefix` and `postfix` to

C++:

```
class Ptr_to_X {
    // ...
    X& operator prefix++();   // prefix ++
    X operator postfix++();   // postfix ++
};
```

or

```
class Ptr_to_X {
    // ...
    X& prefix operator++();   // prefix ++
    X postfix operator++();   // postfix ++
};
```

However, I received the usual howl of outrage from people who dislike new key-words. Several alternatives that did not involve new keywords were suggested. For example:

```
class Ptr_to_X {
    // ...
    X& ++operator();   // prefix ++
    X operator++();    // postfix ++
};
```

or

```
class Ptr_to_X {
    // ...
    X& operator++();   // prefix because it
                       // returns a reference
    X operator++();    // postfix because it
                       // doesn't return a reference
};
```

I considered the former too cute and the latter too subtle. Finally, I settled on:

```
class Ptr_to_X {
    // ...
    X& operator++();      // prefix: no argument
    X operator++(int);    // postfix: because of
                          // the argument
};
```

This may be both too cute and too subtle, but it works, requires no new syntax, and has a logic to the madness. Other unary operators are prefix and take no arguments when defined as member functions. The "odd" and unused dummy int argument is used to indicate the odd postfix operators. In other words, in the postfix case, ++ comes between the first (real) operand and the second (dummy) argument and is thus postfix.

These explanations are needed because the mechanism is unique and therefore a bit of a wart. Given a choice, I would probably have introduced the `prefix` and `postfix` keywords, but that didn't appear feasible at the time. However, the only really important point is that the mechanism works and can be understood and used by the few programmers who really need it.

11.5.4 Overloading `->*`

Operator `->*` was made overloadable primarily because there wasn't any reason not to (because of orthogonality, if you must). It turns out to be useful for expressing binding operations that somehow have semantics that parallel those of the built-in meaning for `->*` (§13.11). No special rules are needed; `->*` behaves just like any other binary operator.

Operator `.*` wasn't included among the operators a programmer could overload for the same reason operator `.` wasn't (§11.5.2).

11.5.5 Overloading the Comma Operator

At the urging of Margaret Ellis, I allowed overloading of the comma operator. Basically, I couldn't find any reason not to at the time. Actually, there is a reason: `a,b` is already defined for any `a` and `b`, so allowing overloading enables the programmer to change the meaning of a built-in operator. Fortunately, that is only possible if either `a` or `b` is a class object. There appear to be few practical uses of `operator,()`. Accepting it was primarily a generalization.

11.6 Adding Operators to C++

There never are enough operators to suit everyone's taste. In fact, it seems that with the exception of people who are against essentially all operators on principle, everyone wants a few extra operators.

11.6.1 An Exponentiation Operator

Why doesn't C++ have an exponentiation operator? The original reason was that C doesn't have one. The semantics of C operators are supposed to be simple to the point where they each correspond to a machine instruction on a typical computer. An exponentiation operator doesn't meet this criterion.

Why didn't I immediately add an exponentiation operator when I first designed C++? My aim was to provide abstraction mechanisms, not new primitive operations. An exponentiation operator would have to be given a meaning for built-in arithmetic types. This was the area of C that I was determined to avoid changing. Further, C and therefore C++ are commonly criticized for having too many operators with a confusing variety of precedences. Despite these significant deterrents, I still considered adding an exponentiation operator and might have done so had there been no technical problems. I wasn't fully convinced that an exponentiation operator was really needed in a language with overloading and inline functions, but it was tempting to add the operator simply to silence the repeated assertions that it was needed.

The exponentiation operator people wanted was `**`. This would cause a problem because `a**b` can be a legal C expression involving a dereference of a pointer `b`:

```
double f(double a, double* b)
{
    return a**b; // meaning a*(*b)
}
```

In addition, there seemed to be some disagreement among proponents of an exponentiation operator about which precedence that operator ought to have:

```
a = b**c**d;   // (b**c)**d or b**(c**d)  ?
a = -b**c;     // (-b)**c or -(b**c)  ?
```

Finally, I had little wish to specify the mathematical properties of exponentiation.

At the time, these reasons convinced me that I could serve users better by focusing on other issues. In retrospect, all of these problems can be overcome. The real question is "Would it be worthwhile to do so?" The issue was brought to a head when Matt Austern presented a complete proposal to the C++ standards committee (§6) in 1992. On its way to the committee this proposal had received a lot of comments and been the subject of much debate on the net.

Why do people want an exponentiation operator?

–   They are used to it from Fortran.
–   They believe that an exponentiation operator is much more likely to be optimized than an exponentiation function.
–   A function call is uglier in the kind of expressions actually written by physicists and other primary users of exponentiation.

Are these reasons sufficient to counterbalance the technical problems and objections? Also, how can the technical problems be overcome? The extensions working group discussed these issues and decided not to add an exponentiation operator. Dag Brück summarized the reasons:

–   An operator provides notational convenience, but does not provide any new functionality. Members of the working group, representing heavy users of scientific/engineering computation, indicated that the operator syntax provides *minor* syntactic convenience.
–   Every user of C++ must learn this new feature.
–   Users have stressed the importance of substituting their own specialized exponentiation functions for the system default, which would not be possible with an intrinsic operator.
–   The proposal is not sufficiently well motivated. In particular, by looking at one 30,000 line Fortran program one cannot conclude that the operator would be widely used in C++.
–   The proposal requires adding a new operator and adding another precedence level, thus increasing the complexity of the language.

This brief statement somewhat understates the depth of the discussion. For example, several committee members reviewed significant bodies of corporate code for use of exponentiation and didn't find the usage as critical as is sometimes asserted. Another key observation was that the majority of occurrences of `**` in the Fortran code examined were of the form `a**n` where n was a small integer literal; writing `a*a` and `a*a*a` seemed viable alternatives in most cases.

Whether it would have been less work in the long run to accept the proposal remains to be seen. However, let me present some of the technical issues. Which operator would be best as a C++ exponentiation operator? C uses all the graphical characters in the ASCII character set with the exception of `@` and `$`, and these were for several reasons not suitable. The operators `!`, `~`, `*~`, `^^`, and even plain `^` when either operand was non-integral were considered. However, `@`, `$`, `~`, and `!` are national characters that don't appear on all keyboards (see §6.5.3.1); `@` and `$` are further perceived by many as ugly for this purpose. The tokens `^` and `^^` read "exclusive or" to C programmers. An added constraint is that it should be possible to combine the exponentiation operator with the assignment operator in the same way other arithmetic operators are; for example, `+` and `=` gives `+=`. This eliminates `!` because `!=` already has a meaning. Matt Austern therefore settled on `*^` and that is probably the best such choice.

All other technical issues were settled by following their resolution in Fortran. This is the only sane solution and saves a lot of work. Fortran is the standard in this area, and it requires very significant reasons to part ways with a de facto standard.

This point led me to revisit `**` as an exponentiation operator for C++. I had, of course, demonstrated that this was impossible using traditional techniques, but when looking at the question again I realized that the C compatibility issues could be overcome by some compiler trickery. Assume we introduced the operator `**`. We could handle the incompatibility by defining it to mean "dereference and multiply" when its second operand is a pointer:

```
void f(double a, double b, int* p)
{
    a**b;   // meaning pow(a,b)
    a**p;   // meaning a*(*p)
    **a;    // error: a is not a pointer
    **p;    // error: means *(*p) and *p is not a pointer
}
```

To fit into the language `**` would of course have to be a token. This implies that when `**` appears as a declarator it must be interpreted as double indirection:

```
char** p; // means char * * p;
```

The main problem with this is that the precedence of `**` must be higher than `*` for `a/b**c` to mean what mathematicians would expect, that is `a/(b**c)`. On the other hand `a/b**p` in C means `(a/b) * (*p)` and would quietly change its meaning to `a/(b*(*p))`. I suspect such code is rare in C and C++. Breaking it would be worthwhile *if* we decided to provide an exponentiation operator – especially because it would be trivial for a compiler to issue a warning where the meaning might change.

However, we decided not to add an exponentiation operator, so the issue is now purely academic. I was amused to see the horror that my semi-serious suggestion to use `**` caused. I am also continuously amused and puzzled over the amount of heat generated by minor syntactic issues such as whether exponentiation should be spelled `pow(a,b)`, `a**b`, or `a*^b`.

11.6.2 User-defined Operators

Could I have avoided the whole discussion about an exponentiation operator by designing a mechanism that allowed users to define their own operators? This would have solved the problem of missing operators in general.

When you need operators you invariably find that the set provided by C and C++ is insufficient to express every desired operation. The solution is to define functions. However, once you can say

```
a*b
```

for some class, functional forms like

```
pow(a,b)
abs(a)
```

start to look unsatisfactory. Consequently, people ask for the ability to define a meaning for

```
a pow b
abs a
```

This can be done. Algol68 showed one way. Further, people ask for the ability to define a meaning for

```
a ** b
a // b
|a
```

etc. This too can be done. The real question is whether allowing user-defined operators is worthwhile. I observed [ARM]:

"This extension, however, would imply a significant extension of complexity of syntax analysis and an uncertain gain in readability. It would be necessary either to allow the user to specify both the binding strength and the associativity of new operators or to fix those attributes for all user-defined operators. In either case, the binding of expressions such as

```
a = b**c**d;      // (b**c)**d or b**(c**d)  ?
```

would be surprising or annoying to many users. It would also be necessary to resolve clashes with the syntax of the usual operators. Consider this, assuming `**` and `//` to be defined as binary operators:

```
a = a**p;    // a**p OR a*(*p)
a = a//p;
*p = 7;      // a = a*p = 7; maybe? ''
```

Consequently, user-defined operators would either have to be restricted to ordinary characters or require a distinguishing prefix such as . (dot):

```
a pow b;     // alternative 1
a .pow b;    // alternative 2
a .** b;     // alternative 3
```

User-defined operators must be given a precedence. The easiest way to do that is to specify the precedence of a user-defined operator to be the same as some built-in operator. However, that would not suffice to define the exponentiation operator "correctly." For that we need something more elaborate. For example:

```
operator pow: binary, precedence between * and unary
```

Also, I am seriously worried about the readability of programs with user-defined operators with user-defined precedences. For example, more than one precedence for exponentiation has been used in programming languages so different people would define different precedences for pow. For example,

```
a = - b pow c * d;
```

would be parsed differently in different programs.

A simpler alternative is to give all user-defined operators the same precedence. The latter seemed very attractive until I discovered that even I and my two closest collaborators at the time, Andrew Koenig and Jonathan Shopiro, were unable to agree on a precedence. The obvious candidates are "very high" (for example, just above multiply) and "very low" (for example, just above assignment). Unfortunately, the number of cases where one seems ideal and the other absurd appeared endless. For example, it seems hard to get even the simplest example "right" with only a single precedence level. Consider:

```
a = b * c pow d;
a = b product c pow d;
a put b + c;
```

Thus, C++ doesn't support user-defined operators.

11.6.3 Composite Operators

C++ supports overloading of unary and binary operators. I suspect it would be useful to support overloading of composite operators. In the ARM, I explained the idea like this:

"For example, the two multiplications in

```
Matrix a, b, c, d;
// ...
a = b * c * d;
```

might be implemented by a specially defined "double multiplication" operator defined like this:

```
Matrix operator * * (Matrix&, Matrix&, Matrix&);
```

that would cause the statement above to be interpreted like this:

```
a = operator * * (b,c,d);
```

In other words, having seen the declaration

```
Matrix operator * * (Matrix&, Matrix&, Matrix&);
```

the compiler looks for patterns of repeated `Matrix` multiplications and calls the function to interpret them. Patterns that are different or too complicated are handled using the usual (unary and binary) operators.

This extension has been independently invented several times as an efficient way of coping with common patterns of use in scientific computing using user-defined types. For example,

```
Matrix operator = * + (
    Matrix&,
    const Matrix&,
    double,
    const Matrix&
);
```

for handling statements like this:

```
a=b*1.7+d; ''
```

Naturally, the placement of whitespace would be very significant in such declarations. Alternatively, some other token could be used to signify the position of the operands:

```
Matrix operator.=.*.+.(
    Matrix&,
    const Matrix&,
    double,
    const Matrix&
);
```

I have never seen this idea explained in print prior to the ARM, but it is a common technique in code generators. I consider the idea promising for supporting optimized vector and matrix operations, but I have never had time to develop it sufficiently to be sure. It would be notational support for the old technique of defining functions performing composite operations given several arguments.

11.7 Enumerations

C enumerations constitute a curiously half-baked concept. Enumerations were not
part of the original conception of C and were apparently reluctantly introduced into
the language as a concession to people who insisted on getting a form of symbolic
constants more substantial than Cpp's parameterless macros. Consequently, the value
of a C enumerator is of type `int`, and so is the value of a variable declared to be of
"enumerator type." An `int` can be freely assigned to any enumeration variable. For
example:

```
enum Color { red, green, blue };

void f() /* C function */
{
    enum Color c = 2; /* ok */
    int i = c;        /* ok */
}
```

I had no need for enumerations in the styles of programming I wished to support and
no particular wish to meddle in the affairs of enumerations, so C++ adopted C's rule
unchanged.

Unfortunately (or fortunately, if you like enumerations), the ANSI C committee
left me with a problem. They changed or clarified the definition of enumerations such
that pointers to different enumerations appeared to be different types:

```
enum Vehicle { car, horse_buggy, rocket };

void g(pc,pv) enum Color* pc; enum Vehicle* pv;
{
    pc = pv; /* probably illegal in ANSI C */
}
```

I had a longish discussion of this point involving C experts such as David Hanson,
Brian Kernighan, Andrew Koenig, Doug McIlroy, David Prosser, and Dennis Ritchie.
The discussion wasn't completely conclusive – that in itself was an ominous sign –
but there was an agreement that the intent of the standard was to outlaw the example,
except maybe leaving a loophole accepting the example if (as is common) `Color` and
`Vehicle` are represented by the same amount of storage.

This uncertainty was unacceptable to me because of function overloading. For
example:

```
void f(Color*);
void f(Vehicle*);
```

must either declare one function twice or two overloaded functions. I had no wish to
accept any weaselwording or implementation dependency. Similarly,

```
void f(Color);
void f(Vehicle);
```

must either declare one function or two overloaded functions. In C and pre-ARM C++, those declarations declared a single function twice. However, the cleanest way out was to deem each enumeration a separate type. For example:

```
void h() // C++
{
    Color c = 2;   // error
    c = Color(2); // ok: 2 explicitly converted to Color
    int i = c;     // ok: col implicitly converted to int
}
```

This resolution had been vocally demanded by someone every time I had discussed enumerations with C++ programmers. I suspect I acted rashly – despite months of delay and endless consulting with C and C++ experts – but nevertheless reached the best resolution for the future.

11.7.1 Overloading based on Enumerations

Having declared each enumeration a separate type, I forgot something obvious: An enumeration is a separate type defined by the user. Consequently, it is a user-defined type just as a class is. Consequently, it is possible to overload operators based on an enumeration. Martin O'Riordan pointed this out at an ANSI/ISO meeting. Together with Dag Brück, he worked out the details and overloading based on enumerations was accepted into C++. For example:

```
enum Season { winter, spring, summer, fall };

Season operator++(Season s)
{
    switch (s) {
    case winter: return spring;
    case spring: return summer;
    case summer: return fall;
    case fall:   return winter;
    }
}
```

I used the switch to avoid integer arithmetic and casts.

11.7.2 A Boolean Type

One of the most common enumerations is

```
enum bool { false, true };
```

Every major program has that one or one of its cousins:

```
#define bool char
#define Bool int
typedef unsigned int BOOL;
typedef enum { F, T } Boolean;
const true = 1;
#define TRUE 1
#define False (!True)
```

The variations are apparently endless. Worse, most variations imply slight variations in semantics, and most clash with other variations when used together.

Naturally, this problem has been well known for years. Dag Brück and Andrew Koenig decided to do something about it:

''The idea of a Boolean data type in C++ is a religious issue. Some people, particularly those coming from Pascal or Algol, consider it absurd that C should lack such a type, let alone C++. Others, particularly those coming from C, consider it absurd that anyone would bother to add such a type to C++.''

Naturally, the first idea was to define an enum. However, an examination of hundreds of thousands of lines of C++ by Dag Brück and Sean Corfield revealed that most Boolean types were used in ways that required free conversion to and from int. This implied that defining a Boolean enumeration would break too much existing code. So why bother with a Boolean type?

[1] The Boolean data type is a fact of life whether it is a part of a C++ standard or not.

[2] The many clashing definitions makes it hard to use *any* Boolean type conveniently and safely.

[3] Many people want to overload based on a Boolean type.

Somewhat to my surprise, the ANSI/ISO accepted this argument so bool is now a distinct integral type in C++ with literals true and false. Non-zero values can be implicitly converted to true, and true can be implicitly converted to 1. Zero can be implicitly converted to false, and false can be implicitly converted to 0. This ensures a high degree of compatibility.

12

Multiple Inheritance

*Because you have
a mother and a father :-)
– comp.lang.c++*

Timing of multiple inheritance — ordinary base classes — virtual base classes — the dominance rule — the object layout model — casting from a virtual base — method combination — the multiple inheritance controversy — delegation — renaming — base and member initializers.

12.1 Introduction

In most people's minds multiple inheritance, the ability to have two or more direct base classes, was *the* feature of 2.0. I disagreed at the time because I felt that the sum of the improvements to the type system was of far greater practical importance.

Also, adding multiple inheritance *in Release 2.0* was a mistake. Multiple inheritance belongs in C++, but is far less important than parameterized types – and to some people, parameterized types are again less important than exception handling. As it happened, parameterized types in the form of templates appeared only in Release 3.0, and exceptions even later. I missed parameterized types much more than I would have missed multiple inheritance.

There were several reasons for choosing to work on multiple inheritance at the time: The design was further advanced, multiple inheritance fits into the C++ type system without major extensions, and the implementation could be done within Cfront. Another factor was purely irrational. Nobody seemed to doubt that I could implement templates efficiently. Multiple inheritance, on the other hand, was widely supposed to be very difficult to implement efficiently. For example, in a summary of C++ in his book on Objective C Brad Cox actually claimed that adding multiple inheritance to C++ was impossible [Cox,1986]. Thus, multiple inheritance seemed more of a challenge. Since I had considered multiple inheritance as early as 1982 (§2.13) and found a simple and efficient implementation technique in 1984, I couldn't resist the challenge. I suspect this to be the only case in which fashion affected the sequence of events.

In September 1984, I presented the C++ operator overloading mechanism at the IFIP WG2.4 conference in Canterbury [Stroustrup,1984b]. There, I met Stein Krogdahl from the University of Oslo, who was just finishing a proposal for adding multiple inheritance to Simula [Krogdahl,1984]. His ideas became the basis for the implementation of ordinary multiple base classes in C++. He and I later learned that the proposal was almost identical to an idea for providing multiple inheritance in Simula. Ole-Johan Dahl considered multiple inheritance in 1966 and rejected it because it would have complicated the Simula garbage collector [Dahl,1988].

12.2 Ordinary Base Classes

The original and fundamental reason for considering multiple inheritance was simply to allow two classes to be combined into one in such a way that objects of the resulting class would behave as objects of either base class [Stroustrup,1986]:

''A fairly standard example of the use of multiple inheritance would be to provide two library classes `displayed` and `task` for representing objects under the control of a display manager and co-routines under the control of a scheduler, respectively. A programmer could then create classes such as

```
class my_displayed_task : public displayed, public task {
        // ...
};


class my_task : public task {   // not displayed
        // ...
};


class my_displayed : public displayed {   // not a task
        // ...
};
```

Using (only) single inheritance, only two of these three choices would be open to the programmer.''

At the time, I was worried about library classes growing too large (''bloated with features'') by trying to serve too many needs. I saw multiple inheritance as a potentially important means of organizing libraries around simpler classes with fewer interclass dependencies. The `task` and `displayed` example shows a way of representing concurrency and output by distinct classes without putting an added burden on application programmers.

''Ambiguities are handled at compile time:

```
class A { public: void f(); /* ... */ };
class B { public: void f(); /* ... */ };
class C : public A, public B {  /* no f() ... */ };

void g()
{
    C* p;
    p->f(); // error: ambiguous
}
```

In this, C++ differs from the object-oriented Lisp dialects that support multiple inheritance [Stroustrup,1987].''

Resolving such ambiguity by an order dependence, say, by preferring A::f because A comes before B in the base class list, was rejected because of negative experience with order dependences elsewhere; see §11.2.2 and §6.3.1. I rejected all forms of dynamic resolution beyond the use of virtual functions as unsuitable for a statically typed language intended for use under severe efficiency constraints.

12.3 Virtual Base Classes

Paraphrasing [Stroustrup,1987]:

"A class can appear more than once in an inheritance DAG (Directed Acyclic Graph):

```
class task : public link { /* ... */ };
class displayed : public link { /* ... */ };
class displayed_task
      : public displayed, public task { /* ... */ };
```

In this case, an object of class displayed_task has two sub-objects of class link: task::link and displayed::link. This is often useful, as in the case of an implementation of lists requiring each element on a list to contain a link element. This allows a displayed_task to be on both the list of displayeds and the list of tasks at the same time."

Or graphically, showing the sub-objects needed to represent a displayed_task:

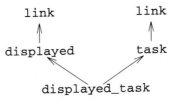

I don't consider this style of list ideal in all situations, but where it fits, it is usually optimal, and I would hate to see it prohibited. Thus, C++ supports the example above. By default, a base class appearing twice will be represented as two sub-objects. However, there is another possible resolution [Stroustrup,1987]:

"I call this *independent multiple inheritance*. However, many proposed uses of multiple inheritance assume a dependence among base classes (for example, the style of providing a selection of features for a window). Such dependencies can be expressed in terms of an object shared between the various derived classes. In other words, there must be a way of specifying that a base class must give rise to only one object in the final derived class even if it is mentioned as a base class several times. To distinguish this usage from independent multiple inheritance such base classes are specified to be virtual:

```
class AW : public virtual W { /* ... */ };
class BW : public virtual W { /* ... */ };
class CW : public AW, public BW { /* ... */ };
```

A single object of class W is to be shared between AW and BW; that is, only one W object must be included in CW as the result of deriving CW from AW and BW. Except for giving rise to a unique object in a derived class, a `virtual` base class behaves exactly like a non-virtual base class.

The "virtualness" of W is a property of the derivation specified by AW and BW and not a property of W itself. Every `virtual` base in an inheritance DAG refers to the same object."

Or graphically:

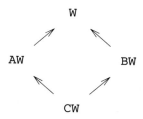

What might W, AW, BW, and CW be in real programs? My original example was a simple windows system, based on ideas from the Lisp literature:

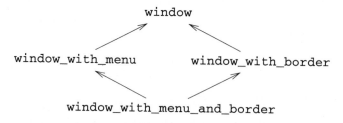

This, in my experience, is a bit contrived, but was based on a real example and, most importantly for presentation, it was intuitive. Several examples can be found in the standard iostreams library [Shopiro,1989]:

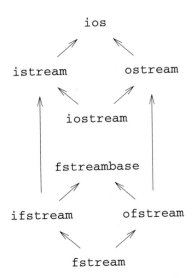

I saw no reason for virtual base classes being more useful or more fundamental than ordinary base classes or vice versa, so I decided to support both. I chose ordinary bases as the default because their implementation is cheaper in run time and space than virtual bases and because "programming using virtual bases is a bit trickier than programming using non-virtual bases. The problem is to avoid multiple calls of a function in a virtual class when that is not desired" [2nd]; see also §12.5.

Because of implementation difficulties, I was tempted not to include the notion of virtual bases in the language. However, I considered the argument that there had to be a way to represent dependencies between sibling classes conclusive. Sibling classes can communicate only through a common root class, through global data, or through explicit pointers. If there were no virtual base classes, the need for a common root would lead to overuse of "universal" base classes. The mixin style described in §12.3.1 is an example of such "sibling communication."

If multiple inheritance should be supported, some such facility had to be included. On the other hand, I consider the simple and unexciting applications of multiple inheritance, such as defining one class with the sum of the attributes of two otherwise independent classes, by far the most useful.

12.3.1 Virtual Bases and Virtual Functions

The combination of abstract classes and virtual base classes was intended to support a style of programming roughly corresponding to the mixin style used in some Lisp systems. That is, an abstract base class defines an interface, and several derived classes contribute to the implementation. Each derived class (each mixin) contributes something to the complete class (mix). The origin of the term *mixin* is reliably reported to be the addition of nuts, raisins, gummy bears, cookies, etc., to ice cream in an ice cream shop somewhere near MIT.

To enable this style, two rules are necessary:

[1] It must be possible to override virtual functions of a base class from different derived classes; otherwise, the essential parts of an implementation must come from a single inheritance chain as in the `slist_set` example in §13.2.2.

[2] It must be possible to determine which function is the one overriding a virtual function and to catch inconsistent overriding in an inheritance lattice; otherwise we would have to rely on order dependencies or run-time resolution.

Consider the example above. Say W had virtual functions `f()` and `g()`:

```
class W {
    // ...
    virtual void f();
    virtual void g();
};
```

and AW and BW each overrode one of those:

```
class AW : public virtual W {
    // ...
    void g();
};
```

```
class BW : public virtual W {
    // ...
    void f();
};
```

```
class CW : public AW, public BW, public virtual W {
    // ...
};
```

Then a CW can be used like this:

```
CW* pcw = new CW;
AW* paw = pcw;
BW* pbw = pcw;

void fff()
{
    pcw->f();   // invokes BW::f()
    pcw->g();   // invokes AW::g()

    paw->f();   // invokes BW::f() !
    pbw->g();   // invokes AW::g() !
}
```

As ever for virtual functions, the same function is called independently of the type of pointer used for the object. The importance of this is exactly that it allows different classes to add to a common base class and benefit from each other's contributions. Naturally, the derived classes have to be designed with this in mind and can sometimes be composed only with care and some knowledge of sibling classes.

Allowing overriding from different branches requires a rule for what is acceptable and for what combinations of overriding are to be rejected as errors. The same function must be invoked by a virtual function call independently of how the class object is specified. Andrew Koenig and I discovered what we consider the only rule that ensures that [ARM]:

"A name B::f *dominates* a name A::f if its class B has A as a base. If a name dominates another, no ambiguity exists between the two; the dominant name is used when there is a choice. For example,

```
class V { public: int f(); int x; };
class B : public virtual V { public: int f(); int x; };
class C : public virtual V { };


class D : public B, public C { void g(); };


void D::g()
{
    x++;      // ok: B::x dominates V::x
    f();      // ok: B::f() dominates V::f()
}
```

Or graphically,

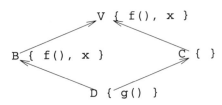

Note that dominance applies to names and not just to functions.

The dominance rule is necessary for virtual functions – since it *is* the rule for which function should be invoked for a virtual call – and experience showed it applying nicely to non-virtual functions as well. Early use of a compiler that did not apply the dominance rule to non-virtual functions led to programmer errors and contorted programs."

From an implementer's point of view, the dominance rule is the usual lookup rule applied to determine whether there is a unique function that can be put in the virtual function table. A laxer rule doesn't ensure this, and a stricter rule would disallow reasonable calls.

The rules for abstract classes and the dominance rule ensure that objects can be created only for classes that provide a complete and consistent set of services. Without these rules, a programmer would have little hope of avoiding serious run-time errors when using nontrivial frameworks.

12.4 The Object Layout Model

Multiple inheritance complicates the object model in two ways:

[1] An object can have more than one virtual function table.

[2] A virtual function table must provide a way of finding the sub-object corresponding to the class that supplied the virtual function.

Consider:

```
class A {
public:
    virtual void f(int);
};

class B {
public:
    virtual void f(int);
    virtual void g();
};

class C : public A , public B {
public:
    void f(int);
};
```

An object of class C might look like this:

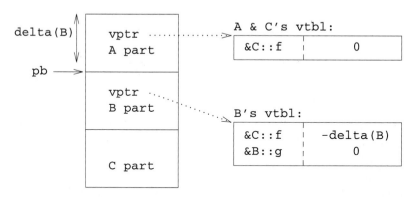

The two `vtbls` are necessary because you can have objects of classes A and B as well as As and Bs that are parts of a C. When you get a pointer to a B, you must be able to invoke a virtual function without knowing whether that B is a "plain B," a "B part" of a C, or some third kind of object containing a B. Thus, every B needs a `vtbl` that is accessed in the same way in all cases.

The delta is necessary because once the `vtbl` is found, the function invoked must be invoked for the sub-object for which it was defined. For example, calling `g()` for a C object requires a `this` pointer pointing to the B sub-object of the C, while a call of `f()` for a C object requires a `this` pointer pointing to the complete C object.

Given the layout suggested above, a call

```
void ff(B* pb)
{
    pb->f(2);
}
```

can be implemented by code like this:

```
/* generated code */
vtbl_entry* vt = &pb->vtbl[index(f)];
(*vt->fct)((B*)((char*)pb+vt->delta),2);
```

This is the implementation strategy I followed when I first implemented multiple inheritance in Cfront. It has the virtue of being easily expressed in C and is therefore portable. The generated code also has the advantage of containing no branching, so it is fast on heavily pipelined machine architectures.

An alternative implementation avoids storing the delta for the this pointer in the virtual function table. Instead, a pointer to code to be executed is stored. When no adjustment to this is needed, the pointer in the vtbl points to the instance of the virtual function to be executed; when this must be adjusted, the pointer in the vtbl points to code that adjusts the pointer then executes the appropriate instance of the virtual function. The class C, declared above, would be represented in this scheme as follows:

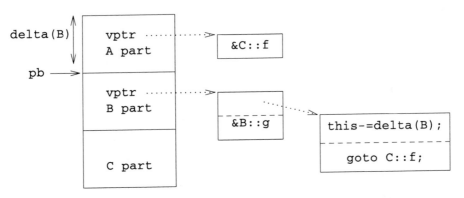

This scheme allows more compact virtual function tables. It also gives faster calls to virtual functions where the delta is 0. Note that the delta is 0 in all single inheritance cases. The change of control after the modification with the delta can be costly on heavily pipelined machines, but these kinds of costs are very architecture-dependent, so no general guidelines can be given. The drawback of such a scheme is that it is less portable. For example, not all machine architectures allow a jump into the body of another function.

The code that adjusts the this pointer is usually called a *thunk*. This name goes back at least as far as the early implementations of Algol60 where such small pieces of code were used to implement call-by-name.

I knew these two implementation strategies for virtual functions at the time I designed multiple inheritance and first implemented it. From a language-design point of view they are almost equivalent, but the thunk implementation has the desirable property that no cost in time or space is incurred for C++ programs using single inheritance – thus fulfilling the zero-overhead "design rule" exactly (§4.5). Both implementation strategies provide acceptable performance in the cases I have looked at.

12.4.1 Virtual Base Layout

Why was a "virtual base class" called `virtual`? Often, I just give the flip explanation "well, `virtual` means magic," and carry on with some more urgent issue, but there is a better explanation. That explanation emerged in discussions with Doug McIlroy long before the first public presentation of multiple inheritance in C++. A virtual function is a function that you find through an indirection through an object. Similarly, the object representing a virtual base class isn't in a fixed position in all classes derived from it and must thus also be accessed through an indirection. Also, a base class is defined as an unnamed member. Consequently, had virtual data members been allowed, a virtual base class would have been an example of a virtual data member. I wish I had implemented virtual bases in the way suggested by this explanation. For example, given a class X with a virtual base V and a virtual function f we'd have:

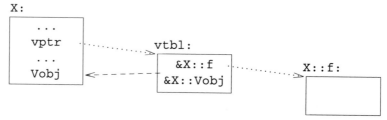

rather than the "optimized" implementation I used in Cfront:

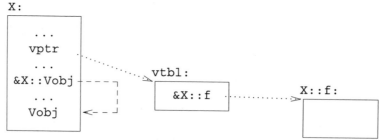

What is called `&X::Vobj` in these figures is the offset of the object representing the virtual base V in X. The former model is cleaner and more general. It wastes a miniscule amount of run time compared to the "optimized" model while saving some space.

Virtual data members is one of the extensions that people keep proposing for C++.

Typically, a proposer wants only "static virtual data," "constant virtual data," or even "constant static virtual data," rather than a more general concept. However, it has been my experience that the proposer typically has a single application in mind: run-time identification of an object's type. There are other ways of getting that; see §14.2.

12.4.2 Virtual Bases and Casting

Sometimes, people express surprise that being a virtual base class is a property of the derivation rather than a property of the base class itself. However, the object layout model described above doesn't provide sufficient information to find a derived class given only a pointer to one of its virtual bases; there is no "back pointer" to the enclosing objects. For example:

```
class A : public virtual complex { /* ... */ };
class B : public virtual complex { /* ... */ };
class C : public A, public B { /* ... */ };

void f(complex* p1, complex* p2, complex* p3)
{
    (A*)p1; // error: can't cast from virtual base
    (A*)p2; // error: can't cast from virtual base
    (A*)p3; // error: can't cast from virtual base
}
```

Given a call:

```
void g()
{
    f(new A, new B, new C);
}
```

the complex pointed to by p1 is unlikely to be in the same position relative to the A as it is in the complex pointed to by p2. Consequently, a cast from a virtual base to a derived class requires a run-time action based on information stored in the base class object. Such information cannot be available in objects of simple classes under layout constraints.

Had I viewed casts with less suspicion, I would have viewed the lack of casting from virtual bases as more serious. Anyway, classes accessed through virtual functions and classes that simply hold a few data items often make the best virtual bases. If a base has only data members, you shouldn't pass a pointer to it around as a representative of the complete class. If, on the other hand, a base has virtual functions you can call those functions. In either case, casting ought to be unnecessary. Also, if you really must cast from a base to its derived class, then dynamic_cast (§14.2.2) solves this problem for bases with virtual functions.

Ordinary bases are in a fixed position in every object of a given derived class and that position is known to the compiler. Therefore, a pointer to an ordinary base class can be cast to a pointer to a derived class without special problems or overhead.

Had it been required that a class should be explicitly declared as a "potential virtual base," special rules could have applied to virtual bases. For example, information could have been added to allow casting from a "virtual base" to a class derived from it. My reason for not making a "virtual base class" a special kind of class was that this would have forced programmers to define two different versions of a concept: one for ordinary class use and another for virtual base use.

Alternatively, we could add the overhead necessary for fully general virtual class use to every class object. However, that would impose significant overhead on applications that don't use virtual bases and would cause layout compatibility problems.

Consequently, I allowed any class to be used as a virtual base and accepted the ban on casting as a restriction on the use of virtual bases.

12.5 Method Combination

It is quite common to synthesize a derived class function from base class versions of the same function. This is often called *method combination* and is supported directly in some object-oriented languages, but – except for constructors, destructors, and copy operations – not in C++. Maybe I should have revived the notion of `call` and `return` functions (§2.11.3) to mimic the CLOS `:before` and `:after` methods. However, people were already worrying about the complexity of the multiple inheritance mechanisms, and I am always reluctant to re-open old wounds.

Instead, I observed that method combination could be achieved manually. The problem is to avoid multiple calls of a function in a virtual class when that is not desired. Here is a possible style:

```
class W {
    // ...
protected:
    void _f() { /* W's own stuff */ }
    // ...
public:
    void f() { _f(); }
    // ...
};
```

Each class provides a protected function `_f()` doing "the class' own stuff" for use by derived classes. It also provides a public function `f()` as the interface for use by the "general public." A derived class's `f()` does its "own stuff" by calling `_f()` and its base classes' "own stuff" by calling their `_f()`s:

```
class A : public virtual W {
    // ...
protected:
    void _f() { /* A's own stuff */ }
    // ...
```

```
public:
    void f() { _f(); W::_f(); }
    // ...
};

class B : public virtual W  {
    // ...
protected:
    void _f() { /* B's own stuff */ }
    // ...
public:
    void f() { _f(); W::_f(); }
    // ...
};
```

In particular, this style enables a class that is (indirectly) derived twice from a class W
to call W::f() only once:

```
class C : public A, public B, public virtual W {
    // ...
protected:
    void _f() { /* C's own stuff */ }
    // ...
public:
    void f() { _f(); A::_f(); B::_f(); W::_f(); }
    // ...
};
```

This is less convenient than automatically generated composite functions, but in some
ways it is more flexible.

12.6 The Multiple Inheritance Controversy

Multiple inheritance in C++ became controversial [Cargill,1991] [Carroll,1991]
[Waldo,1991] [Sakkinen,1992] [Waldo,1993] for several reasons. The arguments
against it centered around the real and imaginary complexity of the concept, its utility,
and the impact of multiple inheritance on other language features and on tool building:

   [1] Multiple inheritance was seen as the first major extension to C++. Some C++
       old-timers saw it as an unnecessary frill, a complication, and possibly as the
       wedge that would open the door to an avalanche of new features into C++. For
       example, at the very first C++ conference in Santa Fe (§7.1.2) Tom Cargill got
       loud applause for the amusing, but not very realistic, suggestion that anyone
       who proposed a new feature for C++ should also propose an old feature of sim-
       ilar complexity to be removed. I approve of the sentiment, but cannot draw the
       conclusion that C++ would be better without multiple inheritance or that C++
       as of 1985 is better than its larger 1993 incarnation. Jim Waldo later followed

up Tom's suggestion with a further idea: Proposers of new features should be required to donate a kidney. That would – Jim pointed out – make people think hard before proposing, and even people without any sense would propose at most two extensions. I note that not everyone is as keen on new features as one might think from reading journals, reading netnews, and listening to questions after talks.

[2] I implemented multiple inheritance in a way that imposed an overhead even if a user didn't use anything but single inheritance. This violated the "you don't pay for what you don't use" rule (§4.5) and led to the (false) impression that multiple inheritance is inherently inefficient. I considered the overhead acceptable because it was small (one array access plus one addition per virtual function call), and because I knew a simple technique for implementing multiple inheritance so that there is absolutely no change in the implementation of a virtual function call in a single inheritance hierarchy (§12.4). I chose the "sub-optimal" implementation because it was more portable.

[3] Smalltalk doesn't support multiple inheritance, and a number of people equate object-oriented programming with both "good" and Smalltalk. Such people often surmise that "if Smalltalk doesn't have it, multiple inheritance must be either bad or unnecessary." Naturally, this doesn't follow. Maybe Smalltalk would benefit from multiple inheritance – and maybe it wouldn't; that is not the issue. However, it was clear to me that several of the techniques that Smalltalk aficionados recommended as alternatives to multiple inheritance didn't apply to a statically typed language such as C++. Language wars are typically silly; the ones that center on single features in isolation are even more silly. Attacks on multiple inheritance that are really misdirected attacks on static type checking or disguised defenses against imagined attacks on Smalltalk are best ignored.

[4] My presentation of multiple inheritance [Stroustrup,1987] was very technical and focused on implementation issues at the expense of explanations of programming techniques using it. This led many people to the conclusion that multiple inheritance had few uses and was horrendously hard to implement. I suspect that if I had presented single inheritance in the same manner, they would have drawn exactly the same conclusions about it.

[5] Some consider multiple inheritance fundamentally bad because "it is too hard to use and thus leads to poor design and buggy code." Multiple inheritance can certainly be overused, but so can every interesting language feature. What matters more to me is that I have seen real programs in which use of multiple inheritance has yielded a structure that the programmers considered superior to the single inheritance alternatives and where I didn't see any obvious alternatives that would simplify the structure of the program or its maintenance. I suspect that some of the claims that multiple inheritance is error-prone are based exclusively on experience with languages that don't provide C++'s level of compile-time error detection.

[6] Others consider multiple inheritance too weak a mechanism and sometimes

point to delegation as an alternative. Delegation is a mechanism to forward operations to another object at run time [Stroustrup,1987]. I liked the idea of delegation, implemented a variant of it for C++, and tried it out. The results were unanimous and discouraging: Every user encountered serious problems due to flaws in their delegation-based designs (§12.7).

[7] It has also been claimed that multiple inheritance itself is acceptable, but having it in C++ leads to difficulties with potential features in the language (such as garbage collection) and makes it unnecessarily hard to build tools (such as database systems) for C++. Certainly, multiple inheritance complicates tool building. Only time will tell if the increase in complexity of tools outweighs the benefits of having multiple inheritance available for application design and implementation.

[8] Finally, it has been argued (mostly years after its introduction into C++) that multiple inheritance itself is a good idea, but that C++'s version of the idea is wrong. Such arguments may be of interest to the designers of ''C++++,'' but I don't find the suggestions very helpful in my work to improve C++, its related tools, and programming techniques. People rarely provide practical evidence to support their suggested improvements, the suggestions are rarely detailed, the various suggested improvements differ radically, and the problems of a transition from the current rules are rarely considered.

I think – as I did then – that the fundamental flaw in these arguments is that they take multiple inheritance far too seriously. Multiple inheritance doesn't solve all of your problems, but it doesn't need to because it is quite cheap. Sometimes multiple inheritance is very convenient to have. Grady Booch [Booch,1991] expresses a slightly stronger sentiment: ''Multiple inheritance is like a parachute; you don't need it very often, but when you do it is essential.'' His opinion is partially based on the experience gained in the reimplementation of the Booch components from Ada into C++ (see §8.4.1). This library of container classes and associated operations, implemented by Grady Booch and Mike Vilot, is one of the better examples of the use of multiple inheritance [Booch,1990] [Booch,1993b].

I have kept out of the multiple inheritance debates: multiple inheritance is in C++ and cannot be taken out or radically changed; I personally find multiple inheritance useful at times; some people insist that multiple inheritance is essential to their approach to design and implementation; it is still too early to have solid data and experience about the value of C++ multiple inheritance in large scale use; and, finally, I don't like to spend my time on sterile discussions.

As far as I can judge, most successful uses of multiple inheritance have followed a few simple patterns:

[1] Merging of independent or almost-independent hierarchies; `task` and `display` is an example of this (§12.2).

[2] Composition of interfaces; stream I/O is an example of this (§12.3).

[3] Composing a class out of an interface and an implementation; `slist_set` is an example of this (§13.2.2).

More examples of multiple inheritance can be found in §13.2.2, §14.2.7, and §16.4.

Most failures have occurred when someone tried to force an alien style onto C++. In particular, a direct transcription of a CLOS design relying on linearization for ambiguity resolution, matching names for sharing within the hierarchy, and `:before` and `:after` methods for creating composite operations tends to get very unpleasant and complicated for large programs.

12.7 Delegation

The original multiple inheritance design as presented to the European UNIX Users' Group (EUUG) conference in Helsinki in May 1987 [Stroustrup,1987] contained a notion of delegation [Agha,1986].

A user was allowed to specify a pointer to some class among the base classes in a class declaration. The object thus designated would be used exactly as if it was an object representing a base class. For example:

```
class B { int b; void f(); };
class C : *p { B* p; int c; };
```

The `:*p` meant that the object pointed to by p would be used exactly as if it represented a base class of C:

```
void f(C* q)
{
    q->f();      // meaning q->p->f()
}
```

An object of class C looked something like this after C::p has been initialized:

This concept looked very promising for representing structures that require more flexibility than is provided by ordinary inheritance. In particular, assignment to a delegation pointer could be used to reconfigure an object at run time. The implementation was trivial and the run-time and space efficiency ideal. Consequently, I tried out an implementation on a few users. In particular, Bill Hopkins contributed significant experience and effort to this issue. Unfortunately, every user of this delegation mechanism suffered serious bugs and confusion. Because of this, the delegation was removed from the design and from the Cfront that was shipped as Release 2.0.

Two problems appeared to be the cause of bugs and confusion:

[1] Functions in the delegating class do not override functions of the class delegated to.

[2] The function delegated to cannot use functions from the delegating class or in other ways "get back" to the delegating object.

Naturally, the two problems are related. Equally naturally, I had considered these potential problems and warned users about them. The warnings didn't help – I even forgot my own rules and got caught. Thus the problems didn't seem to belong to the category of minor blemishes that can be handled through a combination of education and compiler warnings. At the time, the problems seemed insurmountable. Even if I had come up with a better idea, I did not have the time to repeat my experiments with a revised concept and implementation.

In retrospect, I think the problems are fundamental. Solving the problem [1] would require the virtual function table of the object delegated to be changed when it is bound to a delegating object. This seems out of line with the rest of the language and very difficult to define sensibly. We also found examples where we wanted to have two objects delegate to the same ''shared'' object. Similarly, we found examples where we needed to delegate through a B* to an object of a derived class D.

Because delegation isn't supported directly in C++, we must use a workaround if we really need it. Often, the solution to a problem requiring delegation involves a smart pointer (§11.5.1). Alternatively, the delegating class provides a complete interface, and then ''manually'' forwards the requests to some other object (§11.5.2).

12.8 Renaming

During late 1989 and early 1990 several people discovered a problem arising from name clashes in multiple inheritance hierarchies [ARM]:

''Merging two class hierarchies by using them as base classes for a common derived class can cause a practical problem where the same name is used in both hierarchies, but where it refers to different operations in the different hierarchies. For example,

```
class Lottery {
    // ...
    virtual int draw();
};

class GraphicalObject {
    // ...
    virtual void draw();
};

class LotterySimulation
    : public Lottery , public GraphicalObject {
    // ...
};
```

In LotterySimulation we would like to override both Lottery::draw() and GraphicalObject::draw(), but with two distinct functions, since draw() has completely different meanings in the two base classes. We would also like LotterySimulation to have distinct, unambiguous names for the inherited functions `Lottery::draw()` and `GraphicalObject::draw()`. This feature came within an inch of becoming the first non-mandated extension to be accepted for C++.

The semantics of this concept are simple, and the implementation is trivial; the problem seems to be to find a suitable syntax. The following has been suggested:

```
class LotterySimulation
    : public Lottery , public GraphicalObject {
    // ...
    virtual int l_draw() = Lottery::draw;
    virtual void go_draw() = GraphicalObject::draw;
};
```

This would extend the pure virtual syntax in a natural manner.''
After some discussion on the extensions working group mail reflector and a few position papers by Martin O'Riordan and by me, the proposal was presented at the standards meeting in Seattle in July 1990. There appeared to be a massive majority for making this the first non-mandated extension to C++. At that point, Beth Crockett from Apple stopped the committee dead in its tracks by invoking what is known as the ''two week rule:'' Any member can postpone voting on a proposal that has not been in the hands of the members at least two weeks before the meeting until the following meeting. This rule protects people against being rushed into things they don't understand and ensures that there will always be time to consult with colleagues.

As you might imagine, Beth didn't gain instant popularity by that veto. However, her caution was well founded, and she saved us from making a bad mistake. Thanks! As we reexamined the problem after the meeting, Doug McIlroy observed that, contrary to our expectations, this problem does have a solution within C++ [ARM]:

''Renaming can be achieved through the introduction of an extra class for each class with a virtual function that needs to be overridden by a function with a different name plus a forwarding function for each such function. For example:

```
class LLottery : public Lottery {
    virtual int l_draw() = 0;
    int draw() { return l_draw(); } // overrides
};

class GGraphicalObject : public GraphicalObject {
    virtual void go_draw() = 0;
    void draw() { go_draw(); } // overrides
};

class LotterySimulation
    : public LLottery , public GGraphicalObject {
    // ...
    int l_draw();   // overrides
    void go_draw(); // overrides
};
```

Consequently, a language extension to express renaming is not *necessary* and is only worthwhile if the need to resolve such name clashes proves common.''

At the next meeting, I presented this technique. During the discussion that followed, we agreed that such name clashes were unlikely to be common enough to warrant a separate language feature. I also observed that merging large class hierarchies is not likely to become everyday work for novices. The experts who most likely will be doing such merging can apply a workaround as easily as a more elegant language feature.

A further – and more general – objection to renaming is that I dislike chasing chains of aliases while maintaining code. If the name I see spelled f is really the g defined in the header that actually is described as h in the documentation and what is called k in your code, then we have a problem. Naturally, this would be an extreme case, but not out of line with examples created by macro-aficionados. Every renaming requires understanding a mapping by both users and tools.

Synonyms can be useful and occasionally essential. However, their use should be minimized to maintain clarity and commonality of code used in different contexts. Further features directly supporting renaming would simply encourage (mis)use of synonyms. This argument resurfaced as a reason for not providing general renaming features in connection with namespaces (§17).

12.9 Base and Member Initializers

When multiple inheritance was introduced, the syntax for initializing base classes and members had to be extended. For example:

```
class X : public A, public B {
    int xx;
    X(int a, int b)
          : A(a),   // initialize base A
            B(b),   // initialize base B
            xx(1)   // initialize member xx
      { }
};
```

This initialization syntax is a direct parallel to the syntax for initializing class objects:

```
A x(1);
B y(2);
```

At the same time, the order of initialization was defined to be the order of declaration. Leaving the initialization order unspecified in the original definition of C++ gave an unnecessary degree of freedom to language implementers at the expense of the users.

In most cases, the order of initialization of members doesn't matter, and in most cases where it does matter, the order dependency is an indication of bad design. In a few cases, however, the programmer absolutely needs control of the order of initialization. For example, consider transmitting objects between machines. An object must be reconstructed by a receiver in exactly the reverse order in which it was decomposed for transmission by a sender. This cannot be guaranteed for objects communicated between programs compiled by compilers from different suppliers unless the language specifies the order of construction. I remember Keith Gorlen, of NIH library fame (§7.1.2), pointing this out to me.

The original definition of C++ neither required nor allowed a base class to be named in a base class initializer. For example, given a class `vector`:

```
class vector {
    // ...
    vector(int);
};
```

we may derive another class `vec`:

```
class vec : public vector {
    // ...
    vec(int,int);
};
```

The `vec` constructor must invoke the `vector` constructor. For example:

```
vec::vec(int low, int high)
    : (high-low-1) // argument for base class constructor
{
    // ...
}
```

This notation caused much confusion over the years.

Using the base class name explicitly as required by 2.0 makes it reasonably clear even to novices what is going on:

```
vec::vec(int low, int high) : vector(high-low-1)
{
    // ...
}
```

I now consider the original syntax as a classic case of a notation being logical, minimal, and too terse. The problems that occurred in teaching base class initialization completely vanished with the new syntax.

The old-style base class initializer was retained for a transition period. It could be used only in the single inheritance case since it is ambiguous otherwise.

13

Class Concept Refinements

Say what you mean,
simply and directly.
– Brian Kernighan

Abstract classes — virtual functions and constructors — `const` members functions — refinement of the `const` concept — static member functions — nested classes — the `inherited::` proposal — relaxation of the overriding rules — multi-methods — protected members — virtual function table allocation — pointers to members.

13.1 Introduction

Because classes are so central in C++, I receive a steady stream of requests for modifications and extensions of the class concept. Almost all requests for modifications must be rejected to preserve existing code, and most suggestions for extensions have been rejected as unnecessary, impractical, not fitting with the rest of the language, or simply "too difficult to handle just now." Here, I present a few refinements that I felt essential to consider in detail and in most cases to accept. The central issue is to make the class concept flexible enough to allow techniques to be expressed within the type system without casts and other low-level constructs.

13.2 Abstract Classes

The very last feature added to Release 2.0 before it shipped was abstract classes. Late modifications to releases are never popular, and late changes to the definition of what will be shipped are even less so. My impression was that several members of

management thought I had lost touch with the real world when I insisted on this feature. Fortunately, Barbara Moo was willing to back up my insistence that abstract
classes were so important that they ought to ship *now* rather than being delayed for
another year or more.

An abstract class represents an interface. Direct support for abstract classes

–   helps catch errors that arise from confusion of classes' role as interfaces and
    their role in representing objects;
–   supports a style of design based on separating the specification of interfaces
    and implementations.

13.2.1 Abstract Classes for Error Handling

Abstract classes directly address a source of errors [Stroustrup,1989b]:

"One of the purposes of static type checking is to detect mistakes and inconsistencies before a program is run. It was noted that a significant class of detectable
errors was escaping C++'s checking. To add insult to injury, the language actually
forced programmers to write extra code and generate larger programs to make this
happen.

Consider the classic "shape" example. Here, we must first declare a class
shape to represent the general concept of a shape. This class needs two virtual
functions rotate() and draw(). Naturally, there can be no objects of class
shape, only objects of specific shapes. Unfortunately C++ did not provide a way
of expressing this simple notion directly.

The C++ rules specify that virtual functions, such as rotate() and draw(),
must be defined in the class in which they are first declared. The reason for this
requirement is to ensure that traditional linkers can be used to link C++ programs
and to ensure that it is not possible to call a virtual function that has not been
defined. So the programmer writes something like this:

```
class shape {
    point center;
    color col;
    // ...
public:
    point where() { return center; }
    void move(point p) { center=p; draw(); }
    virtual void rotate(int)
        { error("cannot rotate"); abort(); }
    virtual void draw()
        { error("cannot draw"); abort(); }
    // ...
};
```

This ensures that innocent errors such as forgetting to define a draw() function
for a class derived from shape and silly errors such as creating a "plain" shape
and attempting to use it cause run-time errors. Even when such errors are not
made, memory can easily get cluttered with unnecessary virtual tables for classes

such as `shape` and with functions that are never called, such as `draw()` and `rotate()`. The overhead for this can be noticeable.

The solution is simply to allow the user to say that a virtual function does not have a definition; that is, it is a "pure virtual function." This is done by an initializer `=0`:

```
class shape {
    point center;
    color col;
    // ...
public:
    point where() { return center; }
    void move(point p) { center=point; draw(); }
    virtual void rotate(int) = 0;   // pure virtual
    virtual void draw() = 0;        // pure virtual
    // ...
};
```

A class with one or more pure virtual functions is an abstract class. An abstract class can be used only as a base for another class. In particular, it is not possible to create objects of an abstract class. A class derived from an abstract class must either define the pure virtual functions from its base or again declare them to be pure virtual functions.

The notion of pure virtual functions was chosen over the idea of explicitly declaring a class to be abstract because the selective definition of functions is much more flexible."

As shown, it was always possible to represent the notion of an abstract class in C++; it just involved a little more work than one would like. It was also understood by some to be an important issue (for example, see [Johnson,1989]). However, not until a few weeks before the release date for 2.0 did it dawn on me that only a small fraction of the C++ community had actually understood the concept. Further, I realized that lack of understanding of the notion of abstract classes was the source of many problems that people experienced with their designs.

13.2.2 Abstract Types

A common complaint about C++ was (and is) that private data is included in the class declaration, so when a class' private data is changed, code using that class must be recompiled. Often, this complaint is expressed as "abstract types in C++ aren't really abstract" and "the data isn't really hidden." What I hadn't realized was that many people thought that because they *could* put the representation of an object in the private section of a class declaration then they actually *had to* put it there. This is clearly wrong (and that is how I failed to spot the problem for years). If you don't want a representation in a class, don't put it there! Instead, delay the specification of the representation to some derived class. The abstract class notation allows this to be made explicit. For example, one can define a `set` of `T` pointers like this:

```
class set {
public:
    virtual void insert(T*) =0;
    virtual void remove(T*) =0;

    virtual int is_member(T*) =0;

    virtual T* first() =0;
    virtual T* next() =0;

    virtual ~set() { }
};
```

This provides all the information that people need to use a set. More importantly in
this context, it contains no representation or other implementation details. Only people who actually create objects of set classes need to know how those sets are represented. For example, given:

```
class slist_set : public set, private slist {
    slink* current_elem;
public:
    void insert(T*);
    void remove(T*);

    int is_member(T*);

    T* first();
    T* next();

    slist_set() : slist(), current_elem(0) { }
};
```

we can create slist_set objects that can be used as sets by users who have never
heard of an slist_set. For example:

```
void user1(set& s)
{
    for (T* p = s.first(); p; p=s.next()) {
        // use p
    }
}

void user2()
{
    slist_set ss;
    // ...
    user1(ss);
}
```

Importantly, a user of the abstract class set, such as user1(), can be compiled without including the headers defining `slist_set` and the classes, such as `slist`, that it in turn depends on.

As mentioned, attempts to create objects of an abstract class are caught at compile time. For example:

```
void f(set& s1)    // fine
{
    set s2;        // error: declaration of object
                   //        of abstract class set.
    set* p = 0;    // fine
    set& s3 = s1;  // fine
}
```

The importance of the abstract class concept is that it allows a cleaner separation between a user and an implementer than is possible without it. An abstract class is purely an interface to the implementations supplied as classes derived from it. This limits the amount of recompilation necessary after a change as well as the amount of information necessary to compile an average piece of code. By decreasing the coupling between a user and an implementer, abstract classes provide an answer to people complaining about long compile times and also serve library providers, who must worry about the impact on users of changes to a library implementation. I have seen large systems in which the compile times were reduced by a factor of ten by introducing abstract classes into the major subsystem interfaces. I had unsuccessfully tried to explain these notions in [Stroustrup,1986b]. With an explicit language feature supporting abstract classes I was much more successful [2nd].

13.2.3 Syntax

The curious =0 syntax was chosen over the obvious alternative of introducing a keyword `pure` or `abstract` because at the time I saw no chance of getting a new keyword accepted. Had I suggested `pure`, Release 2.0 would have shipped without abstract classes. Given a choice between a nicer syntax and abstract classes, I chose abstract classes. Rather than risking delay and incurring the certain fights over `pure`, I used the traditional C and C++ convention of using 0 to represent ''not there.'' The =0 syntax fits with my view that a function body is the initializer for a function and also with the (simplistic, but usually adequate) view of the set of virtual functions being implemented as a vector of function pointers (§3.5.1). In fact, =0 is not best implemented by putting a 0 in the `vtbl`. My implementation places a pointer to a function called `__pure_virtual_called` in the `vtbl`; this function can then be defined to give a reasonable run-time error.

I chose a mechanism for specifying individual functions pure rather than a way of declaring a complete class abstract because the pure virtual function notion is more flexible. I value the ability to define a class in stages; that is, I find it useful to define some virtual functions and leave the definition of the rest to further derived classes.

13.2.4 Virtual Functions and Constructors

The way an object is constructed out of base classes and member objects (§2.11.1) has
implications on the way virtual functions work. Occasionally, people have been confused and even annoyed by some of these implications. Let me therefore try to
explain why I consider the way C++ works in this respect almost necessary.

13.2.4.1 Calling a Pure Virtual Function

How can a pure virtual function – rather than a derived class function overriding it –
ever be called? Objects of an abstract class can only exist as bases for other classes.
Once the object for the derived class has been constructed, a pure virtual function has
been defined by an overriding function from the derived class. However, during construction it is possible for the abstract class' own constructor to call a pure virtual
function by mistake:

```
class A {
public:
    virtual void f() = 0;
    void g();
    A();
};


A::A()
{
    f();      // error: pure virtual function called
    g();      // looks innocent enough
}
```

The illegal call of A::f() is easily caught by the compiler. However, A::g() may
be declared like this

```
void A::g() { f(); }
```

in some other translation unit. In that case, only a compiler that does cross-
compilation-unit analysis can detect the error, and a run-time error is the alternative.

13.2.4.2 Base-first Construction

I strongly prefer designs that do not open the possibility of run-time errors to those
that do. However, I don't see the possibility of making programming completely
safe. In particular, constructors create the environment in which other member functions operate (§2.11.1). While that environment is under construction, the programmer must be aware that fewer guarantees can be made. Consider this potentially confusing example:

```
class B {
public:
    int b;
    virtual void f();
    void g();
    // ...
    B();
};

class D : public B {
public:
    X x;
    void f();
    // ...
    D();
};

B::B()
{
    b++;     // undefined: B::b isn't yet initialized.
    f();     // calls: B::f(); not D::f().
}
```

A compiler can easily warn about both potential problems. If you really mean to call B's own f() say so explicitly: B::f().

The way this constructor behaves contrasts with the way an ordinary member function can be written (relying on the proper behavior of the constructor):

```
void B::g()
{
    b++;     // fine, since B::b is a member
    //         B::B should have initialized it.
    f();     // calls: D::f() if B::g is called for a D.
}
```

The difference in the function invoked by f() in B::B() and B::g() when invoked for a B part of a D can be a surprise to novices.

13.2.4.3 What if?

However, consider the implication of the alternative, that is, to have *every* call of the virtual function f() invoke the overriding function:

```
void D::f()
{
    // operation relying on D::X having been properly
    // initialized by D::D
}
```

If an overriding function could be called during construction, then no virtual function could rely on proper initialization by constructors. Consequently, every overriding function would have to be written with the degree of resilience (and paranoia) usually reserved for constructors. Actually, writing an overriding function would be *worse* than writing a constructor because in a constructor it is relatively easy to determine what has and hasn't yet been initialized. In the absence of the guarantee that the constructor has been run, the writer of an overriding function would always have two choices:

[1] Simply hope/assume that all necessary initializations have been done.

[2] Try to guard against uninitialized bases and members.

The first alternative makes constructors unattractive. The second alternative becomes truly unmanageable because a derived class can have many direct and indirect base classes and because there is no run-time check that you can apply to an arbitrary variable to see if it has been initialized.

```
void D::f() // nightmare (not C++)
{
    if (base_initialized) {
        // operation relying on D::X having
        // been initialized by D::D
    }
    else {
        // do what can be done without relying
        // on D::X having been initialized
    }
}
```

Consequently, had constructors called overriding functions, the use of constructors would have had to be severely restricted to allow reasonable coding of overriding functions.

The basic design point is that until the constructor for an object has run to completion the object is a bit like a building during construction: You have to suffer the inconveniences of a half-completed structure, often rely on temporary scaffolding, and take precautions commensurate with the more hazardous environment. In return, compilers and users are allowed to assume that an object is usable after construction.

13.3 const Member Functions

In Cfront 1.0, "constness" had been incompletely enforced and when I tightened up the implementation, we found a couple of holes in the language definition. We needed a way to allow a programmer to state which member functions update the state of their object and which don't:

```
class X {
    int aa;
public:
    void update() { aa++; }
```

```
        int value() const { return aa; }
        void cheat() const { aa++; } // error: *this is const
    };
```

A member function declared const, such as X::value(), is called a const member function and is guaranteed not to change the value of an object. A const member function can be used on both const and non-const objects, whereas non-const member functions, such as X::update(), can only be called for non-const objects:

```
    int g(X o1, const X& o2)
    {
        o1.update();       // fine
        o2.update();       // error: o2 is const
        return o1.value() + o2.value(); // fine
    }
```

Technically, this behavior is achieved by having the this pointer point to an X in a non-const member function of X and point to a const X in a const member function of X.

The distinction between const and non-const functions allows the useful logical distinction between functions that modify the state of an object and functions that don't to be directly expressed in C++. Const member functions were among the language features that received a significant boost from the discussions at the Estes Park implementers workshop (§7.1.2).

13.3.1 Casting away const

As ever, C++ was concerned with the detection of accidental errors, rather than with the prevention of fraud. To me, that implied that a function should be allowed to "cheat" by "casting away const." It was not considered the compiler's job to prevent the programmer from *explicitly* subverting the type system. For example [Stroustrup,1992b]:

"It is occasionally useful to have objects that appear as constants to users but do in fact change their state. Such classes can be written using explicit casts:

```
    class XX {
        int a;
        int calls_of_f;
        int f() const { ((XX*)this)->calls_of_f++; return a; }
        // ...
    };
```

The explicit type conversion indicates that something is not quite right. Changing the state of a const object can be quite deceptive, is error-prone in some contexts, and won't work if the object is in read-only memory. It is often better to represent the variable part of such an object as a separate object:

```
class XXX {
    int a;
    int& calls_of_f;
    int f() const { calls_of_f++; return a; }
    // ...
    XXX() : calls_of_f(*new int) { /* ... */ }
    ~XXX() { delete &calls_of_f; /* ... */ }
    // ...
};
```

This reflects that the primary aim of const is to specify interfaces rather than to help optimizers, and also the observation that though the freedom/flexibility is occasionally useful it can be misused.''
The introduction of const_cast (§14.3.4) enables programmers to distinguish casts intended to ''cast away const'' from casts intended to do other forms of type manipulation.

13.3.2 Refinement of the Definition of const

To ensure that some, but not all, const objects could be placed in read-only memory (ROM), I adopted the rule that any object that has a constructor (that is, required run-time initialization) can't be placed in ROM, but other const objects can. This ties in to a long-running concern of what can be initialized and how and when. C++ provides both static (link time) and dynamic (run-time) initialization (§3.11.4) and this rule allows run-time initialization of const objects while still allowing for the use of ROM for objects that don't require run-time initialization. The typical example of the latter is a large array of simple objects, such as a YACC parser table.

Tying the notion of const to constructors was a compromise between my ideal for const, realities of available hardware, and the view that programmers should be trusted to know what they are doing when they write an explicit type conversion. At the initiative of Jerry Schwarz, this rule has now been replaced by one that more closely reflects my original ideal. An object declared const is considered immutable from the completion of its constructor until the start of its destructor. The result of a write to the object between those points is deemed undefined.

When originally designing const, I remember arguing that the ideal const would be an object that is writable until the constructor had run, then becomes read-only by some hardware magic, and finally upon the entry into the destructor becomes writable again. One could imagine a tagged architecture that actually worked this way. Such an implementation would cause a run-time error if someone attempted to write to an object defined const. On the other hand, someone could write to an object not defined const that had been passed as a const reference or pointer. In both cases, the user would have to cast away const first. The implication of this view is that casting away const for an object that was originally defined const and then writing to it is at best undefined, whereas doing the same to an object that wasn't originally defined const is legal and well defined.

Note that with this refinement of the rules, the meaning of const doesn't depend on whether a type has a constructor or not; in principle, they all do. Any object declared const now may be placed in ROM, be placed in code segments, be protected by access control, etc., to ensure that it doesn't mutate after receiving its initial value. Such protection is not required, however, because current systems cannot in general protect every const from every form of corruption.

An implementation still retains a large degree of discretion over how a const is managed. There is no logical problem in having a garbage collector or a database system change the value of a const object (say, moving it to disk and back) as long as it ensures that the object appears unmodified to a user.

13.3.3 Mutable and Casting

Casting away const is still objectionable to some because it is a cast, and even more so because it is not guaranteed to work in all cases. How can we write a class like XX from §13.3.1 that doesn't require casting and doesn't involve an indirection as in class XXX? Thomas Ngo suggested that it ought to be possible to specify that a member should never be considered const even if it is a member of a const object. This proposal was kicked around in the committee for years until Jerry Schwarz successfully championed a variant to acceptance. Originally ~const was suggested as a notation for "can't ever be const." Even some of the proponents of the notion considered that notation too ugly, so the keyword mutable was introduced into the proposal that the ANSI/ISO committee accepted:

```
class XXX {
    int a;
    mutable int cnt; // cnt will never be const
public:
    int f() const { cnt++; return a; }

    // ...
};

XXX var;        // var.cnt is writable (of course)

const XXX cnst; // cnst.cnt is writable because
                // XXX::cnt is declared mutable
```

The notion is still somewhat untried. It does reduce the need for casts in real systems, but not as much as some people hoped for. Dag Brück and others reviewed considerable amounts of real code to see which casts were casting away const and which of those could be eliminated using mutable. This study confirmed the conclusion that "casting away const" cannot be avoided in general (§14.3.4) and that mutable appears to eliminate casting away const in less than half of the cases where it is needed in the absence of mutable. The benefits of mutable appear to be very dependent on programming style. In some cases, every cast could be eliminated by using mutable; in others, not a single cast could be eliminated.

Some people had expressed hope that a revised `const` notion plus `mutable` would open the door to significant new optimizations. This doesn't appear to be the case. The benefits are largely in code clarity and in increasing the number of objects that can have their values precomputed so that they can be placed in ROM, code segments, etc.

13.4 Static Member Functions

A `static` data member of a class is a member for which there is only one copy rather than one per object. Consequently, a `static` member can be accessed without referring to any particular object. Static members are used to reduce the number of global names, to make obvious which `static` objects logically belong to which class, and to be able to apply access control to their names. This is a boon for library providers since it avoids polluting the global namespace and thereby allows easier writing of library code and safer use of multiple libraries.

These reasons apply to functions as well as objects. In fact, *most* of the names a library provider wants non-global are function names. I observed that nonportable code, such as `((X*)0)->f()`, was used to simulate `static` member functions. This trick is a time bomb because sooner or later someone will declare an `f()` called this way to be `virtual`. Then, the call will fail horribly because there is no X object at address zero. Even when `f()` is not virtual, such calls will fail under some implementations of dynamic linking.

At a course I was giving for EUUG (the European UNIX Users' Group) in Helsinki in 1987, Martin O'Riordan pointed out to me that `static` member functions were an obvious and useful generalization. That was probably the first mention of the idea. Martin was working for Glockenspiel in Ireland at the time and later went on to become the main architect of the Microsoft C++ compiler. Later, Jonathan Shopiro championed the idea and made sure it didn't get lost in the mass of work for Release 2.0.

A `static` member function is a member so that its name is in the class scope, and the usual access control rules apply. For example:

```
class task {
    // ...
    static task* chain;
public:
    static void schedule(int);
    // ...
};
```

A `static` member declaration is only a declaration and the object or function it declares must have a unique definition somewhere in the program. For example:

```
task* task::chain = 0;
void task::schedule(int p) { /* ... */ }
```

A `static` member function is not associated with any particular object and need not
be called using the special member function syntax. For example:

```
void f(int priority)
{
    // ...
    task::schedule(priority);
    // ...
}
```

In some cases, a class is used simply as a scope in which to put otherwise global
names as `static` members so they don't pollute the global namespace. This is one
of the origins of the notion of namespaces (§17).

   `Static` member functions were among the language features that received a significant boost from the discussions at the Estes Park implementers workshop (§7.1.2).

13.5 Nested Classes

As mentioned in §3.12, nested classes were reintroduced into C++ by the ARM. This
made the scope rules more regular and improved the facilities for localization of information. We could now write:

```
class String {
    class Rep {
        // ...
    };
    Rep* p; // String is a handle to Rep
    static int count;
    // ...
public:
    char& operator[](int i);
    // ...
};
```

to keep the `Rep` class local. Unfortunately, this led to an increase in the amount of
information placed in class declarations and consequently to an increase in compile
times and in the frequency of recompilations. Too much interesting and occasionally
changing information was put into nested classes. In many cases, such information
was not really of interest to the users of classes such as `String` and should therefore
be put elsewhere along with other implementation details. Tony Hansen proposed to
allow forward declaration of a nested class in exact parallel to the way member functions and `static` members are handled:

```
// file String.h (the interface):

    class String {
        class Rep;
        Rep* p; // String is a handle to Rep
        static int count;
        // ...
    public:
        char& operator[](int i);
        // ...
    };
```

```
// file String.c (the implementation):

    class String::Rep {
        // ...
    };


    static int String::count = 1;


    char& String::operator[](int i)
    {
        // ...
    }
```

This extension was accepted as something that simply corrected an oversight. The technique it supports shouldn't be underestimated, though. People still load up their header files with all kinds of unnecessary stuff and suffer long compile times in consequence. Therefore, every technique and feature that helps reduce unnecessary coupling between users and implementers is important.

13.6 Inherited::

At one of the early standards meetings Dag Brück submitted a proposal for an extension that several people had expressed interest in [Stroustrup,1992b]:

"Many class hierarchies are built "incrementally," by augmenting the behavior of the base class with added functionality of the derived class. Typically, the function of the derived class calls the function of the base class, and then performs some additional operations:

```
    struct A { virtual void handle(int); };
    struct D : A { void handle(int); };
```

```
void D::handle(int i)
{
    A::handle(i);
    // other stuff
}
```

The call to `handle()` must be qualified to avoid a recursive loop. The example could with the proposed extension be written as follows:

```
void D::handle(int i)
{
    inherited::handle(i);
    // other stuff
}
```

Qualifying by the keyword `inherited` can be regarded as a generalization of qualifying by the name of a class. It solves a number of potential problems of qualifying by a class name, which is particularly important for maintaining class libraries.''

I had considered this early on in the design of C++, but had rejected it in favor of qualification with the base class name because that solution could handle multiple inheritance, and `inherited::` clearly can't. However, Dag observed that the combination of the two schemes would deal with all problems without introducing loopholes:

''Most class hierarchies are developed with single inheritance in mind. If we change the inheritance tree so class D is derived from both A and B, we get:

```
struct A { virtual void handle(int); };
struct B { virtual void handle(int); };
struct D : A, B { void handle(int); };

void D::handle(int i)
{
    A::handle(i);              // unambiguous
    inherited::handle(i);      // ambiguous
}
```

In this case `A::handle()` is legal C++ and possibly wrong. Using `inherited::handle()` is ambiguous here, and causes an error message at compile time. I think this behavior is desirable, because it forces the person merging two class hierarchies to resolve the ambiguity. On the other hand, this example shows that `inherited` may be of more limited use with multiple inheritance.''

I was convinced by these arguments and by the meticulous paperwork that documented its details. Here was a proposal that was clearly useful, easily understood, and trivial to implement. It also had genuine experience behind it since a variant of it had been implemented by Apple based on their experiences with Object Pascal. It is also a variant of the Smalltalk `super`.

After the final discussion of this proposal in the committee Dag volunteered it for use as a textbook example of a good idea that shouldn't be accepted [Stroustrup,1992b]:

"The proposal is well-argued and – as is the case with most proposals – there was more expertise and experience available in the committee itself. In this case the Apple representative had implemented the proposal. During the discussion we soon agreed that the proposal was free of major flaws. In particular, in contrast to earlier suggestions along this line (some as early as the discussions about multiple inheritance in 1986) it correctly dealt with the ambiguities that can arise when multiple inheritance is used. We also agreed that the proposal was trivial to implement and would in fact be helpful to programmers.

Note that this is *not* sufficient for acceptance. We know of dozens of minor improvements like this and at least a dozen major ones. If we accepted all the language would sink under its own weight (remember the Vasa!). We will never know if this proposal would have passed, though, because at this point in the discussion, Michael Tiemann walked in and muttered something like "but we don't need that extension; we can write code like that already." When the murmur of "but of course we can't!" had died down Michael showed us how:

```
class foreman : public employee {
    typedef employee inherited;
    // ...
    void print();
};

class manager : public foreman {
    typedef foreman inherited;
    // ...
    void print();
};

void manager::print()
{
    inherited::print();
    // ...
}
```

A further discussion of this example can be found in [2nd,pp205]. What we hadn't noticed was that the reintroduction of nested classes into C++ had opened the possibility of controlling the scope and resolution of type names exactly like other names.

Given this technique, we decided that our efforts were better spent on some other standards work. The benefits of `inherited::` as a built-in facility didn't sufficiently outweigh the benefits of what the programmer could do with existing features. In consequence, we decided not to make `inherited::` one of the very few extensions we could afford to accept for C++."

13.7 Relaxation of Overriding Rules

Consider writing a function that returns a copy of an object. Assuming a copy constructor, this is trivially done like this:

```
class B {
public:
    virtual B* clone() { return new B(*this); }
    // ...
};
```

Now any object of a class derived from B that overrides B::clone can be correctly cloned. For example:

```
class D : public B {
public:
        // old rule:
        // clone() must return a B* to override B::clone():
    B* clone()  { return new D(*this); }

    void h();
    // ...
};

void f(B* pb, D* pd)
{
    B* pb1 = pb->clone();
    B* pb2 = pd->clone(); // pb2 points to a D
    // ...
}
```

Unfortunately, the fact that pd points to a D (or something derived from D) is lost:

```
void g(D* pd)
{
    B* pb1 = pd->clone(); // ok
    D* pd1 = pd->clone(); // error: clone() returns a B*
    pd->clone()->h();       // error: clone() returns a B*

    // ugly workarounds:

    D* pd2 = (D*)pd->clone();
    ((D*)pd->clone())->h();
}
```

This proved a nuisance in real code, and several people observed that the rule that an overriding function must have *exactly* the same type as the overridden could be relaxed without opening the hole in the type system or imposing serious implementation complexity. For example, this might be allowed:

```
class D : public B {
public:
        // note, clone() returns a D*:
    D* clone() { return new D(*this); }

    void h();
    // ...
};

void gg(B* pb, D* pd)
{
    B* pb1 = pd->clone();  // ok
    D* pd1 = pd->clone();  // ok
    pd->clone()->h();      // ok

    D* pd2 = pb->clone();  // error (as always)
    pb->clone()->h();      // error (as always)
}
```

This extension was originally proposed by Alan Snyder and happens to be the first extension ever to be officially proposed to the committee. It was accepted in 1992.

Two questions had to be asked before we could accept it:

[1] Were there any serious implementation problems (say, in the area of multiple inheritance or pointers to members)?

[2] Out of all the conversions that could possible be handled for return types of overriding functions which – if any – are worthwhile?

Personally, I didn't worry much about [1] because I thought I knew how to implement the relaxation in general, but Martin O'Riordan did worry and produced papers for the committee demonstrating implementability in detail.

My main problem was to try to determine whether this relaxation was worthwhile and for exactly which set of conversions? How common is the need for virtual functions called for an object of a derived type and needing operations to be performed of a return value of that derived type? Several people, notably John Bruns and Bill Gibbons, argued strongly that the need was common and not restricted to a few computer science examples such as `clone`. The data that finally convinced me was the observation by Ted Goldstein that almost two thirds of all casts in a multi-100,000-line system he was involved in at Sun were workarounds that would be eliminated by this relaxation of the overriding rules. In other words, what I find most attractive is that the relaxation allows people to do something important within the type system instead of using casts. This brought the relaxation of return types for overriding functions into the mainstream of my effort to make C++ programming safer, simpler, and more declarative. Relaxing the overriding rule would not only eliminate many ordinary casts, but also remove one temptation for misuse of the new dynamic casts that were being discussed at the same time as this relaxation (§14.2.3).

After some consideration of the alternatives, we decided to allow overriding of a B* by a D* and of a B& by a D& where B is an accessible base of D. In addition, `const` can be added or subtracted wherever that is safe. We decided not to relax the rules to allow technically feasible conversions such as a D to an accessible base B, a D to an X for which D has a conversion, `int*` to `void*`, `double` to `int`, etc. We felt that the benefits from allowing such conversions through overriding would not outweigh the implementation cost and the potential for confusing users.

13.7.1 Relaxation of Argument Rules

One major reason that I had been suspicious about relaxing the overriding rules for return types was that in my experience it invariably had been proposed together with an unacceptable ''equivalent'' relaxation for argument types. For example:

```
class Fig {
public:
    virtual int operator==(const Fig&);
    // ...
};


class ColFig: public Fig {
public:
    // Assume that Colfig::operator==()
    // overrides Fig::operator==()
    // (not allowed in C++).

    int operator==(const ColFig& x);
    // ...
private:
    Color col;
};


int ColFig::operator==(const ColFig& x)
{
    return col == x.col && Fig::operator==(x);
}
```

This looks very plausible and allows useful code to be written. For example:

```
void f(Fig& fig, ColFig& cf1, ColFig& cf2)
{
    if (fig==cf1) { // compare Figs
        // ...
    } else if (cf1==cf2) { // compare ColFigs
        // ...
    }
}
```

Unfortunately, this also leads to an implicit violation of the type system:

```
void g(Fig& fig, ColFig& cf)
{
    if (cf==fig) {// compare what?
        // ...
    }
}
```

If `ColFig::operator==()` overrides `Fig::operator==()` then `cf==fig`
will invoke `ColFig::operator==()` with a plain `Fig` argument. This would be
a disaster because `ColFig::operator==()` accesses the member `col`, and `Fig`
does not have such a member. Had `ColFig::operator==()` written to its argument, memory corruption would have resulted. I had considered this scenario when I
first designed the rules for virtual functions and deemed it unacceptable.

Consequently, had this overriding been allowed, a run-time check would have
been needed for every argument to a virtual function. Optimizing these tests away
would not be easy. In the absence of global analysis, we never know if an object
might originate in some other file and thus possibly be of a type that did a dangerous
overriding. The overhead of this checking is unattractive. Also, if every virtual function call became a potential source of exceptions, users would have to prepare for
those. That was considered unacceptable.

The alternative for the programmer is to explicitly test when a different kind of
processing is needed for an argument of a derived class. For example:

```
class Figure {
public:
    virtual int operator==(const Figure&);
    // ...
};

class ColFig: public Figure {
public:
    int operator==(const Figure& x);
    // ...
private:
    Color col;
};

int ColFig::operator==(const Figure& x)
{
    if (Figure::operator==(x)) {
        const ColFig* pc = dynamic_cast<const ColFig*>(&x);
        if (pc) return col == pc->col;
    }
    return 0;
}
```

In this way, the run-time checked cast `dynamic_cast` (§14.2.2) is the complement
to the relaxed overriding rules. The relaxation safely and declaratively deals with

return types; the dynamic_cast operator explicitly and relatively safely deals with argument types.

13.8 Multi-methods

I repeatedly considered a mechanism for a virtual function call based on more than one object, often called *multi-methods*. I rejected multi-methods with regret because I liked the idea, but couldn't find an acceptable form under which to accept it. Consider:

```
class Shape {
    // ...
};

class Rectangle : public Shape {
    // ...
};

class Circle : public Shape {
    // ...
};
```

How would I design an intersect() that is correctly called for both of its arguments? For example,

```
void f(Circle& c, Shape& s1, Rectangle& r, Shape& s2)
{
    intersect(r,c);
    intersect(c,r);
    intersect(c,s2);
    intersect(s1,r);
    intersect(r,s2);
    intersect(s1,c);
    intersect(s1,s2);
}
```

If r and s refers to a Circle and a Shape, respectively, we would like to implement intersect by four functions:

```
bool intersect(const Circle&, const Circle&);
bool intersect(const Circle&, const Rectangle&);
bool intersect(const Rectangle&, const Circle&);
bool intersect(const Rectangle&, const Rectangle&);
```

Each call ought to call the right function in the same way a virtual function does. However, the right function must be selected based on the run-time type of both arguments. The fundamental problems, as I saw them, were to find

   [1] A calling mechanism that was as simple and efficient as the table lookup used for virtual functions.

[2] A set of rules that allowed ambiguity resolution to be exclusively a compile-time matter.

I don't consider the problem unsolvable, but I have never found this issue pressing enough to reach the top of my stack of pending issues for long enough to work out the details of a solution.

One worry I had was that a fast solution seemed to require a lot of memory for the equivalent of a virtual function table, whereas anything that didn't "waste" a lot of space by replicating table entries would be slow, have unpredictable performance characteristics, or both. For example, any implementation of the `Circle`-and-`Rectangle` example that doesn't involve a run-time search for the function to invoke seems to require four pointers to functions. Add an extra class `Triangle`, and we seem to need nine pointers to functions. Derive a class `Smiley` from `Circle` and we seem to need sixteen, though we should be able to save the last seven entries by using entries involving `Circle` for all `Smiley`s.

Worse, the arrays of pointers to functions that would be equivalent to virtual function tables could not be composed until the complete program was known, that is, by the linker. The reason is that there is no one class to which all overriding functions belong. There couldn't be such a class exactly because any interesting overriding function will depend on two or more argument types. At the time, this problem was unsolvable because I was unwilling to have a language feature that depended on non-trivial linker support. Experience had taught me that such support would not be available for years.

Another problem that bothered me, though it didn't seem unsolvable, was how to handle ambiguities. The obvious answer is that calls of multi-methods must obey exactly the same ambiguity rules as other calls. However, this answer was obscured for me because I was looking for a special syntax and special rules for calling multi-methods. For example:

```
(r@s)->intersect(); // rather than intersect(r,s)
```

This was a dead end.

Doug Lea suggested a much better solution [Lea,1991]: Allow arguments to be explicitly declared `virtual`. For example:

```
bool intersect(virtual const Shape&, virtual const Shape&);
```

A function that matches in name and in argument types using a relaxed matching rule along the lines adopted for the return type overrides. For example:

```
bool intersect(const Circle&, const Rectangle&) // overrides
{
    // ...
}
```

Finally, multi-methods can be called with the usual call syntax exactly as shown above.

Multi-methods is one of the interesting what-ifs of C++. Could I have designed and implemented them well enough at the time? Would their applications have been important enough to warrant the effort? What other work might have been left undone to provide the time to design and implement multi-methods? Since about 1985, I have always felt some twinge of regret for not providing multi-methods. To wit: The only official talk I ever gave at an OOPSLA conference was part of a panel making a statement against language bigotry and pointless ''religious'' language wars [Stroustrup,1990]. I presented some bits of CLOS that I particularly liked and emphasized multi-methods.

13.8.1 Workarounds for Multi-methods

So how do we write functions such as `intersect()` without multi-methods?

Until the introduction of run-time type identification (§14.2) the only support for resolution based on type at run time was virtual functions. Since we wanted to resolve based on two arguments we somehow needed two virtual function calls. For the `Circle` and `Rectangle` example above, there are three possible static argument types for a call, so we can provide three different virtual functions:

```
class Shape {
    // ...
    virtual bool intersect(const Shape&) const =0;
    virtual bool intersect(const Rectangle&) const =0;
    virtual bool intersect(const Circle&) const =0;
};
```

The derived classes override the virtual functions appropriately:

```
class Rectangle : public Shape {
    // ...
    bool intersect(const Shape&) const;
    bool intersect(const Rectangle&) const;
    bool intersect(const Circle&) const;
};
```

Any call of `intersect()` will resolve to the appropriate `Rectangle` or `Circle` function. We then have to ensure that the functions taking a nonspecific `Shape` argument use a second virtual function call to resolve that argument to a more specific one:

```
bool Rectangle::intersect(const Shape& s) const
{
    return s.intersect(*this);  // *this is a Rectangle:
                                // resolve on s
}
```

```
bool Circle::intersect(const Shape& s) const
{
    return s.intersect(*this); // *this is a Circle:
                               // resolve on s
}
```

The other `intersect()` functions simply do their job on two arguments of known types. Note that only the first `Shape::intersect()` function is necessary for this technique. The other two `Shape::intersect()` functions are an optimization that can be done where a derived class is known when the base class is designed.

This technique is called *double dispatch* and was first presented in [Ingalls,1986]. In the context of C++, double dispatch has the weakness that adding a class to a hierarchy requires changes to existing classes. A derived class such as `Rectangle` must know about all of its sibling classes to include the right set of virtual functions. For example, adding class `Triangle` requires changes to both `Rectangle`, `Circle`, and – if the optimization used above is desired – also `Shape`:

```
class Rectangle : public Shape {
    // ...
    bool intersect(const Shape&);
    bool intersect(const Rectangle&);
    bool intersect(const Circle&);
    bool intersect(const Triangle&);
};
```

Basically, in C++ double dispatch is a reasonably efficient and reasonably elegant technique for navigating hierarchies where one can modify class declarations to accommodate new classes and where the set of derived classes doesn't change too often.

Alternative techniques involve storing some kind of type identifier in objects and selecting functions to be called based on those. Use of `typeid()` for run-time type identification (§14.2.5) is simply one example of this. One can maintain a data structure containing pointers to functions and use the type identifier to access that structure. This has the advantage that the base class doesn't have to have any knowledge of which derived classes exist. For example, with suitable definitions

```
bool intersect(const Shape* s1, const Shape* s2)
{
    int i = find_index(s1.type_id(),s2.type_id());
    if (i < 0) error("bad_index");
    extern Fct_table* tbl;
    Fct f = tbl[i];
    return f(s1,s2);
}
```

will call the right function for every possible type of the two arguments. Basically, this manually implements the multi-method virtual function table hinted at above.

The relative ease with which each specific example of multi-methods can be simulated is a major reason that multi-methods never stayed at the top of my to-do list long enough to be worked out in detail. In a very real sense, this technique is the same as the one used to simulate virtual functions in C. Such workarounds are acceptable if they are needed only infrequently.

13.9 Protected Members

The simple private/public model of data hiding served C++ well where C++ was used essentially as a data abstraction language and for a large class of problems where inheritance was used for object-oriented programming. However, when derived classes are used, there are two kinds of users of a class: derived classes and "the general public." The members and friends that implement the operations on the class operate on the class objects on behalf of these users. The private/public mechanism allows the programmer to distinguish clearly between the implementers and the general public, but does not provide a way of catering specifically to derived classes.

Shortly after Release 1.0, Mark Linton stopped by my office and made an impassioned plea for a third level of access control to directly support the style used in the Interviews library (§8.4.1) being developed at Stanford. We coined the word protected to refer to members of a class that were "like public" to members of a class and its derived classes yet "like private" to anyone else.

Mark was the main architect of Interviews. He argued persuasively based on genuine experience and examples from real code that protected data was essential for the design of an efficient and extensible X windows toolkit. The alternative to protected data was claimed to be unacceptable inefficiency, unmanageable proliferation of inline interface functions, or public data. Protected data, and in general, protected members seemed the lesser evil. Also, languages claimed "pure" such as Smalltalk supported this – rather weak – notion of protection over the – stronger – C++ notion of private. I had written code where data was declared public simply to be usable from derived classes and had seen code where the friend notion had been clumsily misused to grant access to explicitly named derived classes.

These were good arguments and essentially the ones that convinced me to allow protected members. However, I regard "good arguments" with a high degree of suspicion when discussing programming. There seem to be "good arguments" for every possible language feature and every possible use of it. What we need is data. Without data and properly evaluated experience, we are like the Greek philosophers who argued brilliantly for several centuries, yet didn't quite manage to determine the four (or maybe even five) fundamental substances from which they were sure everything in the universe was composed.

Five years or so later, Mark banned the use of protected data members in Interviews because they had become a source of bugs: "novice users poking where they shouldn't in ways that they ought to have known better than." They also seriously complicate maintenance: "now it would be nice to change this, do you think someone out there might have used it?" Barbara Liskov's OOPSLA keynote [Liskov,1987] gives a detailed explanation of the theoretical and practical problems with access control based on the `protected` notion. In my experience, there have always been alternatives to placing significant amounts of information in a common base class for derived classes to use directly. In fact, one of my concerns about `protected` is exactly that it makes it too easy to use a common base the way one might sloppily have used global data.

Fortunately, you don't have to use protected data in C++; `private` is the default in classes and is usually the better choice. Note that none of these objections are significant for protected member *functions*. I still consider `protected` a fine way of specifying operations for use in derived classes.

Protected members were introduced into Release 1.2. Protected base classes were first described in the ARM and provided in Release 2.1. In retrospect, I think that `protected` is a case where "good arguments" and fashion overcame my better judgement and my rules of thumb for accepting new features.

13.10 Improved Code Generation

To some people, the most important "feature" of Release 2.0 wasn't a feature at all, but a simple space optimization. From the beginning, the code generated by Cfront tended to be pretty good. As late as 1992, Cfront generated the fastest running code in a benchmark used to evaluate C++ compilers on a SPARC. Except for the implementation of the return value optimization suggested in [ARM,§12.1c] in Release 3.0, there have been no significant improvements in Cfront's code generation since Release 1.0. However, Release 1.0 wasted space because each compilation unit generated its own set of virtual function tables for all the classes used in that unit. This could lead to megabytes of waste. At the time (about 1984), I considered the waste necessary in the absence of linker support and asked for such support. By 1987, that linker support hadn't materialized. Consequently, I rethought the problem and solved it by the simple heuristic of laying down the virtual function table of a class right next to the definition of its first non-pure virtual non-inline function. For example:

```
class X {
public:
    virtual void f1() { /* ... */ }
    void f2();
    virtual void f3() = 0;
    virtual void f4(); // first non-inline non-pure virtual
    // ...
};

// in some file:

    void X::f4() { /* ... */ }

    // Cfront will place X's virtual function table here
```

I chose that heuristic because it doesn't require cooperation from the linker. The heuristic isn't perfect because space is still wasted for classes that don't have a non-inline virtual function, but the space taken up by virtual function tables ceased to be a practical problem. Andrew Koenig and Stan Lippman were involved in the discussion of the details of this optimization. Naturally, other C++ compilers can and do choose their own solutions to this problem to suit their environments and engineering tradeoffs.

As an alternative, we considered simply generating virtual function table definitions in every compilation unit and then having a pre-linker eliminate all but one. This, however, was not easy to do portably. It was also plain inefficient. Why generate all those tables just to waste time throwing most away later? Alternative strategies are available to people who are willing to supply their own linker.

13.11 Pointers to Members

Originally, there was no way of expressing the concept of a pointer to a member function in C++. This led to the need to ''cheat'' the type system in cases, such as error handling, where pointers to functions are traditionally used. Given

```
struct S {
        int mf(char*);
};
```

people wrote code like this:

```
typedef void (*PSmem)(S*,char*);

PSmem m = (PSmem)&S::mf;

void g(S* ps)
{
        m(ps,"Hello");
}
```

This only worked with a liberal sprinkling of explicit casts that never ought to have worked in the first place. It also relied on the assumption that a member function is passed its object pointer (''the this pointer'') as the first argument in the way Cfront implements it (§2.5.2).

I considered this unacceptable as early as 1983, but felt no urgency to fix it. I considered it to be a purely technical issue that had to be answered to close a hole in the C++ type system, but of little practical importance. After finishing Release 1.0, I finally managed to find some time to plug this hole, and Release 1.2 implemented the solution. As it happened, the advent of environments relying on callbacks as a primary communication mechanism made the solution to this problem crucial.

The term *pointer to member* is a bit misleading because a pointer to member is more like an offset, a value that identifies a member of an object. However, had I called it ''offset'' people would have made the mistaken assumption that a pointer to member was a simple index into an object and would also have assumed that some forms of arithmetic could be applied. This would have caused even more confusion than the term *pointer to member*, which was chosen because I designed the mechanism as a close syntactic parallel to C's pointer syntax.

Consider the C/C++ function syntax in all its glory:

```
int f(char* p) { /* ... */ }    // define function.
int (*pf)(char*) = &f;          // declare and initialize
                                // pointer to function.
int i = (*pf)("hello");         // call through pointer.
```

Inserting S:: and p-> in the appropriate places, I constructed a direct parallel for member functions:

```
class S {
    // ...
    int mf(char*);
};

int S::mf(char*p) { /* ... */ }   // define member function.
int (S::*pmf)(char*) = &S::mf;    // declare and
                                  // initialize pointer to
                                  // member function.
S* p;
int i = (p->*pmf)("hello");       // call function through
                                  // pointer and object.
```

Semantically and syntactically, this notion of pointer-to-member functions makes sense. All I needed to do was to generalize it to include data members and find an implementation strategy. The acknowledgment section of [Lippman,1988] has this to say:

> "The design of the pointer to member concept was a cooperative effort by Bjarne Stroustrup and Jonathan Shopiro with many useful comments by Doug McIlroy. Steve Dewhurst contributed greatly to the redesign of the pointer to member implementation to cope with multiple inheritance."

At the time I was fond of saying that we discovered pointers to members more than we designed it. Most of 2.0 felt that way.

For a long time, I considered pointers to data members an artifact of generalization rather than something genuinely useful. Again, I was proven wrong. In particular, pointers to data members has proven a useful way of expressing the layout of a C++ class in an implementation-independent manner [Hübel,1992].

14

Casting

*Reasonable men
do not change the world.*
– G.B.Shaw

Major and minor extensions — the need for run-time type information (RTTI) — `dynamic_cast` — syntax — which types support RTTI — casting from a virtual base — uses and misuses of RTTI — `typeid()` — class `type_info`— extended type information — a simple object I/O system — rejected alternatives new casts — `static_cast` — `reinterpret_cast` — `const_cast` — using new-style casts.

14.1 Major Extensions

Templates (§15), exceptions (§16), run-type type information (§14.2), and name-spaces (§17) are often referred to as *major* extensions. What makes them major – whether seen as extensions or as integral features of C++ – is that they affect the way programs can be organized. Since C++ was created primarily to allow new ways of organizing programs rather than simply to provide more convenient ways of express-ing traditional designs, the major features are the ones that matter.

Minor features are therefore considered minor because they don't affect the over-all structure of a program. They don't affect design. They are not minor because they involve only a few lines of manual text to define or require only a few lines of com-piler code to implement. In fact, some major features are easier to describe and implement than some minor features.

Naturally, not every feature fits neatly into the simple minor and major categories. For example, nested functions could be seen as either minor or major depending on how important you consider their use in expressing iteration. However, my policy over the years has been to work hard on a few major extensions while trying to mini-mize minor extension. Curiously enough, the volume of interest and public debate is often inversely proportional to the importance of a feature. The reason is that it is much easier to have a firm opinion on a minor feature than on a major one; minor fea-tures fit directly into the current state of affairs, whereas major ones – by definition – do not.

Because support for building libraries and for composing software out of semi-independent parts is a key aim of C++, the major extensions relate to that: templates, exception handling, run-time type identification, and namespaces. Of these, templates and exception handling were part of my view of what C++ should be even in the pre-Release-1.0 days (§2.9.2 and §3.15). Run-time type identification was considered even in the first draft of C++ (§3.5), but postponed in the hope that it would prove unnecessary. Namespaces is the only major extension beyond the original conception of C++, yet even it is a response to a problem that I unsuccessfully tried to solve in the first version of C++ (§3.12).

14.2   Run-Time Type Information

In many ways, the discussion about mechanisms for run-time determination of the type of an object resembled the discussions about multiple inheritance (§12.6). Multi-ple inheritance was perceived as the first major extension to the original C++ defini-tion. Run-Time Type Information, often called RTTI, was the first major extension beyond the features mandated for the standardization process and presented in the ARM.

Again, a new style of programming was being directly supported by C++. Again some
- Declared the support unnecessary
- Declared the new style inherently evil (''against the spirit of C++'')
- Deemed it too expensive
- Thought it too complicated and confusing
- Saw it as the beginning of an avalanche of new features

In addition, RTTI attracted criticism related to the C/C++ casting mechanism in gen-eral. For example, many dislike that (old-style) casts can be used to bypass the access control for private base classes and can cast away `const`. These criticisms are well founded and important; they are discussed in §14.3.

Again, I defended the new feature on the grounds that it was important to some, harmless to people who didn't use it, that if we didn't support it directly people would simply simulate it, and that it was easy to implement. To support the last claim, I pro-duced an experimental implementation in two mornings. This makes RTTI at least two orders of magnitude simpler than exceptions and templates, and more than an order of magnitude simpler than multiple inheritance.

The original impetus for adding facilities for determining the type of an object at run time to C++ came from Dmitry Lenkov [Lenkov,1991]. Dmitry in turn built on experience from major C++ libraries such as Interviews [Linton,1987], the NIH library [Gorlen,1990], and ET++ [Weinand,1988]. The dossier mechanism [Interrante,1990] was also available for examination.

The RTTI mechanisms provided by libraries are mutually incompatible, so they become a barrier to the use of more than one library. Also, all require considerable foresight from base class designers. Consequently, a language-supported mechanism was needed.

I got involved in the detailed design for such mechanisms as the coauthor with Dmitry of the original proposal to the ANSI/ISO committee and as the main person responsible for the refinement of the proposal in the committee [Stroustrup,1992]. The proposal was first presented to the committee at the London meeting in July 1991 and accepted at the Portland, Oregon meeting in March 1993.

The run-time type information mechanism consists of three parts:

- An operator, dynamic_cast, for obtaining a pointer to an object of a derived class given a pointer to a base class of that object. The operator dynamic_cast delivers that pointer only if the object pointed to really is of the specified derived class; otherwise it returns 0.
- An operator, typeid, for identifying the exact type of an object given a pointer to a base class.
- A structure, type_info, acting as a hook for further run-time information associated with a type.

To conserve space, the RTTI discussion is almost completely restricted to pointers.

14.2.1 The Problem

Assume that a library supplies class dialog_box and that its interfaces are expressed in terms of dialog_boxes. I, however, use both dialog_boxes and my own dbox_w_strs:

```
class dialog_box : public window {   // library class
    // ...
public:
    virtual int ask();
    // ...
};

class dbox_w_str : public dialog_box {   // my class
    // ...
public:
    int ask();
    virtual char* get_string();
    // ...
};
```

So, when the system/library hands me a pointer to a dialog_box, how can I know whether it is one of my dbox_w_strs?

Note that I can't modify the library to know my dbox_w_str class. Even if I could, I wouldn't, because then I would have to worry about dbox_w_strs in new versions of the library and about errors I might have introduced into the "standard" library.

14.2.2 The dynamic_cast Operator

A naive solution would be to find the type of the object pointed to and compare that to my dbox_w_str class:

```
void my_fct(dialog_box* bp)
{
    if (typeid(*bp) == typeid(dbox_w_str)) {   // naive

        dbox_w_str* dbp = (dbox_w_str*)bp;

        // use dbp
    }
    else {

        // treat *bp as a ''plain'' dialog box
    }
}
```

Given the name of a type as the operand, the typeid() operator returns an object that identifies it. Given an expression operand, typeid() returns an object that identifies the type of the object that the expression denotes. In particular, typeid(*bp) returns an object that allows the programmer to ask questions about the type of the object pointed to by bp. In this case, we asked if that type was identical to the type dbox_w_str.

This is the simplest question to ask, but it is typically *not* the right question. The reason to ask is to see if some detail of a derived class can be safely used. To use it, we need to obtain a pointer to the derived class. In the example, we used a cast on the line following the test. Further, we typically are not interested in the *exact* type of the object pointed to, but only in whether we can safely perform that cast. This question can be asked directly using the dynamic_cast operator:

```
void my_fct(dialog_box* bp)
{
    if (dbox_w_str* dbp = dynamic_cast<dbox_w_str*>(bp)) {

        // use dbp
    }
    else {

        // treat *pb as a ''plain'' dialog box
    }
}
```

The dynamic_cast<T*>(p) operator converts its operand p to the desired type

T* if *p really is a T or a class derived from T; otherwise, the value of
dynamic_cast<T*>(p) is 0.

There are several advantages to merging the test and the cast into a single operation:

- A dynamic cast makes it impossible to mismatch the test and the cast.
- By using the information available in the type-information objects, it is possible to cast to types that are not fully defined in the scope of the cast.
- By using the information available in the type information objects, it is often possible to cast from a virtual base class to a derived class (§14.2.2.3).
- A static cast can't give the correct result in all cases (§14.3.2.1).

The dynamic_cast operator serves the majority of needs I have encountered. I consider dynamic_cast to be the most important part of the RTTI mechanism and the construct users should focus on.

dynamic_cast operator can also be used to cast to a reference type. In case of failure, a cast to a reference throws a bad_cast exception. For example:

```
void my_fct(dialog_box& b)
{
    dbox_w_str& db = dynamic_cast<dbox_w_str&>(b);

    // use db
}
```

I use a reference cast when I want an assumption about a reference type checked and consider it a failure for my assumption to be wrong. If, instead, I want to select among plausible alternatives, I use a pointer cast and test the result.

I don't recall exactly when I settled on a run-time-checked cast as my preferred way of dealing with run-time type checking should direct language support become necessary. The idea was first suggested to me by someone at Xerox PARC during a visit there in 1984 or 1985. The suggestion was to have ordinary casts do checking. As mentioned in §14.2.2.1, this variant has problems with overhead and compatibility, but I saw that some form of casts would help minimize the misuses that a switch-on-type mechanism, such as Simula's INSPECT, makes so tempting.

14.2.2.1 Syntax

The discussion of what the dynamic_cast operator should look like reflected both pure syntactic concerns and concerns about the nature of conversions.

Casts are one of the most error-prone facilities in C++. They are also one of the ugliest syntactically. Naturally, I considered if it would be possible to

[1] Eliminate casts.

[2] Make casts safe.

[3] Provide a cast syntax that makes it obvious that an unsafe operation is used.

[4] Provide alternatives to casting and discourage the use of casts.

Basically, dynamic_cast reflects the conclusion that a combination of [3] and [4] seems feasible, whereas [1] and [2] are not.

Considering [1], we observed that no language supporting systems programming has completely eliminated the possibility of casting and that even effective support for numeric work requires some form of type conversion. Thus, the aim must be to minimize the use of casts and make them as well behaved as possible. Starting from that premise, Dmitry and I devised a proposal that unified dynamic and static casts using the old-style cast syntax. This seemed a good idea, but upon closer examination several problems were uncovered:

[1] Dynamic casts and ordinary unchecked casts are fundamentally different operations. Dynamic casts look into objects to produce a result and may fail with a run-time indication of that failure. Ordinary casts perform an operation that is determined exclusively by the types involved and doesn't depend on the value of the object involved (except for occasional checking for null pointers). An ordinary cast doesn't fail; it simply produces a new value. Using the cast syntax for both dynamic and static casts led to confusion about what a given cast expression really did.

[2] If dynamic casts are not syntactically distinguished, it is not possible to find them easily (grep for them, to use Unix-speak).

[3] If dynamic casts are not syntactically distinguished, it is not possible for the compiler to reject unsuitable uses of dynamic casts; it must simply perform whatever kind of cast can be done for the types involved. If distinguished, it can be an error to attempt a dynamic cast for objects that don't support run-time checking.

[4] The meaning of programs using ordinary casts would change if run-time checking were applied wherever feasible. Examples are casts to undefined classes and casts within multiple inheritance hierarchies (§14.3.2). We did not manage to convince ourselves that this change would leave the meaning of all reasonable programs unchanged.

[5] The cost of checking would be incurred even for old programs that already carefully checked that casts were viable using other means.

[6] The suggested way of "turning off checking," casting to and from `void*`, wouldn't be perfectly reliable because the meaning would be changed in some cases. These cases might be perverted, but because understanding of the code would be required, the process of turning off checking would be manual and error-prone. We are also against techniques that would add yet more uncheckable casts to programs.

[7] Making some casts "safe" would make casting more respectable; yet the long-term aim is to decrease the use of all casts (including dynamic casts).

After much discussion, we found this formulation: "Would our ideal language have more than one notation for type conversion?" For a language that distinguishes fundamentally different operations syntactically the answer is yes. Consequently, we abandoned the attempt to "hijack" the old cast syntax.

We considered if it would be possible to deprecate the old cast syntax in favor of something like:

```
Checked<T*>(p); // run-time checked conversion of p to a T*
Unchecked<T*>(p); // unchecked conversion of p to a T*
```

This would eventually make all conversions obvious, thus eliminating problems arising from traditional casts being hard to spot in C and C++ programs. It would also give all casts a common syntactic pattern based on the `<T*>` template notation for types (§15). This line of thought led to the alternative cast syntax presented in §14.3.

Not everyone likes the template syntax, though, and not everyone who likes the template syntax likes its use for cast operators. Consequently, we discussed and experimented with alternatives.

The `(?T*)p` notation was popular for some time because it mirrors the traditional cast syntax `(T*)p`. Others disliked it for exactly that reason, and many considered `(?T*)p` "far too cryptic." Worse, I discovered a critical flaw. The most common mistake when using `(?T*)p` was to forget the `?`. What was meant to be a relatively safe and checked conversion becomes a completely different, unchecked, and unsafe operation. For example:

```
if (dbox_w_string* p = (dbox_w_string*)q) // dynamic cast
{
    // *q is a dbox_w_string
}
```

Oops! Forgetting the `?` and thus turning the comment into a lie was found to be uncomfortably common. Note that we cannot grep for occurrences of old-style casts to protect against this kind of mistake, and those of us with a strong C background are most prone to make the mistake and to miss it when reading the code.

Among the other alternatives considered, the notation

```
(virtual T*)p
```

was the most promising. It is relatively easy to spot for humans and for tools, the word `virtual` indicates the logical connection to classes with virtual functions (polymorphic types), and the general syntactic pattern is that of a traditional cast. However, it too was considered "too cryptic" by many and attracted the hostility of people who disliked the old cast syntax. Personally, I weakly agreed with that criticism, feeling that the `dynamic_cast` syntax simply fit better into C++ (as many who had significant experience using templates did). I also considered it an advantage that `dynamic_cast` provided a cleaner syntactic pattern that might eventually be used as an alternative to the old casts (§14.3).

14.2.2.2 When can we use Dynamic Casts?

The introduction of run-time type identification separates objects into two categories:
- [1] Ones that have run-time type information associated so that their type can be determined (almost) independently of context.
- [2] Those that haven't.

Why? We cannot impose the burden of being able to identify an object's type at run-time on built-in types such as `int` and `double` without unacceptable costs in run-time, space, and layout-compatibility problems. A similar argument applies to simple class objects and C-style structs. Consequently, from an implementation point of view, the first acceptable dividing line is between objects of classes with virtual functions and classes without. The former can easily provide run-time type information, the latter cannot.

Further, a class with virtual functions is often called a *polymorphic class*, and polymorphic classes are the only ones that can be safely manipulated through a base class. By "safely," I here mean that the language provides guarantees that objects are used only according to their defined type. Naturally, individual programmers can in specific cases demonstrate that manipulations of a non-polymorphic class don't violate the type system.

From a programming point of view, it therefore seems natural to provide run-time type identification for polymorphic types only: They are exactly the ones for which C++ supports manipulation through a base class. Supporting RTTI for a non-polymorphic type would simply provide support for switch-on-type-field programming. Naturally the language should not make that style impossible, but I saw no need to complicate the language solely to accommodate it.

Experience shows that providing RTTI for polymorphic types (only) works acceptably. However, people can get confused about which objects are polymorphic and thus about whether a dynamic cast can be used or not. Fortunately, the compiler will catch the errors when the programmer guesses wrong. I looked long and hard for an acceptable way of explicitly saying "this class supports RTTI (whether it has virtual functions or not)," but didn't find one that was worth the effort of introducing it.

14.2.2.3 Casting from Virtual Bases

The introduction of the `dynamic_cast` operator allowed us to provide a way to circumvent an old problem. It is not possible to cast from a virtual base class to a derived class using an ordinary cast. The reason for the restriction is that there is insufficient information available in an object to implement a cast from a virtual base to one of the classes derived from it; see §12.4.1.

However, the information needed to provide run-time type identification includes the information needed to implement the dynamic cast from a polymorphic virtual base. Therefore, the restriction against casting from a virtual base need not apply to dynamic casts from polymorphic virtual base classes:

```
class B { /* ... */ virtual void f(); };
class V { /* ... */ virtual void g(); };
class X { /* no virtual functions */ };

class D: public B, public virtual V, public virtual X {
    // ...
};
```

```
void g(D& d)
{
    B* pb = &d;
    D* p1 = (D*)pb;                    // ok, unchecked
    D* p2 = dynamic_cast<D*>(pb);      // ok, run-time checked

    V* pv = &d;
    D* p3 = (D*)pv; // error: cannot cast from virtual base
    D* p4 = dynamic_cast<D*>(pv); // ok, run-time checked

    X* px = &d;
    D* p5 = (D*)px; // error: cannot cast from virtual base
    D* p6 = dynamic_cast<D*>(px); // error: can't cast from
                                  // non-polymorphic type
}
```

Naturally, such a cast can only be performed when the derived class can be unambiguously determined.

14.2.3 Uses and Misuses of RTTI

One should use explicit run-time type information only when one has to. Static (compile-time) checking is safer, implies less overhead, and – where applicable – leads to better-structured programs. For example, RTTI can be used to write thinly disguised switch statements:

```
    // misuse of run-time type information:

void rotate(const Shape& r)
{
    if (typeid(r) == typeid(Circle)) {
        // do nothing
    }
    else if (typeid(r) == typeid(Triangle)) {
        // rotate triangle
    }
    else if (typeid(r) == typeid(Square)) {
        // rotate square
    }
    // ...
}
```

I have heard this style described as providing "the syntactic elegance of C combined with the run-time efficiency of Smalltalk," but that is really too kind. The real problem is that this code does not handle classes derived from the ones mentioned correctly and needs to be modified whenever a new class is added to the program.

Such code is usually best avoided through the use of virtual functions. It was my experience with Simula code written this way that caused facilities for run-time type identification to be left out of C++ in the first place (§3.5).

For many people trained in languages such as C, Pascal, Modula-2, Ada, etc., there is an almost irresistible urge to organize software as a set of switch statements. This urge should most often be resisted. Please note that even though the standards committee approved a RTTI mechanism for C++, we did not support it with a type-switch statement (such as Simula's INSPECT statement). I still don't consider a type switch a model of software organization worth supporting directly. The examples where it is appropriate are far fewer than most programmers believe at first – and by the time a programmer has second thoughts, the reorganization needed most likely will involve too much work to be done.

Many examples of proper use of RTTI arise where some service code is expressed in terms of one class and a user wants to add functionality through derivation. The dialog_box example from §14.2.1 is an example of this. If the user is willing and able to modify the definitions of the library classes, say dialog_box, then the use of RTTI can be avoided; if not, it is needed. Even if the user is willing to modify the base classes, such modification may have its own problems. For example, it may be necessary to introduce dummy implementations of virtual functions such as get_string() in classes for which the virtual functions are not needed or not meaningful. This problem is discussed in some detail in [2nd,§13.13.6] under the heading of "Fat Interfaces." A use of RTTI to implement a simple object I/O system can be found in §14.2.7.

For people with a background in languages that rely heavily on dynamic type checking, such as Smalltalk, it is tempting to use RTTI in conjunction with overly general types. For example:

```
// misuse of run-time type information:

class Object { /* ... */ };

class Container : public Object {
public:
    void put(Object*);
    Object* get();
    // ...
};

class Ship : public Object { /* ... */ };

Ship* f(Ship* ps, Container* c)
{
    c->put(ps);
    // ...
    Object* p = c->get();
    if (Ship* q = dynamic_cast<Ship*>(p)) // run-time check
        return q;

    // do something else (typically, error handling)
}
```

Here, class `Object` is an unnecessary implementation artifact. It is overly general because it does not correspond to an abstraction in the application domain and forces the application programmer to operate at a lower level of abstraction. Problems of this kind are often better solved by using container templates holding only a single kind of pointer:

```
template<class T> class Container {
public:
    void put(T*);
    T* get();
    // ...
};

Ship* f(Ship* ps, Container<Ship>* c)
{
    c->put(ps);
    // ...
    return c->get();
}
```

Combined with the use of virtual functions, this technique handles most cases.

14.2.4 Why Provide a "Dangerous Feature?"

So, if I confidently predict misuses of RTTI, why did I design the mechanism and work for its adoption?

Good programs are achieved through good education, good design, adequate testing, etc., not by providing language features that supposedly can be used only in "the right way." Every useful feature can be misused, so the question is not whether a feature can be misused (it can), or whether it will be misused (it will). The questions are whether the good uses are sufficiently critical to warrant the effort of providing a feature, whether the effort of simulating a feature using other language features is manageable, and whether the misuses can be kept to a reasonable level by proper education.

Having considered RTTI for some time, I became convinced that we faced a classical standardization problem:

- Most major libraries provide a RTTI feature.
- Most provide it in a form that requires significant and error-prone user cooperation for it to work correctly.
- All provide it in incompatible ways.
- Most provide it in a non-general way.
- Most present it as a "neat feature" that users ought to try rather than a dangerous mechanism to be used as a last resort.
- In every major library there seem to be (only) a few cases where RTTI is critical in the sense that without it there would be a facility that the library couldn't offer or could only offer by imposing a significant burden on users and implementers.

By providing standard RTTI, we can overcome one barrier to the use of libraries from different sources (see §8.2.2). We can provide a coherent view of the use of RTTI and try to make it as safe as possible and provide warnings against misuse.

Finally, it has been a guideline in the design of C++ that when all is said and done the programmer must be trusted. What good can be done is more important than what mistakes might be made. C++ programmers are supposed to be adults and need only minimal "nannyism."

Not everyone is convinced, though. Some, notably Jim Waldo, argue strongly that RTTI is needed so infrequently and the misconceptions that are the roots of misuses of RTTI are so widespread that the net effect of RTTI must be detrimental to C++. Only time will tell for sure. The greatest danger from misuse comes from programmers who consider themselves so expert that they see no need to consult a C++ textbook before starting to use C++ (§7.2).

14.2.5 The `typeid()` Operator

I had hoped that the `dynamic_cast` operator would serve all common needs so that no further RTTI features needed to be presented to users. However, most other people I discussed the issue with disagreed and pointed to two further needs:

[1] A need to find the exact type of an object; that is, being told that an object is of class X, rather than just that it is of class X or some class derived from class X the way `dynamic_cast` does.

[2] Using the exact type of an object as a gateway to information describing properties of that type.

Finding the exact type of an object is sometimes referred to as *type identity*, so I named the operator yielding it `typeid`.

The reason people want to know the exact type of an object is usually that they want to perform some standard service on the whole object. Ideally, such services are presented as a virtual function so that the exact type needn't be known, but when – for some reason – no such function is available, finding the exact type and then performing the operation is necessary. People have designed object I/O and database systems working this way. In those cases, no common interface can be assumed for every object manipulated so the detour through the exact type becomes necessary. Another, much simpler, use has been to obtain the name of a class for diagnostic output:

```
cout << typeid(*p).name();
```

The `typeid()` operator is used explicitly to gain access to information about types at run time; `typeid()` is a built-in operator. Had it been a function, its declaration would have looked something like this:

```
class type_info;
const type_info& typeid(type-name);  // pseudo declaration
const type_info& typeid(expression); // pseudo declaration
```

That is, `typeid()` returns a reference to an unknown type called `type_info`†.

---

† The standards committee is still discussing naming conventions for standard library classes. I have picked the names I consider the most likely outcome of these discussions.

Given a *type-name* as its operand, `typeid()` returns a reference to a `type_info` that represents the *type-name*. Given an *expression* as its operand, `typeid()` returns a reference to a `type_info` that represents the type of the object denoted by the *expression*.

The reason `typeid()` returns a reference to `type_info` rather than a pointer is that we wanted to disable the usual pointer operators such as `==` and `++` on the result of `typeid()`. For example, it is not clear that every implementation will be able to guarantee uniqueness of type identification objects. This implies that comparing `typeid()`s can't simply be defined as comparing pointers to `type_info` objects. With `typeid()` returning a `type_info&`, there is no problem defining `==` to cope with possible duplication of `type_info` objects for a single type.

14.2.5.1 Class `type_info`

Class `type_info` is defined in the standard header file `<type_info.h>`, which needs to be included for the result of `typeid()` to be used. The exact definition of class `type_info` is implementation dependent, but it is a polymorphic type that supplies comparisons and an operation that returns the name of the type represented:

```
class type_info {
  // implementation-dependent representation

private:
  type_info(const type_info&);              // users can't
  type_info& operator=(const type_info&);   // copy type_info

public:
  virtual ~type_info();                     // is polymorphic

  int operator==(const type_info&) const;   // can be compared
  int operator!=(const type_info&) const;
  int before(const type_info&) const;       // ordering

  const char* name() const;                 // name of type
};
```

More detailed information can be supplied and accessed as described below. However, because of the great diversity of the "more detailed information" desired by different people and because of the desire for minimal space overhead by others, the services offered by `type_info` are deliberately minimal.

The `before()` function is intended to allow `type_infos` to be sorted so that they can be accessed through hash tables, etc. There is no relation between the relationships defined by `before` and inheritance relationships (see §14.2.8.3). Further, there is no guarantee that `before()` yields the same results in different programs or different runs of the same programs. In this, `before()` resembles the address-of operator.

14.2.5.2 Extended Type Information

Sometimes knowing the exact type of an object is simply the first step to acquiring and using more detailed information about that type.

Consider how an implementation or a tool could make information about types available to users at run time. Say we have a tool that generates a table of My_type_info objects. The preferred way of presenting this to the user is to provide an associative array (map, dictionary) of typenames and such tables. To get such a member table for a type, a user would write:

```
#include <type_info.h>

extern Map<My_type_info,const char*> my_type_table;

void f(B* p)
{
    My_type_info& mi = my_type_table[typeid(*p).name()];
    // use mi
}
```

Someone else might prefer to index tables directly with typeids rather than requiring the user to use the name() string:

```
extern Map<Your_type_info,type_info*> your_type_table;

void g(B* p)
{
    Your_type_info& yi = your_type_table[&typeid(*p)];
    // use yi
}
```

This way of associating typeids with information allows several people or tools to associate different information to types without interfering with each other:

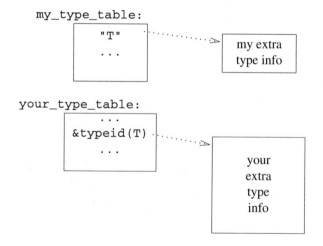

my_type_table:

"T"

. . .

my extra
type info

your_type_table:

. . .

&typeid(T)

. . .

your
extra
type
info

This is most important because the likelihood that someone can come up with a set of information that satisfies all users is zero. In particular, any set of information that would satisfy most users would be so large that it would be unacceptable overhead for users who need only minimal run-time type information.

An implementation may choose to provide additional implementation-specific type information. Such system-provided extended type information could be accessed through an associative array exactly as user-provided extended type information is. Alternatively, the extended type information could be presented as a class `Extended_type_info` derived from class `type_info`:

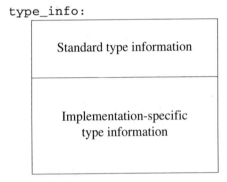

```
type_info:
```

> Standard type information
>
> Implementation-specific
> type information

A `dynamic_cast` can then be used to determine if a particular kind of extended type information is available:

```
#include <type_info.h>

typedef Extended_type_info Eti;

void f(Sometype* p)
{
    if (Eti* p = dynamic_cast<Eti*>(&typeid(*p))) {
        // ...
    }
}
```

What "extended" information might a tool or an implementation make available to a user? Basically any information that a compiler can provide and that some program might want to take advantage of at run time. For example:

- Object layouts for object I/O and/or debugging.
- Pointers to functions creating and copying objects.
- Tables of functions together with their symbolic names for calls from interpreter code.
- Lists of all objects of a given type.
- References to source code for the member function.
- Online documentation for the class.

The reason such things are supported through libraries, possibly standard libraries, is that there are too many needs, too many potentially implementation-specific details, and too much information to support every use in the language itself. Also, some of these uses subvert the static checking provided by the language. Others impose costs in run time and space that I do not feel appropriate for a language feature.

14.2.6 Object Layout Model

Here is a plausible memory layout for an object with a virtual function table and type information object:

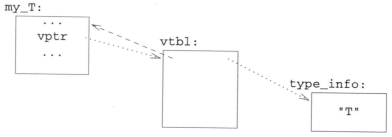

The dashed arrow represents an offset that allows the start of the complete object to be found given only a pointer to a polymorphic sub-object. It is equivalent to the offset (delta) used in the implementation of virtual functions (§12.4).

For each type with virtual functions, an object of type `type_info` is generated. These objects need not be unique. However, a good implementation will generate unique `type_info` objects wherever possible and only generate `type_info` objects for types where some form of run-time type information is actually used. An easy implementation simply places the `type_info` object for a class right next to its `vtbl`.

Cfront-based implementations and implementations that borrowed Cfront's virtual table layout can be updated to support RTTI without even requiring recompilation of old code. The reason is that I considered providing RTTI at the time I implemented Release 2.0 and left two empty words at the start of each `vtbl` to allow such an extension. At the time, I didn't add RTTI because I wasn't certain that it was needed or – assuming that it was needed – exactly how the facility should be presented to users. As an experiment, I implemented a simple version in which every object of a class with virtual functions could be made to print out its name. Having done that, I was satisfied that I knew how to add RTTI should it ever become necessary – and removed the feature.

14.2.7 An Example: Simple Object I/O

Let me present a sketch of how a user might use RTTI together with a simple object I/O system and outline how such an object I/O system might be implemented. Users want to read objects from a stream, determine that they are of the expected types, and then use them. For example:

```
void user()
{
    // open file assumed to hold shapes, and
    // attach ss as an istream for that file
    // ...

    io_obj* p = get_obj(ss); // read object from stream

    if (Shape* sp = dynamic_cast<Shape*>(p)) {
        sp->draw(); // use the Shape
        // ...
    }
    else {
        // oops: non-shape in Shape file
    }
}
```

The function `user()` deals with shapes exclusively through the abstract class `Shape` and can therefore use every kind of shape. The use of `dynamic_cast` is essential because the object I/O system can deal with many other kinds of objects and the user may accidentally have opened a file containing perfectly good objects of classes that this user has never heard of.

This object I/O system assumes that every object read or written is of a class derived from `io_obj`. Class `io_obj` must be a polymorphic type to allow us to use `dynamic_cast`. For example:

```
class io_obj { // polymorphic
    virtual io_obj* clone();
};
```

The critical function in the object I/O system is `get_obj()` that reads data from an `istream` and creates class objects based on that data. Let me assume that the data representing an object on an input stream is prefixed by a string identifying the object's class. The job of `get_obj()` is to read that string prefix and call a function capable of creating and initializing an object of the right class. For example:

```
typedef io_obj* (*PF)(istream&);

Map<String,PF> io_map; // maps strings to creation functions

io_obj* get_obj(istream& s)
{
    String str;
    if (get_word(s,str) == 0) // read initial word into str
        throw no_class;

    PF f = io_map[str]; // lookup 'str' to get function
    if (f == 0) throw unknown_class; // no match for 'str'
```

```
        io_obj* p = f(s); // construct object from stream
        if (debug) cout << typeid(*p).name() << '\n';
    }
```

The Map called `io_map` is an associative array that holds pairs of name strings and functions that can construct objects of the class with that name. The Map type is one of the most useful and efficient data structures in any language. One of the first widely used implementations of the idea in C++ was written by Andrew Koenig [Koenig,1988]; see also [2nd,§8.8].

Note the use of `typeid()` for debugging purposes. In this particular design, that is the only use of RTTI in the implementation.

We could, of course, define class `Shape` the usual way except deriving it from `io_obj` as required by `user()`:

```
    class Shape : public io_obj {
        // ...
    };
```

However, it would be more interesting (and in many cases more realistic) to use some previously defined `Shape` class hierarchy unchanged:

```
    class iocircle : public Circle, public io_obj {
    public:
        iocircle* clone() // override io_obj::clone()
            { return new iocircle(*this); }

        iocircle(istream&); // initialize from input stream

        static iocircle* new_circle(istream& s)
        {
            return new iocircle(s);
        }
        // ...
    };
```

The `iocircle(istream&)` constructor initializes an object with data from its `istream` argument. The `new_circle` function is the one put into the `io_map` to make the class known to the object I/O system. For example:

```
    io_map["iocircle"]=&iocircle::new_circle;
```

Other shapes are constructed in the same way:

```
    class iotriangle : public Triangle, public io_obj {
        // ...
    };
```

If the provision of the object I/O scaffolding becomes tedious, a template might be used:

```
template<class T>
class io : public T, public io_obj {
public:
    io* clone() // override io_obj::clone()
        { return new io(*this); }

    io(istream&); // initialize from input stream

    static io* new_io(istream& s)
    {
        return new io(s);
    }
    // ...
};
```

Given this, we could define `iocircle` like this:

```
typedef io<Circle> iocircle;
```

We would still have to define `io<Circle>::io(istream&)` explicitly, though, because it needs to know about the details of `Circle`.

This simple object I/O system may not do everything anyone ever wanted, but it almost fits on a single page, and the key mechanisms have many uses. In general, these techniques can be used to invoke a function based on a string supplied by a user.

14.2.8 Alternatives Considered

The RTTI mechanism provided is an "onion design." As you peel off the layers of the mechanism you find more powerful facilities – which if badly used might make you cry.

The basic notion of the RTTI mechanisms described here is that for maximal ease of programming and to minimize implementation dependencies, we should minimize the use of RTTI:

[1] Preferably, we should use no run-time type information at all and rely exclusively on static (compile-time) checking.

[2] If that is not possible, we should use only dynamic casts. In that case, we don't even have to know the exact name of the object's type and don't need to include any header files related to RTTI.

[3] If we must, we can compare `typeid()`s, but to do that, we need to know the exact name of at least some of the types involved. It is assumed that "ordinary users" will never need to examine run-time type information further.

[4] Finally, if we absolutely do need more information about a type – say, because we are trying to implement a debugger, a database system, or some other form of object I/O system – we can use operations on `typeid`s to obtain more detailed information.

This approach of providing a series of facilities of increasing involvement with run-time properties of classes contrasts to the approach of providing a class giving a single standard view of the run-time type properties of classes – a meta-class. The C++ approach encourages greater reliance on the (safer and more efficient) static type system, has a smaller minimal cost (in time and comprehensibility) to users, and is also more general because of the possibility of providing multiple views of a class by providing more detailed type information.

Several alternatives to this "onion approach" were considered.

14.2.8.1 Meta-Objects

The onion approach differs from the approaches taken by Smalltalk and CLOS. Such systems have also repeatedly been proposed for C++. In such systems, `type_info` is replaced by a "meta-object" capable of accepting – at run time – requests to perform any operation that can be requested of an object in the language. In essence, having a meta-object mechanism embeds an interpreter for the complete language in the run-time environment. I saw that as a danger to the basic efficiency of the language, a potential way of subverting the protection mechanisms, and at odds with the basic notions of design and documentation relating to static type checking.

These objections to basing C++ on a notion of meta-objects doesn't mean that meta-objects can't be useful. They most certainly can be, and the notion of extended type information opens the door for people who really need those techniques to supply them through libraries. I did, however, reject the idea of burdening *every* C++ user with those mechanisms, and I cannot recommend those design and implementation techniques for general C++ programming; see [2nd,§12] for details.

14.2.8.2 The Type-inquiry Operator

To many people, an operator that answers the question "is *pb of class D or a class derived from D?" seems more natural than `dynamic_cast` that performs a cast if and only if the answer to that question is affirmative. That is, they want to write code like this:

```
void my_fct(dialog_box* bbp)
{
    if (dbp->isKindOf(dbox_w_str)) {

        dbox_w_str* dbsp = (dbox_w_str*)dbp;

        // use dbsp
    }
    else {

        // treat *dbp as a ''plain'' dialog box
    }
}
```

There are several problems with this. The most serious is that the cast will, in some cases, not give the desired result (see §14.3.2.1). This is an example of how difficult it can be to import notions from a different language. Smalltalk provides `isKindOf` for type inquiry, but Smalltalk doesn't need the subsequent cast and therefore cannot suffer any problems relating to it. However, importing the `isKindOf` idea into C++ would cause both technical and stylistic problems.

In fact, stylistic arguments had settled the issue for me in favor of some form of conditional cast before I discovered those technical "killer" arguments against type-inquiry operators along the line of `isKindOf`. Separating the test and the type conversion causes verbosity and makes it possible to mismatch the test and the cast.

14.2.8.3 Type Relations

Several people suggested defining `<`, `<=`, etc., on `type_info` objects to express relationships in a class hierarchy. That is easy, but too cute. It also suffers from problems with an explicit type comparison operation as described in §14.2.8.2. We need a cast in any event so we can just as well use a dynamic cast.

14.2.8.4 Multi-methods

A more promising use of RTTI would be to support "multi-methods," that is, the ability to select a virtual function based on more than one object. Such a language facility would be a boon to writers of code that deals with binary operations on diverse objects; see §13.8. It appears that the `type_info` objects could easily hold the information necessary to accomplish this. This makes multi-methods more of a possible further extension than an alternative to the approach we adopted.

I made no such proposal, however, because I could not clearly grasp the implications of such a change and did not want to propose a major new extension without experience in the context of C++.

14.2.8.5 Unconstrained Methods

Given RTTI, one can support "unconstrained methods;" that is, one could hold enough information in the `type_info` object for a class to check at run time whether a given function was supported or not. Thus, one could support Smalltalk-style run-time-checked function calls. However, I felt no need for that and considered that extension as contrary to my effort to encourage efficient and type-safe programming. The dynamic cast enables a check-and-call strategy:

```
if (D* pd = dynamic_cast<D*>(pb)) { // is *pb a D?
    pd->dfct(); // call D function
    // ...
}
```

rather than the call-and-have-the-call-check strategy of Smalltalk:

```
pb->dfct(); // hope pb points to something that
            // has a dfct; handle failed calls
            // somewhere (else)
```

The check-and-call strategy provides more static checking (we know at compile time that `dfct` is defined for class D), doesn't impose an overhead on the vast majority of calls that don't need the check, and provides a visible clue that something beyond the ordinary is going on.

14.2.8.6 Checked Initialization

We also considered checking assignments and/or initialization in a way similar to what is done in languages such as Beta and Eiffel. For example:

```
void f(B* pb)
{
    D* pd1 = pb; // error: type mismatch
    D* pd2 ?= pb; // ok, check if is *pb a D at run time

    pd1 = pb; // error: type mismatch
    pd2 ?= pb; // ok, check if is *pb a D at run time
}
```

However, I thought the ? was too hard to spot in real code and too error-prone because it wouldn't be combined with a test. Also, it sometimes requires the introduction of an otherwise unnecessary named variable. The alternative, allowing ?= only in conditions seemed very attractive:

```
void f(B* pb)
{
    D* pd1 ?= pb;          // error: unchecked
                           // conditional initialization

    if (D* pd2 ?= pb) { // ok: checked
                        // conditional initialization
        // ...
    }
}
```

However, you would have to distinguish between cases where exceptions are thrown in the case of failure and cases where 0 is returned. Also, a ?= operator would lack the odium attached to ugly casts and would therefore encourage misuse.

By allowing declarations in conditions (§3.11.5.2), I made it possible to use `dynamic_cast` in the style suggested by this alternative:

```
void f(B* pb)
{
    if (D* pd2 = dynamic_cast<D*>(pb)) { // ok: checked
        // ...
    }
}
```

14.3 A New Cast Notation

Syntactically and semantically, casts are one of the ugliest features of C and C++. This has led to a continuous search for alternatives to casts: Function declarations enabling implicit conversion of arguments (§2.6), templates (§14.2.3), and the relaxation of the overriding rules for virtual functions (§13.7) each remove the need for some casts. The `dynamic_cast` operator (§14.2.2), on the other hand, provides a safer alternative to old-style casts for a specific usage. This led to a complementary approach to try to factor out the logically separate uses of casting and support them with operators similar to `dynamic_cast`:

```
static_cast<T>(e)        // reasonably well-behaved casts.
reinterpret_cast<T>(e)   // casts yielding values that must
                         // be cast back to be used safely.
const_cast<T>(e)         // casting away const.
```

This section can be read as an analysis of the problems with old-style casts or as a synthesis of a new feature. It is both. The definition of these operators owes much to the efforts of the extensions working group where strong opinions both for and against have been heard. Dag Brück, Jerry Schwarz, and Andrew Koenig have made particularly constructive contributions. These new cast operators were accepted at the San Jose meeting in November of 1993.

To conserve space the discussion is almost completely restricted to the most difficult case: pointers. The treatment of arithmetic types, pointers to members, references, etc., is left as an exercise for the reader.

14.3.1 The Problem

The C and C++ cast is a sledgehammer: `(T)expr` will – with very few exceptions – yield a value of type `T` based in some way on the value of `expr`. Maybe a simple reinterpretation of the bits of `expr` is involved, maybe an arithmetic narrowing or widening is involved, maybe some address arithmetic is done to navigate a class hierarchy, maybe the result is implementation dependent, maybe a `const` or `volatile` attribute is removed, etc. It is not possible for a reader to determine what the writer intended from an isolated cast expression. For example:

```
const X* pc = new X;
// ...
pv = (Y*)pc;
```

Did the programmer intend to obtain a pointer to a type unrelated to `X`? Cast away the `const` attribute? Both? Was the intent to gain access to a base class `Y` of `X`? The possibilities for confusion are endless.

Further, an apparently innocent change to a declaration can quietly change the meaning of an expression dramatically. For example:

```
class X : public A, public B { /* ... */ };

void f(X* px)
{
    ((B*)px)->g();    // call B's g
    px->B::g();       // a more explicit, better, way
}
```

Change the definition of X so that B no longer is a base class and the meaning of (B*)px changes completely without giving the compiler any chance to diagnose a problem.

Apart from the semantic problems with old-style casts, the notation is unfortunate. The notation is close to minimal and uses only parentheses – the most overused syntactic construct in C. Consequently, casts are hard for humans to spot in a program and also hard to search for using simple tools such as grep. The cast syntax is also a major source of C++ parser complexity.

To sum up, old-style casts:

[1] Are a problem for understanding: they provide a single notation for several weakly related operations.

[2] Are error-prone: almost every type combination has some legal interpretation.

[3] Are hard to spot in code and hard to search for with simple tools.

[4] Complicate the C and C++ grammar.

The new cast operators represent a classification of the old cast's functionality. To have a chance of wide acceptance in the user population, they have to be able to perform any operation that the old casts can do. Otherwise, a reason for future use of old-style casts would have been provided. I have found only one exception: an old-style cast can cast from a derived class to its private base class. There is no reason for this operation; it is dangerous and useless. There is no mechanism for granting oneself access to the complete private representation of an object – and none is needed. The fact that an old-style cast can be used to gain access to the part of a representation that is a private base is an unfortunate historical accident. For example:

```
class D : public A, private B {
private:
    int m;
    // ...
};


void f(D* pd) // f() is not a member or a friend of D
{
    B* pb1 = (B*)pd;              // gain access to D's
                                 // private base B.
                                 // Yuck!
    B* pb2 = static_cast<B*>(pd); // error: can't access
                                 // private. Fine!
}
```

Except by manipulating pd as a pointer to raw memory, there is no way for f() to get to D::m. Thus, the new cast operators close a loophole in the access rules and provide a greater degree of consistency.

The long names and the template-like syntax of the new casts put off some people. That may be all for the better because one of the purposes of the new casts is to remind people that casting is a hazardous business and to emphasize that there are different kinds of danger involved in the use of the different operators. In my experience, the strongest dislike is expressed by people who use C++ mostly as a dialect of C and think they need to cast frequently. Also, people who haven't yet made serious use of templates find the notation odd. The dislike for the template-like notation wears off as people gain experience with templates.

14.3.2 The static_cast Operator

The static_cast<T>(e) notation is meant to replace (T)e for conversions such as Base* to Derived*. Such conversions are not always safe but frequent and well-defined even in the absence of a run-time check. For example:

```
class B { /* ... */ };

class D : public B { /* ... */ };

void f(B* pb, D* pd)
{
    D* pd2 = static_cast<D*>(pb);  // what we used
                                   // to call (D*)pb.

    B* pb2 = static_cast<B*>(pd);  // safe conversion
    // ...
}
```

One way of thinking of static_cast is as the explicit inverse operation to the implicit conversions. Except that static_cast respects constness, it can do S->T provided T->S can be done implicitly. This implies that in most cases the result of static_cast can be used without further casting. In this, it differs from reinterpret_cast (§14.3.3).

In addition, conversions that may be performed implicitly – such as standard conversions and user-defined conversions – are invoked by static_cast.

In contrast to dynamic_cast, no run-time check is required for the static_cast conversion of pb. The object pointed to by pb might not point to a D in which case uses of *pd2 are undefined and probably disastrous.

In contrast to the old-style cast, pointer and reference types must be complete; that is, trying to use static_cast to convert to or from a pointer to a type for which the declaration hasn't been seen is an error. For example:

```
class X;   // X is an incomplete type
class Y;   // Y is an incomplete type

void f(X* px)
{
    Y* p = (Y*)px;   // allowed, dangerous
    p = static_cast<Y*>(px);   // error:
                               // X and Y undefined
}
```

This eliminates yet another source of errors. If you need to cast incomplete types, use reinterpret_cast (§14.3.3) to make it clear that you are not trying to do hierarchy navigation, or use dynamic_cast (§14.2.2).

14.3.2.1 Static Casts and Dynamic Casts

The effect of both dynamic_cast and static_cast on pointers to classes is navigation in a class hierarchy. However, static_cast relies exclusively on static information (and can therefore be fooled). Consider:

```
class B { /* ... */ };

class D : public B { /* ... */ };

void f(B* pb)
{
    D* pd1 = dynamic_cast<D*>(pb);
    D* pd2 = static_cast<D*>(pb);
}
```

If pb really points to a D, then pd1 and pd2 get the same value. So do they if pb==0. However, if pb points to a B (only) then dynamic_cast will know enough to return 0, whereas static_cast must rely on the programmer's assertion that pb points to a D and returns a pointer to the supposed D object. Worse, consider:

```
class D1 : public D { /* ... */ };
class D2 : public B { /* ... */ };
class X : public D1, public D2 { /* ... */ };

void g()
{
    D2* pd2 = new X;
    f(pd2);
}
```

Here, g() will call f() with a B that is not a sub-object of a D. Consequently, dynamic_cast will correctly find the sibling sub-object of type D, whereas static_cast will return a pointer to some inappropriate sub-object of the X. I think it was Martin O'Riordan who first brought this phenomenon to my attention.

14.3.3 The **reinterpret_cast** Operator

The reinterpret_cast<T>(e) notation is meant to replace (T)e for conversions, such as char* to int* and Some_class* to Unrelated_class*, that are inherently unsafe and often implementation dependent. Basically, reinterpret_cast returns a value that is a crude reinterpretation of its argument. For example:

```
class S;
class T;

void f(int* pi, char* pc, S* ps, T* pt, int i)
{
    S* ps2 = reinterpret_cast<S*>(pi);
    S* ps3 = reinterpret_cast<S*>(pt);
    char* pc2 = reinterpret_cast<char*>(pt);
    int* pi2 = reinterpret_cast<int*>(pc);
    int i2 = reinterpret_cast<int>(pc);
    int* pi3 = reinterpret_cast<int*>(i);
}
```

The reinterpret_cast operator allows any pointer to be converted into any other pointer type and also any integral type to be converted into any pointer type and vice versa. Essentially, all of these conversions are unsafe, implementation dependent, or both. Unless the desired conversion is inherently low-level and unsafe, the programmer should use one of the other casts.

Unlike static_cast, the result of a reinterpret_cast can't safely be used for anything except being cast back to its original type. Other uses are at best non-portable. This is why pointer-to-function and pointer-to-member conversions are reinterpret_casts rather than static_casts. For example:

```
void thump(char* p) { *p = 'x'; }

typedef void (*PF)(const char*);
PF pf;

void g(const char* pc)
{
    thump(pc); // error: bad argument type

    pf = &thump; // error

    pf = static_cast<PF>(&thump); // error!

    pf = reinterpret_cast<PF>(&thump); // ok: on your
                                       // head be it
    pf(pc); // not guaranteed to work!
}
```

Clearly, getting pf to point to thump is dangerous because doing so fools the type system and allows the address of a const to be passed to something that tries to modify it. That is why we must use a cast and in particular why the "nasty" reinterpret_cast must be used. It comes as a surprise to many, though, that a call through pf to thump is still not guaranteed to work (in C++ exactly as in C). The reason is that an implementation is allowed to use different calling sequences for different function types. In particular, there are good reasons why an implementation would use different calling sequences for const and non-const arguments.

Note that reinterpret_cast does *not* do class hierarchy navigation. For example:

```
class A { /* ... */ };
class B { /* ... */ };
class D : public A, public B { /* ... */ };

void f(B* pb)
{
    D* pd1 = reinterpret_cast<D*>(pb);
    D* pd2 = static_cast<D*>(pb);
}
```

Here, pd1 and pd2 will typically get different values. In a call

```
f(new D);
```

pd2 will point to the start of the D object passed, whereas pd1 will point to the start of D's B sub-object.

The reinterpret_cast<T>(arg) operation is almost as bad as (T)arg. However, reinterpret_cast is more visible, never performs class hierarchy navigation, does not cast away const, and the other casts provide alternatives; reinterpret_cast is an operation for performing low-level and usually implementation-dependent conversions – only.

14.3.4 The const_cast Operator

The thorniest issue in finding a replacement for old-style casts was finding an acceptable treatment of const. The ideal is to ensure that "constness" is never quietly removed. For this reason reinterpret_cast, dynamic_cast, and static_cast were conceived as respecting constness; that is, they can't be used to "cast away const."

The const_cast<T>(e) notation is meant to replace (T)e for conversions used to gain access to data specified const or volatile. For example:

```
extern "C" char* strchr(char*, char);

inline const char* strchr(const char* p, char c)
{
    return strchr(const_cast<char*>(p), char c);
}
```

In `const_cast<T>(e)`, the type argument `T` must be identical to the type of the argument `e` except for `const` and `volatile` modifiers. The result is identical to `e` except that its type is `T`.

Note that the result of casting away `const` from an object originally defined `const` is undefined (§13.3).

14.3.4.1 Problems with `const` Protection

There are, unfortunately, subtleties in the type system that open loopholes in the protection against implicit violation of ''constness.'' Consider:

```
const char cc = 'a';
const char* pcc = &cc;
const char** ppcc = &pcc;
void* pv = ppcc; // no cast needed:
                    // ppcc isn't a const, it only points to one,
                    // but const vanished!
char** ppc = (char**)pv; // points to pcc

void f()
{
    **ppc = 'x'; // Zap!
}
```

However, having `void*` unsafe can be considered acceptable because everybody knows – or at least ought to know – that casts *from* `void*` are inherently tricky.

Such examples become interesting when you start building classes that can contain a variety of pointer types (for example, to minimize generated code, see §15.5).

Unions and the use of the ellipsis to suppress type checking of function arguments provide other loopholes in the protection against implicit violation of ''constness.'' However, I prefer a system that leaves a few loopholes to one that provides no protection at all. As with `void*`, programmers should know that unions and unchecked function arguments are inherently dangerous, should be avoided wherever possible, and should be handled with special care when actually needed.

14.3.5 Impact of the New-style Casts

The new-style casts are part of a continuing effort to eliminate holes in the C++ type system. The aim is to minimize and localize unsafe and error-prone programming practices. Here, I discuss how to cope with related problem areas (old-style casts, implicit narrowing conversions, and function style conversions) and how to convert existing code to use the new cast operators.

14.3.5.1 Old-style Casts

I intended the new-style casts as a complete replacement for the `(T)e` notation. I proposed to deprecate `(T)e`; that is, for the committee to give users warning that the `(T)e` notation would most likely not be part of a future revision of the C++ standard.

I saw a direct parallel between this and the introduction of C++-style function proto-types in the ANSI/ISO C standard together with the deprecation of unchecked calls. However, that idea didn't gain a majority, so that cleanup of C++ will probably never happen.

What is more important, though, is that the new cast operators provide individual programmers and organizations with an opportunity to avoid the insecurities of old-style casts when type safety is more important than backward compatibility with C. The new casts can further be supported by compiler warnings for the use of old-style casts.

The new cast operators provide an evolution path to a safer, yet no less efficient, style of programming. This is likely to increase in importance over the years as the general quality of code improves and tools assuming type safety come into widespread use – in C++ and in other languages.

14.3.5.2 Implicit Narrowing Conversions

The idea of minimizing violations of the static type system and making such viola-tions as obvious as possible is fundamental to the work on new casts. Naturally, I also reconsidered the possibility of eliminating implicit narrowing conversions such as long to int and double to char (§2.6.1). Unfortunately, a general ban is not just infeasible, it would also be counterproductive. The main problem is that arith-metic can overflow:

```
void f(char c, short s, int i)
{
    c++; // result might not fit in a char
    s++; // result might not fit in a short
    i++; // might overflow
}
```

If we prohibited implicit narrowing, c++ and s++ would become illegal because chars and shorts are promoted to ints before arithmetic operations are per-formed. Requiring explicit casts for narrowing conversions would require a rewrite:

```
void f(char c, short s, int i)
{
    c = static_cast<char>(c+1);
    s = static_cast<short>(s+1);
    i++;
}
```

I don't see any hope for imposing such a notational burden without a corresponding *major* benefit. And where is the benefit? Littering the code with explicit casts will not improve code clarity and won't even reduce the number of errors because people would add the casts thoughtlessly. The i++ isn't safe, either, because of the possibil-ity of overflow. Adding the casts might even be counterproductive because an imple-mentation might by default catch overflow at run time, and the explicit use of a cast would suppress such a check. A better way would be to define dynamic_cast to perform a run-time check on the value of a numeric operand. That way users who consider checking important could then use `dynamic_cast` where their experience tells them that the check is actually worthwhile. Alternatively, people can just write a function that checks and use that. For example (§15.6.2):

```
template<class V, class U> V narrow(U u)
{
    V v = u;
    if (v!=u) throw bad_narrowing;
    return v;
}
```

Even though a ban on narrowing conversions is infeasible and would require a thorough overhaul of the rules governing arithmetic operations, there are still quite a few conversions that an implementation could warn against with a good degree of confidence: floating type to integral type, `long` to `short`, `long` to `int`, and `long` to `char`. Cfront always did that. In my experience, other potentially narrowing conversions such as `int` to `float` and `int` to `char` are harmless too often for warnings to be accepted by users.

14.3.5.3 The Constructor Call Notation

C++ supports the constructor notation `T(v)` as a synonym for the old-style cast notation `(T)v`. A better solution would be to redefine `T(v)` as a synonym for valid object construction as in initializations such as

```
T val(v);
```

(that we don't have a good name for). Such a change would require a transition because – like the suggested deprecation of `(T)v` – this breaks existing code. Like the deprecation of the `(T)e` notation, this failed to gain acceptance in the committee. Fortunately, people who want to use an explicit form of otherwise implicit conversions, say for disambiguation, can write a class template to do so (§15.6.2).

14.3.5.4 Using the New Casts

Can the new casts be used without understanding the subtleties presented here? Can code using old-style casts be converted to use the new-style casts without programmers getting bogged down in language law? For the new casts to become widely preferred over old-style casts, the answer to both questions must be yes.

A simple conversion strategy is to use `static_cast` in all cases and see what the compiler says. If the compiler doesn't like `static_cast` in some case, then that case is worth examining. If the problem is a `const` violation, look to see if the result of the cast does lead to an actual violation; if not, `const_cast` should be used. If the problem is incomplete types, pointer to functions, or casting between unrelated pointer types, try to determine that the resulting pointer is actually cast back again before use. If the problem is something like a pointer to `int` conversion one ought to think harder about what should be going on. If such a cast can't be eliminated, `reinterpret_cast` will do exactly what an old-style cast would do in such cases.

In most cases this analysis and its resulting elimination of old-style casts can be done by a not-too-complicated program. In all cases, it would be better if the cast – new or old – could be eliminated.

15

Templates

There is nothing more difficult to carry out,
nor more doubtful of success, nor more dangerous
to handle, than to initiate a new order of things.
– Niccolo Macchiavelli

Support for parameterized types — class templates — constraints on template arguments — avoiding storage overhead — function templates — deducing function template arguments — explicit specification of function template arguments — conditionals in templates — syntax — composition techniques — relationships among template classes — member templates — template instantiation — name binding in templates — specialization — explicit instantiation — a model for templates in files — importance of templates.

15.1 Introduction

Templates and exceptions were explicitly mentioned in the "whatis" paper [Stroustrup,1986b] (§3.15) as desirable for C++, the designs for the two features were presented in papers [Stroustrup,1988b] [Koenig,1989b] [Koenig,1990], in the ARM, and their inclusion into the language was mandated in the proposal for standardization of C++. Thus, even though the implementation and availability of templates and exception handling in C++ post-dates the start of the standardization effort, their design and the desire for them goes much further back in C++'s history.

The roots of templates lie in the wish to express parameterization of container classes. Exceptions come from a desire to provide a standard way to handle run-time errors. In both cases, the mechanisms inherited from C were in actual use found to be too primitive. The C features didn't allow programmers to directly express their aims and didn't interact well with key features of the C++ language. We had used macros to parameterize containers since the earliest days of C with Classes (§2.9.2), but C macros fail to obey scope and type rules and don't interact well with tools. The mechanisms used for error handling in early C++ such as `setjmp/longjmp` and error indicators (for example, `errno`) don't interact well with constructors and destructors.

The lack of these features led to warped designs, to unnecessarily low-level coding styles, and eventually to problems with combining libraries from more than one provider. In other words, the absence of these features made it unnecessarily difficult for people to maintain a consistent (high) level of abstraction.

To my mind, templates and exceptions are two sides of the same coin: templates allow a reduction in the number of run-time errors by extending the range of problems handled by static type checking; exceptions provide a mechanism for dealing with the remaining run-time errors. Templates make exception handling manageable by reducing the need for run-time error handling to the essential cases. Exceptions make general template-based libraries manageable by providing a way for such libraries to report errors.

15.2 Templates

In the original design of C++, parameterized types were considered but postponed because there wasn't time to do a thorough job of exploring the design and implementation issues and because of fear of the complexity they might add to an implementation. In particular, I worried that a poor design would cause slow compilation and linking. I also assumed that a well-supported parameterized type mechanism would significantly increase porting times. Unfortunately, my fears proved well founded.

Templates were considered essential for the design of proper container classes. I first presented the design for templates at the 1988 USENIX C++ conference in Denver [Stroustrup,1988b]. I summarized the issues like this:

"In the context of C++, the problems are

[1] Can type parameterization be easy to use?

[2] Can objects of a parameterized type be used as efficiently as objects of a "hand-coded" type?

[3] Can a general form of parameterized types be integrated into C++?

[4] Can parameterized types be implemented so that the compilation and linking speed is similar to that achieved by a compilation system that does not support type parameterization?

[5] Can such a compilation system be simple and portable?"

These were my design criteria for templates. Naturally, my answer to all these questions was yes. I stated the fundamental design alternatives like this:

"For many people, the largest single problem using C++ is the lack of an extensive standard library. A major problem in producing such a library is that C++ does not provide a sufficiently general facility for defining "container classes" such as lists, vectors, and associative arrays. There are two approaches for providing such classes/types:

    [1] The Smalltalk approach: rely on dynamic typing and inheritance.

    [2] The Clu approach: rely on static typing and a facility for arguments of type *type*.

The former is very flexible, but carries a high run-time cost, and more importantly defies attempts to use static type checking to catch interface errors. The latter approach has traditionally given rise to fairly complicated language facilities and also to slow and elaborate compile/link time environments. This approach also suffered from inflexibility because languages where it was used, notably Ada, had no inheritance mechanism.

    Ideally, we would like a mechanism for C++ that is as structured as the Clu approach with ideal run-time and space requirements, and with low compile-time overheads. It also ought to be as flexible as Smalltalk's mechanisms. The former is possible; the latter can be approximated for many important cases.''

Thus, the key issues were seen to be notational convenience, run-time efficiency, and type safety. The main constraints were portability and reasonably efficient compilation and linkage – including the instantiation of template classes and functions directly or indirectly used in a program.

    The key activity in determining what we needed from a parameterized type facility was to write programs using macros to fake parameterized types. In addition to me, Andrew Koenig, Jonathan Shopiro, and Alex Stepanov wrote many template-style macros to help determine what language features were needed to support this style of programming. Ada didn't feature in my thinking about templates except as the source of my dislike for template instantiation operators (§15.10.1). Alex Stepanov knew Ada well, though, and some Ada styles may have entered our thinking through his examples.

    The earliest implementation of templates that was integrated into a compiler was a version of Cfront that supported class templates (only) written by Sam Haradhvala at Object Design Inc. in 1989. This version was later expanded into a full implementation by Stan Lippman and supported by a template instantiation mechanism designed by Glen McCluskey with input from Tony Hansen, Andrew Koenig, Rob Murray, and me [McCluskey,1992]. Mary Fontana and Martin Neath from Texas Instruments wrote a public-domain preprocessor that implemented a variant of templates [Fontana,1991].

    These and other implementations gave us significant experience. However, I and others were still nervous about putting something not completely well-understood into a standard, so the template mechanism defined in the ARM was deliberately minimal. It was understood at the time that it was probably *too* minimal, but it is much harder to remove unfortunate features than to add features shown to be needed.

    The template mechanisms presented in the ARM were accepted by the ANSI C++ committee in July 1990. An important argument for the acceptance of templates into the draft standard was the observation that the committee members discussing the issue in a working group found that among ourselves, we had more than half a million lines of C++ using templates and ''fake templates'' in real use.

In retrospect, templates fell into a crack between two strategies for refining the design of a new C++ language feature. Before templates, I refined all features through a process of implementation, use, discussion, and reimplementation. After templates, features were extensively discussed in the standards committee and usually implemented concurrently with that discussion. The discussion about templates wasn't as extensive or wide-ranging as it ought to have been, and I lacked the crucial implementation experience. This has led to a revision of many aspects of templates based on implementation and usage experience. For post-exception-handling extensions, I have resurrected the practice of acquiring personal implementation experience as a key design activity.

Despite their rough corners and need for revision, templates did what they were supposed to do. In particular, templates allowed efficient, compact, and type-safe C++ container classes to be designed and conveniently used. Without templates, design choices were being pushed towards weakly typed or dynamically typed alternatives to the detriment of both program structure and efficiency.

I do, however, think that I was too cautious and conservative when it came to specifying template features. I could have included features such as explicit specification of function template arguments (§15.6.2), deduction of non-type function template arguments (§15.6.1), and nested templates (§15.9.3). These features would not have added greatly to the burden of the implementers, and users would have been helped. On the other hand, I failed to give enough guidance and support to implementers in the area of template instantiation (§15.10). What I cannot know is whether I would have done more harm than good had I proceeded with the design of templates without the benefit of experience that implementation and use of the initial design have given me.

The presentation here reflects the state of affairs after much experience has been gained and resolutions reflecting this experience passed by the ANSI/ISO standards committee. The name binding rules, the explicit instantiation mechanism, the restrictions on specialization, and the explicit qualification of template function calls were voted into C++ at the San Jose meeting in November 1993 as part of a general cleanup of the definition of templates.

The discussion of templates is organized like this:

15.3 Class Templates

The key constructs were explained like this [Stroustrup,1988b]:

"A C++ parameterized type will be referred to as a *class template*. A class template specifies how individual classes can be constructed much like the way a class specifies how individual objects can be constructed. A vector class template might be declared like this:

```
template<class T> class vector {
    T* v;
    int sz;
public:
    vector(int);
    T& operator[](int);
    T& elem(int i) { return v[i]; }
    // ...
};
```

The `template <class T>` prefix specifies that a template is being declared and that an argument T of type *type* will be used in the declaration. After its introduction, T is used exactly like other type names within the scope of the template declaration. Vectors can then be used like this:

```
vector<int> v1(20);
vector<complex> v2(30);

typedef vector<complex> cvec;   // make cvec a synonym
                                // for vector<complex>.
cvec v3(40);   // v2 and v3 are of the same type.

void f()
{
    v1[3] = 7;
    v2[3] = v3.elem(4) = complex(7,8);
}
```

Clearly class templates are no harder to use than classes. The complete names of instances of a class template, such as `vector<int>` and `vector<complex>`, are quite readable. They might even be considered more readable than the notation for the built-in array type: `int[]` and `complex[]`. When the full name is considered too long, abbreviations can be introduced using `typedef`.

It is only trivially more complicated to declare a class template than it is to declare a class. The keyword `class` is used to indicate arguments of type *type* partly because it appears to be an appropriate word, partly because it saves introducing a new keyword. In this context, `class` means "any type" and not just "some user-defined type."

The `<...>` brackets are used in preference to the parentheses `(...)` to emphasize the different nature of template arguments (they will be evaluated at compile time) and because parentheses are already hopelessly overused in C++.

The keyword `template` is introduced to make template declarations easy to
find, for humans and for tools, and to provide a common syntax for class templates and function templates.''

Templates provide a mechanism for generating types. They are not themselves types
and have no run-time representation. Therefore, they have no effect on the object layout model.

One reason for the emphasis on run-time efficiency comparable to macros was
that I wanted templates to be efficient enough in time and space to be used for low-
level types such as arrays and lists. For that, I considered inlining essential. In particular, I saw standard array and vector templates as the only realistic way to allow C's
low-level array concept to be confined to the guts of implementations where it serves
well. Higher-level alternatives – say, a range-checked array with a `size()` operation, a multidimensional array, a vector type with proper numeric vector operations
and copy semantics, etc. – would be accepted by users only if their run-time, space,
and notational convenience approached those of built-in arrays.

In other words, the language mechanism supplying parameterized types should be
such that a concerned user should be able to afford to eliminate the use of arrays in
favor of a standard library class (§8.5). Naturally, built-in arrays would still be there
for people who wanted them and for the millions of lines of old code that use them.
However, I intended to provide an efficient alternative to people who value convenience and type safety over compatibility.

Also, C++ supports virtual functions and through them a variant of every concept
for which the obvious implementation technique is a jump table. For example, a
''truly abstract'' set of `T` would be implemented as a template that was an abstract
class with its virtual functions operating on `T` objects (§13.2.2). For this reason, I felt
I could concentrate on source-text-based, compile-time intensive solutions that provided near optimal run-time and space performance.

15.3.1 Non-type Template Arguments

In addition to type arguments, C++ allows non-type template arguments. These were
primarily seen as necessary for supplying sizes and limits to container classes. For
example:

```
template<class T, int i> class Buffer {
    T v[i];
    int sz;
public:
    Buffer() :sz(i) {}
    // ...
};
```

Such templates are important when competing head on with C arrays and structs
where run-time efficiency and compactness are important. Passing a size allows the
implementer of a container to avoid free store use.

Had non-type arguments not been available, users would have encoded sizes in array types. For example:

```
template<class T, class A> class Buf {
    A v;
    int sz;
public:
    Buf() :sz(sizeof(A)/sizeof(T)) {}
    // ...
};


Buf<int,int[700]> b;
```

This seemed indirect, error-prone, and doesn't extend cleanly to types other than integers. In particular, I wanted pointer to function template arguments for flexibility.

In the original template design, namespaces and templates could not be template arguments. This restriction was another case of simple caution. I now see no reason prohibit such arguments and they would obviously be useful. Class templates as template arguments were approved at the March 1994 meeting in San Diego.

15.4 Constraints on Template Arguments

Template arguments are not constrained in any way. Instead, all type checking is postponed to template instantiation time [Stroustrup,1988b]:

"   "Should a user be required to specify the set of operations that may be used for a template argument of type *type*?" For example:

```
            // The operations =, ==, <, and <=
            // must be defined for an argument type T

    template <
        class T {
            T& operator=(const T&);
            int operator==(const T&, const T&);
            int operator<=(const T&, const T&);
            int operator<(const T&, const T&);
        };
    >
    class vector {
        // ...
    };
```

No. Requiring the user to provide such information decreases the flexibility of the parameterization facility without easing the implementation or increasing the safety of the facility. ... It has been argued that it is easier to read and understand parameterized types when the full set of operations on a type parameter is specified. I see two problems with this: such lists would often be long enough to be unreadable and a higher number of templates would be needed for many applications."

In retrospect, I underestimated the importance of constraints in readability and early error detection, but I also discovered further problems with expressing constraints: a function type is too specific to be an effective constraint. If taken literally, a function type seriously overconstrains the solution. In the `vector` example, one would imagine that any < accepting two arguments of type T should be acceptable. However, in addition to the built-in operator < we have several plausible alternatives:

```
int X::operator<(X);
int Y::operator<(const Y&);
int operator<(Z,Z);
int operator<(const ZZ&,const ZZ&);
```

If taken literally, only ZZ would be an acceptable argument `vector`.

The idea of constraining templates repeatedly surfaced:

– Some people thought that better code could be generated if template arguments were constrained – I don't believe that.
– Some people thought static type checking was compromised by the absence of constraints – it isn't, but some parts of static type checking are postponed until link time and that is indeed a practical problem.
– Some people thought that template declarations would be easier to understand given constraints – often, that is indeed the case.

The following sections present two alternative ways of expressing constraints. Generating member functions only if actually needed (§15.5) and specialization (§15.10.3) are alternatives to constraints in some cases.

15.4.1 Constraints through Derivation

Doug Lea, Andrew Koenig, Philippe Gautron, I, and many others independently discovered the trick of using the inheritance syntax to express constraints. For example:

```
template <class T> class Comparable {
    T& operator=(const T&);
    int operator==(const T&, const T&);
    int operator<=(const T&, const T&);
    int operator<(const T&, const T&);
};

template <class T : Comparable>
    class vector {
        // ...
    };
```

This makes sense. The various proposals differ in details, but they would all have the desired effect of pushing error detection and reporting forward to the compilation of an individual compilation unit. Proposals along this line are still under discussion in the C++ standards groups.

I do, however, have a fundamental objection to expressing constraints through derivation. It would encourage programmers to organize their programs so that anything that is a reasonable constraint is a class and thus encourage the use of inheritance to express every constraint. For example, instead of saying "T must have a less-than function," one must say "T must be derived from `Comparable`." This is an indirect and somewhat inflexible way of expressing constraints and can easily lead to an overuse of inheritance.

Because there are no inheritance relationships among built-in types, such as `int` and `double`, derivation cannot be used to constrain such types. Similarly, derivation cannot be used to express constraints that apply to both a user-defined and a built-in type. For example, the reasons that an `int` and a `complex` are often acceptable alternatives as template arguments cannot be expressed through derivation.

Further, a template writer can't foresee every possible use of a template. This leads to programmers initially overconstraining template arguments, and then later – out of experience – underconstraining them. The logical outcome of constraints-through-derivation is the introduction of a universal base class to express "no constraints." However, such a base class would become the cause of much sloppy coding both within the context of templates and elsewhere (see §14.2.3).

Using derivation to constrain template arguments also fails to address what has been discovered to be a nuisance: Derivation constraints do not allow a programmer to write two templates with the same name so that one is used for pointer types and the other for non-pointer types. This problem was first brought to my attention by Keith Gorlen. It can be addressed through template function overloading (§15.6.3.1).

A more fundamental criticism of this approach is that it uses inheritance for something that isn't primarily sub-typing. I see constraints expressed in terms of inheritance as an example of inheritance being used just because it is fashionable rather than for any fundamental reason. Inheritance relationships are not the only useful relationships, and not all relationships between types and statements about types should be shoehorned into an inheritance framework.

15.4.2 Constraints through Use

When I first gained access to a template implementation, I solved the constraint problem by expressing constraints as use in an inline function. For example:

```
template<class T> class X {
    // ...
    void constraints(T* tp)
    {                   // T must have:
        B* bp = tp;    //    an accessible base B
        tp->f();       //    a member function f
        T a(1);        //    a constructor from int
        a = *tp;       //    assignment
        // ...
    }
};
```

Unfortunately, this takes advantage of a local implementation detail: Cfront does a complete syntax and semantic check of all inline functions when a template declaration is instantiated. However, a version of a function shouldn't be generated for a particular set of template arguments unless it is called (§15.5).

The approach allows the template writer to specify a constraint function and a template user can check the constraint by calling the function when such a check is convenient for the user.

If the template writer does not want to bother the user, the template writer can call `constraints()` from every constructor. However, this can be tedious when there are many constructors and when those constructors wouldn't ordinarily be inline.

If necessary, the notion could be formalized as a language feature:

```
template<class T>
    constraints {
        T* tp;          // T must have:
        B* bp = tp;     //    an accessible base B
        tp->f();        //    a member function f
        T a(1);         //    a constructor from int
        a = *tp;        //    assignment
        // ...
    }
    class X {
        // ...
    };
```

This would allow constraints on template arguments for function templates, but I doubt this extension would be worthwhile. It is, however, the only constraint system I have seen that comes close to satisfying my desire not to overconstrain template arguments while remaining fully general, reasonably terse, comprehensible, and trivial to implement.

See §15.9.1 and §15.9.2 for examples of essential constraints expressed through use in template functions.

15.5 Avoiding Code Replication

Avoiding unnecessary space overheads caused by too many instantiations was considered a first order – that is, design- and language-level – problem rather than an implementation detail. The rules requiring "late" instantiation of template functions (§15.10, §15.10.4) ensure that code is not replicated when a template is used with the same template arguments in different translation units. I considered it unlikely that early (or even late) template implementations would be able to look at instantiations of a class for different template arguments and figure out when all or part of the instantiated code could be shared. Yet I also considered it essential that gross code replication – as experienced with macro expansion and in languages with primitive instantiation mechanisms – could be avoided [Stroustrup,1988b]:

"Among other things, derivation (inheritance) ensures code sharing among different types (the code for a non-virtual base class function is shared among its derived classes). Different instances of a template do not share code unless some clever compilation strategy has been employed. I see no hope for having such cleverness available soon. So, can derivation be used to reduce the problem of code replicated because templates are used? This would involve deriving a template from an ordinary class. For example [Stroustrup,1988b]:

```
template<class T> class vector { // general vector type
    T* v;
    int sz;
public:
    vector(int);
    T& elem(int i) { return v[i]; }
    T& operator[](int i);
    // ...
};

template<class T> class pvector : vector<void*> {
        // build all vector of pointers
        // based on vector<void*>
public:
    pvector(int i) : vector<void*>(i) {}
    T*& elem(int i)
        { return (T*&) vector<void*>::elem(i); }
    T*& operator[](int i)
        { return (T*&) vector<void*>::operator[](i); }
    // ...
};

pvector<int*> pivec(100);
pvector<complex*> icmpvec(200);
pvector<char*> pcvec(300);
```

The implementations of the three vector of pointer classes will be completely shared. They are all implemented exclusively through derivation and inline expansion relying on the implementation of `vector<void*>`. The `vector<void*>` implementation is a good candidate for a standard library.''

This technique proved successful in curbing code bloat in real use. People who do not use a technique like this (in C++ or in other languages with similar facilities for type parameterization) have found that replicated code can cost megabytes of code space even in moderate size programs.

Addressing the same concern, I considered it essential to allow an implementation to instantiate only the template functions actually used. For example, given a template `T` with member functions `f` and `g`, an implementation should be allowed to instantiate only `f` if `g` isn't used for a given template argument.

I also felt that generating versions of a template function for a given set of template arguments only if that function was called added an important degree of flexibility [Stroustrup,1988b]:

"Consider `vector<T>`. To provide a sort operation one must require that type `T` has some order relation. This is not the case for all types. If the set of operations on T must be specified in the declaration of `vector` one would have to have two vector types: one for objects of types with an ordering relation and another for types without one. If the set of operations on T need not be specified in the declaration of `vector` one can have a single vector type. Naturally, one still cannot sort a vector of objects of a type `glob` that does not have an order relation. If that is tried, the generated sort function `vector<glob>::sort()` would be rejected by the compiler.''

15.6 Function Templates

In addition to class templates, C++ offers function templates. Function templates were introduced partly because we clearly needed member functions for class templates and partly because the template concept seemed incomplete without them. Naturally, there were also quite a few textbook examples, such as `sort()` functions. Andrew Koenig and Alex Stepanov were the main contributors of examples requiring function templates. Sorting an array was considered the most basic example:

```
// declaration of a template function:
template<class T> void sort(vector<T>&);

void f(vector<int>& vi, vector<String>& vs)
{
    sort(vi);    // sort(vector<int>& v);
    sort(vs);    // sort(vector<String>& v);
}

// definition of a template function:
template<class T> void sort(vector<T>& v)
/*
    Sort the elements into increasing order

    Algorithm: bubble sort (inefficient and obvious)
*/
{
    unsigned int n = v.size();

    for (int i=0; i<n-1; i++)
        for (int j=n-1; i<j; j--)
            if (v[j] < v[j-1]) { // swap v[j] and v[j-1]
                T temp = v[j];
                v[j] = v[j-1];
                v[j-1] = temp;
            }
}
```

As expected, function templates proved extremely useful in their own right, and they also proved essential for supporting class templates when non-member functions are preferred over member functions for providing services (for example, friends; §3.6.1). The following subsections examine technical details related to template functions.

15.6.1 Deducing Function Template Arguments

For function templates, one doesn't need to explicitly specify the template arguments. As shown above, the compiler can deduce them from the actual arguments of a call. Naturally, every template argument that is not explicitly specified (§15.6.2) must be uniquely determined by a function argument. That was about all the original manual said. During the standardization process, it became clear that it is necessary to specify how smart a compiler is required to be when deducing template argument types from actual function arguments. For example, is this legal?:

```
template<class T, int i>
    T lookup(Buffer<T,i>& b, const char* p);

int f(Buffer<int,128>& buf, const char* p)
{
    return lookup(buf,p); // use the lookup() where
                          // T is int and i is 128
}
```

The answer used to be no because non-type arguments couldn't be deduced. This was a real problem because it meant that one couldn't define non-inlined non-member functions operating on a template class that took a non-type template argument. For example:

```
template<class T, int i> class Buffer {
    friend T lookup(Buffer&, const char*);
    // ...
};
```

requires a previously illegal template function definition.

The revised list of acceptable constructs in a template function argument list is:

```
T
const T
volatile T
T*
T&
T[n]
some_type[I]
CT<T>
CT<I>
T (*)(args)
some_type (*) (args_containing_T)
some_type (*) (args_containing_I)
T C::*
C T::*
```

Here, T is a template type argument, I is a template non-type argument, C is a class name, CT is the name of a previously declared class template, and args_containing_T is an argument list from which T can be determined by application of these rules. This makes the lookup() example legal. Fortunately, users need not memorize this list because it simply formalizes the obvious deductions.

Another example is:

```
template<class T, class U> void f(const T*, U(*)(U));

int g(int);

void h(const char* p)
{
    f(p,g); // T is char, U is int
    f(p,h); // error: can't deduce U
}
```

Looking at the arguments of the first call of f(), we easily deduce the template arguments. Looking at the second call of f(), we see that h() doesn't match the pattern U(*)(U) because h()'s argument and return type differ.

John Spicer helped clarify this and many other similar issues.

15.6.2 Specifying Function Template Arguments

At the time of the original template design, I considered allowing explicit specification of template arguments for template functions in the same way template arguments are explicitly specified for template classes. For example:

```
vector<int> v(10); // class, template argument 'int'
sort<int>(v);      // function, template argument 'int'
```

However, I rejected the idea because explicit specification of template arguments wasn't needed for most examples. I also feared "obscurity" and parsing problems. For example, how would we parse this example?:

```
void g()
{
    f<1>(0); // (f) < (1>(0)) or (f<1>) (0) ?
}
```

I now don't consider this a problem. If f is a template name, f< is the beginning of a qualified template name and the subsequent tokens must be interpreted based on that; if not, < means less-than.

One reason explicit specification is useful is that we can't deduce a return type from a call of a template function:

```
template<class T, class U> T convert(U u) { return u; }
```

```
void g(int i)
{
    convert(i);                 // error: can't deduce T.
    convert<double>(i);         // T is double, U is int.
    convert<char,double>(i);    // T is char, U is double.
    convert<char*,double>(i);   // T is char*, U is double
                                // error: cannot convert
                                // a double to a char*.
}
```

As for default function arguments, only trailing arguments can be left out of a list of explicit template arguments.

Explicit specification of template arguments allows the definition of families of conversion functions and object creation functions. An explicit conversion that performs what can be done by implicit conversion only, such as convert() is frequently requested and a good candidate for a library. Another variant would apply a check to ensure that narrowing conversions would cause a run-time error (§14.3.5.2).

The syntax for the new cast operators (§14.3) and for explicitly qualified template function calls were chosen to match. The new casts express operations that cannot be specified using other language features. Similar operations, such as convert() can be expressed as template functions, so they need not be built-in operators.

Another use of explicitly specified function template arguments is to control the algorithm used by specifying the type or value of a local variable. For example:

```
template<class TT, class AT> void f(AT a)
{
    TT temp = a;    // use TT to control
                    // precision of computation
    // ...
}

void g(Array<float>& a)
{
    f<float>(a);
    f<double>(a);
    f<Quad>(a);
}
```

Explicit specification of function template arguments was voted into C++ at the November 1993 San Jose meeting.

15.6.3 Function Template Overloading

Once function templates existed, the issue of how to handle overloading had to be resolved. To avoid language definition trouble, I chose to allow only exact matches for template functions and to bias overload resolution in favor of ordinary functions of the same name:

    "Overloading resolution for template functions and other functions of the same

name is done in three steps [ARM]:
   [1] Look for an exact match [ARM,§13.2] on functions; if found, call it.
   [2] Look for a function template from which a function that can be called with
       an exact match can be generated; if found, call it.
   [3] Try ordinary overloading resolution [ARM,§13.2] for the functions; if a
       function is found, call it.
   If no match is found, the call is an error. In each case, if there is more than one
   alternative in the first step that finds a match, the call is ambiguous and is an
   error.''

In retrospect, this seems too restrictive and too special purpose. Though it works, it
opens the door for many minor surprises and annoyances.

   Even at the time, it was clear that the best solution was somehow to unify the rules
for ordinary and template functions; I just didn't know how. Here is an outline of an
alternative approach in a formulation suggested by Andrew Koenig:
   ''For a call, find the set of functions that could possibly be called; this will in general include functions generated from different templates. Apply the usual overload resolution rules to this set of functions.''

This would allow for conversions to be applied to template function arguments and
provide a common framework for all function overloading. For example:

```
template<class T> class B { /* ... */ };
template<class T> class D : public B<T> { /* ... */ };

template<class T> void f(B<T>*);

void g(B<int>* pb, D<int>* pd)
{
    f(pb);   // f<int>(pb)
    f(pd);   // f<int>((B<int>*)pd); standard conversion used
}
```

This is necessary to make template functions interact properly with inheritance. Also:

```
template<class T> T max(T,T);

const int s = 7;


void k()
{
    max(s,7); // max(int(s),7); trivial conversion used
}
```

The need to relax the rule against all conversions for template function arguments was
anticipated in the ARM and many implementations currently allow the examples
above. This issue remains to be formally resolved, though.

15.6.3.1 Conditionals in Templates

When writing a template function, it is sometimes tempting to have the definition depend on properties of the template argument. For example, paraphrasing [Stroustrup,1988b]:

"Consider providing a print function for a vector type that sorts the elements before printing if and only if sorting is possible. A facility for inquiring if a certain operation, such as <, can be performed on objects of a given type can be provided. For example:

```
template<class T> void vector<T>::print()
{
    // if T has a < operation sort before printing

    if (?T::operator<) sort();
    for (int i=0; i<sz; i++) { /* ... */ }
}
```

Printing a vector of elements that can be compared will involve a sort() whereas printing a vector of elements that cannot be compared will not."
I decided against providing this kind of type inquiry facility because I was – as I still am – convinced that it would lead to ill-structured code. In some ways, this technique combines the worst aspects of macro hackery and overreliance of type inquiries (§14.2.3).

Instead, specialization can be used to provide separate versions for specific template argument types (§15.10.3). Alternatively, operations that cannot be guaranteed for every template argument type can be isolated in separate member functions called only for types that actually have those operations (§15.5). Finally, template function overloading can be used to provide different implementations for different types. For example, let me show a reverse() template function that can reverse the order of elements in a container given iterators identifying the first and last element to be considered. User code should look like this:

```
void f(ListIter<int> l1, ListIter<int> l2, int* p1, int* p2)
{
    reverse(p1,p2);
    reverse(l1,l2);
}
```

where a ListIterator can be used to access elements from some user-defined container and an int* can be used to access an ordinary array of integers. To do that, different implementations of reverse() must somehow be selected for the two calls.

The reverse() template function simply chooses an implementation based on its argument type:

```
template <class Iter>
inline void reverse(Iter first, Iter last)
{
    rev(first,last,IterType(first));
}
```

Overload resolution is used to select `IterTypes`:

```
class RandomAccess { };

template <class T> inline RandomAccess IterType(T*)
{
    return RandomAccess();
}

class Forward { };

template <class T> inline Forward IterType(ListIterator<T>)
{
    return Forward();
}
```

Here, the `int*` will choose the `RandomAccess` and `ListIter` will choose the `Forward`. In turn, these iterator types will determine the version of `rev()` used:

```
template <class Iter>
inline void rev(Iter first, Iter last, Forward)
{
    // ...
}

template <class Iter>
inline void rev(Iter first, Iter last, RandomAccess)
{
    // ...
}
```

Note, that the third argument isn't actually used in `rev()`; it is simply an aid to the overloading mechanism.

The fundamental observation is that every property of a type or an algorithm can be represented by a type (possibly defined specifically to do exactly that). That done, such a type can be used to guide the overload resolution to select a function that depends on the desired property. Unless the type used to select represents a fundamental property, this technique is a bit indirect, but very general and effective.

Please note that thanks to inlining this resolution is done at compile time, so the appropriate `rev()` function will be called directly without any run-time overhead. Note also that this mechanism is extensible in that new implementations of `rev()` can be added without touching old code. This example is based on ideas from Alex Stepanov [Stepanov,1993].

If all other alternatives fail, run-time type identification can sometimes help (§14.2.5).

15.7 Syntax

As ever, syntax was a problem. Initially, I had aimed for a syntax in which a template argument was placed immediately after the template name:

```
class vector<class T> {
    // ...
};
```

However, this didn't cleanly extend to function templates [Stroustrup,1988b]:

"The function syntax at first glance also looks nicer without the extra keyword:

```
T& index<class T>(vector<T>& v, int i) { /* ... */ }
```

There is typically no parallel (to class templates) in the usage, though, since function template arguments are not usually specified explicitly:

```
int i = index(vi,10);
char* p = index(vpc,29);
```

However, there appear to be nagging problems with this "simpler" syntax. It is too clever. It is relatively hard to spot a template declaration in a program because the template arguments are deeply embedded in the syntax of functions and classes and the parsing of some function templates is a minor nightmare. It is possible to write a C++ parser that handles function template declarations where a template argument is used before it is defined, as in index() above. I know, because I wrote one, but it is not easy nor does the problem appear amenable to traditional parsing techniques. In retrospect, I think that not using a keyword and not requiring a template argument to be declared before it is used would result in a set of problems similar to those arising from the clever and convoluted C and C++ declarator syntax."

Using the final template syntax the declaration of index() becomes:

```
template<class T> T& index(vector<T>& v, int i) { /* ... */ }
```

At the time, I seriously discussed the possibility of providing a syntax that allowed the return value of a function to be placed after the arguments. For example

```
index<class T>(vector<T>& v, int i) return T& { /* ... */ }
```

or

```
index<class T>(vector<T>& v, int i) : T& { /* ... */ }
```

This would solve the parsing problem, but most people like having a keyword to help recognize templates, so that line of reasoning became redundant.

The <...> brackets were chosen in preference to parentheses because users found them easier to read and because parentheses are overused in the C and C++ grammar. As it happens, Tom Pennello proved that parentheses would have been easier to parse, but that doesn't change the key observation that (human) readers prefer `<...>`.

One problem is a consistent nuisance:

```
List<List<int>> a;
```

appears to declare a list of a list of integers. In fact, it is a syntax error because the token `>>` (right shift or output) isn't the same as the two tokens `>` `>`. Naturally, a simple lexical trick could solve this problem, but I decided to keep both the grammar and the lexical analyzer clean. I have now seen this mistake so often and heard so many complaints about

```
List<List<int>> a;
```

that I am sorely tempted to apply some glorious hack to make the problem go away. I find it more painful to listen to complaints from users than to listen to complaints from language lawyers.

15.8 Composition Techniques

Templates support several safe and powerful composition techniques. For example, templates can be applied recursively:

```
template<class T> class List { /* ... */ };

List<int> li;
List< List<int> > lli;
List< List< List<int> > > llli;
```

If specific "composed types" are needed, they can be specifically defined using derivation:

```
template<class T> class List2 : public List< List<T> > { };
template<class T> class List3 : public List2< List<T> > { };

List2<int> lli2;
List3<int> llli3;
```

This is a somewhat unusual use of derivation because no members are added. No overhead in time or space is implied by this use of derivation; it is simply a composition technique. Had derivation not been available for composition, templates would have had to be augmented with specific composition mechanisms, or the language would have been much poorer. The smooth interaction between derivation and templates has been a continuous source of pleasant surprises to me.

Variables of such composed types can be used like their explicitly defined types, but not vice versa:

```
void f()
{
    lli = lli2;  // ok
    lli2 = lli;  // error
}
```

The reason is that public derivation defines a subtype relationship.

Allowing assignment in both directions would require a language extension to allow the introduction of genuine parameterized synonyms. For example:

```
template<class T> typedef List< List<T> > List4;

void (List< List<T> >& lst1, List4& lst2)
{
    lst1 = lst2;
    lst2 = lst1;
}
```

The extension is technically trivial, but I'm not sure how wise it would be to introduce yet another renaming feature.

Derivation also allows for partial specification of template arguments in the definition of a new type:

```
template<class U, class V> class X { /* ... */ };
template<class U> class XX : public X<U,int> { };
```

In general, deriving from a template class gives you the opportunity to tailor the base with information to suit the derived class. This allows for extremely powerful patterns of composition. For example:

```
template<class T> class Base { /* ... */ };

class Derived : public Base<Derived> { /* ... */ };
```

Such techniques make it possible for information about a derived class to flow into the definition of its base class. See also §14.2.7.

15.8.1 Representing Implementation Policies

Another use of derivation and templates for composition is the technique of passing in objects representing implementation policies. For example, the meaning of comparison for sorting or the means of allocating and deallocating storage for a container class can be supplied through template arguments [2nd]:

"One way is to use a template to compose a new class out of the interface to the desired container and an allocator class using the placement technique described in [2nd,§6.7.2]:

```
template<class T, class A> class Controlled_container
    : public Container<T>, private A {

    // ...
    void some_function()
    {
        // ...
        T* p = new(A::operator new(sizeof(T))) T;
        // ...
    }
    // ...
};
```

Here, it is necessary to use a template because we are designing a container. Derivation from `Container` is needed to allow a `Controlled_container` to be used as a container. The use of the template argument `A` is necessary to allow a variety of allocators to be used. For example:

```
class Shared : public Arena { /* ... */ };
class Fast_allocator { /* ...*/ };
class Persistent : public Arena { /* ... */ };

Controlled_container<Process_descriptor,Shared> ptbl;

Controlled_container<Node,Fast_allocator> tree;

Controlled_container<Personnel_record,Persistent> payroll;
```

This is a general strategy for providing nontrivial implementation information for a derived class. It has the advantage of being systematic and allowing inlining to be used. It does tend to lead to extraordinarily long names, though. As usual, `typedef` can be used to introduce synonyms for type names of undesirable length.''

The Booch components [Booch,1993] uses such composition techniques extensively.

15.8.2 Representing Ordering Relationships

Consider a sorting problem: We have a container template. We have an element type. We have a function sorting the container based on element values.

We can't hardwire the sorting criteria into the container because the container can't (in general) impose its needs on the element types. We can't hardwire the sorting criteria into the element type because there are many different ways of sorting elements.

Consequently, the sorting criteria are neither built into the container nor into the element type. Instead, the criteria are supplied when a specific operation needs to be performed. For example, given strings of characters representing names of Swedes, what collating criteria would I like to use for a comparison? Two different collating sequences are in common use for sorting Swedish names. Naturally, neither a general

string type nor a general sorting algorithm should have to know about the conventions
for sorting names in Sweden.

Consequently, any general solution involves the sorting algorithm expressed in
general terms that can be defined not just for a specific type but for a specific use of a
specific type. For example, let us generalize the standard library function `strcmp()`
for strings of any type `T`.

First, I define a class template giving the default meaning of comparison of objects
of a type `T`:

```
template<class T> class CMP {
public:
    static int eq(T a, T b) { return a==b; }
    static int lt(T a, T b) { return a<b; }
};
```

The template function `compare()` uses this form of comparison by default to compare `basic_strings`:

```
template<class T> class basic_string {
    // ...
};


template<class T, class C = CMP<T> >
int compare(const basic_string<T>& str1,
        const basic_string<T>& str2)
{
    for(int i=0; i<str1.length() && i< str2.length(); i++)
        if (!C::eq(str1[i],str2[i]))
            return C::lt(str1[i],str2[i]);
    return str2.length()-str1.length();
}


typedef basic_string<char> string;
```

Given member templates (§15.9.3), `compare()` could alternatively be defined as a
member of `basic_string`.

If someone wants a `C<T>` to ignore case, to reflect locale, to return the largest of
the unicode values of the two elements that compared `!C<T>::eq()`, etc., that can
be done by defining suitable `C<T>::eq()` and `C<T>::lt()` in terms of operators
"native" to `T`. This allows any (comparison, sorting, etc.) algorithm that can be
described in terms of the operations supplied by `CMP` and the container to be
expressed. For example:

```
class LITERATE {
    static int eq(char a, char b) { return a==b; }
    static int lt(char,char); // use literary convention
};
```

```
void f(string swede1, string swede2)
{
    compare(swede1,swede2); // ordinary/telephone order
    compare<char,LITERATE>(swede1,swede2); // literary order
}
```

I pass the comparison criteria as a template parameter because that's a way of passing
several operations without imposing a run-time cost. In particular, the comparison
operators `eq()` and `lt()` are trivial to inline. I use a default argument to avoid
imposing a notational cost on everyone. Other variants of this technique can be found
in [2nd,§8.4].

   A less esoteric example (for non-swedes) is comparing with and without taking
case into account:

```
void f(string s1, string s2)
{
    compare(s1,s2); // case sensitive
    compare<char,NOCASE>(s1,s2); // not sensitive to case
}
```

   Note that the `CMP` template class is never used to define objects; its members are
all `static` and `public`. It therefore ought to be a namespace (§17):

```
template<class T> namespace CMP {
    int eq(T a, T b) { return a==b; }
    int lt(T a, T b) { return a<b; }
}
```

Unfortunately, namespace templates are not (yet) part of C++.

15.9 Template Class Relationships

A template is usefully understood as a specification of how particular types are to be
created. In other words, the template implementation is a mechanism that generates
types when needed based on the user's specification.

   As far as the C++ language rules are concerned, there is no relationship between
two classes generated from a single class template. For example:

```
template<class T> class Set { /* ... */ };

class Shape { /* ... */ };
class Circle : public Shape { /* ... */ };
```

Given these declarations, people sometimes want to treat a `Set<Circle>` as a
`Set<Shape>` or to treat a `Set<Circle*>` to be a `Set<Shape*>`. For example:

```
void f(Set<Shape>&);

void g(Set<Circle>& s)
{
    f(s);
}
```

This won't compile because there is no built-in conversion from `Set<Circle>&` to
`Set<Shape>&`. Nor should there be; thinking of `Set<Circle>` as a
`Set<Shape>` is a fundamental – and not uncommon – conceptual error. In particular, `Set<Circle>` guarantees that its members are `Circle`s, so that users can
safely and efficiently apply `Circle`-specific operations, such as determining the
radius, on its members. If we allowed a `Set<Circle>` to be treated as a
`Set<Shape>`, we could no longer maintain that guarantee because it is presumably
acceptable to put arbitrary `Shape`s such as `Triangle`s into a `Set<Shape>`.

15.9.1 Inheritance Relationships

Therefore, there cannot be any *default* relationship between classes generated from
the same templates. However, sometimes we would like such a relationship to exist.
I considered whether a special operation was needed to express such relationships, but
decided against it because many useful conversions could be expressed as inheritance
relationships or by ordinary conversion operators. However, this leaves us without a
way of expressing some of the most interesting such relationships. For example,
given:

```
template<class T> class Ptr { // pointer to T
    // ...
};
```

we would often like to provide the inheritance relationships we are accustomed to for
built-in pointers for these user-defined `Ptr`s. For example:

```
void f(Ptr<Circle> pc)
{
    Ptr<Shape> ps = pc;   // can this be made to work?
}
```

We would like to allow this if and only if `Shape` really is a direct or indirect public
base class of `Circle`. In particular, David Jordan asked the standards committee for
that property for smart pointers on behalf of a consortium of Object-Oriented database
suppliers.
    Member templates – which are not currently part of C++ – provide a solution:

```
template<class T1> class Ptr { // pointer to T1
    // ...
    template<class T2> operator Ptr<T2> ();
};
```

We need to define the conversion operator so that the `Ptr<T1>` to `Ptr<T2>` conversion is accepted if and only if a `T1*` can be assigned to a `T2*`. This can be done by providing `Ptr` with an extra constructor:

```
template<class T> class Ptr { // pointer to T
    T* p;
public:
    Ptr(T*);
    template<class T2> operator Ptr<T2> () {
        return Ptr<T2>(p); // works iff p can be
                           // converted to a T2*
    }
    // ...
};
```

This solution has the nice property that it doesn't use any casts. The return statement will compile if and only if p can be an argument to `Ptr<T2>`'s constructor. Now, p is a `T1*` and the constructor expects a `T2*` argument. This is a subtle application of the constraints through use technique (§15.4.2). If you prefer to keep the extra constructor private, you can use a technique suggested by Jonathan Shopiro:

```
template<class T> class Ptr { // pointer to T
    T*   tp;
    Ptr(T*);
    friend template<class T2> class Ptr<T2>;
public:
    template<class T2> operator Ptr<T2> ();
    // ...
};
```

Member templates are described in §15.9.3.

15.9.2 Conversions

A closely related problem is that there is no general way of defining conversions between different classes generated from a class template. For example, consider a `complex` template that defines complex numbers for a range of scalar types:

```
template<class scalar> class complex {
    scalar re, im;
public:
    // ...
};
```

Given that we can use `complex<float>`, `complex<double>`, etc. However, when doing that, we would like to convert from a `complex` with lower precision to one with higher precision. For example:

```
complex<double> sqrt(complex<double>);

complex<float> c1(1.2f,6.7f);
complex<double> c2 = sqrt(c1); // error, type mismatch:
                               // complex<double> expected
```

We would like a way of making the call of sqrt legal. This leads programmers to abandon the template approach to complex in favor of replicated class definitions:

```
class float_complex {
    float re, im;
public:
    // ...
};

class double_complex {
    double re, im;
public:
    double_complex(float_complex c) :re(c.re), im(c.im) {}
    // ...
};
```

The purpose of the replication is to define the constructor that defines the conversion.

Again, all solutions I can think of require the combination of nested templates and some form of constraints. Again, the actual constraint can be implicit:

```
template<class scalar> class complex {
    scalar re, im;
public:
    template<class T2> complex(const complex<T2>& c)
        : re(c.re), im(c.im) { }
    // ...
};
```

In other words, you can construct a complex<T1> from a complex<T2> if and only if you can initialize a T1 by a T2. That seems reasonable. Interestingly enough, this definition subsumes the usual copy constructor.

This definition makes the sqrt() example above legal. Unfortunately, this definition also allows narrowing conversions of complex numbers simply because C++ allows narrowing conversions for scalars. Naturally, given this definition of complex, an implementation that warns against narrowing conversions of scalars will automatically also warn against narrowing conversions of complex values.

We can get the "traditional" names back by using typedef:

```
typedef complex<float> float_complex;
typedef complex<double> double_complex;
typedef complex<long double> long_double_complex;
```

Personally, I find the un-typedef'd versions more readable.

15.9.3 Member Templates

The only reason templates weren't allowed as class members in C++ as defined in the ARM is that I couldn't prove to my own satisfaction that such nesting wouldn't be a serious implementation problem. Member templates were part of the original template design, I am in principle for nested forms of all scope constructs (§3.12, §17.4.5.4), I didn't doubt that member templates would be useful, and I didn't have any solid reason for suspecting implementation problems. It was fortunate that I hesitated, though. Had I simply admitted member templates into C++ without constraints, I would inadvertently have broken the C++ object layout model and would then have had to retract part of the feature. Consider this promising-looking idea for a more elegant variant of double dispatch (§13.8.1):

```
class Shape {
    // ...
    template<class T>
        virtual Bool intersect(const T&) const =0;
};


class Rectangle : public Shape {
    // ...
    template<class T>
        virtual Bool intersect(const T& s) const;
};


template<class T>
virtual Bool Rectangle::intersect(const T& s) const
{
    return s.intersect(*this);  // *this is a Rectangle:
                                // resolve on s
}
```

This *must* be illegal, otherwise we would have to add another entry to the virtual table for class Shape each time someone called Shape::intersect() with a new argument type. This would imply that only the linker could make virtual function tables and assign table positions to functions. Consequently, a member template cannot be virtual.

I found this problem only after the publication of the ARM and was thus saved by the restriction that templates must be defined in the global scope. On the other hand, the conversion problems mentioned in §15.9 have no solution in the absence of member templates. Member templates were voted into C++ at the March 1994 meeting in San Diego.

Please note that explicit specification of template arguments for function templates is an alternative to nested template classes in many cases (§15.6.2).

15.10 Template Instantiation

Originally [Stroustrup,1988b] [ARM], C++ had no operator for ''instantiating'' a template; that is, there was no operation for explicitly generating a class declaration and function definitions for a particular set of template arguments. The reason was that only when the program is complete can it be known which templates need to be instantiated. Many templates will be defined in libraries, and many instantiations will be directly and indirectly caused by users who don't even know of the existence of those templates. It therefore seemed unreasonable to require the user to request instantiations (say, by using something like Ada's ''new'' operator). Worse, if a template instantiation operator existed, it would have to correctly handle the case where two otherwise unrelated parts of a program both request the same template function instantiated for the same set of template arguments. This would have to be done without code replication and without making dynamic linking infeasible.

The ARM comments on this problem without giving a definite answer:

''These rules imply that the decision of what functions to generate from function template definitions cannot be made until a program is complete, that is, not until it is known what function definitions are available.

As stated, error detection has been postponed to the last possible moment: the point after initial linking where definitions are generated for template functions. This is too late for many people's tastes.

As stated, the rules also place the maximum reliance on the programming environment. It will be up to the system to find the definitions of the class templates, function templates, and classes needed for generating those template function definitions. This will be unacceptably complicated for some environments.

Both problems can be alleviated by the introduction of mechanisms allowing a programmer to say ''generate these template functions here for these template arguments.'' This can be made simple enough for any environment and will ensure that errors relating to a specific template function definition are detected on request.

It is not clear, however, whether such mechanisms should be considered part of the language or part of the programming environment. It was felt that more experience was needed and, for that reason, such mechanisms belonged in the environment – at least temporarily.

The simplest mechanism for ensuring proper generation of template function definitions is to leave the problem to the programmer. The linker will tell which definitions are needed, and a file containing non-inline template function definitions can be compiled together with an indication of which template arguments are to be used. More sophisticated systems can be built based on this fully manual base.''

Now, a variety of implementations are available. Experience shows that the problem was at least as hard as suspected and that something better than the existing implementations was needed.

The Cfront implementation [McCluskey,1992] automates template instantiation completely as suggested by the original template design [Stroustrup,1988b] and the ARM. Basically, the linker is run, and if some template function instantiations are missing, the compiler is invoked to produce the missing object code from the template source. This process is repeated until all templates used have been instantiated. Template and argument-type definitions are (when needed) found based on a file naming convention. Where needed, this convention is supplemented by a user-supplied directory file that maps template and class names to the files that contain their definitions. The compiler has a special mode for processing template instantiations. This strategy often works very well, but in some contexts three very annoying problems were discovered:

[1] Poor compile- and link-time performance: Once a linker has determined that the instantiation is needed, the compiler has to be invoked to generate the needed functions. That done, the linker needs to be invoked again to link the new functions. In a system where the compiler and linker are not permanently running, this can be surprisingly costly. A good library mechanism can significantly reduce the number of times the compiler has to be run.

[2] Poor interaction with some source control systems: Some source control systems have very definite ideas about what source code is and how object code is produced from it. Such systems don't interact well with a compilation system where the linker, the compiler, and a library interact to produce a complete program (in the way outlined in [1]). This is not a fault of the language, but that is no consolation to programmers who have to live with such a source-control system.

[3] Poor hiding of implementation details: If I use templates in the implementation of a library, then the source of those templates must be included with my library for a user to link my library. The reason is that the need to generate template instantiations will only be noticed at the final link time. This problem can only be bypassed by (somehow) producing object code that contains every version of the templates I use in my implementation. This can lead to object-code bloat as the implementer tries to cover every possible use – any one application will use only a subset of the possible template instantiations. Note also, that if the instantiation of implementation templates depends directly on which templates a user instantiates, late instantiation is necessary.

15.10.1 Explicit Instantiation

The most promising approach for mitigating these problems seems to be optional explicit instantiation. Such a mechanism could be either an extralinguistic tool, an implementation-dependent #pragma, or a directive in the language proper. All of these approaches have been tried with some success. Of these approaches, I like the #pragma the least. If we need an explicit instantiation mechanism in the language, we need one that is generally available and has well-defined semantics.

What would be the benefit of an optional instantiation operator?

[1] Users would be able to specify the environment for instantiation.

[2] Users would be able to pre-create libraries of common instantiations in a relatively implementation-independent manner.

[3] These pre-created libraries would be independent of changes in the environment of the program that used them (depending only on the context of instantiation).

The instantiation request mechanism described here was adopted at the San Jose meeting; it has its roots in a proposal by Erwin Unruh. The syntax was chosen to match the way template arguments are explicitly specified in uses of class templates (§15.3), template function calls (§15.6.2), the new cast operators (§14.2.2, §14.3), and template specializations (§15.10.3). An instantiation request looks like this:

```
template class vector<int>;                    // class
template int& vector<int>::operator[](int);   // member
template int convert<int,double>(double);     // function
```

The keyword `template` was recycled for this use in preference to introducing a new keyword `instantiate`. A template declaration is distinguished from an instantiation request by the template argument list: `template<` begins a template definition, whereas plain `template` begins an instantiation request. The fully specified form of the functions was chosen over possible abbreviated forms such as

```
// not C++:

template vector<int>::operator[];   // member
template convert<int,double>;       // function
```

to avoid ambiguities for overloaded template functions, to provide the compiler with redundancy needed for consistency checks, and because instantiation requests are infrequent enough to cast doubt on the value of a terse notation. However, as in template function calls, the template arguments that can be deduced from the function arguments can be omitted (§15.6.1). For example:

```
template int convert<int>(double);    // function
```

When a class template is explicitly instantiated, every member function presented to the compiler (§15.10.4) is also instantiated. This implies that an explicit instantiation can be used as a constraints check (§15.4.2).

The link-time and recompilation efficiency impact of instantiation requests can be significant. I have seen examples in which bundling all template instantiations into a single compilation unit cut the compile time from a number of hours to the equivalent number of minutes. For this magnitude of speedup, I am willing to accept a mechanism for manual optimization.

What should happen if a template is explicitly instantiated twice for the same set of template arguments? This question was (rightly, I think) considered critical. If that is an unconditional error, explicit instantiation becomes a serious obstacle to composition of programs out of separately developed parts. This was the original reason for not introducing an explicit instantiation operator. On the other hand, suppressing redundant explicit instantiations could in general be very difficult.

The committee decided to dodge the issue slightly by leaving some freedom to the implementers: Multiple instantiations is a nonrequired diagnostic. This allows a smart implementation to ignore redundant instantiations and thereby avoid the problems related to composition of programs from libraries using explicit instantiation mentioned above. However, the rule does not require implementations to be smart. Users of "less smart" implementations must avoid multiple instantiations, but the worst that will happen if they don't is that their program won't load; there will be no silent changes of meaning.

As ever, no explicit instantiation is required by the language. Explicit instantiation is a mechanism for manual optimization of the compile-and-link process.

15.10.2 Point of Instantiation

The most difficult aspect of the definition of templates is to pin down exactly which declarations the names used in a template definition refer to. This problem is often referred as "the name binding problem."

The revised name binding rules described in this section are the result of work by many people over the last few years, notably members of the extensions working group, Andrew Koenig, Martin O'Riordan, Jonathan Shopiro, and me. By the time they were accepted (November 1993, San Jose) they had also benefited from significant implementation experience.

Consider this example:

```
#include<iostream.h>
#include<vector.h>

void db(double);
                                                      // #1
template<class T> T sum(vector<T>& v)
{
    T t = 0;
    for (int i = 0; i<v.size(); i++) t = t + v[i];
    if (DEBUG) {
        cout << "sum is " << t << '\n';
        db(t);
        db(i);
    }
    return t;
}
// ...

#include<complex.h>
                                                      // #2
void f(vector<complex>& v)
{
    complex c = sum(v);
}
```

The original definition says that names used in the template are all bound at the point of instantiation and that the point of instantiation is just before the global declaration in which a template is first used (#2 above). This has at least three undesirable properties:

[1] No error checking can be performed at the point of the template definition. For example, if DEBUG is undefined at that point, no error message can be produced.

[2] Names defined *after* the template definition can be found and used. This is often (but not always) a surprise to the reader of the template definition. For example, one might expect the call db(i) to be resolved to the db(double) declared above, but if the ... contains a declaration of db(int) then db(int) would be preferred over db(double) under the usual overload resolution rules. On the other hand, if a db(complex) is defined in complex.h, we need db(t) to resolve to db(complex) rather than being an error by not being a valid call of the db(double) visible from the template definition.

[3] The set of names available at the point of instantiation will differ when sum is used in two different compilations. If sum(vector<complex>&) thereby gets two different definitions the resulting program is illegal under the one-definition rule (§2.5). However, the checking of the one-definition rule in such cases is beyond a traditional C++ implementation.

In addition, this original rule doesn't explicitly cover the case where the definition of the template function isn't included in this particular compilation unit. For example:

```
template<class T> T sum(vector<T>& v);

// ...

#include<complex.h>
                                                    // #2
void f(vector<complex>& v)
{
    complex c = sum(v);
}
```

No guidance was given to implementers or users about how the definition of the sum() function templates was supposed to be found. In consequence, different implementers used different heuristics.

The general problem is that three contexts are involved in a template instantiation and they cannot be cleanly separated:

[1] The context of the template definition.
[2] The context of the argument type declaration.
[3] The context of the use of the template.

The overall aim of the template design is to assure that enough context is available for the template definition to make sense in terms of its actual arguments without picking up ''accidental'' stuff from the environment at the call point.

The original design relied exclusively on the one-definition rule (§2.5) to maintain sanity. The assumption was that if accidental stuff affected the definition of the generated function, it was most unlikely to happen consistently over all uses of a template function. This is a good assumption, but – for good reasons – implementations usually don't check for inconsistencies. The net effect is that reasonable programs work. However, people who wish that templates were really macros can get away with writing programs that take advantage of the calling environment in undesirable (according to me) ways. Also, implementers have a major headache when they want to synthesize a context for a template definition to speed up instantiation.

Refining the definition of *point of definition* in such a way that it is both better than the original and doesn't break reasonable programs was difficult, but necessary.

A first attempt would be to require every name used in the template to be defined at the point of the template definition. This would make the definition readable, guarantee that nothing undesirable was picked up accidentally, and allow perfect early error detection. Unfortunately, that wouldn't allow the template to apply operations on objects of its template class. In the example above, +, f (), and the constructor for T are undefined at the point of the template definition. We can't declare them in the template either because we can't specify their types. For example, + may be a built-in operator, a member function, or a global function. If it is a function, it may take arguments of type T, const T&, etc. This is exactly the problem of specifying template argument constraints (§15.4).

Given that neither the point of the template definition nor the point of template use provides a good enough context for template instantiation, we must look for a solution that combines aspects of both.

The solution is to separate names used in a template definition into two categories:
 – The ones that depend on a template argument.
 – The ones that don't.
The latter can be bound in the context of the template definition, the former in the context of an instantiation. This concept is clean to the extent that the definition of ''depends on a template argument'' can be made clean.

15.10.2.1 Defining ''Depend on T''

The first candidate for a definition of ''depends on a template argument T'' is ''member of T.'' Built-in operators would be considered ''members'' where T was a built-in type. Unfortunately, this doesn't quite suffice. Consider:

```
class complex {
    // ...
    friend complex operator+(complex,complex);
    complex(double);
};
```

For this to work, the definition ''depends on a template argument T'' must at least be extended to include T's friends. However, even that isn't enough because crucial nonmember functions don't always need friendship:

```
class complex {
    // ...
    complex operator+=(complex);
    complex(double);
};

complex operator+(complex a, complex b)
{
    complex r = a;
    return r+=b;
}
```

It would also be unreasonable and constraining to require the designer of a class to provide all the functions that a writer of a template might possibly need in the future; 20/20 foresight is rare.

Consequently, ''depends on a template argument T'' must rely on the context of the point of instantiation to at least the extent of finding the global functions used for Ts. This will inevitably open the possibility of some unexpected function being used. However, that problem is minimized. We define ''depends on a template argument T'' in the most general way; that is, a function call *depends on* a template argument if the call would have a different resolution or no resolution if the actual template type were missing from the program. This condition is reasonably straightforward for a compiler to check. Examples of calls that depend on an argument type T are:

[1] The function called has a formal parameter that depends on T according to the type deduction rules (§15.6.1). For example: `f(T)`, `f(vector<T>)`, and `f(const T*)`.

[2] The type of the actual argument depends on T according to the type deduction rules (§15.6.1). For example: `f(T(1))`, `f(t)`, `f(g(t))`, and `f(&t)` assuming that t is a T.

[3] A call is resolved by the use of a conversion to T without either an actual argument or a formal argument of the called function being of a type that depended on T as specified in [1] and [2].

The last example was found in real code, and the code that relied on it seemed quite reasonable. A call `f(1)` didn't look dependent on T, and neither did the function `f(B)` that it invoked. However, the template argument type T had a constructor from int and was derived from B, so the resolution of `f(1)` was `f(B(T(1)))`.

These three kinds of dependencies exhaust the examples I have seen.

15.10.2.2 Ambiguities

What should be done when different functions are found by lookup #1 (at the point of the template definition, point #1 in the example in §15.10.2) and lookup #2 (at the point of use, point #2 in the example in §15.10.2)? Basically we could:

[1] Prefer lookup #1.
[2] Prefer lookup #2.
[3] Make it an error.

Note that lookup #1 can only be done for nonfunctions and for functions where the types of all arguments are known at the point of use in the template definition; the lookup of other names must be postponed to point #2.

Essentially, the original rule says ''prefer lookup #2,'' and this implies that the usual ambiguity resolution rules are applied because only if a better match was found by lookup #2 could it have found a different function from lookup #1. Unfortunately, this makes it very hard to trust what you see when you read the text of a template definition. For example:

```
double sqrt(double);

template<class T> void f(T t)
{
    double sq2 = sqrt(2);
    // ...
}
```

It seems obvious that `sqrt(2)` will call `sqrt(double)`. However, there just might be a `sqrt(int)` found in lookup #2. In most cases, that wouldn't matter because the ''must depend on a template argument'' rule would ensure that the ''obvious'' resolution to `sqrt(double)` would be used. However, if T was int then the call `sqrt(2)` would depend on the template argument, so the call would resolve to `sqrt(int)`. This is an inescapable consequence of taking lookup #2 into account, but I considered it most confusing and would like to avoid it.

On the other hand, I thought it necessary to give preference to lookup #2 because only that could resolve uses of base class members as an ordinary class would have. For example:

```
void g();

template<class T> class X : public T {
    void f() { g(); }
    // ...
};
```

If T has a `g()` then that `g()` ought to be called to match the way nontemplate classes behave:

```
void g();

class T { public: void g(); }

class Y : public T {
    void f() { g(); }   // calls T::g
    // ...
};
```

On the other hand, in the usual ''non-perverted'' cases sticking with what was found in lookup #1 seems right. This is how lookup of global names is done in C++, this is what allows the largest amount of early error-detection, this is what allows the largest amount of pre-compilation of templates, and this is what provides the most protection against "accidental" hijacking of names by context unknown to the template writer. Over the years I have come to appreciate the importance of these matters and several implementers, notably Bill Gibbons, argued persuasively for preferring lookup #1.

For a while, I favored making it an error for different functions to be found in the two lookups, but that complicates matters for the implementers without giving significant benefits to the users. Also, this would allow names in the context of a use of a template to "break" otherwise good template code written by a programmer who intended names in scope at the point of the template definition to be used. Finally, after hours of work in the extensions working group, I changed my mind. The argument that clinched the case for preferring lookup #1 was that the really tricky examples can trivially be resolved by the template writer. For example:

```
double sqrt(double);

template<class T> void f(T t)
{
    // ...
    sqrt(2);        // resolve in lookup #1
    sqrt(T(2));     // clearly depends on T
                    // bind in lookup #2
    // ...
}
```

and:

```
int g();

template<class T> class X : public T {
    void f()
    {
        g();        // resolve in lookup #1
        T::g();     // clearly depends on T
                    // bind in lookup #2
    }
    // ...
};
```

Essentially, this requires the template writer to be more explicit when the intent is to use some function that isn't actually visible from the template definition. That seems to put the burden in the right place and have the right default behavior.

15.10.3 Specialization

A template specifies how a function or a class is defined for any template argument. For example,

```
template<class T> class Comparable {
    // ...
    int operator==(const T& a, const T& b) { return a==b; }
};
```

specifies that for every T, you compare elements with the == operator. Unfortunately, that is quite restrictive. In particular, C strings represented by char*s are usually better compared using strcmp().

During the initial design, we found that such examples abounded and that the ''special cases'' were often essential for generality or critical for performance reasons. C-style strings are a good example of this.

I therefore concluded that we needed a mechanism for ''specializing'' templates. This could be done either by accepting general overloading or by some more specific mechanism. I chose a specific mechanism because I thought I was primarily addressing irregularities caused by irregularities in C and because suggestions of overloading invariably creates a howl of protests. I was trying to be cautious and conservative; I now consider that a mistake. Specialization as originally defined was a restricted and anomalous form of overloading that fitted poorly with the rest of the language.

A class or function template can be ''specialized.'' For example, given a template

```
template<class T> class vector {
    // ...
    T& operator[](int i);
};
```

one can provide specializations, that is separate declarations, for, say vector<char> and vector<complex>::operator[](int):

```
class vector<char> {
    // ...
    char& operator[](int i);
};
```

```
complex& vector<complex>::operator[](int i) { /* ... */ }
```

This enables a programmer to provide specialized implementations for classes that are either particularly important from a performance point of view or have semantics that differ from the default. This mechanism is crude and very effective.

My original idea was that such specializations would be put into libraries and automatically used where necessary without programmer intervention. This proved a costly and questionable service. Specialization caused comprehension and implementation problems because there was no way of knowing what a template meant for a particular set of template arguments – even if we were looking at the template definition – because the template may have been specialized in some other compilation unit. For example:

```
template<class T> class X {
    T v;
public:
    T read() const { return v; }
    void write(int vv) { v=vv; }
};

void f(X<int> r)
{
    r.write(2);
    int i = r.read();
}
```

It would seem reasonable to assume that f() uses the member functions defined above. However, that was not guaranteed. Some other compilation unit may have defined X<int>::write() to do something completely different.

Specialization can also be considered as opening a protection loophole in C++ because a specialized member function can access a template class' private data in a way that is not discernible from reading the template definition. There were even more technical problems.

I concluded that specialization as originally defined was a botch and also provided essential functionality. How might we provide the functionality while remedying the botch? After many complicated arguments, I proposed a trivially simple solution that was accepted at the San Jose meeting: *A specialization must be declared before it is used.* This simply brings specialization into line with the rules for ordinary overloading. If no specialization is in scope at a point of use, the general template definition will be used. For example:

```
template<class T> void sort(vector<T>& v)
    { /* ... */ }

void sort<char*>(vector<char*>& v);   // specialization

void f(vector<char*>& v1, vector<String>& v2)
{
    sort(v1); // use specialization
              // sort(vector<char*>&)

    sort(v2); // use general template
              // sort(vector<T>&), T is String
}

void sort<String>(vector<String>& v); // error: specialize
                                       // after use

void sort<>(vector<double>& v); // fine: sort<double>
                                // hasn't yet been used
```

We considered an explicit keyword for requesting a specialization. For example:

```
specialise void sort(vector<String>&);
```

but the mood of the committee at the San Jose meeting was strongly against new keywords and I would never have managed to get agreement on the spelling of *specialize*
vs. *specialise* in that thoroughly international gathering.

15.10.4 Finding Template Definitions

Traditionally, C++ programs, like C programs, have consisted of sets of files that were
composed into compilation units, compiled and linked into programs by a host of programs relying on conventions. For example, .c files are source code and include .h
files to gain information about other parts of the program. From .c files, the compiler can produce object code files, often called .o files. The executable version of
the program is obtained by simply linking the .o files together. Archives and dynamically linked libraries complicate matters without changing the overall picture.

Templates don't fit neatly into this picture. That is the root of many of the problems with template implementations. A template isn't just source code (what is
instantiated from a template is more like traditional source code), so template definitions don't quite belong in .c files. On the other hand, templates are not just types
and interface information, so they don't quite belong in .h files either.

The ARM didn't offer sufficient guidance to implementers (§15.10), and this has
led to a proliferation of schemes that are becoming a barrier to portability. Some
implementations have required templates to be placed in .h files. This can lead to
performance problems because too much information is supplied for each compilation
and because each compilation unit appears to depend on all the templates in its .h
files. Basically, template function definitions don't belong in header files. Other
implementations have required template function definitions to be placed in .c files.
This leads to problems with finding a template function definition when an instantiation is needed, and it also complicates the composition of a context for an instantiation.

I suspect that any solution to these problems must be based on the recognition that
a C++ program is more than a set of unrelated separately compiled units. This is true
even during compilation. Somehow, the concept of a central point where information
related to templates and other issues that affect multiple compilation units must be
recognized. Here I will call that point *the repository* because its role is to keep information that the compiler needs between compilations of the separate parts of a program.

Think of the repository as a persistent symbol table with one entry per template
that the compiler uses to keep track of declarations, definitions, specializations, uses,
etc. Given that concept, I can outline a model of instantiation that supports all language facilities, accommodates the current uses of .h and .c files, doesn't require
the user to know about the repository, and provides the alternatives for error checking,
optimization, and compiler/linker efficiencies that implementers have asked for. Note
that this is a model for an instantiation system, rather than a language rule or a

specific implementation. Several alternative implementations are possible, but I suspect a user could ignore the details (most of the time) and think of the system this way.

Let me outline what might happen in a number of cases from the point of view of a compiler. As usual, .c files are fed to the compiler, and they contain #include directives for .h files. The compiler knows only about code that has been presented to it. That is, it never looks around in the file system to try to find a template definition that it hasn't already been presented with. However, the compiler uses the repository to "remember" which templates it has seen and where they came from. This scheme can easily be extended to include the usual notions of archives. Here is a brief description of what a compiler does at critical points:

- A template declaration is seen: The template can now be used. Enter the template into the repository.
- A function template definition is seen in a .c file: The template is processed as far as necessary to enter it into the repository. If it is already entered, we give a double-definition error unless it is a new version of same template.
- A function template definition is seen in a .h file: The template is processed as far as necessary to enter it into the repository. If it is already entered, we check that the already-entered template did in fact originate in the same header. If not, we give a double-definition error. We check that the one-definition rule hasn't been violated by checking that this definition is in fact identical to the previous one. If not, we give a double-definition error unless it is a new version of same template.
- A function template specialization declaration is seen: If necessary, give a used-before-specialized error. The specialization can now be used. Enter the declaration into the repository.
- A function template specialization definition is seen: If necessary, give a used-before-specialized error. The specialization can now be used. Enter the definition into the repository.
- A use is encountered: Enter the fact that the template has been used with this set of template arguments into the repository. Look into the repository to see if a general template or a specialization has been defined. If so, error checking and/or optimizations may be performed. If the template has not previously been used for this set of template arguments, code may be generated. Alternatively, code generation can be postponed until link time.
- An explicit instantiation request is encountered: Check if the template has been defined. If not, give a template-not-defined error. Check if a specialization has been defined. If so, give an instantiated-and-specialized error. Check if the template has already been instantiated for this set of template arguments. If so, a double-instantiation error may be given, or the instantiation request may be ignored. If not, code may be generated. Alternatively, code generation can be postponed until link time. In either case, code is generated for every template class member function presented to the compiler.
- The program is linked: Generate code for every template use for which code

hasn't already been generated. Repeat this process until all instantiations have been done. Give a use-but-not-defined error for any missing template functions.

Code generation for a template and a set of template arguments involves lookup #2 mentioned in §15.10.2. Naturally, checking against illegal uses, unacceptable overloadings, etc., must also be performed.

An implementation can be more or less thorough in checking for violations of the one-definition rule and the rule against multiple instantiations. These are nonrequired diagnostics, so the exact behavior of the implementation is a quality-of-implementation issue.

15.11 Implications of Templates

The absence of templates in early C++ had important negative implications on the way C++ is used. Now that templates are widely available, what can we do better?

In the absence of templates, there was no way in C++ to implement container classes without extensive use of casting and the manipulation of objects through pointers to common base classes or void*. In principle, this can all be eliminated. However, I suspect that misuses of inheritance stemming from misguided application of Smalltalk techniques in C++ (for example, see §14.2.3) and overuse of weakly typed techniques stemming from C will be very hard to root out.

On the other hand, I expect that it will be possible to slowly get rid of many of the unsafe practices involving arrays. The ANSI/ISO standard library has the dynarray template class (§8.5) so that people can use it or some ''home brew'' array template to minimize the unchecked uses of arrays. People often criticize C and C++ for not checking array bounds. Much of that criticism is misguided because people forget that just because you can make a range error on a C array, you don't have to. Array templates allow us to relegate the low-level C arrays to the bowels of an implementation where they belong. Once the frequency of C-style array usage goes down and their use becomes more stylized within class and template implementations, the number of errors that can be attributed to C arrays will be drastically reduced. This has been slowly happening for years and templates, especially templates in libraries, accelerate this trend.

The third important aspect of templates is that they open completely new possibilities for library design when used for composition in combination with derivation (§15.8). In the long run, that might be the most important aspect.

Even though implementations supporting templates are no longer uncommon, they they are not yet universally available, either. Furthermore, most such implementations are at the time of writing immature. This currently limits the impact of templates on people's thinking about C++ and the design of programs. The ANSI/ISO resolutions of the various dark corners ought to solve both problems so that we will see templates take the central place in the C++ programmer's tool box that they were designed for.

15.11.1 Separation of Implementation and Interface

The template mechanism is completely a compile-time and link-time mechanism. No part of the template mechanism needs run-time support. This is of course deliberate, but leaves the problem of how to get the classes and functions generated (instantiated) from templates to depend on information known only at run time. The answer is, as ever in C++: use virtual functions.

Many people expressed concern that templates relied too heavily on the availability of source code. This was seen as having two bad side-effects:

[1] You can't keep your implementation a trade secret.

[2] If a template implementation changes, user code must be recompiled.

This is certainly the case for the most obvious implementation, but the trick of deriving template classes from classes that provide a clean interface limits the impact of these problems. Often, a template simply provides interface code to something that can be "secret" and can be changed without affecting users. The pvector example from §15.5 is a simple example of that. A template version of the set example from §13.2.2 would be another. My view was that people who were concerned with these matters had an alternative in the virtual function concept and I needn't provide another variant of the jump table.

It is also possible to devise a partially compiled form of templates that will keep the implementer's secrets as safe – or maybe as unsafe – as ordinary object code.

To some, the problem is to ensure that no new versions of templates meant to be secret are instantiated – directly or indirectly – by the user. This can be ensured simply by not supplying their source. That approach is feasible if the supplier can pre-instantiate (§15.10.1) all versions needed. Those versions (and only those) can then be shipped as object code libraries.

15.11.2 Flexibility and Efficiency

Because templates have to compete directly with macros the demands on their flexibility and efficiency are severe. In retrospect, the result has been a mechanism of unsurpassed flexibility and efficiency without compromising the static type checking. When it comes to expressing algorithms, I occasionally wish for higher-order functions, but rarely for run-time type checking. I suspect that most suggestions for "improvements" to templates through constraints and restrictions would seriously limit the utility of templates without providing added safety, simplicity, or efficiency to compensate. To quote Alex Stepanov summarizing the experience of writing and using a major library of data structures and algorithms:

"C++ is a powerful enough language – the first such language in our experience – to allow the construction of generic programming components that combine mathematical precision, beauty, and abstractness with the efficiency of non-generic hand-crafted code."

We have yet to discover the full power of the combination of templates, abstract classes, exception handling, etc. I don't consider the factor-ten difference in the size of the Booch Ada and C++ components [Booch,1993b] a freak example (§8.4.1).

15.11.3 Impact on the Rest of C++

A template argument can be either a built-in type or a user-defined type. This has created constant pressure for user-defined and built-in types to look and behave as similarly as possible. Unfortunately, user-defined and built-in types cannot be made to behave in a completely uniform manner. The reason is that the irregularity of the built-in types cannot be removed without causing serious incompatibilities with C. In many small ways, however, the built-in types have benefited from the progress made with templates.

When I first considered templates and also when I used them later, I found several cases in which built-in types were treated slightly differently than classes. This became an obstacle to writing templates that could be used with both classes and built-in type arguments. I therefore set out to ensure that minor syntactic and semantic details applied uniformly to all types. This effort continues to this day.

Consider:

```
vector v(10);    // vector of 10 elements
```

This initializer syntax used to be illegal for built-in types. To allow it, I introduced the notion that built-in types have constructors and destructors. For example:

```
int a(1);    // pre-2.1 error, now initializes a to 1
```

I considered extending this notion to allow derivation from built-in classes and explicit declaration of built-in operators for built-in types. However, I restrained myself.

Allowing derivation from an `int` doesn't actually give a C++ programmer anything significantly new compared to having an `int` member. This is primarily because `int` doesn't have any virtual functions for the derived class to override. More seriously though, the C conversion rules are so chaotic that pretending that `int`, `short`, etc., are well-behaved ordinary classes is not going to work. They are either C compatible or they obey the relatively well-behaved C++ rules for classes, but not both.

Allowing the definition of built-in operators such as `operator+(int,int)` would also have made the language mutable. However, allowing such functions to be synthesized so that one could pass pointers to them and in other ways refer directly to them seems attractive.

Conceptually, built-in types do have constructors and destructors, though. For example:

```
template<class T> class X {
    T a;
    int i;
    complex c;
```

```
public:
    X() :a(T()), i(int()), c(complex()) { }
    // ...
};
```

The constructor for X initializes each of its members by calling the member's default constructor. The default constructor for any type T is defined to yield the same value as a global variable of type T that hasn't been explicitly initialized. This is an improvement over the ARM where X() is defined to yield an undefined value unless a default constructor is defined for X.

16

Exception Handling

Don't Panic!
– The Hitchhiker's Guide to the Galaxy

Aims for exception handling — assumptions about exception handling — syntax — grouping of exceptions — resource management — errors in constructors — resumption vs. termination semantics — asynchronous events — multi-level exception propagation — static checking — implementation issues — invariants.

16.1 Introduction

In the original design of C++, exceptions were considered, but postponed because there wasn't time to do a thorough job of exploring the design and implementation issues and because of fear of the complexity they might add to an implementation (§3.15). In particular, it was understood that a poor design could cause run-time overhead and a significant increase in porting times. Exceptions were considered important for error handling in programs composed out of separately designed libraries.

The actual design of the C++ exception mechanism stretched over years (1984 to 1989) and was the first part of C++ to be designed in the full glare of public interest. In addition to the innumerable blackboard iterations that every C++ feature went through, several designs were worked out on paper and widely discussed. Andrew Koenig was closely involved in the later iterations and is the coauthor (with me) on the published papers [Koenig,1989a] [Koenig,1990]. Andy and I worked out significant parts of the final scheme en route to the Santa Fe USENIX C++ conference in November 1987. I also had meetings at Apple, DEC (Spring Brook), Microsoft, IBM (Almaden), Sun, and other places where I presented draft versions of the design and received valuable input. In particular, I searched out people with real experience with systems that provide exception handling to compensate for my personal inexperience in that area. The first serious discussion of exception handling for C++ that I recall was in Oxford in the summer of 1983. The focus of that discussion with Tony Williams from the Rutherford Lab was the design of fault-tolerant systems and the value of static checking in exception-handling mechanisms.

At the time when the debate about exception handling started in the ANSI C++ committee, experience with exception handling in C++ was limited to library-based implementations by Apple, Mike Miller [Miller,1988], and others, and to a single compiler-based implementation by Mike Tiemann [Tiemann,1990]. This was worrying, though there was fairly wide agreement that exception handling in some suitable form was a good idea for C++. In particular, Dmitry Lenkov expressed a strong wish for exception handling based on experiences at Hewlett-Packard. A notable exception to this agreement was Doug McIlroy, who stated that the availability of exception handling would make systems less reliable because library writers and other programmers will throw exceptions rather than try to understand and handle problems. Only time will tell to what extent Doug's prediction will be true. Naturally, no language feature can prevent programmers from writing bad code.

The first implementations of exception handling as defined in the ARM started appearing in the spring of 1992.

16.2 Aims and Assumptions

The following assumptions were made for the design:
- Exceptions are used primarily for error handling.
- Exception handlers are rare compared to function definitions.
- Exceptions occur infrequently compared to function calls.
- Exceptions are a language-level concept – not just implementation, and not an error-handling policy.

This formulation, like the list of ideals below, is taken from slides I used for presentations of the evolving design from about 1988.

What is meant is that exception handling
- Isn't intended as simply an alternative return mechanism (as was suggested by some, notably David Cheriton), but specifically as a mechanism for supporting the construction of fault-tolerant systems.
- Isn't intended to turn every function into a fault-tolerant entity, but rather as a mechanism by which a subsystem can be given a large measure of fault tolerance even if its individual functions are written without regard for overall error-handling strategies.
- Isn't meant to constrain designers to a single ''correct'' notion of error handling, but to make the language more expressive.

Throughout the design effort, there was an increasing influence of systems designers of all sorts and a decrease of input from the language design community. In retrospect, the greatest influence on the C++ exception handling design was the work on fault-tolerant systems started at the University of Newcastle in England by Brian Randell and his colleagues in the seventies and continued in many places since.

The following ideals evolved for C++ exception handling:

[1] Type-safe transmission of arbitrary amounts of information from a throw-point to a handler.

[2] No added cost (in time or space) to code that does not throw an exception.

[3] A guarantee that every exception raised is caught by an appropriate handler.

[4] A way of grouping exceptions so that handlers can be written to catch groups of exceptions as well as individual ones.

[5] A mechanism that by default will work correctly in a multi-threaded program.

[6] A mechanism that allows cooperation with other languages, especially with C.

[7] Easy to use.

[8] Easy to implement.

Most of these ideals were achieved, others ([3], [8]) were considered too expensive or too constraining and were only approximated. I consider it given that error handling is a difficult task for which the programmer needs all the help that can be provided. An over-zealous language designer might provide features and/or constraints that would actually complicate the task of designing and implementing a fault-tolerant system.

My view that fault-tolerant systems must be multi-level helped me resist the clamor for ''advanced'' features. No single unit of a system can recover from every error that might happen in it, and every bit of violence that might be done to it from ''the outside.'' In extreme cases, power will fail or a memory location will change its value for no apparent reason.

At some point, the unit must give up and leave further cleanup to a ''higher'' unit. For example, a function may report a catastrophic failure to a caller, a process may have to terminate abnormally and leave recovery to some other process, a processor may ask for help from another, and a complete computer may have to request help from a human operator. Given this view, it makes sense to emphasize that the error handling at each level should be designed so that relatively simple code using relatively simple exception handling features will have a chance of actually working.

Trying to provide facilities that allow a single program to recover from all errors is misguided and leads to error-handling strategies so complex that they themselves become a source of errors.

16.3 Syntax

As ever, syntax attracted more attention than its importance warranted. In the end, I settled on a rather verbose syntax using three keywords and lots of brackets:

```
int f()
{
    try {                    // start of try block
        return g();
    }
    catch (xxii) {    // start of exception handler

            // we get here only if 'xxii' occurs
        error("g() goofed: xxii");
        return 22;
    }
}

int g()
{
    // ...
    if (something_wrong) throw xxii();   // throw exception
    // ...
}
```

The try keyword is completely redundant and so are the { } brackets except where multiple statements are actually used in a try-block or a handler. For example, it would have been trivial to allow:

```
int f()
{
    return g() catch (xxii) {   // not C++
        error("g() goofed: xxii");
        return 22;
    };
}
```

However, I found this so difficult to explain that the redundancy was introduced to save support staff from confused users. Because of the C community's traditional aversion to keywords, I tried hard to avoid having three new keywords for exception handling, but every scheme I cooked up with fewer keywords seemed overly clever and/or confusing. For example, I tried to use catch for both throwing an exception and for catching it. This can be made logical and consistent, but I despaired over explaining that scheme.

The word throw was chosen partly because the more obvious words raise and signal had already been taken by standard C library functions.

16.4 Grouping

Having talked to dozens of users of more than a dozen different systems supporting some form of exception handling, I concluded that the ability to define groups of exceptions is essential. For example, a user must be able to catch "any I/O library exception'' without knowing exactly which exceptions that includes. There are work-arounds when a grouping mechanism isn't available. For example, one might encode what would otherwise have been different exceptions as data carried by a single exception, or simply list all exceptions of what we consider a group everywhere a catch of the group is intended. However, every such workaround was experienced – by most if not everybody – to be a maintenance problem.

Andrew Koenig and I first tried a grouping scheme based on groups dynamically constructed by constructors for exception objects. However, this seemed somewhat out of style with the rest of C++ and many people, including Ted Goldstein and Peter Deutsch, noted that most such groups were equivalent to class hierarchies. We there-fore adopted a scheme inspired by ML where you throw an object and catch it by a handler declared to accept objects of that type. The usual C++ initialization rules then allow a handler for a type B to catch objects of any class D derived from B. For exam-ple:

```
class Matherr { };
class Overflow: public Matherr { };
class Underflow: public Matherr { };
class Zerodivide: public Matherr { };
// ...



void g()
{
    try {
        f();
    }
    catch (Overflow) {
        // handle Overflow or anything derived from Overflow
    }
    catch (Matherr) {
        // handle any Matherr that is not Overflow
    }
}
```

It was later discovered that multiple inheritance (§12) provided an elegant solution to otherwise difficult classification problems. For example, one can declare a network file error like this:

```
class network_file_err
    : public network_err , public file_system_err { };
```

An exception of type `network_file_err` can be handled both by software expecting network errors and software expecting file system errors. I believe that Daniel Weinreb was the first one to spot this usage.

16.5 Resource Management

The central point in the exception handling design was the management of resources. In particular, if a function grabs a resource, how can the language help the user to ensure that the resource is correctly released upon exit even if an exception occurs? Consider this simple example borrowed from [2nd]:

```
void use_file(const char* fn)
{
    FILE* f = fopen(fn,"w");   // open file fn

    // use f

    fclose(f);   // close file fn
}
```

This looks plausible. However, if something goes wrong after the call of fopen() and before the call of fclose(), an exception may cause use_file() to be exited without calling fclose(). Please note that exactly the same problem can occur in languages that do not support exception handling. For example, a call of the standard C library function longjmp() would have the same bad effects. If we want to write a fault-tolerant system, we must solve this problem. A primitive solution looks like this:

```
void use_file(const char* fn)
{
    FILE* f = fopen(fn,"r");   // open file fn
    try {
        // use f
    }
    catch (...) {    // catch all
        fclose(f);   // close file fn
        throw;       // re-throw
    }
    fclose(f);   // close file fn
}
```

All the code using the file is enclosed in a try block that catches every exception, closes the file, and re-throws the exception.

The problem with this solution is that it is verbose, tedious, and potentially expensive. Furthermore, any verbose and tedious solution is error-prone because programmers get bored. We can make this solution ever so slightly less tedious by providing a specific finalization mechanism to avoid the duplication of the code releasing the resource (in this case fclose(f)), but that does nothing to address the fundamental problem: writing resilient code requires special and more complicated code than traditional code.

Fortunately, there is a more elegant solution. The general form of the problem looks like this:

```
void use()
{
        // acquire resource 1
        // ...
        // acquire resource n

        // use resources

        // release resource n
        // ...
        // release resource 1
}
```

It is typically important that resources are released in the reverse order of their acquisition. This strongly resembles the behavior of local objects created by constructors and destroyed by destructors. Thus we can handle such resource acquisition and release problems by a suitable use of objects of classes with constructors and destructors. For example, we can define a class `FilePtr` that acts like a `FILE*`:

```
class FilePtr {
        FILE* p;
public:
        FilePtr(const char* n, const char* a) { p = fopen(n,a); }
        FilePtr(FILE* pp) { p = pp; }
        ~FilePtr() { fclose(p); }

        operator FILE*() { return p; }
};
```

We can construct a `FilePtr` given either a `FILE*` or the arguments required for `fopen()`. In either case, a `FilePtr` will be destroyed at the end of its scope and its destructor closes the file. Our program now shrinks to this minimum

```
void use_file(const char* fn)
{
        FilePtr f(fn,"r");   // open file fn
        // use f
} // file fn implicitly closed
```

and the destructor will be called independently of whether the function is exited normally or because an exception is thrown.

I called this technique ''resource acquisition is initialization.'' It extends to partially constructed objects and thus addresses the otherwise difficult issue of what to do when an error is encountered in a constructor; see [Koenig,1990] or [2nd].

16.5.1 Errors in Constructors

To some, the most important aspect of exceptions is that they provide a general mechanism for reporting errors detected in a constructor. Consider the constructor for

`FilePtr`; it didn't test whether the file was opened correctly. A more careful coding would be:

```
FilePtr::FilePtr(const char* n, const char* a)
{
    if ((p = fopen(n,a)) == 0) {
        // oops! open failed - what now?
    }
}
```

Without exceptions, there is no direct way of reporting the failure because a constructor doesn't have a return value. This has led people to use workarounds such as putting the constructed objects into an error state, leaving return value indicators in agreed upon variables, etc. Surprisingly enough, this was rarely a significant practical problem. However, exceptions provide a general solution:

```
FilePtr::FilePtr(const char* n, const char* a)
{
    if ((p = fopen(n,a)) == 0) {
        // oops! open failed
        throw Open_failed(n,a);
    }
}
```

Importantly, the C++ exception handling mechanism guarantees that partly constructed objects are correctly destroyed, that is, completely constructed sub-objects are destroyed and yet-to-be-constructed sub-objects are not. This allows the writer of a constructor to concentrate on the error handling for the object in which the failure is detected. For details see [2nd,§9.4.1].

16.6 Resumption vs. Termination

During the design of the exception handling mechanism, the most contentious issue turned out to be whether it should support termination semantics or resumption semantics; that is, whether it should be possible for an exception handler to require execution to resume from the point where the exception was thrown. For example, wouldn't it be a good idea to have the routine invoked because of memory exhaustion, find some extra memory, and then return? To have the routine invoked because of a divide-by-zero return with a user-defined value? To have the routine invoked because a read routine found the floppy drive empty, request the user to insert a disk, and then return?

My personal starting point was: "Why not? That seems a useful feature. I can see quite a few situations where I could use resumption." Over the next four years, I learned otherwise, and thus the C++ exception handling mechanism embodies the opposite view, often called the *termination model*.

The main resumption vs. termination debate took place in the ANSI C++ committee where the issue was discussed in the committee as a whole, in the extensions working group, at evening technical sessions, and on the committee's electronic mailing lists. That debate lasted from December 1989 when the ANSI committee was formed to November 1990. Naturally, the issues were also the topic of much interest in the C++ community at large. In the committee, the resumption point of view was ably presented and defended primarily by Martin O'Riordan and Mike Miller. Andrew Koenig, Mike Vilot, Ted Goldstein, Dag Brück, Dmitry Lenkov, and I were usually the most vocal proponents of termination semantics. I conducted most of the discussions in my role as chairman of the extensions working group. The outcome was a 22 to 1 vote for termination semantics in the extensions working group after a long meeting where experience data was presented by representatives of DEC, Sun, TI, and IBM. This was followed by the acceptance of the exception handling proposal as presented in the ARM (that is, with termination semantics) by a 30 to 4 vote by the full committee.

After a long debate at the Seattle meeting in July 1990, I summarized the arguments for resumption like this:

- More general (powerful, includes termination).
- Unifies similar concepts/implementations.
- Essential for very complex, very dynamic systems (that is, OS/2).
- Not significantly more complex/expensive to implement.
- If you don't have it, you must fake it.
- Provides simple solutions for resource exhaustion problems.

The arguments for termination were similarly summarized:

- Simpler, cleaner, cheaper.
- Leads to more manageable systems.
- Powerful enough for everything.
- Avoids horrendous coding tricks.
- Significant negative experience with resumption.

These lists trivialize the debate, which was very technical and thorough. It also got quite heated at times with less restrained proponents expressing the view that termination proponents were somehow trying to impose an arbitrary and restrictive view of programming on them. Clearly, the termination/resumption issue touches deep issues of how software ought to be designed. The debate was never between two equal-sized groups. The proponents of termination semantics always seemed to be in a 4-to-1 or larger majority in every forum.

The most repeated and most persuasive arguments for resumption were that

[1] because resumption is a more general mechanism than termination, it should be accepted even if there was doubt about the usefulness;

[2] there are important cases where a routine finds itself blocked because of the lack of a resource (for example, memory exhaustion or an empty floppy disk drive). In that case, resumption will allow the routine to throw an exception, have the exception handler provide the missing resource, and then resume the execution as if the resource had never been missing.

The most repeated and convincing arguments (to me) for termination were that

[1] Termination is significantly simpler than resumption. In fact, resumption

requires the key mechanisms for continuations and nested functions without providing the benefits of those mechanisms.

[2] The method of dealing with resource exhaustion proposed in argument [2] for resumption is fundamentally bad. It leads to error-prone and hard-to-comprehend tight bindings between library code and users.

[3] Really major systems in many application areas have been written using termination semantics so resumption cannot be necessary.

The last point is also backed up by a theoretical argument by Flaviu Cristian that given termination, resumption isn't needed [Cristian,1989].

After a couple of years of discussion, I was left with the impression that one could concoct a convincing logical argument for either position. Even the original paper on exception handling [Goodenough,1975] had done so. We were in the position of the ancient Greek philosophers debating the nature of the universe with such intensity and subtlety that they forgot to study it. Consequently, I kept asking anyone with genuine experience with large systems to come forward with data. On the side of resumption, Martin O'Riordan reported that "Microsoft had several years of positive experience with resumable exception handling," but the absence of specific examples and doubts about the value of OS/2 Release 1 as a proof of technical soundness weakened his case. Experiences with PL/I's ON-conditions were mentioned as arguments both for and against resumption.

Then, at the Palo Alto meeting in November 1991, we heard a brilliant summary of the arguments for termination semantics backed with both personal experience and data from Jim Mitchell (from Sun, formerly from Xerox PARC). Jim had used exception handling in half a dozen languages over a period of 20 years and was an early proponent of resumption semantics as one of the main designers and implementers of Xerox's Cedar/Mesa system. His message was

"termination is preferred over resumption; this is not a matter of opinion but a matter of years of experience. Resumption is seductive, but not valid."

He backed this statement with experience from several operating systems. The key example was Cedar/Mesa: It was written by people who liked and used resumption, but after ten years of use, there was only one use of resumption left in the half million line system – and that was a context inquiry. Because resumption wasn't actually necessary for such a context inquiry, they removed it and found a significant speed increase in that part of the system. In each and every case where resumption had been used it had – over the ten years – become a problem and a more appropriate design had replaced it. Basically, every use of resumption had represented a failure to keep separate levels of abstraction disjoint.

Mary Fontana presented similar data from the TI Explorer system where resumption was found to be used for debugging only, Aron Insinga presented evidence of the very limited and nonessential use of resumption in DEC's VMS, and Kim Knuttilla related exactly the same story as Jim Mitchell for two large and long-lived projects inside IBM. To this we added a strong opinion in favor of termination based on experience at L.M.Ericsson relayed to us by Dag Brück.

Thus, the C++ committee endorsed termination semantics.

16.6.1 Workarounds for Resumption

It appears that most of the benefits of resumption can be obtained by combining a function call and a (terminating) exception. Consider a function that a user calls to acquire some resource X:

```
X* grab_X() // acquire resource  X
{
    for (;;) {
        if (can_acquire_an_X) {
            // ...
            return some_X;
        }

        // oops! can't acquire an X, try to recover:

        grab_X_failed();
    }
}
```

It is the job of `grab_X_failed()` to make it possible to make an X available for acquisition. If it can't, it can throw an exception:

```
void grab_X_failed()
{
    if (can_make_X_available) { // recovery
        // make X available
        return;
    }

    throw Cannot_get_X; // give up
}
```

This technique is a generalization of the `new_handler` approach to memory exhaustion (§10.6). There are, of course, many variants of this technique. My favorites use a pointer to function somewhere to allow a user to ''tailor'' the recovery action. This technique doesn't burden the system with the complexity of a resumption implementation. Often, it doesn't imply the negative impact on system organization that general resumption does.

16.7 Asynchronous Events

The C++ exception handling mechanism is explicitly *not* for handling asynchronous events directly:

''Can exceptions be used to handle things like signals? Almost certainly not in most C environments. The trouble is that C uses functions like `malloc` that are not re-entrant. If an interrupt occurs in the middle of `malloc` and causes an exception, there is no way to prevent the exception handler from executing `malloc` again.

A C++ implementation where calling sequences and the entire run-time library are designed around the requirement for re-entrancy would make it possible for signals to throw exceptions. Until such implementations are commonplace, if ever, we must recommend that exceptions and signals be kept strictly separate from a language point of view. In many cases, it will be reasonable to have signals and exceptions interact by having signals store away information that is regularly examined (polled) by some function that in turn may throw appropriate exceptions in response to the information stored by the signals [Koenig,1990].''

My view, which appears to reflect a large majority view in the part of the C/C++ community concerned with exception handling, is that to produce reliable systems you need to map asynchronous events into some form of process model as quickly as possible. Having exceptions happen at random points in the execution and having to stop the processing of one exception to deal with an unrelated exception is a prescription for chaos. A low-level interrupt system should be separated from general programs as far as possible.

This view precludes the direct use of exceptions to represent something like hitting a DEL key and replacing UNIX signals with exceptions. In such cases, a low-level interrupt routine must somehow do its minimal job and possibly map into something that could trigger an exception at a well-defined point in a program's execution. Note that signals, as defined in the C standard, are not allowed to call functions because during signal handling the machine state isn't guaranteed to be consistent enough to handle a function call and return.

Similarly, low-level events, such as arithmetic overflows and divide by zero, are assumed to be handled by a dedicated lower-level mechanism rather than by exceptions. This enables C++ to match the behavior of other languages when it comes to arithmetic. It also avoids the problems that occur on heavily pipelined architectures where events such as divide by zero are asynchronous. Making divide by zero, etc., synchronous is not possible on all machines. Where it is possible, flushing the pipelines to ensure that such events are caught before unrelated computation has happened slows the machine down (often by an order of magnitude).

16.8 Multi-level Propagation

There are several good reasons to allow an exception to be implicitly propagated from a function to its immediate caller only. However, this was not an option for C++:

[1] There are millions of C++ functions that couldn't reasonably be expected to be modified to propagate or handle exceptions.

[2] It is not a good idea to try to make every function a fire-wall. The best error-handling strategies are those in which only designated major interfaces are concerned with non-local error handling issues.

[3] In a mixed-language environment, it is not possible to require a specific action of a function because that function may be written in another language. In

particular, a C++ function throwing an exception may be called by a C function
that was called by a C++ function willing to catch the exception.

The first reason is pragmatic, the other two are fundamental: [2] is a statement about
systems design strategies, and [3] is a statement about what kind of environments C++
code is assumed to be able to work in.

16.9 Static Checking

By allowing multi-level propagation of exceptions, C++ loses one aspect of static
checking. One cannot simply look at a function to determine which exceptions it may
throw. In fact, it may in principle throw any exception even if there isn't a single
`throw` statement in the body of that function. Functions called by it may do the
throwing.

Several people, notably Mike Powell, bemoaned this and tried to figure out how
stronger guarantees could be provided for C++ exceptions. Ideally, we would like to
guarantee that every exception thrown is caught by a suitable user-provided handler.
Often, we would like to guarantee that only exceptions from an explicitly specified
list can escape from a function. The C++ mechanism for specifying a list of exceptions that a function may throw was essentially designed by Mike Powell, Mike Tiemann, and me on a blackboard at Sun sometime in 1989.

''In effect, writing this:

```
void f() throw (e1, e2)
{
    // stuff
}
```

is equivalent to writing this:

```
void f()
{
    try {
        // stuff
    }
    catch (e1) {
        throw;   // re-throw
    }
    catch (e2) {
        throw;   // re-throw
    }
    catch (...) {
        unexpected();
    }
}
```

The advantage of the explicit declaration of exceptions that a function can
throw over the equivalent checking in the code is not just that it saves typing. The
most important advantage is that the function *declaration* belongs to an interface

that is visible to its callers. Function *definitions*, on the other hand, are not universally available and even if we do have access to the source code of all our libraries we strongly prefer not to have to look at it very often.

"Another advantage is that it may still be practical to detect many uncaught exceptions during compilation [Koenig,1990]."

Ideally, exception specifications would be checked at compile time, but that would require that every function cooperate in the scheme, and that isn't feasible. Further, such static checking could easily become a source of much recompilation. Worse, such recompilation would only be feasible for users who had all the source code to recompile:

"For example, a function must potentially be changed and recompiled if a function it calls (directly or indirectly) changes the set of exceptions it catches or throws. This could lead to major delays in the production of software produced (partly) by composition of libraries from different sources. Such libraries would *de facto* have to agree on a set of exceptions to be used. For example, if subsystem X handles exceptions from subsystem Y and the supplier of Y introduces a new kind of exception, then X's code will have to be modified to cope. A user of X and Y will not be able to upgrade to a new version of Y until X has been modified. Where many subsystems are used this can cause cascading delays. Even where the 'multiple supplier problem' does not exist this can lead to cascading modifications of code and to large amounts of recompilation.

Such problems would cause people to avoid using the exception specification mechanism or else subvert it [Koenig,1990]."

Thus we decided to support run-time checking only and leave static checking to separate tools.

"An equivalent problem occurs when dynamic checking is used. In that case, however, the problem can be handled using the exception grouping mechanism presented in §16.4. A naive use of the exception handling mechanism would leave a new exception added to subsystem Y uncaught or converted into a call to `unexpected()` by some explicitly-called interface. However, a well-defined subsystem Y would have all its exceptions derived from a class `Yexception`. For example

```
class newYexception : public Yexception { /* ... */ };
```

This implies that a function declared

```
void f() throw (Xexception, Yexception, IOexception);
```

would handle a `newYexception` by passing it to callers of `f()` ".

For a further discussion see [2nd,§9].

In 1995, we found a scheme that allows some static checking of exception specifications and improved code generation without causing the problems described above. Consequently, exception specifications are now checked so that pointer to function assignments, initializations, and virtual function overriding cannot lead to violations. Some unexpected exceptions can still occur, and those are caught at run time as ever.

16.9.1 Implementation Issues

As ever, efficiency was a major concern. It was obvious that one could design an exception handling mechanism that could only be implemented with significant direct overhead in the function-calling sequences or indirectly through optimizations that were prevented by the possibility of exceptions. It appears that these concerns were successfully addressed so that in theory at least, the C++ exception handling mechanism can be implemented without any time overhead to a program that doesn't throw an exception. An implementation can arrange that all run-time cost is incurred when an exception is thrown [Koenig,1990]. It is also possible to limit space overhead, but it is hard to simultaneously avoid run-time overhead and an increase in code size. Several implementations now support exceptions so the tradeoffs will become clear; see for example [Cameron,1992].

Curiously, exception handling doesn't affect the object layout model to any real extent. It is necessary to represent a type at run time to communicate between a throw point and a handler. However, it appears that can be done by a special-purpose mechanism that doesn't affect objects in general. Alternatively, the data structures supporting run-time type identification (§14.2.6) can be used. A much more critical point is that keeping track of the exact lifetimes of every automatic object becomes essential. Straightforward implementations of that can lead to some code bloat even where the number of added instructions actually executed is low.

My ideal implementation technique derives from work done with Clu and Modula-2+ [Rovner,1986] implementations. The fundamental idea is to lay down a table of code address ranges that corresponds to the state of the computation as relates to exception handling. For each range, the destructors that need to be called and the handlers that can be invoked are recorded. When an exception is thrown the exception handling mechanism compares the program counter to the addresses in the range table. If the program counter is in a range found in the range table, the appropriate actions are taken; otherwise the stack is unwound and the program counter from the calling function is looked up in the range table.

16.10 Invariants

Being a relatively new, evolving, yet heavily used language, C++ attracts more than its share of suggested improvements and extensions. In particular, every feature of every language that is fashionable somewhere will eventually be proposed for C++. Bertrand Meyer popularized the old idea of preconditions and postconditions and provided direct language support for it in Eiffel [Meyer,1988]. Naturally, direct language support was suggested for C++.

Segments of the C community have always relied heavily on the `assert()` macro, but there has been no good way of reporting a violation of some assertion at run time. Exceptions provided such a way, and templates provided a way of avoiding reliance on macros. For example, one can write an `Assert()` template that mimics the C `assert()` macro:

```
template<class T, class X> inline void Assert(T expr,X x)
{
    if (!NDEBUG)
        if (!expr) throw x;
}
```

will throw exception x if expr is false and we have not turned off checking by setting NDEBUG. For example:

```
class Bad_f_arg { };

void f(String& s, int i)
{
    Assert(0<=i && i<s.size(),Bad_f_arg());
    // ...
}
```

This is the least-structured variant of such techniques. I personally prefer defining invariants for classes as member functions rather than using assertions directly. For example:

```
void String::check()
{
    Assert(p
            && 0<=sz
            && sz<TOO_LARGE
            && p[sz-1]==0 , Invariant);
}
```

The ease with which assertions and invariants can be defined and used within the existing C++ language has minimized the clamor for extensions that specifically support program verification features. Consequently, most of the effort related to such techniques has gone into suggestions for standardizing techniques [Gautron,1992], much more ambitious verification systems [Lea,1990], or simple use within the existing framework.

17

Namespaces

*Always design a thing by considering
it in its next larger context.*
– Eliel Saarinen

Global scope problems — ideals for a solution — namespaces, using-declarations, and using-directives — how to use namespaces — namespaces and classes — C compatibility.

17.1 Introduction

C provides a single global namespace for all names that don't conveniently fit into a single function, a single `struct`, or a single translation unit. This causes problems with name clashes. I first grappled with this problem in the original design of C++ by defaulting all names to be local to a translation unit and requiring an explicit `extern` declaration to make them visible to other translation units. As described in §3.12, this idea was neither sufficient to solve the problem nor sufficiently compatible to be acceptable, so it failed.

When I devised the type-safe linkage mechanism (§11.3), I reconsidered the problem. I observed that a slight change to the

```
extern "C" { /* ... */ }
```

syntax, semantics, and implementation technique would allow us to have

```
extern XXX { /* ... */ }
```

mean that names declared in XXX were in a separate scope XXX and accessible from other scopes only when qualified by XXX:: in exactly the same way static class members are accessed from outside their class.

For various reasons, mostly related to lack of time, this idea lay dormant until it resurfaced in the ANSI/ISO committee discussions early in 1991. First, Keith Rowe from Microsoft presented a proposal that suggested the notation

```
bundle XXX { /* ... */ };
```

as a mechanism for defining a named scope and an operator `use` for bringing all names from a `bundle` into another scope. This led to a – not very vigorous – discussion among a few members of the extensions group including Steve Dovich, Dag Brück, Martin O'Riordan, and me. Eventually, Volker Bauche, Roland Hartinger, and Erwin Unruh from Siemens refined the ideas discussed into a proposal that didn't use new keywords:

```
:: XXX :: { /* ... */ };
```

This led to a serious discussion in the extensions group. In particular, Martin O'Riordan demonstrated that this `::` notation led to ambiguities with `::` used for class members and for global names.

By early 1993, I had – with the help of multi-megabyte email exchanges and discussions at the standards meetings – synthesized a coherent proposal. I recall technical contributions on namespaces from Dag Brück, John Bruns, Steve Dovich, Bill Gibbons, Philippe Gautron, Tony Hansen, Peter Juhl, Andrew Koenig, Eric Krohn, Doug McIlroy, Richard Minner, Martin O'Riordan, John Skaller, Jerry Schwarz, Mark Terribile, and Mike Vilot. In addition, Mike Vilot argued for immediate development of the ideas into a definite proposal so that the facilities would be available for addressing the inevitable naming problems in the ISO C++ library. Namespaces were voted into C++ at the Munich meeting in July 1993. At the San Jose meeting in November 1993, it was decided to use namespaces to control names in the standard C and C++ libraries.

17.2 The Problem

Having only a single global scope makes it unnecessarily difficult to write program fragments that can be linked together without fear of name clashes. For example:

```
// my.h:
    char f(char);
    int f(int);
    class String { /* ... */ };

// your.h:
    char f(char);
    double f(double);
    class String { /* ... */ };
```

Given these definitions, a third party cannot easily use both my.h and your.h.

Note that some of these names will appear in object code, and that some programs will be shipped without source. This implies that macro-like schemes that change the appearance of programs without actually changing the names presented to a linker are insufficient.

17.2.1 Workarounds

There are several workarounds. For example:

```
// my.h:
    char my_f(char);
    int my_f(int);
    class my_String { /* ... */ };


// your.h:
    char yo_f(char);
    double yo_f(double);
    class yo_String { /* ... */ };
```

This approach is not uncommon, but it is quite ugly and – unless the prefix strings are short – unpleasant for the user. Another problem is that there are only a few hundred two-letter prefixes and already hundreds of C++ libraries. This is one of the oldest problems in the book. Old-time C programmers will be reminded of the time when `struct` member names were given one or two letter suffixes to avoid clashes with members of other `structs`.

Macro hackery can make this approach even nastier (or even nicer, if you happen to like macros):

```
// my.h:
    #define my(X) myprefix_##X

    char  my(f)(char);
    int my(f)(int);
    class my(String) { /* ... */ };


// your.h:
    #define yo(X) your_##X

    char yo(f)(char);
    double yo(f)(double);
    class yo(String) { /* ... */ };
```

The idea is to allow longer prefixes in the name used for linkage while leaving the names used in the program short. As with all macro schemes, this creates a problem for tools: Either the tool keeps track of the mapping (complicating the tool) or the user will have to do so (complicating programming and maintenance).

An alternative approach – often preferred by people who dislike macros – is to wrap related information into a class:

```
// my.h:
    class My {
    public:
        static char f(char);
        static int f(int);
        class String { /* ... */ };
    };

// your.h:
    class Your {
    public:
        static char f(char);
        static double f(double);
        class String { /* ... */ };
    };
```

Unfortunately, this approach suffers from many little inconveniences. Not all global declarations can be simply transferred into a class and some change their meaning if you do so. For example, global functions and variables must be specified as `static` members to avoid semantic changes and the function bodies, and initializers must in general be separated from their declarations.

17.3 Ideals for a Solution

Many mechanisms can be used to provide solutions to namespace problems. Indeed, most languages can claim to have at least the rudiments of one. For example, C has its static functions, Pascal its nested scopes, C++ its classes, but we need to go to languages such as PL/I, Ada, Modula-2, Modula-3 [Nelson,1991], ML [Wikström,1987], and CLOS [Kiczales,1992] for more complete solutions.

So what would a good namespace mechanism give us in C++? A lengthy and voluminous discussion on the ANSI/ISO committee's extensions working group mailing list provided a list:

[1] The ability to link two libraries without name clashes.
[2] The ability to introduce names without fear of clashing with someone else's names (for example, names used in a library I haven't heard of, or names I haven't heard of in a library I thought I knew).
[3] The ability to add a name to the implementation of a library without affecting its users.
[4] The ability to select names from two different libraries even if those two libraries use the same names.
[5] The ability to resolve name clashes without modifying functions (that is, through declarations manipulating the namespace resolution).
[6] The ability to add a name to a namespace without fear of causing a quiet change to code using other namespaces (we cannot provide such a guarantee for code using the namespace being added to).

[7]   The ability to avoid clashes among namespace names (in particular, the ability to have the "real" or linkage name longer than the name used in user code).

[8]   The ability to use the namespace mechanism to deal with the standard libraries.

[9]   C and C++ compatibility.

[10] No added cost in link time or run time for the users of namespaces.

[11] No added verbosity for the users of namespaces compared to users of global names.

[12] The ability to indicate explicitly where a name is supposed to come from in code using the name.

In addition, a good solution must be simple. I defined *simple* as:

[1]   A mechanism that can be explained to the degree needed for serious use in less than ten minutes. Explaining any mechanism to the satisfaction of language lawyers takes much longer.

[2]   Something a C++ compiler writer can implement in less than two weeks.

Naturally, simplicity in this sense cannot be proven rigorously. For example, the time needed to understand something will vary greatly between people with different backgrounds and different levels of abilities.

There were also some properties that were asked for that we deliberately excluded from the criteria for the namespace mechanism:

[1]   The ability to take binaries with clashing link names and link them together. This can be done by tools in every system, but I don't see a language mechanism that could easily be implemented without significant effort or overhead on *all* systems. There are too many linkers and too many object code formats around to make it feasible to change them. For a solution to be useful for C++ it must require only facilities provided by almost all current linkers.

[2]   The ability to provide arbitrary synonyms for names used in libraries. Existing mechanisms, such as `typedef`, references, and macros provide mechanisms for providing synonyms only in specific cases, and I distrust general renaming facilities; see §12.8.

This implies that disambiguation must be compiled into the object code by providers of program fragments. In particular, library providers will have to use a technique that allows users to disambiguate. Fortunately, the library providers will be some of the main beneficiaries from a systematic use of namespaces because they (partly through their users) are the main sufferers in the current situation.

Naturally, it is possible to add criteria to these lists, and no two people will agree to the exact importance of the criteria. Nevertheless, these lists give an idea of the complexity of the problem and the demands that a solution must meet.

After first presenting these criteria, I had the opportunity to test the namespace design for simplicity according to these criteria. Peter Juhl completed a pilot implementation in five days, and I explained the basics of namespaces to several people in less than ten minutes using just a couple of foils. Their follow-up questions showed understanding and the ability to deduce some of the uses of namespaces that I hadn't explained. That satisfied me that the namespace facilities were simple enough. Further implementation experience, discussion of the namespace concept, and some use have increased my confidence in that conclusion.

17.4 The Solution: Namespaces

The adopted solution is fundamentally simple. It provides four new mechanisms:

[1] A mechanism for defining a scope that holds what have traditionally been global declarations in C and C++: a namespace. Such scopes can be named and a namespace's members can be referred to using the traditional notation for class members: `namespace_name::member_name`. In fact, a class scope can be seen as a special case of a namespace scope.

[2] A mechanism for defining a local synonym for a namespace name.

[3] A mechanism allowing a member of a namespace to be accessed without the explicit `namespace_name::` qualification: a *using-declaration*.

[4] A mechanism allowing *all* members of a namespace to be accessed without the explicit `namespace_name::` qualification: a *using-directive*.

This meets the criteria from §17.3. In addition, it solves a long-standing problem with access to base class members from a derived class scope (see §17.5.1, §17.5.2) and renders `static` redundant as used for global names (see §17.5.3).

Consider:

```
namespace A {
    void f(int);
    void f(char);
    class String { /* ... */ };
    // ...
}
```

The names declared within the *namespace* braces are in namespace A and do not collide with global names or names in any other namespace. Namespace declarations (including definitions) have exactly the same semantics as global declarations, except that the scope of their names is restricted to the namespace.

Programmers can use such names by explicitly qualifying uses:

```
A::String s1 = "Annemarie";

void g1()
{
    A::f(1);
}
```

Alternatively, we can explicitly make an *individual* name from a specific library available for use without qualification by a *using-declaration*:

```
using A::String;
String s2 = "Nicholas";   // meaning A::String
```

```
void g2()
{
    using A::f;    // introduce local synonym for A's f
    f(2);          // meaning A::f
}
```

A *using-declaration* introduces a synonym for the name it mentions into the local scope.

Alternatively, we can explicitly make *all* names from a specific library available for use without qualification by a *using-directive*:

```
using namespace A;      // make all names from A accessible
String s3 = "Marian";   // meaning A::String

void g3()
{
    f(3);               // meaning A::f
}
```

A *using-directive* doesn't introduce names into the local scope; it simply makes the names from the namespace accessible.

My original design used a simpler and less verbose syntax for *using-directives*:

```
using A; // meaning ``using namespace A;''
```

This created total confusion between *using-directives* and *using-declarations*. Most of this confusion disappeared when I introduced the more explicit syntax. The more explicit form also simplified the parser.

I anticipated a need to avoid repetition of long namespace names. Therefore, the original design allowed for several member names to be mentioned in a single *using-declaration*:

```
using X::(f,g,h);
```

This is syntactically ugly, and so were all the alternatives we considered. More precisely: every alternative we considered was considered unbearably ugly by several people. Having used namespaces a bit, I found far less need for such lists than I had expected. I also tended to overlook such lists when reading code because they resemble function declarations too much, so I fell into the habit of using repeated *using-declarations* instead:

```
using X::f;
using X::g;
using X::h;
```

Consequently, there is no special form of a *using-declaration* that specifies a list of member names.

Namespaces provide an example of a feature that became noticeably simpler through experimentation. Namespaces are also easy to implement because they fit exactly with C++'s view of scope and class.

17.4.1 Views on Namespace Use

The three ways of accessing names from a namespace are the result of long discussions trying to address apparently irreconcilable views on what is important for naming in a large program. Some people insist that reliable and maintainable programs can be obtained only if every use of a non-local name is explicitly qualified. Naturally, these people insist on the use of explicit qualification and express serious doubts about the value of *using-declaration*s and even more about *using-directive*s.

Other people denounce explicit qualification as unacceptably verbose, making code too hard to change, limiting flexibility, and making a transition to the use of namespaces infeasible. Naturally, these people argue for *using-directive*s and other mechanisms for mapping ordinary short names into namespaces.

I am sympathetic to the less radical variants of both views. Consequently, namespaces allow each style to be used and enforce neither. Local style guidelines can – as usual – be used to enforce restrictions that would be unwise to impose on all users through a language rule.

Many people – quite reasonably – worry about ordinary unqualified names being "hijacked;" that is, being bound to an object or a function different from the one intended by the programmer. Every C programmer has suffered from this phenomenon at some time or other. Explicit qualification greatly alleviates such problems. A similar, yet distinct, worry is that it can be hard to find the declaration of a name and hard to guess the meaning of an expression containing it. Explicit qualification gives such a strong clue that it often isn't necessary to look for the declaration: The name of a library plus the name of a function often makes the meaning of an expression obvious. For these reasons, explicit qualification should be preferred for unusual or infrequently used non-local names. The increase of code clarity can be significant.

On the other hand, explicit qualification of names that everybody knows (or at least ought to know) and of frequently used names can become a real nuisance. For example, writing `stdio::printf`, `math::sqrt`, and `iostream::cout` is not going to help anyone acquainted with C++. The added visual clutter easily becomes a source of errors. This argues strongly for a mechanism like *using-declaration*s or *using-directive*s. Of these, a *using-declaration* is the more discriminating and by far the less dangerous. A *using-directive*:

```
using namespace X;
```

makes an unknown set of names available. In particular, this directive may make one set of names available today, but if changes are made to X, a different set of names may be made available tomorrow. People who find this worrying will prefer to list the names they want to use from X explicitly in *using-declaration*s:

```
using X::f;
using X::g;
using X::h;
```

However, the ability to gain access to every name from a namespace without having

to name them and to have that set of available names change with the definition of X
without having to modify user code is occasionally exactly what is desired.

17.4.2 Getting Namespaces into Use

Given the millions of lines of C++ code relying on global names and existing libraries,
I considered the most important question about namespaces to be: How can we get
namespaces into use? It doesn't matter how elegant namespace-based code can be if
there is no simple transition path that users and library providers can follow to introduce namespaces. Requiring major rewrites didn't seem a viable option.

Consider the canonical first C program:

```
#include <stdio.h>

int main()
{
    printf("Hello, world\n");
}
```

Breaking this program wouldn't be a good idea. I didn't consider making standard
libraries special cases a good idea either. I considered it important to ensure that the
namespace mechanism was good enough to serve the standard libraries. In this way,
the standards committee can't demand privileges for their libraries that they are not
willing to extend to purveyors of other libraries. In other words, don't impose rules
on others unless you are willing to live by those rules yourself.

The *using-directive* is the key to achieving this. For example, stdio.h is
wrapped in a namespace like this:

```
// stdio.h:

namespace std {
    // ...
    int printf(const char* ... );
    // ...
}
using namespace std;
```

This achieves backwards compatibility, and a new header file stdio is defined for
people who don't want the names implicitly available:

```
// stdio:

namespace std {
    // ...
    int printf(const char* ... );
    // ...
}
```

People who worry about replication of declarations will of course define stdio.h
by including stdio:

```
// stdio.h:

    #include<stdio>
    using namespace std;
```

Personally, I consider *using-directive*s primarily as a transition tool. Most programs can be expressed more clearly using explicit qualification and *using-declaration*s when referring to names from other namespaces.

Naturally, names from an enclosing namespace require no qualification:

```
namespace A {
    void f();
    void g()
    {
        f(); // call A::f; no qualifier necessary
        // ...
    }
}

void A::f()
{
    g(); // call A::g; no qualifier necessary
    // ...
}
```

In this respect, namespaces behave exactly like classes.

17.4.3 Namespace Aliases

If users give their namespaces short names, the names of different namespaces will clash:

```
namespace A { // short namespace name:
                // will clash (eventually)
    // ...
};

A::String s1 = "asdf";
A::String s2 = "lkjh";
```

However, long namespace names can be tedious:

```
namespace American_Telephone_and_Telegraph { // too long
                                              // to use in
                                              // real code
    // ...
}

American_Telephone_and_Telegraph::String s3 = "asdf";
American_Telephone_and_Telegraph::String s4 = "lkjh";
```

This dilemma can be resolved by providing a short alias for a longer namespace name:

```
// use namespace alias to shorten names:

namespace ATT = American_Telephone_and_Telegraph;

ATT::String s3 = "asdf";
ATT::String s4 = "lkjh";
```

This feature also allows a user to refer to "the library" without having to say exactly which library is actually used each time. In fact, namespaces can be used to compose interfaces out of names from more than one namespace:

```
namespace My_interface {
    using namespace American_Telephone_and_Telegraph;
    using My_own::String;
    using namespace OI;
      // resolve clash of definitions of 'Flags'
      // from OI and American_Telephone_and_Telegraph:
    typedef int Flags;
    // ...
}
```

17.4.4 Using Namespaces to Manage Releases

As an example of namespaces, I'll show how a library supplier might use namespaces to manage incompatible changes between releases. This technique was first pointed out to me by Tanj Bennett. Here is my `release1`:

```
namespace release1 {
    // ...
    class X {
        Impl::Xrep* p;
    public:
        virtual void f1() = 0;
        virtual void f2() = 0;
        // ...
    };
    // ...
}
```

`Impl` is some namespace where I keep my implementation details.

A user will write code like this:

```
class XX : public release1::X {
    int xx1;
    // ...
public:
    void f1();
    void f2();
    virtual void ff1();
    virtual void ff2();
    // ...
};
```

This implies that I, as a library provider, cannot change the size of `release1::X` objects (for example, by adding data members), add or rearrange virtual functions, etc., because that would imply that the user's code would have to be recompiled to readjust the object layout to accommodate my changes. There are implementations of C++ that insulate users from such changes, but they are not common, so as a library provider I cannot rely on them without tying myself to a single compiler supplier. I might encourage users not to derive from my library classes in this way, but they'll do it anyway and complain about having to recompile even when they have been warned.

I need a better solution. Using namespaces to distinguish different versions, my `release2` might look like this:

```
namespace release1 { // release1 supplied for compatibility
    // ...
    class X {
        Impl::Xrep* p; // Impl::Xrep has changed
                       // to accommodate release2
    public:
        virtual void f1() = 0;
        virtual void f2() = 0;
        // ...
    };
    // ...
}

namespace release2 {
    // ...
    class X {
        Impl::Xrep* p;
    public:
        virtual void f2() = 0;  // new ordering
        virtual void f3() = 0;  // more functions
        virtual void f1() = 0;
        // ...
    };
    // ...
}
```

Old code uses `release1`, and new code uses `release2`. New and old code not

only work, but coexist. The headers for `release1` and `release2` are distinct so
that the user need only `#include` the necessary minimum. To ease upgrades, a user
can use a namespace alias to localize the effect of a version change. A single file

```
// lib.h:
    namespace lib = release1;
    // ...
```

can include all the version-dependent stuff and be used everywhere like this:

```
#include "lib.h"

class XX : public lib::X {
    // ...
};
```

which is upgraded to use a new release by a single change:

```
// lib.h:
    namespace lib = release2;
    // ...
```

This update is done only when there is a reason to use `release2`, time to recompile,
and time to deal with possible source code incompatibilities between the releases.

17.4.5 Details

This section presents technical details relating to scope resolution, the global scope,
overloading, nested namespaces, and composition of namespaces from separate parts.

17.4.5.1 Convenience vs. Safety

A *using-declaration* adds to a local scope. A *using-directive* does not; it simply renders names accessible. For example:

```
namespace X {
    int i, j, k;
}

int k;

void f1()
{
    int i = 0;
    using namespace X; // make names from X accessible
    i++;               // local i
    j++;               // X::j
    k++;               // error: X::k or global k ?
    ::k++;             // the global k
    X::k++;            // X's k
}
```

```
void f2()
{
    int i = 0;
    using X::i; // error: i declared twice in f2()
    using X::j;
    using X::k; // hides global k

    i++;
    j++;            // X::j
    k++;            // X::k
}
```

This preserves the important property that a locally declared name (declared either by an ordinary declaration or by a *using-declaration*) hides non-local declarations of the same name, and any illegal overloadings of the name are detected at the point of declaration.

As shown, giving no preference to the global scope over namespaces made accessible in the global scope provides some protection against accidental name clashes.

Non-local names, on the other hand, are found in the context in which they were declared and treated just like other non-local names. In particular, errors relating to a *using-directive* are detected only at the point of use. This saves the programmer from having a program fail because of potential errors. For example:

```
namespace A {
    int x;
}

namespace B {
    int x;
}

void f()
{
    using namespace A;
    using namespace B;   // ok: no error here

    A::x++;   // ok
    B::x++;   // ok
    x++;      // error: A::x or B::x ?
}
```

17.4.5.2 The Global Scope

With the introduction of namespaces, the global scope becomes just another namespace. The global namespace is odd only in that you don't have to mention its name in an explicit qualification: ::f means "the f declared in the global namespace," whereas X::f means "the f declared in namespace X." Consider:

```
int a;

void f()
{
    int a = 0;
    a++;        // local a
    ::a++;      // global a
}
```

If we wrap a namespace around this and add yet another variable called a, we get:

```
int a;

namespace X {
    int a;

    void f()
    {
        int a = 0;
        a++;        // local a
        X::a++;     // X::a
        ::a++;      // X::a or global a ? -- the global a !
    }
}
```

In other words, qualification by unary : : means "global" rather than "in the nearest enclosing namespace." The latter would ensure that wrapping arbitrary code in a namespace implied no change of meaning. However, then the global scope would not have a name, and that would be in variance with the view that the global namespace is just an ordinary namespace with an odd name. Consequently, we chose the former meaning so that : : a refers to the a declared in the global scope.

I expect to see a radical decrease in the use of global names. The rules for namespaces were specifically crafted to give no advantages to a "lazy" user of global names over someone who takes care not to pollute the global scope.

Note that a *using-directive* does *not* declare names in the scope in which it occurs:

```
namespace X {
    int a;
    int b;
    // ...
}

using namespace X; // make all names from X accessible
using X::b;        // declare local synonym for X::b

int i1 = ::a; // error: no ''a'' declared in global scope
int i2 = ::b; // ok: find the local synonym for X::b
```

This implies that old code using explicit : : to access global library functions will break when the library is put into a namespace. The solution is either to modify the code to explicitly mention the new library namespace name or to introduce suitable global *using-declarations*.

17.4.5.3 Overloading

The most controversial aspect of the namespace proposal was the decision to allow overloading across namespaces according to the usual overloading rules. Consider:

```
namespace A {
    void f(int);
    // ...
}
using namespace A;

namespace B {
    void f(char);
    // ...
}
using namespace B;

void g()
{
    f('a');   // calls B::f(char)
}
```

A user who hasn't looked carefully at namespace B might expect A::f(int) to be called. Worse, a user who looked carefully at the program last year and didn't notice that a declaration of f(char) was added to B in a later release might get surprised.

However, this problem occurs only when you maintain programs that explicitly use using namespace twice for the same scope – a non-recommended practice for newly written software. A call of a function that has two legal resolutions from different namespaces is also an obvious candidate for an optional compiler warning even if the ordinary overload resolution rules prefer the one resolution over the other. I see *using-directives* as primarily a transition aid and writers of new code can avoid many theoretical and a few real problems by sticking to explicit qualification and *using-declarations* wherever possible.

My reason for allowing overloading across namespaces is that this is the simplest rule ("the usual overloading rules apply"), and it is the only rule I can think of that allows us to migrate existing libraries to use namespaces with minimal source code changes. For example:

```
// old code:

    void f(int);     // from A.h
    // ...

    void f(char);    // from B.h
    // ...
```

```
    void g()
    {
        f('a');   // calls the f from B.h
    }
```

can be upgraded to the version using namespaces shown above without changing anything but the header files.

17.4.5.4 Nesting of Namespaces

One obvious use of namespaces is to wrap a complete set of declarations and definitions in a separate namespace:

```
namespace X {
    // all my declarations
}
```

The list of declarations will in general contain namespaces. Thus, for practical reasons – as well as for the simple reason that constructs ought to nest unless there is a
strong reason for them not to – nested namespaces are allowed. For example:

```
void h();

namespace X {
    void g();
    // ...
    namespace Y {
        void f();
        void ff();
        // ...
    }
    // ...
}
```

The usual scope and qualification rules apply:

```
void X::Y::ff()
{
    f();   g();   h();
}


void X::g()
{
    f();       // error: no f() in X
    Y::f();
}
```

```
void h()
{
    f();        // error: no global f()
    Y::f();     // error: no global Y
    X::f();     // error: no f() in X
    X::Y::f();
}
```

17.4.5.5 Namespaces are Open

A namespace is open; that is, you can add names to it from several namespace declarations. For example:

```
namespace A {
    int f(); // now A has member f()
};

namespace A {
    int g(); // now A has two members f() and g()
}
```

The aim was to support large program fragments within a single namespace the way a current library or application lives within the single global namespace. To do this, it is necessary to distribute the namespace definition over several header and source code files. This openness was also seen as a transition aid. For example:

```
// my header:
    extern void f(); // my function
    // ...
    #include<stdio.h>
    extern int g(); // my function
    // ...
```

can be rewritten without reordering of the declarations:

```
// my header:

    namespace Mine {
        void f(); // my function
        // ...
    }

    #include<stdio.h>

    namespace Mine {
        int g(); // my function
        // ...
    }
```

Current taste (including mine) favors the use of many smaller namespaces over putting really major pieces of code into a single namespace. That style could be enforced by requiring all members to be declared in a single namespace declaration in the same way all members of a class must be declared in a single class declaration. However, I saw no point in foregoing the many small conveniences I find with open namespaces in favor of a more restrictive system just to conform to some current taste.

17.5 Implications for Classes

It has been suggested that a namespace should be a kind of class. I don't think that is a good idea because many class facilities exist exclusively to support the notion of a class being a user-defined type. For example, facilities for defining the creation and manipulation of objects of that type has little to do with scope issues.

The opposite, that a class is a kind of namespace, seems almost obviously true. A class is a namespace in the sense that all operations supported for namespaces can be applied with the same meaning to a class unless the operation is explicitly prohibited for classes. This implies simplicity and generality, while minimizing implementation effort. I consider this view vindicated by the smooth way namespaces fit into C++ and because solutions to apparently unrelated long-standing problems naturally follow from the basic namespace mechanisms.

17.5.1 Derived Classes

Consider the old problem of a class member hiding a member of the same name in a base class:

```
class B {
public:
    f(char);
};

class D : public B {
public:
    f(int);   // hides f(char)
};

void f(D& d)
{
    d.f('c'); // calls D::f(int)
}
```

Naturally, the introduction of namespaces doesn't change the meaning of such examples. A new explanation is possible, though: Because D is a class, the scope it provides is a namespace. The namespace D is nested in the namespace B, so D::f(int) hides B::f(char). Consequently, D::f(int) is called. If this resolution isn't what is wanted, we can use a *using-declaration* to bring B's f() into scope:

```
class B {
public:
    f(char);
};

class D : public B {
public:
    f(int);
    using B::f;    // bring B::f into D to enable overloading
};

void f(D& d)
{
    d.f('c');    // calls D::f(char)  !
}
```

We suddenly have a choice!

As ever, names from different sibling base classes can cause ambiguities (independently of what they name):

```
struct A { void f(int); };
struct B { void f(double); };

struct C : A, B {
    void g() {
        f(1);      // error: A::f(int) or B::f(double)
        f(1.0);    // error: A::f(int) or B::f(double)
    }
};
```

However, if we want to resolve these ambiguities, we can now do so by adding a couple of *using-declaration*s to bring A::f and B::f into the scope of C:

```
struct C : A, B {
    using A::f;
    using B::f;

    void g() {
        f(1);     // A::f(1)
        f(1.0);   // B::f(1.0)
    }
};
```

An explicit mechanism along these lines has been suggested repeatedly over the years. I remember discussing the possibility with Jonathan Shopiro while working on release 2.0, but rejecting it as being ''too specialized and unique'' to include. The *using-declaration*, on the other hand, is a general mechanism that just happens to provide a solution to this problem.

17.5.2 `Using` Base Classes

To avoid confusion, a *using-declaration* that is a class member must name a member of a (direct or indirect) base class. To avoid problems with the dominance rule (§12.3.1) *using-directives* are not allowed as class members.

```
struct D : public A {
    using namespace A; // error: using-directive as member
    using ::f;   // error: ::f not a member of a base class
};
```

A *using-declaration* naming a base class member has an important role to play in adjusting access:

```
class B {
public:
    f(char);
};

class D : private B {
public:
    using B::f;
};
```

This achieves in a general and more obvious way what *access-declarations* (§2.10) were introduced to do:

```
class D : private B {
public:
    B::f;   // old way: access declaration
};
```

Thus, *using-declarations* make the specialized *access-declarations* redundant. Consequently, *access-declarations* are deprecated. That is, *access-declarations* are slated to be removed sometime in the distant future after users have had ample time to upgrade.

17.5.3 Eliminating Global `static`

It is often useful to wrap a set of declarations in a namespace simply to avoid interference from declarations in header files or to avoid having the names used interfere with global declarations in other compilation units. For example:

```
#include <header.h>
namespace Mine {
    int a;
    void f() { /* ... */ }
    int g() { /* ... */ }
}
```

In many cases, we aren't really interested in the name of the namespace as long as it doesn't clash with other namespace names. To serve that need more elegantly, we allow a namespace to be unnamed:

```
#include <header.h>
namespace {
    int a;
    void f() { /* ... */ }
    int g() { /* ... */ }
}
```

Except for overloading by names in the header, this is equivalent to

```
#include <header.h>

static int a;
static void f() { /* ... */ }
static int g() { /* ... */ }
```

Such overloading is usually undesirable, but easy to achieve when desired:

```
namespace {
#include <header.h>
    int a;
    void f() { /* ... */ }
    int g() { /* ... */ }
}
```

Thus, the namespace concept allows us to deprecate the use of `static` for control of visibility of global names. That leaves `static` with a single meaning in C++: statically allocated, don't replicate.

The unnamed namespace is just like any other namespace except that we don't need to utter its name. Basically,

```
namespace { /* ... */ }
```

is semantically equivalent to

```
namespace unique_name { /* ... */ }
using namespace unique_name;
```

Every unnamed namespace in a single scope share the same unique name. In particular, all global unnamed namespaces in a single translation unit are part of the same namespace and differ from the global unnamed namespace of other translation units.

17.6 C Compatibility

A function with C linkage can be placed in a namespace:

```
namespace X {
    extern "C" void f(int);
    void g(int)
}
```

This allows functions with C linkage to be used like other members of a namespace. For example:

```
void h()
{
    X::f();
    X::g();
}
```

However, in a single program one cannot have two different functions with C linkage and the same name in different namespaces; both would resolve to the same C function. The unsafe rules of C linkage make such errors hard to find.

One alternative to this design would be to disallow functions with C linkage in namespaces. That would lead to disuse of namespaces by forcing people who need to interface to C to pollute the global namespace. This non-solution was deemed unacceptable.

Another alternative would be to ensure that two functions of the same name in different namespaces were really different functions even if they had C linkage. For example:

```
namespace X {
    extern "C" void f(int);
}

namespace Y {
    extern "C" void f(int);
}
```

The problem is then how to call such a function from a C program. Since the C language doesn't have a mechanism for disambiguating based on namespaces, we would have to rely on an (almost certainly implementation-dependent) naming convention. For example, the C program might have to refer to __X__f and __Y__f. This solution was deemed unacceptable, so we stuck with the unsafe C rules. C pollutes the linker's namespace, but not the global namespace of a C++ translation unit.

Note that this is a C problem (a compatibility hack) and not a problem with C++ namespaces. Linking to a language that has a mechanism analogous to C++'s namespaces should be obvious and safe. For example, I'd expect this

```
namespace X {
    extern "Ada" void f(int);
}

namespace Y {
    extern "Ada" void f(int);
}
```

to be the way for a C++ program to map to functions in different Ada packages.

18

The C Preprocessor

Furthermore, I am of the opinion
that Cpp must be destroyed.
– Cato the Elder (Marcus Porcius Cato)

Problems with the C preprocessor, Cpp — alternatives to Cpp constructs — banning Cpp.

18.1 Cpp

Among the facilities, techniques, and ideas C++ inherited from C was the C preprocessor, Cpp. I didn't like Cpp at all, and I still don't like it. The character and file orientation of the preprocessor is fundamentally at odds with a programming language designed around the notions of scopes, types, and interfaces. For example, consider this innocent-looking code fragment:

```
#include<stdio.h>
extern double sqrt(double);

main()
{
    printf("The square root of 2 is %g\n",sqrt(2));
    fflush(stdout);
    return(0);
}
```

What does it do? Print

```
The square root of 2 is 1.41421
```

maybe? That seems plausible, but actually I compiled it with

```
cc -Dsqrt=rand -Dreturn=abort
```

so it printed

```
The square root of 2 is 7.82997e+28
abort - core dumped
```

and left a core image behind.

This example may be extreme, and you might consider the use of compiler options to define Cpp macros not quite sportsmanlike, but the example is not unrealistic. Macro definitions can lurk in environments, compiler directives, and header files. Macro substitution cuts across all scope barriers, can indeed change the scope structure of a program by inserting braces, quotes, etc., and allows a programmer to change what the compiler proper sees without even touching the source code. Occasionally, even the most extreme uses of Cpp are useful, but its facilities are so unstructured and intrusive that they are a constant problem to programmers, maintainers, people porting code, and tool builders.

In retrospect, maybe the worst aspect of Cpp is that it has stifled the development of programming environments for C. The anarchic and character-level operation of Cpp makes nontrivial tools for C and C++ larger, slower, less elegant, and less effective than one would have thought possible.

Cpp isn't even a very good macroprocessor. Consequently, I set out to make Cpp redundant. That task turned out to be far harder than expected. Cpp may be ugly, but it is hard to find better-structured and efficient alternatives for all of its varied uses.

The C preprocessor has four fundamental directives†:

[1] #include to copy source text from another file.

[2] #define to define a macro (with or without arguments).

[3] #ifdef to include lines of code dependent on a condition.

[4] #pragma to affect the compilation in an implementation-dependent manner.

These directives are used to express a variety of basic programming tasks:

#include
  – Make interface definitions available.
  – Compose source text.

#define
  – Define symbolic constants.
  – Define open subroutines.
  – Define generic subroutines.
  – Define generic "types."
  – Renaming.
  – String concatenation.
  – Define special purpose syntax.
  – General macro processing.

---

† The #if, #line, and #undef directives can be important, but they do not impinge on this discussion.

```
#ifdef
```
    –   Version control.

    –   Commenting out code.

```
#pragma
```
    –   Control of layout.

    –   Informing the compiler about unusual control flow.

Cpp does all of these tasks pretty badly, mostly by indirect means, but cheaply and often adequately. Most important, Cpp is available everywhere C is, and it is well known. This has often made it more useful than far better, but less widely available and less widely known, macroprocessors. This aspect is so important that the C preprocessor is frequently used for tasks that have very little to do with the C language, but that is not a C++ problem.

C++ provides alternatives for the main uses of `#define`:

–   `const` for constants (§3.8).

–   `inline` for open subroutines (§2.4.1).

–   `template` for functions parameterized by types (§15.6).

–   `template` for parameterized types (§15.3).

–   `namespace` for more general naming (§17).

C++ provides no alternative for `#include`, though namespaces provide a scope mechanism that supports composition in a way that can be used to make `#include` better behaved.

I have suggested that an `include` directive might be added to C++ proper as an alternative to Cpp's `#include`. A C++ `include` directive would differ from Cpp's `#include` in three ways:

[1] If a file is `included` twice, the second `include` is ignored. This solves a practical problem that is currently solved inefficiently and awkwardly by `#defines` and `#ifdefs`.

[2] Macros defined outside `included` text don't get expanded within the `included` text. This provides a mechanism for insulating information from interference from macros.

[3] Macros defined inside `included` text don't get expanded in text processed after the `included` text. This ensures that macros in `included` text don't impose order dependencies on the including compilation unit and generally protects against surprises caused by macros.

This mechanism would be a boon to systems that precompile header files and, in general, for people who compose software out of independent parts. Please note, however, that this is only an idea, not an accepted language feature.

This leaves `#ifdef` and `#pragma`. I could live without `#pragma` because I have never seen a pragma that I liked. Too often, `#pragma` seems to be used to sneak variations of language semantics into a compiler and to provide extensions with very specialized semantics and awkward syntax. We don't yet have a good alternative for `#ifdef`. In particular, using *if-statements* and constant expressions is not a complete alternative. For example:

```
const C = 1;

// ...

if (C) {
    // ...
}
```

This technique cannot be used to control declarations and the text of an *if-statement* must be syntactically correct and type check even if it is part of a branch that an execution will never take.

I'd like to see Cpp abolished. However, the only realistic and responsible way of doing that is first to make it redundant, then encourage people to use the better alternatives, and *then* – years later – banish Cpp into the program development environment with the other extra-linguistic tools where it belongs.

I

Index

F

O